The Great Open Dance

The Great Open Dance

A Progressive Christian Theology

Jon Paul Sydnor

PICKWICK *Publications* · Eugene, Oregon

THE GREAT OPEN DANCE
A Progressive Christian Theology

Pickwick Publications
An Imprint of Wipf and Stock Publishers
199 W. 8th Ave., Suite 3
Eugene, OR 97401

www.wipfandstock.com

PAPERBACK ISBN: 978-1-6667-7515-0
HARDCOVER ISBN: 978-1-6667-7516-7
EBOOK ISBN: 978-1-6667-7517-4

Cataloguing-in-Publication data:

Names: Sydnor, Jon Paul, author.

Title: The great open dance : a progressive Christian theology / Jon Paul Sydnor.

Description: Eugene, OR: Pickwick Publications, 2024. | Includes bibliographical references and index.

Identifiers: ISBN 978-1-6667-7515-0 (paperback). | ISBN 978-1-6667-7516-7 (hardcover). | ISBN 978-1-6667-7517-4 (ebook).

Subjects: LSCH: Theology. | Process theology. | Ethics.

Classification: BT83.6 S99 2024 (print). | BT83.6 (epub).

VERSION NUMBER 04/22/24

All sorrow, labor, suffering, I, tallying it, absorb in myself;
Many times have I been rejected, taunted, put in prison,
and crucified—and many times shall be again;
All the world have I given up for my dear [siblings'] sake—for the soul's sake;
Wending my way through the homes of [all], rich or poor,
with the kiss of affection;
For I am affection—I am the cheer-bringing God,
with hope, and all-enclosing Charity;
(Conqueror yet—for before me all the armies and soldiers
of the earth shall yet bow—
and all the weapons of war become impotent).
With indulgent words, as to children—
with fresh and sane words, mine only;
Young and strong I pass, knowing well I am destin'd myself to an early death:
But my Charity has no death—
my Wisdom dies not, neither early nor late,
And my sweet Love, bequeath'd here and elsewhere,
Never dies.

—Walt Whitman, "Chanting the Square Deific"

to my wife, Abby, who shares the love of God with the world

Contents

Figures

Abbreviations

Books of the Bible

Gen	Genesis	Mic	Micah
Exod	Exodus	Zech	Zechariah
Lev	Leviticus	Mal	Malachi
Num	Numbers	Matt	Matthew
Deut	Deuteronomy	Rom	Romans
Josh	Joshua	1 Cor	1 Corinthians
Judg	Judges	2 Cor	2 Corinthians
1 Sam	1 Samuel	Gal	Galatians
2 Sam	2 Samuel	Eph	Ephesians
1 Kgs	1 Kings	Phil	Philippians
2 Kgs	2 Kings	Col	Colossians
1 Chr	1 Chronicles	1 Thess	1 Thessalonians
2 Chr	2 Chronicles	2 Thess	2 Thessalonians
Neh	Nehemiah	1 Tim	1 Timothy
Ps/Pss	Psalm/s	2 Tim	2 Timothy
Prov	Proverbs	Heb	Hebrews
Eccl	Ecclesiastes	Jas	James
Song	Song of Songs	1 Pet	1 Peter
Isa	Isaiah	2 Pet	2 Peter
Jer	Jeremiah	3 Pet	3 Peter
Lam	Lamentations	Rev	Revelation
Ezek	Ezekiel	Wis	Wisdom
Dan	Daniel	Sir	Sirach
Hos	Hosea		

Journals

AThR	Anglican Theological Review
AYBRL	Anchor Yale Bible Reference Library
BA	Biblical Archaeologist
BAR	Biblical Archaeology Review
Di	Dialog
HvTSt	Hervormde teologiese studies
JRH	Journal of Religious History
LCL	Loeb Classical Library
MelT	Melita Theologica
NBf	New Blackfriars
RelS	Religious Studies
SJT	Scottish Journal of Theology
ThTo	Theology Today
VC	Vigiliae Christianae

Introduction

I believe that love is the main key to open the doors to the "growth" of
[humankind]. Love and union with someone or something outside
of oneself, union that allows one to put oneself into relationship with
others, to feel one with others, without limiting the sense of integrity
and independence.... I believe that the experience of love is the most
human and humanizing act that it is given to us to enjoy and that it,
like reason, makes no sense if conceived in a partial way.

—ERICH FROMM[1]

LOVE IS THE GROUND, meaning, and destiny of the cosmos. We need love
to flourish, and we will find flourishing only in love. Too often, other
forces tempt us into their servitude, always at the cost of our own suffering. Greed prefers money to love, ambition prefers power to love, fear
prefers hatred to love, expediency prefers violence to love. And so we find
ourselves in a hellscape of our own making, wondering how personal
advantage degenerated into collective agony. Then, seeing the cynicism at
work in society, we accept its practicality and prioritize personal advantage again, investing ourselves in brokenness.

The world need not be this way. Love is compatible with our highest
ideals, such as well-being, excellence, courage, and peace. It is the only
reliable ground for human well-being, both individual and collective. Yet
the sheer momentum of history discourages us from trusting love's promise. Despondent about our condition, we subject the future to the past.

1. Fromm, *On Being Human*, 102–3 (gender neutralized).

1

Historically, one institution charged with resisting despair, sustaining hope, and propagating love has been the Christian church. Its record is spotty, as it has promoted both peace and war, love and hate, generosity and greed. The church can do better, and must do better, if it is to survive.

Today, the church's future is in doubt as millions of disenchanted members vote with their feet. A slew of recent studies has attempted to understand why both church attendance and religious affiliation are declining. To alarmists, this decline corresponds to the overall collapse of civilization, which (so they worry) is falling into ever deepening degeneracy. But to others, this decline simply reveals an increasing honesty about the complexity and variety of our religious lives. In this more optimistic view, people can at last speak openly about religion, including their lack thereof, without fear of condemnation.

Historians suggest that concerns about the decline are exaggerated, produced by a fanciful interpretation of the past in which everyone belonged to a church that they attended every Sunday in a weekly gathering of clean, well-dressed, happy nuclear families. In fact, this past has never existed, not once over the two-thousand-year history of Christianity. These historians report that church leaders have *always* worried about church decline, church membership has *always* fluctuated wildly, and attendance has *always* been spotty. Today is no different.[2]

To some advocates of faith, this decline in church attendance and religious affiliation is a healthy development, *even for the church.* When a culture compels belief, even nonbelievers must pretend to believe. During the Cold War, believers in the Soviet Union had to pretend to be atheists, and atheists in America had to pretend to be believers. Such compelled duplicity helps no one; as anyone living under tyranny can tell you, rewards for belief and punishment for disbelief produce only inauthenticity. Even today, many people claim faith solely for the social capital that a religious identity provides. If perfectly good atheists can't win elections because atheism is considered suspect, then politically ambitious atheists will just pretend to be Christians. But coerced conformity and artificial identity show no faith; Jesus needs committed disciples, not political opportunists. Hopefully, after this period of church decline, what Christianity loses in power it may gain in credibility.

Self-centeredly, faith leaders often blame the decline in attendance and affiliation on the people. More frequently, the leaders themselves are

2. Stark, "Secularization, R.I.P.," 252–64.

to blame. In the past, people may have stayed home in protest of corruption, or in resistance to state authority, or due to their own uncon-
ventional ideas about God. Today, sociologists identify different reasons
for avoiding organized religion. Most of their studies focus on young
people, who often reject Christian teachings as *insufficiently loving and
open*. Their responses to surveys suggest that the faith's failure to attract
or retain them is largely theological, and they won't change their minds
until Christian theology changes its focus.

Christianity shouldn't change its theology to attract young people;
Christianity should change its theology because the young people are
right. *They are arguing that Christianity fails to express the love of Christ,*
and they have very specific complaints. For example, traditional teachings about other religions often offend contemporary minds. Our world
is multireligious, so most people have friends from different religions. On
the whole, these friends are kind, reasonable people. This warm interpersonal experience doesn't jibe with doctrines asserting that other religions
are false and their practitioners condemned. If forced to choose between
an exclusive faith and a kind friend, most people will choose their kind
friends, *which they should*. Rightfully, they want to be members of a
beloved community, not insiders at an exclusive club.[3] The new generations' preference for inclusion also extends to the LGBTQ+ community.
One of the main reasons young adults reject religious affiliation today is
negative teachings about sexual and gender minorities.[4] Many preachers assert that being LGBTQ+ is "unnatural," or "contrary to the will of
God," or "sinful." But to young adults, LGBTQ+ identity is an expression of authenticity; neither they nor their friends must closet their true
selves any longer, a development for which all are thankful. A religion
that would force LGBTQ+ persons back into the closet, back into a lie,
must be resisted.

Regarding gender, most Christians, both young and old, are tired of
church-sanctioned sexism. Although 79 percent of Americans support
the ordination of women to leadership positions, most denominations
ordain only men.[5]

The traditionalism and irrationalism that rejects women's ordination
often extends into Christianity's relationship to science. We now live in an

---

3. Kinnaman with Hawkins, *You Lost Me*, 178–79.

4. PRRI Staff, "Religion and Congregations," 16.

5. Barna Group, "Women in Power," para. 12.

age that recognizes science as a powerful tool for understanding the universe, yet some denominations reject the most basic insights of science, usually due to a literal interpretation of the Bible. The evidence for evolution, to which almost all high school students are exposed, is overwhelming. Still, fundamentalist churches insist on reading Genesis like a science and history textbook, thereby creating an artificial conflict with science. This insistence drives out even those who were raised in faith, 23 percent of whom have "been turned off by the creation-versus-evolution debate."[6]

Tragically, although most young adults would like to nurture their souls in community, many are leaving faith because they find it narrow-minded and parochial. They can access all kinds of religious ideas on the internet and want to process those ideas with others, but their faith leaders pretend these spiritual options do not exist. Blessed with a spirit of openness, this globalized generation wants to learn how to *navigate* the world, not *fear* the world. Churches that acknowledge only one perspective, and try to impose that perspective, render a disservice that eventually produces resentment.[7] Over a third of people who have left the church lament that they could not "ask my most pressing life questions" there.[8]

Why are Christian denominations so slow to change? Perhaps because, as a third of young adults complain, "Christians are too confident they know all the answers."[9] Increasingly, people want church to be a safe place for spiritual conversation, not imposed dogma, and they want faith to be a sanctuary, not a fortress. They want to dwell in the presence of God, and feel that presence *everywhere*, not just with their own people in their own church. This change is good, because it reveals an increasing celebration of the *entirety* of creation that God sustains, including other nations, other cultures, and other religions. Faith is beginning to celebrate reality itself as sanctuary, rather than walling off a small area within, declaring it pure, and warning that everything outside is depraved.

As Christians change, Christian theology must change, replacing defensive theology with sanctuary theology. This sanctuary theology will provide a thought world within which the human spirit can flourish, where it feels free to explore, confident of love and acceptance, in a God-centered community. Such faith will not be a mere quiet place of repose for the individual; its warmth will radiate outward, to all. In so doing, it

6. Kinnaman with Hawkins, *You Lost Me*, 136–37.
7. Kinnaman with Hawkins, *You Lost Me*, 102–3.
8. Kinnaman with Hawkins, *You Lost Me*, 193–94.
9. Barna Group, "Six Reasons," para. 6.

will at last implement the prophet Isaiah's counsel, offered 2500 years ago: "Enlarge the site of your tent, and let the curtains of your habitations be stretched out; do not hold back; lengthen your cords and strengthen your stakes" (Isa 54:2 NRSV).

What follows is my attempt to provide one such sanctuary theology. My hope is that it will help readers flourish in life, both as individuals and in community, in the presence of God.

Flourishing needs community, and I could not have written this book without the support of many, to whom I express my gratitude. I thank you, dear reader, for risking your time on these thoughts; I pray that the risk pays off for you. I also thank Priests for Equality for their work on The Inclusive Bible, the first egalitarian translation of the Bible, and I thank them for permission to use that translation freely. All biblical quotations in this book are from The Inclusive Bible unless otherwise noted.

My employer, Emmanuel College, Boston, granted me a yearlong sabbatical to write. I thank the administration for this freedom, and I thank my students for the innumerable conversations we have had, through which I have learned so much. I also thank the members of Grace Community Boston, a progressive Christian gathering where I serve as theologian in residence, who have joined me in Sacred Conversation every Sunday for thirteen years. Without a doubt, I have learned more from them than they have from me.

Every writer needs readers who will provide honest feedback, and I am blessed with many, each of whom played a special role in the development of this book. Erin Umlauf clarified and updated my writing, making sure it was accessible to nonspecialists. John Gilmer challenged me whenever my arguments were weak or self-congratulatory and provided his own suggestions for improvement. I have focused this theology on spiritual experience, and psychotherapist Judith Anhammer-Sauer guided me in that effort. Jennifer Bird scrutinized my interpretation of the Bible and was gracious enough to allow me some theological play; any bogus interpretations are solely my responsibility. Rabbi Natan Margalit helped me scrub my work of the anti-Judaism, purposeful or accidental, that has so long stained the Christian tradition. Again, any remaining anti-Judaism is solely my responsibility, for which I apologize beforehand. Paul March and Allen Price reviewed the scientific passages and kept me from embarrassing myself, for which I am grateful. Amanda Udis-Kessler reviewed and improved the LGBTQ+ advocacy.

The artist Scotty Utz offers his own theological reflections in this book, in iron (well, photos of iron) rather than words. His blacksmithing has inspired my thinking, as I hope my thinking has inspired his blacksmithing. Julio Nieves, my friend and fellow podcaster at The Progressive Sacred, reminds me that theology is worthless until it comes back down to earth, to the people, as God does in Christ.

Most importantly, I thank my family. My parents raised me in the religious tradition that I practice today. I thank God that they taught me to pray, read the Bible, and say grace before meals. These regular practices kept me from forgetting God. I thank my late father, Rev. Dr. Clement A. Sydnor III, an ordained minister in the Presbyterian Church (USA), who taught me a love of words.

My own children, Josiah, Isaac, and Lydia, have always humored their dad, gamely expressing interest in all the strange topics I bring up for table conversation; any one of them can discuss nondualism intelligently. They are and always will be my most important contribution to this world.

Finally, my greatest conversation partner, friend, and editor is my wife, Rev. Abby Henrich. She is the immensely gifted pastor of both Grace Community Boston and Stratford Street United, two churches that truly manifest the love of God for the world. At this point in our marriage, I don't know where I stop and she begins, so united are we in mind and spirit. I trust her theological instincts more than my own, and her suggestions have transformed this book. I love you, Abby.

1

Unifying Love

Your life and my life flow into each other as wave flows into wave, and
unless there is peace and joy and freedom for you, there can be no real
peace or joy or freedom for me. To see reality—not as we expect it to
be but as it is—is to see that unless we live for each other and in and
through each other, we do not really live very satisfactorily; that there
can really be life only where there really is, in just this sense, love.

— FREDERICK BUECHNER[1]

This Universe Must Become Our Home

WE ARE BORN INTO this universe much like we move into a house. The
house will meet our material needs, providing us with shelter, protecting
our bodies from the cold and rain, shading us from the sun. Here we will
prepare our meals and sleep in safety. A good house provides much to be
thankful for. In the same way, we may be thankful *for* the universe, and
thankful *to* the universe, for granting us life.

But humans are more than bodies, so a house must provide more
than shelter. A house must become a *home*. A house may protect our
lives, but a home gives us life. A house sustains us, but a home nurtures

1. Buechner, *Magnificent Defeat*, 20.

7

us. It is more than shelter; it is sanctuary. Home is where our spirit settles, troubles are shared, and relationships deepen. The walls of a house still the wind, while the walls of a home still the soul.

By default, the universe is our house. We live within its walls, abide by its rules, and look to it for sustenance. But again, this minimal state is not enough. We need more from life than to eat, survive, and reproduce. We need the universe to become our home, a place with more than struggle and anxiety, a place of meaning and purpose.

I believe that the universe has this potential, and not by accident. The universe was designed to offer us more than mere existence; it was designed to offer us abundance. *The universe is designed to become our home.* However, the universe does not become our home automatically. It becomes our home through activity, in all its forms. The most important contribution comes from those who love us unconditionally when we are first born, who welcome us into life with care and concern and attentiveness, who make us feel unique and uniquely important. Not all of us are so blessed, but such love, when shared between family and child, paints the entire universe for that child.

Yet, as the child matures, they must accept responsibility for their personal destiny and emotional well-being. They must choose to live well or live badly, since different people can experience the exact same event in different ways. One person can do chores and be thankful for the usefulness of their body and the opportunity to feel productive; another person will resent the tedium. One person can be wronged and will work for reconciliation; another person will plot revenge. After new legislation is passed one person will interpret it as progress and another as decline. Hence, events do not come with an objective meaning; they meet us within our freedom of interpretation. To live well is to interpret well, and to live badly is to interpret badly.[2]

Life is extravagant and offers riches, but we must *act* to receive them; we must cooperate with the plan if we are to benefit from its beneficence. One important action that we may take is to pay close attention to how we *think*, because how we think influences what we *do* and what we *feel*—just as what we do and feel influences our thinking. These are three aspects of the one person, *triune*, distinguishable but inseparable, each in constant reciprocal activity with the other two. Together thinking, doing, and feeling constitute us.

2. Tracy, *Plurality and Ambiguity*, 9.

Historically, much of our thinking has turned our universe into a hell instead of a home. We create scarcity from abundance, division from unity, and war from peace. Often, this thinking is *dualistic*—it projects false binaries or false oppositions onto a reality that should be kept whole. Politically, we create negative reference groups, hated others, in the hope that our shared hatred of *them* will bind *us* together. Spiritually, finding ourselves embodied, we reject the body and try to identify with the soul alone. Finding ourselves in time, we posit a superior state of timelessness and call it eternity. Finding ourselves immersed in matter, we declare spirit to be divine. Finding ourselves on earth, we fantasize about heaven. Such binary, divisive *dualities*, in which one pole is deemed good and the other evil, turn the universe into a prison.

We are discussing spirituality—our most basic interpretation of life, the interpretation that undergirds all other interpretations, the interpretation that most profoundly influences what we think, do, and feel. Everyone's life has a mood, a disposition that colors every experience and influences every action. This mood is the abiding musical key to which all notes relate, the interpreting matrix through which life itself flows. As interpreters of life, if we change our interpretation, then we will change the very texture of our being. In effect, by changing our worldview, we can change the universe that we inhabit.

Religions have overpromised for too long. This book will not make you happy, increase your income, protect you from illness, or free you from all regret. My hope for this book is more modest, yet equally important: I hope that this book might help you experience life more vividly, face its challenges more confidently, and feel more at home in the universe. It will address our most basic experience, that depth experience that shapes all other experience, in an attempt to discover more meaning, purpose, and joy.

Human Thought Is Evolving from Separation to Relation

We are constantly discovering how deeply connected the world is. This discovery is not new. The Buddha argued 2500 years ago that reality is characterized by *pratitya-samutpada*, co-arising or co-origination. By co-origination, he meant that reality is one interconnected web of becoming, a flow within which everything influences everything else, all the time.

Because reality flows like water, there is no point grasping after things you want or clinging to things that you have. Within a flow, there are no "things" to grasp after and no "things" to cling to, any more than we can grasp water or cling to air. Events arise, and events cease, and events cannot be held. Together, all events constitute a process, such that everything is changing all the time, everywhere. Our challenge is to *affirm change itself*, even when it brings us sadness and disappointment.

Despite this ancient teaching, and the spread of Buddhism throughout the world today, we still tend to think of things as separate from each other. Philosophers call this interpretation of the universe "atomism" or "dualism." The term *atomism* derives from the Greek philosopher Democritus, who taught that "atoms," the smallest particles in existence, are independent, self-sustaining, and self-identical, combining in different ways with other atoms to create different things, but never changing in themselves. The term *dualism* asserts that any two things really are two *separate* things, independent until contact. According to atomism and dualism, any *one* thing is just there, loitering alone, until something else comes near it and acts on it in some way, usually only superficially. They provide an understanding of the universe that is mechanical, not organic.

Such a mechanistic universe is best represented by a pool table, where separate balls lie still until hit by another ball, bouncing off at a certain angle, all according to the hard laws of physics. These interactions are very well described by Sir Isaac Newton, who treated space, time, and matter as separate aspects of the physical universe, just as they appear in everyday experience. But the more physicists studied the universe, the more Newtonian mechanics failed them. Newton's equations seemed to break down at high speeds, great mass, and exceedingly tiny mass. Astrophysicists, for example, were befuddled by Mercury's shifting perihelion (point at which it is closest to the Sun), whose behavior did not match Newton's predictions. As experimental and observational evidence accumulated, physicists found it increasingly difficult to think of objects as interacting with each other against a shared background of absolute, unchanging space and time.

Eventually, Einstein discovered that space and time are not two *separate* aspects of the universe; they are deeply related expressions of *one aspect* of the universe, now called space-time. He also discovered that energy and mass are not two *different* qualities of an object; matter is better understood as energy, as described by the formula $E=mc^2$. Moreover, energy as mass (which some physicists call "rest energy") curves space-time. So pronounced is this curvature that Einstein had to utilize Bernhard Riemann's geometry of curved space to articulate his new theory. The perihelion of Mercury did not shift according to Newtonian expectations because the Sun warps space-time, such that time moves more slowly for Mercury than for Earth.

Following this revolution, physicists began to think *relatively*: everything is defined by its relation to other things. A thing is not a thing *in itself*; a thing is what it is through its *interactions*. Rethinking the physical universe as a *relational* universe, Einstein developed his general theory of relativity, a theory that has been repeatedly confirmed by predicted observations.

Unfortunately, our spiritual thinking has not caught up with our scientific thinking. In our interpretation of the universe, we still tend to think of it as a collection of independent objects that bounce off each other. Socially, we are individualistic: we see ourselves as separate from other people, except maybe when we interact with some of them, some of the time. Ecologically, we see ourselves as separate from the environment, so we can harm it with impunity.

This simplistic view of reality has a certain attractiveness. It resonates with unstudied experience. I am me, and you are not-me, so how could our destinies possibly entwine? Moreover, I am *always* me. I was born and given a name that I carry with me throughout my life, an ongoing identity that remains constant. Sure, I may grow over time, but am I not always more or less the same person? But if we really think hard about our *self*, as the physicists have thought hard about our *universe*, then our interior reality also becomes characterized by relatedness, such that any illusion of separation evaporates. Reality, both outer and inner, physical and spiritual, is characterized by *interdependence*, not independence. Nothing has a pure way of being, a way that it is when it is alone, that is its true identity. Instead, everything co-creates everything else.

We find our source in one another. We are not islands but one teeming ecology. Zulu philosophy expresses this sentiment through the term *ubuntu*, which has been loosely translated as: "I am because you are." Reality is not atomic or dualistic; reality is characterized by *infinite relatedness*.

How Can We Express Infinite Relatedness, as a Concept, in English?

The English language, and Western languages generally, lack a word to describe the infinite relatedness that underlies the universe. Problematically, humans have difficulty thinking a concept that they cannot speak. For instance, regarding color, people have difficulty seeing subtle colors for which their language has no word.[3] Speakers of languages without numbers have a hard time visually determining the size of groups, such as six or seven fish, whereas speakers of languages with numbers can determine which group is larger, even without counting.[4] People choose different responses to crime, varying if it is referred to in the abstract, or as a virus, or as a beast.[5] Due to the subtle influence of language on our interpretation of reality, the sentiment of infinite relatedness demands a word. One candidate comes from Sanskrit, the sacred language of Hinduism and Mahayana Buddhism. This term is *nondualism*. Nondualism is a literal translation of the Sanskrit terms *advaita* and *advaya*, both of which mean "not-two." Whatever we think of as "two"—as separated or divided, is actually "not-two"—is united. "Not-two" does *not* mean that they are one homogeneous whole. Instead, "not-two" refers to the unity-in-difference upon which our universe is based, within which all diversity is integrated. Nondualism, as a concept, asserts that the universe is *both many and one.*[6]

In philosophical terms, nondualism is a *fundamental ontology of relation.* That is, it interprets reality as entirely interdependent. Moreover, that interdependence is entirely unified. This unity does not erase difference but instead *harmonizes* it. Philosophers and theologians have used many terms to describe these fundamental ontologies of relation, many of which are more accessible and marketable than nondualism. *Relativity* describes the physical universe, *process* describes the time-full quality of reality, *ecologism* describes our embeddedness in nature, *organicism* describes the interrelatedness of all things. We could simply use the most obvious choice, relationalism, as obvious as it is unpoetic. But nondualism offers two advantages. First, it makes an implicit claim about reality: that whatever we think of as divided is united. Explicitly, whatever we

3. Zheng et al., "Color Adaptation."
4. P. Gordon, "Numerical Cognition."
5. Thibodeau and Boroditsky, "Natural Language Metaphors," 3–5.
6. J. P. Sydnor, *Rāmānuja and Schleiermacher,* 7–9.

think of as "two" is actually "not-two." Second, and perhaps more importantly, the term *nondualism*, as a translation of *advaita* and *advaya*, refers us to an extremely rich heritage of thought stretching from India to Japan, from 500 BCE to the present, especially in the traditions of Hinduism and Buddhism. This thought presents tremendous opportunities to the evolving human mind.

To Flourish, We Must Mend What Is Torn

As noted above, much religion is *binary*. It divides reality into good and evil, God and Satan, heaven and hell, angels and demons, saints and sinners. At its worst, such binary religion pits soul against body, spirit against matter, and time against eternity. Then, having posited these absolutes, binary religion posits salvation as the eradication of one absolute in favor of the other, sometimes in apocalyptic battle, sometimes in an event of gnostic liberation (soul freed from body, spirit freed from matter, ignorance replaced by knowledge, time yielding to eternity, etc.).

Interpreting the universe as an assortment of opposing binaries splinters human experience. But instead of separating the different aspects of life from each other and choosing one over another, we can embrace them all as divinely gifted. Matter and spirit, soul and body, time and eternity are meant to infuse each other, not annihilate each other. The relationship is the gift. Hence, the poles are not *opposites*—they do not *oppose* one another. Instead, they are *mutually amplifying contrasts*, cooperating to intensify experience. The embrace of both poles grants us the fullness of life. To choose between the two, to prefer one to the neglect of the other, impoverishes.

If we choose one contrast over another, then we lose the power they derive through their relationship. Consider, for example, light and darkness. Each is incomplete because it lacks what the other has. At the same time, each is incomplete because it depends on the other for the contrast that grants it fullness of being. Alone, light is just light. But in contrast, light is *not darkness*, so light has an added quality, so light has become *more*. At the same time, light grants darkness the quality of being *not light*, so that darkness too has an added quality and has become *more*. Through this one relationship, light has become light, light has become *not darkness*, and light has become the gift of *not light* to darkness.[7] Re-

7. Bahm, "Polarity," 348.

lationship creates excess. For this reason, wanting us to live vividly, God creates the light *and* the darkness (Gen 1:1–5). They are separated so that they contrast, then set side by side so that they can relate. To choose one over against the other creates a breach.

The universe is not separated into parts; it is united as a whole. Although nondualism is a concept, it is not a bald assertion or cold belief. It is a vibrant way to live. Many people who have lived their lives well have concluded that the world is truly nondual—a shimmering matrix of dynamic relations. The American naturalist John Muir, for example, observes, "When we try to pick out anything by itself, we find it hitched to everything else in the Universe."[8] For Muir, reality is a vast tapestry, infinite threads bound together as beauty. Anything that happens to one thread happens to the tapestry, and anything that happens to the tapestry happens to the thread. We are many, and we are one. We are *nondual*.

Nondualism Is Active

Here, we are proposing *pluralistic* nondualism, the belief that reality is composed of real difference harmonized into perfect unity. Below, we will clarify how *pluralistic* nondualism differs from *monistic* nondualism, which argues that ultimate reality is absolute homogeneity without difference. In a universe characterized by pluralistic nonduality, everything is correlated to everything else. Nothing has "self-identity" or any pure presentation without reference to context. While everything is unique and offers unique qualities to the play of relations, the effect of that uniqueness will change with context. If anything were so isolated as to be in a pure, self-identical state, then it would be irrelevant. The only quality that is natural to all beings is the quality of being correlated through time, and to be constantly changed by those changing correlations.

The assertions above may sound abstract, but they are daily experiences. For example, consider the musical note E. The note E has a defined wavelength (a unique quality) but no inherent identity; E is what it is through its relations. For example, E becomes a cheerful C major chord when played alongside the notes C and G. But E acquires a certain sadness when played with C# and G#, forming the lilting C# minor chord, as in Chopin's posthumous "Nocturne in C# Minor." Likewise, if E is played sequentially with C and G rather than concurrently. Our experience of E

8. Muir, *My First Summer*, 211.

changes, so that we do not know what E will be until we know its context. E always makes its own unique contribution, but the context influences the character of the contribution, just as the character of the contribution influences the context.

Or, consider the atom. Without relations an atom is free, but it lacks versatility. If united with other atoms, it becomes more. *It transcends its own potential.* For example, hydrogen can combine with oxygen to form water, or nitrogen to form ammonia, or carbon to form methane. Each of these combinations is effectively different from hydrogen itself. Water serves purposes that neither hydrogen nor oxygen could serve alone. By combining, hydrogen and oxygen have become something new, greater than the sum of their parts. Indeed, they have become *other than* the sum of their parts. So, what is the "essence" of hydrogen? Is it the solitary hydrogen atom when it's alone? Or is it the hydrogen atom in water, methane, or ammonia? Perhaps the "essence" of hydrogen is to combine with another hydrogen atom and become helium in a star. Or better yet, perhaps hydrogen has no essence and is what it is only in context, through its relations.

"Essence" is a limiting concept, asserting that things are what they are and cannot be otherwise. We can even think of ourselves as having an essence, a fixed identity that is who we are and will never change. If we become addicted to this essence and want to protect it, then we must insulate it from the relationships that threaten change; we must be free *from*. But the freedom that offers the greatest transcendence is not freedom *from*, it is freedom *with* and *for*. Only through combination can we exceed our potential. The elements of the universe, including ourselves, are much like the notes in a musical composition, meaningless without relationships. We are not simply arbitrary, nor are we fully determined. Instead, we are free to create through the relativity that time offers, thereby offering our own particular increase to the divine harmony.

The above provides a brief presentation of what nondualism *is*. To clarify the concept, we must also explain what nondualism is *not*.

Nondualism Is not Monism

As noted above, "nondual" is the English translation of the Sanskrit terms *advaita* or *advaya*, which literally mean "not-two." Some schools of Hinduism interpret "not-two" to mean "only one." They then propound *monism*, the belief that everything is just one thing, a pure unity, such that all differentiation is illusion. For example, the Ashtavakra Gita states, "I am always one / without two."[9] The poem also declares:

> Two from one!
> This is the root of suffering.
> Only perceive
> That I am one without two,
> Pure awareness, pure joy,
> And all the world is false.
> There is no other remedy![10] . . .
>
> The world with all its wonders
> Is nothing.
> When you know this,
> Desire melts away.
> For you are awareness itself.
> When you know in your heart
> That there is nothing,
> You are still.[11]

The Ashtavakra Gita is a monistic text that rejects belief in a personal God. *Monism* teaches that everything is really *one* thing. In this case, the Ashtavakra Gita teaches that all reality is Brahman: pure being, pure bliss, and pure consciousness. Only Brahman is real; everything else is illusion. The poem grants everyday life a certain *provisional* reality, like that of a dream. But in the end, salvation is the recognition of one's own *identity* with Brahman. "Identity" is more than "unity." If only Brahman exists, then your *self* is false, and the universe in which you live is an illusion. If Brahman is everything, then in truth, you are *identical* with Brahman; you *are* Brahman.[12]

But nondualism, as we are interpreting it, is not monism. In our view, nondualism means *indivisibly united yet internally distinguished*. Nondualism discerns the unity in difference that underlies all things. For this-worldly examples, we may think of the light and heat of a fire, which are distinguishable but inseparable, both one and two. Physicists may think of space and time, which they call space-time. Psychologists may

---

9. Byrom, *Heart of Awareness*, 74, §20.2.

10. Byrom, *Heart of Awareness*, 9, §2.16.

11. Byrom, *Heart of Awareness*, 30, §11.8.

12. See Chandogya Upanishad, in Olivelle, *Upaniṣads*, 6.8.7.

think of memory, intelligence, emotions, and will, those various aspects that constitute one mind.

Nondualism Is not Atomism or Separatism

Nondualism charges the cosmos with dynamic reciprocity, such that we can never determine where one thing stops and another starts. All transitions are gradual, as the river flows into the sea, the grassland transitions into the forest, or the plains meet the hills. The universe is one expansive continuum, without demarcation. And if reality is a continuum without demarcation, if all boundaries are arbitrary and artificial, then difference does not oppose, and difference certainly doesn't annihilate. Instead, *difference generates energy*. For fullness of life, safety needs danger, warmth needs cold, day needs night, and light needs darkness.[13]

We call the far shore of a river the "opposite bank," but it opposes nothing. Instead, it *cooperates* with the near shore to grant the river its being and direction. We call the front and back of a coin "opposite sides," but which could exist without the other? If we take away the front, the back ceases to be, and vice versa. They do not oppose; they co-originate. So thorough is this universal interdependence that, as Barbara Holmes observes, "The light . . . pierces but does not castigate the darkness."[14]

Nondualism Is not a Perennial Philosophy

Some scholars of religion believe that all religions are fundamentally the same. In their view, differences between religions are accidents of history, geography, and culture, while similarities result from their shared sacred source. So, we should put away our differences and instead act together on our shared values, to make the world a better place. These scholars frequently gather quotes from the mystical traditions of various religions, and these quotes do share a certain resonance. Since the scholars find these quotes in different times and places, they deem their collective teaching to be the "perennial philosophy," the recurring, universal truth. For these scholars, the perennial philosophy is the eternal heart of all religion.[15]

---

13. Habito, *Living Zen, Loving God*, 46–47.

14. B. Holmes, *Joy Unspeakable*, 31.

15. Huxley, *Perennial Philosophy*, vii.

There are several problems with this belief. Religions tend to be vast, long lasting, and literate. They produce vast amounts of writing, which makes it easy to find similar quotes in different traditions. By way of analogy, we can find similar rocks in each of the seven continents, even though the continents themselves are quite different geologically. Moreover, the endeavor of the perennial philosophers is basically evaluative: "If we take the world's enduring religions at their *best*, we discover the distilled wisdom of the human race," argues Huston Smith.[16] Perennialists go to each religion, find that part within the religion that is most attractive to them, lift it out of context, and declare it to be the core truth. But this process simply reveals their own religious preference, to which they ascribe transcendent authority. Anyone could do this in the way that pleases them most. The perennial philosophers tend to be mystics, but legalists could just as easily select legalistic passages from multiple traditions and declare legalism the perennial philosophy. Or, more dangerously, militants could select militant passages from different religions and declare militancy to be the perennial philosophy. The choice is that of the selector.

Even worse, the perennial philosophy erases *difference*. If all religions are basically the same, then differences in thought, feeling, and practice are irrelevant. Nondualism, by contrast, finds *wealth* in difference. *Their* ritual practice (that of other religions), and the transformation that it offers, stimulates *our* ritual practice to reform. Their ethics give us a unique perspective and new insight into our own. Their thought worlds and lifeways open new perspectives onto our own. If all religions were the same, then no religion could challenge another. Religions frequently advocate transformation, and the engines of transformation are difference, disagreement, and debate.[17] Sameness is impotent.

Nondualism Offers Hope

We live in an age of metaphysical divorce, an age in which corrupt worldviews and philosophies fracture that which is naturally united. Nondualism asserts that all reality is inherently related. Nothing is separable from anything else, and no one is separable from anyone else. Thus, nondualism offers intellectual resistance to the false divisions that cause our

16. Huston Smith, in Center for Action and Contemplation, "Distilled Wisdom," para. 2 (emphasis added).

17. Clooney, *Seeing through Texts*, 54.

suffering, implicitly condemning sexism, racism, classism, nationalism, co-religionism, neoliberalism, and every other divisive worldview.

Many movements assert our fundamental relatedness and countless groups are working to make the world a better place. Humanists work to improve the human condition, because they believe that humans are inseparable from one another. Ecologists work to protect nature because they believe that we are part of it. Religious leaders help people recognize their embeddedness in the sacred. All assert *connectedness*: humanists call it humanism, naturalists call it ecologism, religious leaders call it God. Nondualism, as an umbrella concept, can help to unite these different groups to act together for a better world.

The Hindu Theologian Ramanuja Describes *Vertical* Nondualism

Now, we can distinguish between two types of nondualism, the vertical and horizontal. Vertical nondualism refers to the inseparability, interpenetration, and shared energy of God, humankind, and the universe. Horizontal nondualism refers to the inseparability, interpenetration, and shared energy between all aspects of creation, including persons. To articulate vertical nondualism, we will turn to the Hindu theologian Ramanuja, the most prominent writer within *Visistadvaita Vedanta*, or the teaching of qualified nondualism. This tradition interprets advaita as *both one and two*, hence makes room for the inherent relatedness between God, humankind, and the universe that we are advocating. Ramanuja argues that everything in the universe, moving and unmoving, feeling and unfeeling, conscious and unconscious, is an expression of God and therefore just as real as God. Ramanuja writes: "This world . . . consisting of spiritual and physical entities, has the supreme spirit [God] as the ground of its origination, maintenance, destruction, and of the liberation of the individual from transmigratory existence."[18] In Ramanuja's interpretation, the difference that distinguishes two things is real, a name and form granted them by their benevolent Sustainer, Vishnu, who also grants them their fundamental unity with, in, and through himself. Both human souls and the physical universe are modes of God, who emanates, sustains, and incorporates real distinctions into the divine. Hence, everything is both one and two, distinguishable yet inseparable.

18. Ramanuja, *Vedartha Sangraha*, 4, §2.

Because this God pervades all human souls and all material objects, we can experience the sacred anywhere—in heaven, in ourselves, in others, in matter, and in reason. Anyone having any *one* of these religious experiences is experiencing an aspect of God. If the experiencer thinks *exclusively*, then they may believe that their experience is the *only* legitimate experience. But, if one divine ontology (or metaphysic) can accommodate the varieties of religious experience, as does Ramanuja's, then such exclusivism is unnecessary. Our religious experience can be plural, making for a richer life. Moreover, Ramanuja's *personalist* panentheism, in which God is a full-fledged person, better serves Christian faith than *impersonalist* Platonic idealism, which has been the intellectual source of Christian panentheism for centuries.[19]

The Buddhist Philosopher Nagarjuna Describes *Horizontal* Nondualism

Ramanuja's nondual vision is primarily vertical: he explains how God emanates individual human souls and the material world of time and change, even while God remains an embodied person in heaven. However, he does not develop *horizontal* interrelatedness. While he advocates the dependence of souls and matter on God, he does not posit any *interdependence* between persons or material objects themselves. Another Indian thinker, the Mahayana Buddhist philosopher Nagarjuna, insists on the absolute interdependence of all this-worldly beings on one another—while denying the existence of any sustaining God. His doctrine is that of *sunyata* (shoon-YAH-tah): literally "emptiness." But this is not a generalized emptiness: he insists that all existents (things) are empty of *svabhava* (swuh-BHUH-vuh)—"own being," unchanging essence, inherent existence, intrinsic nature, or independent reality. Instead, everything derives its existence from everything else, even as it grants existence to everything else, in one pulsing flow of infinite relatedness.

As mentioned above, *sunyata* translates literally as "emptiness." Even in the modern Indian language of Hindi, *sunya* (SHOON-yah) can be translated as "zero," "empty," "nothing," or "nothingness." Due to this literal meaning, many opponents of Nagarjuna have interpreted *sunyata* as voidness and accused him of nihilism.[20] Nihilism is belief in

19. J. P. Sydnor, "God in All Things," 154.
20. R. King, "Early Yogacara," 669–70.

nothingness. These philosophers argue that, if everything depends on its relations for existence, then nothing can exist, because things must exist *before* they come into relationship.[21] This argument belies our tendency to believe in separate things, each of which possesses its proper substance, unchanging essence, or enduring nature. This misinterpretation is sometimes encouraged when teachers of *sunyata* critique our attachment to *things*. If we consider a "thing" to be an abiding object with stable qualities that will grant us permanent satisfaction, then there is no "thing." But to assert that there is "no thing" and that there is "nothing" makes a fine distinction that careless readers may overlook, leading once again to the accusation of nihilism.[22] When Buddhists assert that there is "no thing," they are asserting that everything flows into everything else, not that there is "nothing" at all.

Properly interpreted, *sunyata* does not assert the *nonexistence* of objects; it asserts the *interdependence* of objects. Things exist contingently, based on their manifold relations, and any object's self-expression will change based on its context, which means the *object* will change based on its context.

Consider an electron. We could argue that it has an unchanging essence since, as an elementary particle, an electron is absolutely simple. It is not composed of any other particles, unlike protons and neutrons, which are both made of three quarks, according to quantum theorists. So, it doesn't *depend* on those other parts for its existence. All electrons share the same negative charge, the same mass, an up or down spin, etc. And, as an elementary particle, electrons last a very, very long time—perhaps 6.6×10^{28} years, according to the most recent experiments.[23] If electrons are perfectly simple, behaviorally identical, and vastly enduring, then don't they refute our assertion of universal interdependence? Don't they have *independent* being?

Even though we may know all the properties of an electron, we cannot describe the behavior of any *particular* electron without knowing its *context*. If I ask you to imagine an electron and tell me what it is doing right now, you must imagine it in a situation. You know that, in general, it has a negative charge, but you cannot know if it is currently being attracted to a proton or repulsed by another electron. You know that, in general, it is immensely stable, but this particular electron may have just

21. Burton, "Is Madhyamaka Buddhism," 181.

22. Kitarô, *Last Writings*, 24.

23. Cullerne, *Penguin Dictionary of Physics*, 239, "Electron."

been birthed by a muon or may be on the verge of annihilation by a posi-
tron or may be about to fall into a neutron star, where it and a proton will
be smashed together to create a neutron. You don't know if it is bound
up in an atom or free, you don't know its energy level, you don't know its
spin, etc. In other words, even though all electrons share the same properties, you cannot know much about any *particular* electron until you
thoroughly know its context. We learn the electron's *general* properties,
and we think we know the *thing-in-itself*. But there is no thing-in-itself.
There is only the *thing-in-relation*.

Since *sunyata* refers to the infinite relatedness of things, to translate
it literally as "emptiness" is misleading. The terms *empty* and *emptiness*
have negative connotations in English: "I feel so empty" is not a celebratory comment. Since Nagarjuna argues for the perfect activity and receptivity permeating the cosmos, a more accurate translation would be
openness.[24] By design, entities within the universe are wholly responsive
to one another. For humans, who are blessed with the freedom to interpret the universe as we wish, this openness can be forgotten, ignored, or
denied, but only at great expense. Those who close themselves off will feel
less. Those who open themselves up will feel *more*.

With regard to persons, Nagarjuna rejects the existence of any
unchanging, eternal, isolated self. Everyone is empty of self-existence.
Again, Nagarjuna is not asserting that each person is a nothingness. He
is neither an eternalist who asserts the existence of an unchanging soul,
nor a nihilist who denies the existence of any self. Instead, he asserts the
existence of a dynamic, impermanent, thoroughly related "self." In other
words, he does not assert that the self does not exist so much as he asserts that all selves exist, together. We are not one self but many selves,
as one—one web, one nexus, one interconnected, interrelated, pulsing
becoming. Everyone is entirely permeated, causally and qualitatively, by
everyone else. And this absolute relatedness is realized through impermanence. *Profound interdependence occurs through time and is dependent
on time.*

To the human being accustomed to craving permanence, the concept of emptiness will initially present as a threat. But it is actually an opportunity. Our related self is as expansive as the universe. For the person
who has realized emptiness, reality is characterized by unceasing novelty.
We do not fear the end of happiness, because we have always known that

24. McCagney, *Nāgārjuna and the Philosophy*, 33–34.

any period of happiness will end. We do not become undone by tribulation, because we know that tribulation will pass. Thus, the person who
has realized emptiness can be buoyant, even through the vicissitudes of
life, because that person recognizes the impermanence of all vicissitudes.
Impermanence, our unceasing passage through time, does not cause
human suffering. Our craving for permanence in the midst of impermanence causes our suffering. The solution to suffering, then, is to stop
craving permanence. The solution to suffering is to love time.

Indra's Net Illustrates the Promise of Openness

The Buddhist tradition provides a powerful illustration of the dynamic
reciprocity that we have been discussing, commonly referred to as "Indra's Net." To please the god Indra, his courtly artist resolved to create a
work of stunning beauty. To do so, the artist spun a net throughout all
universes, reaching forever in every direction. At every link in the net, he
hung a sparkling jewel. Each jewel catches the light of every other jewel
and reflects it, thereby containing within itself the sprawling splendor of
the entire cosmos. At the same time, the light of each jewel is caught in
all others, so that it is also active within them. Any one jewel contains
the universe, and is expressed throughout the universe, in one glittering
cascade of light.[25]

In the vision of Indra's net, we are the universe, and the universe is
us. Spiritual wealth lies beyond the bounds of any narrow ego. Instead,
the infinity and exteriority of reality invite the self beyond the self into the
whole. Abundance surges as the outer becomes the inner, until there is no
outer and inner, only an open expanse of shared energy.[26] How much we
contain, how big we are, is determined by how open we are to the universe.
If absolutely open, then we can contain the whole universe. If absolutely
closed, then we contain naught but our empty self. In the Buddhist view,
we are as full as we are empty, and we are as empty as we are full.

25. Cook, *Hua-Yen Buddhism*, 2.
26. Siderits and Katsura, *Nagarjuna's Middle Way*, 197.

Nondualism Has Always Been Implicit in the Christian Tradition

The concept of nondualism may be an Eastern import, yet surprisingly, we find a correlate to advaita in the Christian tradition. As noted above, prior to its encounter with Indian philosophy, the West had no *explicit* concept for nondualism, and introduced the word *nondual* only as a translation of advaita. But prior to this encounter, for centuries Christianity had declared God to be *triune* (tri-une, "three-one"), both three and one. From the compound *tri-unity* we derive the term *Trinity*. And we find a powerful statement of Trinitarian paradox in the sixth-century Athanasian Creed, the first creed to specifically address relations *within* the Trinity:

> We worship one God in trinity
> and the Trinity in unity,
> neither confusing the persons
> nor dividing the divine being.
> For the Father is one person,
> the Son is another,
> and the Spirit is still another.
> But the deity of the Father, Son, and Holy Spirit
> is one, equal in glory,
> coeternal in majesty.
> What the Father is,
> the Son is,
> as is the Holy Spirit.[27]

For the author of the Athanasian Creed (who was in all likelihood *not* Athanasius), the Christian God is fully three and fully one. We can refer to the persons of the Trinity as individuals or as a collective. Either way is accurate, because they are three individuals forming one indivisible society. *If nondualism is a fundamental ontology of relation, in which the one and the many are perfectly harmonized, then the Christian Trinity is a form of nondualism.* That is, the Trinity is not *either* three or one. The Trinity is *both* three *and* one. The Trinity is triune; they are nondual. In the words of Richard Rohr, "If the mystery of the Trinity is the template of all reality, what we have in the trinitarian God is the perfect balance between union and differentiation, autonomy and mutuality, identity and community."[28]

---

27. Commission on Worship, *Lutheran Service Book*, 239.
28. Rohr, *Adam's Return*, 75.

The Trinity is a treasure chest for Christian theology, but for too long Christianity has been embarrassed by its riches, defensively asserting its membership in the club of monotheistic religions, proudly proclaiming the One while insecurely mumbling the Three. The reason for this prefer- ence is far from obvious. Historians of religion report tremendously more interreligious violence between monotheistic religions than other forms of religion. In China, Taoists, Confucians, and Buddhists occasionally persecuted each other, but they rarely slaughtered each other.[29] Mono- theism also seems to produce higher levels of *intra*-religious violence, between sects within the same religion.[30] Islam, for example, fought the First Fitna, a struggle between Sunnis and Shi'a, from 656 to 661 CE, and Christianity fought the Thirty Years War between Protestants and Catholics from 1618 to 1638 CE. Certainly, both religious conflicts were complicated by ethnic, political, and economic factors. Nevertheless, historians have made sound arguments that monotheism distorts faith into a motivation for war.[31] Anyone who yearns for a reduction in violence must consider monotheism with a critical eye.

Reflecting its embarrassment, the Christian tradition's *language* for the Trinity has never fit its *theology* of the Trinity. The Athanasian Creed continues: "So the Father is God, the Son is God, and the Holy Ghost is God. And yet they are not three Gods, but one God. . . . For like as we are compelled by the Christian verity to acknowledge every Person by himself to be both God and Lord, so are we forbidden by the Catholic Religion to say there be three Gods, or three Lords."[32]

In conversation, when referring to three persons, we say "they." But in theology, when referring to God the Trinity, we usually say "he." How can three persons as one God take a singular pronoun? If a vocal trio performs a beautiful song in three-part harmony, so perfectly that they sing as both three and one, we still don't refer to them as "he"; we refer to them as "they." Likewise, trust of Trinitarian revelation must express itself grammatically: *God the Trinity takes they/them pronouns.* Anything less risks Arianism, which rejects the divinity of Jesus (and, by implication, the Holy Spirit). Therefore, for the rest of this book, we shall refer to God the Trinity as "they." This pluralistic reference does not assert any *division*

29. Kang, "No Religious War," 970–75.

30. Strathern, "Religion and War," 157–59.

31. Drake, "Monotheism and Violence," 255–56.

32. Episcopal Church, *Book of Common Prayer*, 864.

within God but does proclaim *differentiation* within God. (Pronouns for each *person* of the Trinity will be applied as the book unfolds.)

The Three-in-One Nature of the Trinitarian God Parallels the Three-in-One Nature of a Musical Chord

By way of analogy, the Trinity is three persons who "interanimate" one another.[33] *Interanimation* is an excellent term for the Trinity and, ideally, for human communal becoming. In the Latin language, the *animus* was that part of the person that lent them vitality, energy, and life. The animus was associated with spirit and courage. So, to "interanimate" one another is to grant one another more vitality, spirit, and courage. We have more life through relationship than we can alone, and the deeper the relationships the greater the life.[34] For this reason the Trinitarian God declares, "Seek me and live" (Amos 5:4).

Nevertheless, the eternal threeness and oneness of the Trinity remain, at first glance, mathematically and logically problematic. From an objectivist or materialist perspective, it is impossible to be both three and one. Rocks can't be both three and one; you pick them up, and count them, and you either have one rock or three, not both one and three. According to some logicians, if rocks can't do it, then humans can't do it—not to mention God.

But, on closer examination, it *is* possible to be three and one in human experience. Above, we considered the effect that its harmonic surroundings have on the musical note E, which can provide definitive character to either a C major chord, making it happy, or a C# minor chord, making it sad. Now we can consider if a musical chord, consisting of the notes C–E–G, is one thing or three things. We can label it as either: *one* C major chord, or *three* notes: C–E–G. Most of us will experience it as one thing, but a trained ear can distinguish the three notes within the chord. So a musical chord, one of the most common, shared experiences we have, is both one and three.

The notes in a chord are played simultaneously, but the same analysis applies to melody, in that the notes played before and after any particular note will determine our experience of that note. If the note E is followed by F# and G#, we recognize it as the beginning of a major scale,

---

33. McDougall, *Pilgrimage of Love*, 97.
34. Gunton, *One, Three and Many*, 152.

which feels happy. If the note E is followed by F# and G, we recognize it as the beginning of a minor scale, which feels sad. According to the doctrine of *sunyata*, or openness, E lacks any self-sufficient, independent reality.[35] For a tone to become a melody, it must be contextualized within relationships of becoming, mediated by the passage of time. Tones *interanimate* each other, both vertically (in harmony) and horizontally (in melody), transforming the other tones played before them, with them, and after them. Moreover, the beauty of this harmony, its experiential power, is predicated upon the tones' *difference*. The symphonic abundance of the C chord, or any melody in the key of C, is not experienced *despite* the tonal differences between C, E, and G; it is experienced *due to* their differences.

Agape Unites the Three Persons into One God

The tones within a chord are united by their underlying mathematics. Each tone has a frequency, and those frequencies will create different effects depending on how they overlap. The tones flow through one another, so that their uniqueness can be discerned but not separated. Similarly, the persons within the Trinity are united by their shared love, a love so perfect that the three persons become one God. In Greek, the word for this divine love is *agapē* (ah-GAHP-ay). Agape refers to the love between the persons of God, the love that God has for humankind, and the love that humans are called to share with one another. Agape is a perfect love, unconditional and universal. As such, we must distinguish it from all the transactional loves that characterize human life: from familial and tribal love (Greek: *storgē*) that grants us security and protection, from the brotherly love (Greek: *philos*) that is of benefit to both parties, and from the erotic love (Greek: *eros*) that brings pleasure to both parties. Agape is not *against* these other loves, but agape *completes* them by divinizing them, by bringing them plumb with the grain of the universe.

Christianity, as an outgrowth of Judaism, has always identified itself as a monotheistic religion, worshiping one God and one God alone. Although the tradition has been soundly Trinitarian for a millennium and a half, some Christians deny that three unique persons can comprise one God. They argue that such a belief would constitute *tritheism*—the worship of three different gods. In their view, tritheism is a form of polytheism that rejects worship of the one God and is, therefore, heretical.

---

35. Streng, *Emptiness*, 63.

However, Christianity has also taught that the love of God is infinitely more perfect than the love of human for human. Therefore, if humans can achieve a love that erases the boundaries between persons, God should be able to as well. Hal and Janice were two parishioners in a former church, married for sixty years. They had an extremely loving relationship, one of those rare near-perfect marriages—unfailing kindness toward one another, patience with each other's foibles, continual gratitude and mutual praise. In his mid-eighties, Hal got sick and, after a three month fight, died. Janice was devastated.

I was having lunch with Janice a few months later. When I asked her about life without Hal, she smiled gently, looked slightly befuddled, and said that she felt like "half a person." She wasn't whole once separated from Hal. She no longer felt complete. Her *self* was lacking. Janice's statement was both tragic and wonderful; tragic because she was in such pain, wonderful because she had known such love. *She was saying that the two of them had become one, so that when one of the two was lost, the one who was left felt like only a half.* They had a nondual relationship, being both two and one. They had a Trinitarian relationship, being united by agapic love, which had completed their familial, friendly, and erotic love.

Crucially, this union was predicated upon their difference, not their sameness. Janice and Hal did not fall in love or continually deepen their love because they saw themselves in each other. They loved one another because they saw someone *different* in each other. They were attracted to one another's uniqueness, not sameness. Certainly, they shared values, ideals, and goals that made their marriage work. But neither saw the other as an extension or reflection of the self. They saw each other as free selves, deeply united.

Janice and Hal's relationship achieved divine unity because neither sought to protect any aspect of themselves from the other. Using Nagarjuna's language, they practiced openness, and found their greatest joy in that openness. Conversely, Hal and Janice denied their *svabhava*, which we can here translate as "separate-being" or "self-sufficiency." In this telling, *svabhava* refers to a withdrawn portion of the soul, an invulnerable hardness in the psyche that shallows our relationships. Nagarjuna asserts that it does not exist in truth, but that our craving for it—our fear of vulnerability—conjures its illusion. And that illusion causes our self-assertion, self-obsession, and ultimately our self-suffering, all of which spread like a disease.

If Janice and Hal can achieve unity through love, if *two* humans can become *one* couple, then certainly the Trinitarian God—Parent, Child, and Spirit—should be able to do the same. To deny God a human capacity would be bad theology. For this reason, accusations of tritheism against Trinitarians do not hold water. God is three persons united through agapic love into one nondual community. God is *agapic nonduality*. Recognizing love as the basis for all Christian thought, Catherine Mowry LaCugna concludes, "The doctrine of the Trinity, in one form or another, is the *sine qua non* for preserving the essentially relational character of God, the relational nature of human existence, and the interdependent quality of the entire universe."[36]

The Persons of the Trinity Relate to One Another in a Divine Dance

When they were younger, Janice and Hal loved to dance. Interestingly, much like the teachers of openness have illustrated their concept through the metaphor of Indra's web, the teachers of the Trinity have illustrated their concept through the metaphor of dance. When a skilled couple dances you cannot detect who is leading. There is no compulsion. Their movements appear spontaneously generated. Each defers to the other to produce perfectly synchronized action, action so spontaneous that it embodies freedom.[37] So it is with the Trinity. They dance freely, spontaneously, always in relation to one another but never determined by one another, co-originating one another in joyful mutuality.[38] Dance creates beauty out of motion and grace out of time. Dance renders impermanence playful. The unique motions of the dancers unite to form the one harmony, so that the sum is greater than the parts. Interactions are spontaneous, the product of trust, attentiveness, and communion.

We, being made in the image of God, are made to dance—with God, with one another, and with the cosmos. In other words, our being is invited into God's dance, and God's dance is invited into our being. Just as importantly, we are called to share God's dance with one another, to relate to

36. LaCugna, *God for Us*, 289.

37. Moltmann, "God Is Unselfish Love," 123–24. Moltmann refers to the metaphor of spontaneity, not to the metaphor of dance.

38. Here, we stray from Moltmann, who continues to insist on the monarch Father as the origin of the history of salvation, including the Son and the Spirit. See Moltmann, *Trinity and the Kingdom*, 177–78.

one another freely and joyfully, spontaneously effecting one another. The energy of this love feels inexhaustible. Without the hindrance of obstinate self-assertion, energy multiplies itself exponentially. An unexpected quantity of joy arises, which is the experience of grace. But all of this can occur only if we first empty ourselves of any grasping self.[39]

Once the open dance begins there is no coercion. Autonomy is not lost, but it is *surpassed* as the dancer's movements become interdependent with their partners', and vice versa. This interdependence does not involve control since the partners fluidly co-originate each other's movements, embodying joyful freedom in spontaneous relationship.[40] The dance expresses mutuality; it proves that many can dance together more gracefully, joyfully, and spontaneously than one can dance alone.

The Divine Dance
(sculpture by Scotty Utz, photo by Daniel Weatherby)

39. Siderits, "Soteriological Significance of Emptiness," 9–10.
40. Bauckham, "Jürgen Moltmann," 158.

This Book Will Draw on Multiple Religious Traditions to Produce a Christian Theology

Above, we have encountered two great images from two great traditions. The Mahayana Buddhist tradition presents us with the image of Indra's web, that glittering network of jewels in which each jewel reflects all others, while simultaneously being reflected within all others, in one shimmering matrix of light. In that tradition, Indra's web symbolizes the fundamental openness of the universe and the beauty that offers itself if we participate in that openness. The Trinitarian Christian tradition presents us with the image of the dance, elegant movement through time, in which the three persons who constitute one God process with, in, and through one another. We have also encountered Ramanuja of the Hindu tradition, who teaches that all reality is divine Being in three modes: that of God, of human souls, and the material universe. Certainly, these three visions hold promise for one another. If we can compare them, if we place them into conversation, then they will transform one another.

Scholars call the deliberate comparison of thought across religions *comparative theology*. The novel and burgeoning discipline of comparative theology is a powerful method for gaining critical insight into our inherited worldviews. More importantly, the critical insights gained through comparison can produce *constructive* theology or, in other words, revised and renewed worldviews. New comparisons produce new questions, new questions produce new answers, and new answers constitute new theology. Through comparison, by placing our worldviews into a new context, we can ask original, unfamiliar questions of our traditions. Then, we can speculatively suggest possible answers to those questions, responding to the challenges raised. This practice demonstrates the incisive power of comparative theology to generate critical tension, as well as the creative power of comparative theology to resolve that very tension.[41]

Comparative theology responds to the times in which we live. Religious plurality (religious "difference") is a fact. Religions have different beliefs, different practices, different symbols, etc. Human beings respond to difference, especially religious difference, in varying ways, some helpful and some harmful. As the world becomes increasingly globalized, and as we are brought into contact with otherness more frequently, how we react to otherness will become increasingly important. Our response will affect us personally, and it will have geopolitical implications. Some

41. Clooney, *Comparative Theology*, 82.

people are repulsed by religious difference and attempt to insulate themselves from it. Other people are fascinated by difference and see it as an opportunity to learn more about "the other"—the one who is different from us, the one whose very existence challenges all our assumptions. For these intellectual extroverts, otherness provides a powerful means of insight. Religiously, the other presents an opportunity to compare and contrast our beliefs, practices, and moods with different beliefs, practices, and moods, and to reform ourselves in the light of difference.

This comparative practice brings hidden aspects of ourselves to awareness. Most of our beliefs and behaviors arise from our subconscious. We are not aware of them, do not choose them, and cannot analyze them. They have been bequeathed to us by our culture, family, and personal history, and we have absorbed them unknowingly from childhood to adulthood. Since these beliefs and behaviors are unchosen, they are unfree. We are determined (unfree) whenever our thoughts or actions are instinctive rather than conscious. If we desire freedom, then we must become aware of who we are. We must bring to consciousness that which now lies hidden. Then we can analyze our beliefs and actions and revise them in accordance with consciously chosen values. This process will never be complete, but the more we do it the more free we become.

Our deepest beliefs and values tend to be associated with our religion. Here, I am using the word *religion* loosely. For our purposes, religion can include theism (believing in God), atheism (not believing in God), agnosticism (not knowing whether God exists or not), materialism (believing only in matter), or nontheism (rejecting belief in God but still believing in transcendence). Everyone has an orientation toward reality, an "ultimate concern," a worldview, a personal philosophy, etc. Much of what we believe may be vague, or we might not even know what we believe, and we may act on beliefs we are unaware of. This, sadly, is the unstudied human condition.

Thankfully, comparison interrogates sameness—the familiar, the obvious, the assumed—through otherness. The other's difference provides a contrast to our subconscious beliefs, raising them into consciousness, depriving them of their obviousness, and subjecting them to the vitalizing scrutiny of doubt. Comparative theology grants us greater awareness of our own faith by encountering a different faith. Once we have encountered this other faith, we have multiple options. We can leave ours the way it was, thankful for the increased awareness. We can revise our faith according to the challenge presented by the other. Or we can borrow aspects of the other faith and incorporate them into our own. We can even attempt to synthesize the two faiths into one. Conversion is the final option, and it must be a real option for comparative theology to be effective. Comparative theology seeks to transform theology, and transformation demands risk.[42]

To gain a place at the table of theological method, comparative theology must become constructive, pastoral theology. In other words, it must produce new (constructive) theology that is helpful to the church—to priests, pastors, and parishioners alike. Once comparative theology achieves this, then theological method will broaden and comparative theology will become theology itself.

On first view, comparative theology might appear colonialist. It does have some similarities to colonialism. It searches the other for resources and appropriates them, usually without the permission of the other, occasionally against the will of the other. It unites other and same into one world economy of ideas, in a process of globalization that will not treat all participants equally. It enriches self by importing the other. At its worst, it merely decorates its theological drawing rooms with curios from foreign lands. For these reasons, comparative theology is condemned by some critics as an inescapably colonialist endeavor.

These critics, however, tell only half the story. Comparative theology seeks *transformation of the self by the other*. To achieve this transformation, comparative theology renders the self existentially vulnerable to the other—not a common practice among colonialists. Indeed, comparative theology acknowledges the other as sacred, as a legitimate revelation of the holy. As holiness relating to holiness, comparative theology seeks *exchange* rather than extraction. Colonialism, on the other hand, denigrates the colonized to justify their colonization. In a sense, comparative theology *reverses colonialism*. Colonialism is a physical, historical invasion of native lands by foreign forces. Comparative theology is an intellectual invitation of the foreign to transform the native.[43] When practiced hospitably it engenders a symbiotic relationship between the compared parties. No longer does only one benefit from the other. Now, both are potentially enriched through a newly established relationship of mutual challenge and mutual benefit. To deem any *beneficial* relationship a *colonial* relationship implicitly rejects all community. If all benefit is parasitic

---

42. Clooney, *Theology after Vedanta*, 8.
43. Hedges, "Old and New," 1130–31.

then isolation becomes the only moral choice and even the possibility of community is denied.[44]

Comparative theology, as a practice of mutual respect and mutual benefit, seeks the construction of *interreligious community*. As such, it is a practice of global citizenship. Its fundamental postulate is that theology profits from comparison, so the religions are (at least intellectually) interdependent. This interdependence is increasingly disclosing itself—we are because they are, and we become more as they become more, together. In the past, difference has been abominated at times, tolerated at times, sometimes even appreciated. Now, difference is becoming sacralized. We are coming to see difference as a gift of God, *from the heart of God*. And through comparative theology, as we have seen, difference becomes a blessing rather than a threat. At its best, comparative theology expresses the hope that we may become benedictions to one another.[45]

 ## This Book Will Tell a Story

We love stories. People read more novels than essays and watch more movies than documentaries. Perhaps because we find ourselves within time—within a story—we also find ourselves intrinsically open to the power of narrative. Recognizing this openness, I have attempted to write this book as *narrative nonfiction*. I do so fully recognizing that, as John Thatamanil notes, "Voyages to uncharted territories cannot be made with map in hand."[46] We will begin our journey with God as Trinity, three persons joined through perfect love into one God (ch. 2). Next, we will consider Creator and creation. The Creator and Sustainer of the universe is YHWH, whom Jesus called Abba, God the Father, whom the prophets recognized as God the Mother, the womb of reality who births being itself (Isa 66:13, etc., ch. 3). Then, we will consider *anthropology*, the relationship of God to humankind and the status of humankind within the cosmos (ch. 4). Having considered humankind, we will examine Jesus of Nazareth, the divine human whom Christians consider to be the perfect window onto God (ch. 5). After his ascension, Jesus bequeathed to us the Holy Spirit, Sophia (ch. 6). Through their combined action, the Sustainer, Christ, and Wisdom offer a cosmic healing (ch. 7). To share this healing

---

44. J. P. Sydnor, *Rāmānuja and Schleiermacher*, 216–17.

45. J. P. Sydnor, *Rāmānuja and Schleiermacher*, 217.

46. Thatamanil, *Immanent Divine*, 172.

with the world, the Holy Spirit animates Jesus's disciples with the same Spirit that animated Christ himself, thereby creating a new (still imperfect) humanity, the church (ch. 8). The church recorded its experience of new life, which it called salvation, in the Bible (ch. 9). Although we may experience despair within this story, we are promised its consummation in the end, which is a new beginning (ch. 10).

This Theology Will Be Systematic: Internally Coherent and Unified in Theme

A theology that is broad in scope, centered around one central insight, and addresses multiple aspects of Christian thought is called *systematic*. To be systematic, a theology should not present internal contradictions. It may utilize *paradox*, tensions in reason that spur the mind to deeper thought: "If you would save your life, you will lose it; but if you would lose your life for my sake, you will find it," says Jesus (Matt 16:25). Contemplation of this challenging statement is intellectually fruitful. But in general, theology should make sense and not *accidentally* present claims that do not cohere with each other. Accidental contradictions produce only confusion.

The uniting theme of this systematic theology is *agapic nondualism.* As noted above, agape is the unconditional, universal love of God for all creation. Nondualism asserts that everything is fundamentally united to everything else. Agapic nondualism, then, claims that *the love of our Trinitarian God, who is three persons united through agape into one God, expresses itself within our infinitely related universe, such that nothing is separable from anything else, and no one is separable from anyone else.* This insight will guide our thinking about God, creation, humankind, etc., allowing us to reinterpret them in a consistent manner.

The danger of systematic theology is over-ambition, the mistaken belief that this particular theology is comprehensive and answers all the important questions, thereby providing resolution. No theology can present a totalized interpretation of reality, and no theology should try, since totalization would reduce the overflowing abundance to an understandable system, thereby eliminating the available riches. Indeed, intellectual resolution would be a spiritual tragedy as it would stop all growth. Any claim to final adequacy masks a manipulative spirit that seeks control over the reader instead of humility before God.

This Theology Is Progressive

Although theology is *about* God, it is *for* humans, and it is for humans in their God-given freedom. Hence, we cannot achieve theological mastery or know God in Godself. Even as we trust that God's self-revelation is truthful, God's inner nature will spill over our minds like an ocean overflows a thimble. By way of consequence, all theological proposals, including this one, are intrinsically partial and inadequate. This book will serve its purpose in its time and eventually be forgotten. Put simply, the power of the transcendent will always shatter any vehicle that tries to contain it. Old wineskins cannot hold new wine, and no wineskin can hold revelation (Mark 2:22). Still, the effort of thinking about God is worth it because our concept of God will influence the quality and conduct of our life: "The belief of a cruel God makes a cruel [person]," writes Thomas Paine.[47] Can belief in a kind God make a kind person?

In respect of our limited nature, and in hope of our transformation, this theology is *progressive*, in two senses of the word. First, the theology presented here will be *ethically* progressive regarding the pressing issues of our day. It will praise LGBTQ+ love, argue for the ordination of women to Christian ministry, advocate equality between all races, cherish the environment, learn from other religions, condemn the militarization of our consciousness, and promote a more generous economics.

Just as importantly, the theology presented here will be *fundamentally* progressive. That is, it will present a *theology of progress* toward universal flourishing. God has not created a steady-state universe; God has created an evolving universe characterized by freedom. As free, we can grow toward God or away from God, toward one another or away from one another, toward joy or into suffering. God wants reunion, with us and between us, but does not impose that desire, allowing us instead to choose the direction of our activity, while always inviting us to work toward the reign of love.

Divine Reality Is a Great Open Dance

Jesus's first miracle was to turn water into wine (John 2:1–11). This miracle suggests a festive aspect of Jesus rarely expressed in Christian art. Jewish weddings in Jesus's day were weeklong affairs of food, music,

---

47. Paine, *Collected Writings*, 205 (gender neutralized).

storytelling, and *dance*. The participants were segregated by gender, but everyone danced. So, although the Bible does not state that Jesus danced, from historical evidence we can infer that he probably did.[48] After all, he wasn't a Calvinist: Jesus inherited a religious tradition, Judaism, that revered dance as an expression of the joy found through relationship with God: "Then the young women will dance with joy, and the young men and the elderly will make merry. I [YHWH, Abba] will turn their mourning into joy; I will comfort them, exchanging gladness for sorrow" (Jer 31:13). Jesus implies his own love of dance. In his story of the prodigal son, the father hosts a party with celebratory dancing upon the lost son's return (Luke 15:21–29). And Jesus condemns his own generation as one that does not dance even when music is played (Matt 11:16–17).

The apocryphal gospel Acts of John (second century) explicitly depicts Jesus dancing with his disciples. In the ascribed words of the disciple John,

> He [Jesus] gathered us all together and said, "Before I am delivered up to them, let us sing a hymn to the Father, and go forth to what lies before us. So he commanded us to make a circle, holding one another's hands, and he himself stood in the middle. He said, "Respond Amen to me." He then began to sing a hymn, and to say:
>
> . . .
>
> "Grace is dancing.
> "I will pipe, dance all of you!" "Amen."
> "I will mourn, lament all of you!" "Amen."
>
> . . .
>
> "The whole universe takes part in the dancing." "Amen."
> "He who does not dance, does not know what is being done." "Amen."[49]

The text reveals not just *that* Jesus dances, but *why* he dances. His dancing is tied to his *openness to life*—music and mourning, play and lament. Indeed, God and heaven join in this dance, as well as the disciples. They ratify Jesus's perfect Amen, his sacred Yes to the agony and ecstasy of this-worldly being. For Jesus, who is the Christ, life is a *great open dance* into which we are all invited.

Jesus's great open dance is intimately connected to the God of love whom he preached. His sense of loving interdependence—agapic

---

48. Hikota, "Christological *Perichōrēsis* and Dance," 195.

49. James, "Acts of John," §§94–95.

nondualism—is not new to the Christian tradition, although it has generally been a minority report. This book will represent the Christian tradition through the lens of agapic nondualism. At times, this representation
may seem untraditional, but traditionalism does not concern us. *Given
Christ's revelation of God as agape, the Christian tradition must justify itself as agapic. Agape need not justify itself as traditional.*

We proceed in the conviction that agapic nondualism dovetails with
Jesus's great open dance, just as Jesus's great open dance dovetails with
agapic nondualism. Too much Christian theology has been soul-stifling
dogma rather than life-giving thought. No longer are people willing to
practice faith out of denominational loyalty, tribal identity, or fear of divine wrath. Instead, people want faith to give them *more life*, and people
want faith to make society *more just*, and people want faith to grant the
world *more peace*. I have written this book in the conviction that Trinitarian, agapic nondualism can do so. To develop agapic nondualism in this
book I will, in the words of Kenneth Burke, use all that can be used,[50]
drawing from multiple thinkers to flesh out a theology of infinite relatedness. In addition to our Indian thinkers, our palette will include process,
feminist, liberationist, womanist, and classical theologians, among others.
To begin our journey, let us first consider our understanding of the Trinity,
developing a concept of God as three persons who cooperatively Sustain,
Exemplify, and Animate the great open dance in which we all participate.

---

50. Burke, *Philosophy of Literary Form*, 13.

2

God of Infinite Relatedness

In God there can be no selfishness, because the Three Selves of God
are Three subsistent relations of selflessness, overflowing and super-
abounding in joy in the gift of their own life.

—THOMAS MERTON[1]

Our Image of God Creates Our Image of Ourselves

OUR IMAGE OF GOD creates us, even if we don't believe in God. A punishing God creates punishing people, just as a merciful God creates merciful people. Sometimes merciful people turn away from a merciless God
and call themselves atheists. Their mercifulness suggests that they have
faith, but if the concept of God bequeathed them is all judgment and fear
and wrath, then atheism becomes the only sensible option. Bad theology
drives good people out of faith.

Theology is what we think and say about God. To define what good
theology is, we must first define what good faith is. Many people believe
that God loathes them for their imperfection, or controls everyone like
a puppeteer, or causes their tribulation as punishment, or hates the same
people they hate. Such faith arrests development, induces anxiety, and

1. Merton, *New Seeds of Contemplation*, 71.

sanctions hatred. But if we truly believe in a benevolent God, then faith becomes something more life-giving. Faith becomes *the enacted conviction that there is more available than the immediately obvious would suggest or even allow.* And within this faith, God becomes the *ever more*—ever more love, ever more joy, ever more peace, meaning, and purpose. Faith is not the assertion of truth claims that we have never experienced; faith is the discernment of a trustworthy extravagance within and beyond the universe. Faith suspects that there is always more than we can receive. This type of faith experiences the world as luminous and trusts the source of that illumination.[2] Rather than discounting religious experience as a disturbance of the psyche or accident of evolution, faith celebrates the capacity of these experiences to render the ordinary extraordinary.

Early humans expanded geographically by chasing the horizon, repeatedly trusting that new opportunities lay beyond. In much the same way, contemporary humans expand *spiritually* by chasing the horizon, trusting that new ways of being await us. And like our distant ancestors, we experience this movement as a journey homeward, toward a land that is where we are supposed to be. Rejecting the path of least resistance, faith instead chooses the path of most promise.

Theology is faith at thought. But faith can express itself only in thought humbly. Theology does not try to "get it right" so much as it tries to help. We can't get our thinking about God right: "For my thoughts are not your thoughts, nor are your ways, my ways," says YHWH. "As high as the heavens are above the earth, so high are my ways above your ways and my thoughts above your thoughts" (Isa 55:8–9). We can't think comprehensively about God, but we can think beneficially for humans, and we can trust that such beneficial thought fulfills the will of God because God is beneficent, a very present help in times of trouble (Ps 46:1).

This practical attitude toward theology includes criteria of evaluation. Since we are made in the image of God, we must ask what kind of self this theology makes. Does it make a loving self or a hateful self? Does it make a courageous self or a fearful self? Our struggle to think as beneficially as possible, to receive the abundance that is already present, requires attentiveness. It also requires perseverance, because so much inherited religious thought blocks the love of God instead of transmitting it. We can ask two questions: What *do* Christians believe? And what

2. Ramanuja, *Vedartha Sangraha*, 186, §242.

should Christians believe? Far too often, the most astute answers to those questions will diverge.

Some Christians have believed and still believe, and some Christian denominations have taught and still teach, that women are subordinate to men, non-Christian religions are demonic, LGBTQ+ identity is unholy, extreme poverty and extreme wealth represent God's will, God gave us the earth to exploit, God loves our nation-state the best, human suffering is divine punishment, dark skin marks the disfavor of God, and God made the universe about seven thousand years ago in six twenty-four-hour periods. Such bad thinking produces diseased feeling and harmful behavior. Recognizing this problem, we must unlearn every destructive *dogma* that we have been taught, then replace that dogma with a life-giving *idea*. Ideas are brighter, lighter, and more life-giving than dogma. Dogma ends the conversation, but ideas fuel it.

This project, of deconstruction followed by reconstruction, demands that we examine every received cultural inheritance and every authoritative dogma, subject them to scrutiny, then renounce those that harm while keeping those that help. Along the way, we will generate new thoughts, or look for thoughts elsewhere, if the tradition doesn't offer those we need. The process is laborious, tricky, and unending, but our ongoing experience of increasing Spirit legitimates the effort.

Questions fuel this project of emancipation. Because God is infinite and we are finite, we are invited to grow perpetually toward God. Because God loves justice and our societies are not perfectly just, we are invited to work perpetually toward their improvement. The infinite God invites finite reality to move like a stream. But without questions, we do not move. With unchanging answers, we do not move. Only ceaseless questioning propels us over the horizon. For persons and communities committed to growth, answers are not the answer. Having questions—intense, consequential, burning questions—is the answer.

Eventually, good questions may produce better theology. When I was a young man, I preferred philosophy to theology. Reason and observation themselves would save me, I reckoned, and I didn't need any old gods or ancient superstitions to cloud the process. But over time, I came to suspect that philosophy itself was either predicated on a hidden abundance (that was the philosophy I liked) or blind to that hidden abundance (that was the philosophy I disliked). Theology always engaged the abundance, even if I did not always find its conclusions attractive. Nevertheless, I saw that theology could ascribe great potential to existence and provide a ground for the experience of all reality as sacred. So, I cast my lot with theology. In so doing, I cast my lot with God.

At the time, I didn't think of God as Trinitarian, I wasn't sure who Jesus was, and the Holy Spirit seemed like an abstraction. But over the years, I have pondered certain questions: What worldview promotes human thriving? What worldview will allow us to say, on our deathbeds, "Yes, that was a good way to live my life"? What worldview produces abundance in all its forms—spiritual, communal, and material? Over the years, I have come to believe that the Trinity—the interpersonal Trinity characterized by agapic nondualism—provides the best intellectual ground for thinking through the fullness of life. Below, I will explain why.

But first, we will have to consider one of the great mysteries of Christian history. Jesus of Nazareth was a Jew, a devout practitioner of a monotheistic religion, a religion that insistently worships only one God. In the Gospel of Mark, drawing from his own Scriptures, Jesus repeats the central monotheistic refrain of Judaism, the Shema: "Hear, O Israel: the Lord our God, the Lord is one" (Deut 6:4; Mark 12:29). How did a monotheistic prophet of a monotheistic religion inaugurate a movement that became Trinitarian? Since all of Jesus's original disciples were Jewish, to the best of our knowledge, how did they end up talking about three persons—Father, Son, and Holy Spirit—whenever they spoke of God and salvation? No consideration of the Trinity can proceed without first delving into this historical mystery. We will begin with the first appearance of Trinitarian language in the tradition.

We Find a Tripersonal (Based in Three Persons) Experience of Salvation in the Christian Scriptures

Within the Christian tradition, the most consequential speculation on the nature of God occurs in the unrecorded period between the resurrection of Christ and the writing of the Christian Scriptures. We have no writings *from* this period, although we do have writings *about* this period, such as Acts.

Most importantly for our purposes, we have no description of the origins of Trinitarian worship or thought. Although the earliest followers of the Way (Acts 9:2; 19:9, 23; etc.) were Jewish worshipers of one God, their experience of salvation was *tripersonal*. That is, they experienced *one* salvation through *three* persons, whom they called the Father, Son, and Holy Spirit. They expressed this tripersonal salvation in their liturgy, their language of worship, which the authors of the Christian Scriptures then incorporated into their writings.

For instance, Paul provides a Trinitarian benediction, drawing on preexisting liturgical language: "May the grace of our savior Jesus Christ and the love of God and the friendship of the Holy Spirit be with you all!" (2 Cor 13:14). The earliest Gospel, Mark, describes the baptism of Jesus in a Trinitarian manner, referring to Jesus himself, the descent of the Spirit upon him in the form of a dove, and a voice from heaven declaring Jesus the Beloved Child of God (Mark 1:11). In the Gospel of John, Jesus declares, "Abba and I are one" (John 10:30) and promises to send a Counselor (the Holy Spirit) to the new community of disciples (John 14:16). So transformative was the community's experience of tripersonal salvation that the rite of entry into the church became a rite of entry into Trinitarian life: "Go, therefore, and make disciples of all the nations, baptizing them in the name of Abba God, and of the Only Begotten, and of the Holy Spirit" (Matt 28:19).

Since no historian recorded the transition from Jewish monotheism to early Christian Trinitarianism, we cannot know exactly how or why it happened. But given the vigor of the young church, we can infer that the liturgical expressions recorded in the earliest Christian Scriptures were generated within the Christian community and resonated with that community's experience. In worship they preached, prayed, and sang the healing that they had received, a healing which came through three persons but led congregants into one body.[3]

In other words, the early Christian community's experience of salvation was Trinitarian—one salvation through three persons as one God. To assert that their *experience* was Trinitarian is not to assert that their *theology* was Trinitarian. The earliest Christians did not think the same way about God that later Christians would think. They felt that their lives had been transformed by the Father, Son, and Holy Spirit, whom they worshiped as one. (Please note: when discussing historical theology, we will use the traditional, gender-specific terminology of Father, Son, and Holy Spirit. As the book progresses, we will substitute our own, gender-inclusive terminology.)

The early Christians' liturgy expressed their experience, and their initial, unrecorded theological speculations reflected it. The early church laid the foundations of tripersonal (three person) theism on the

---

3. Keating, "Trinity and Salvation," 445–49.

experience of tripersonal salvation.[4] By the time the church wrote its new Scriptures, it could not talk about God without talking about Jesus and the Holy Spirit. Euclideans needed three lines to draw a triangle; Christians needed three persons to talk about God. So John writes: "There are three who give testimony in heaven, the Father, the Word, and the Holy Ghost. And these three are one" (1 John 5:7 DRA).

The Concept of the Trinity Coheres with the Most Fundamental Summation of Jesus's Message: God Is Love

As mentioned above, Jesus and his followers practiced Judaism, a religion replete with commandments to worship God alone: "I am YHWH, who brought you out of the land of Egypt, out of the house of bondage. Do not worship any gods except me!" (Exod 20:2–3). Jesus's favored prophet, Isaiah, reiterates the exclusive status of the one God: "Thus says the Lord, the King of Israel, and his Redeemer, the Lord of hosts: I am the first and I am the last; besides me there is no god" (Isa 44:6 NRSV).

As noted above, Jesus himself affirms Jewish monotheism. When a scribe approaches Jesus and asks him which commandment is the greatest of all, Jesus responds by quoting (and embellishing) the Jews' beloved Shema: "This is the foremost: 'Hear, O Israel, God, our God, is one. You must love the Most High God with all your heart, with all your soul, with all your mind, and with all your strength'" (paraphrasing Deut 6:4–5). Jesus then couples love of God to love of neighbor by quoting Lev 19b: "The second is this: 'You must love your neighbor as yourself.' There is no commandment greater than these" (Mark 12:29–31).

So, when asserting the greatest commandment in Mark, Jesus offers the preamble of Deut 6:4 ("Hear, O Israel: The Lord our God, the Lord is one"). Deuteronomy refers to God with the proper name of YHWH. For the Deuteronomist, God is one deity with one personality bearing one name. But in Matt 22:35–40 and Luke 10:25–28, the greatest commandment conspicuously lacks the monotheistic preamble: "One of them, an expert on the Law, attempted to trick Jesus with this question: 'Teacher, which commandment of the Law is the greatest?' Jesus answered: 'You must love the Most High God with all your heart, with all your soul, and with all your mind.' That is the greatest and first commandment.

---

4. Moltmann, *Trinity and the Kingdom*, 58–60.

The second is like it: 'You must love your neighbor as yourself.' On these two commandments the whole Law is based—and the Prophets as well" (Matt 22:35–39). Both Matthew and Luke were written fifteen to twenty years after Mark.

Was the early Christian community already shying away from pure monotheism? This historical development may seem to come out of nowhere, but it has some precedents in Hebrew thought. Prior to the rise of Christianity, and presaging the Trinitarian inclination, Judaism had a "rich tradition of speculation about heavenly intermediaries."[5] These celestial beings could be the angel of the Lord (Zech 1:12), or personified Wisdom (Prov 8:22–36), or the sons of God (Gen 6:2–7), or Satan the accuser (Job 1:6), all of whom fulfilled roles within the heavenly court.

For this reason, the earliest preachers of Jesus and the Holy Spirit, all of whom were Jews, could have initially identified Jesus and the Spirit as figures in the heavenly court, then seen their status increase over time. In his analysis of John's Prologue (John 1:1–14), Jewish scholar Daniel Boyarin quotes this passage from Philo of Alexandria, a Hellenistic (Greek speaking) Jew who wrote before the birth of Jesus:

> To His Word [Greek: *Logos*], His chief messenger [Greek: *Archangelos*], highest in age and honor, the Father [Greek: *Patēr*] of all has given the special prerogative, to stand on the border and separate the creature from the Creator. This same [*Logos*] both pleads with the immortal as suppliant for afflicted mortality and acts as ambassador of the ruler to the subject. He glories in this prerogative and proudly proclaims, "And I stood between the Lord and you" [Deut 5:5].[6]

This passage presages the early Christians' experience of Jesus as an advocate for humankind to the Father, and as a revelation from the Father to humankind.

Further, in his speculative work *On Dreams*, Philo goes on to offer language anticipatory of the Trinity itself: "The Divine Word [*Theios Logos*] descends from the fountain of wisdom [*Sophia*] like a river. . . . [The psalmist] represents the Divine Word as full of the stream of wisdom [*Sophia*]."[7] Philo is now working with an explicitly tripartite spiritual experience: of a Sustaining God who provides a Mediator to humankind,

5. Juel, "Trinity and New Testament," 314.

6. Boyarin, "John's Prologue as Midrash," 689; quoting Philo, "Who Is the Heir," 205–6.

7. Boyarin, "John's Prologue as Midrash," 689; quoting Philo, *On Dreams*, 2.242–45.

that Mediator being full of Wisdom. If read in a Christian context, then Philo's Logos anticipates Christ and Philo's Sophia anticipates the Holy Spirit. While we cannot know the exact genesis of his thought, Philo's theology may represent a widespread, preexisting notion among Hellenized Jews. If so, then for some this expectation was fulfilled by Jesus of Nazareth, then ratified by the appearance of the Holy Spirit at Pentecost.

Whatever the historical source of Trinitarian thought, these first Jewish-Christians sensed the love of the Parent, salvation through the Child, and inhabitation by the Spirit. They sensed that three persons were producing one salvation. They sensed the Trinity. In keeping with their monotheistic tradition, they also sensed a unifying quality of those three persons: love. Whenever Jesus speaks of God, Jesus speaks of love—love of God, love of neighbor, and love of self (Matt 22:37–40). This law of love admits neither exception nor compromise: Jesus teaches his followers that outsiders will recognize them by their love (John 13:35) and commands them to love their enemies (Luke 6:35). Indeed, Jesus so deeply associates God with love that John later declares, "God is love" (1 John 4:8).

Love cannot be abstract; love needs a beloved. All love is *love of;* hence all love implies relation. If God is love then God must be love between persons: biblically, the Father, Son, and Holy Spirit.[8] The early American theologian Jonathan Edwards writes: "God is Love shews that there are more persons than one in the deity, for it shews Love to be essential & necessary to the deity so that his nature consists in it, & this supposes that there is an Eternal & necessary object, because all Love respects another that is the beloved."[9] So, according to Edwards, when John asserts that God is love, he necessarily asserts that God is *internally related.* Indeed, if he asserts that God in Godself is love, then he asserts that God in Godself is *interpersonal*—inherently more than one. Love is not the Godhead beyond God, a singular, pure abstraction. Instead, love is the self-forming activity of the triune God, the most salient quality of each divine person, and the disposition of each person toward the other—and toward creation.[10]

Paradoxically, Christianity has inherited an experience of God as one and many, singular and plural. The tradition has articulated this experience by adopting a both/and epistemology, a way of knowing that preserves creative tensions rather than resolving them into a simplistic

8. Boff, *Trinity and Society,* 58–60.

9. Jonathan Edwards, in Fisher, *Unpublished Essay,* 79.

10. Moltmann, *Trinity and the Kingdom,* 58–60.

absolute. God is both three and one; God is tri-unity; God is Trinity. This concept of God presents Christianity with its greatest challenge and its greatest opportunity: to think, act, and feel as *many who are becoming one.*

The Early Church Theologians Laid the Foundations for the Social, Tripersonal Doctrine of the Trinity

The early Church's theologians were not *social* Trinitarians, or fully developed *tripersonal* Trinitarians, in the contemporary sense of the concept. However, much of their thought regarding the Trinity lays the groundwork for social Trinitarian thought. Like any theorist of the Trinity, they could have interpreted the three as superficial modes of the one, as did Sabellius in the third century. Or, they could have claimed that the human being Jesus was adopted by YHWH/Abba in response to his sinless devotion, as the Ebionites claimed. Or, they could have described Jesus as subordinate to God by nature, a "secondary god," as Origen asserted. But the early Christians rejected these proposals in favor of a thoroughgoing Trinitarianism.[11]

Theophilus of Antioch, who wrote circa 170–80 CE, was the first Christian to use the word *Trinity.* Writing in Greek, he states: "In like manner also the three days which were before the luminaries, are types of the Trinity [*trias*], of God, and His Word, and His Wisdom."[12] Due to the brevity of the reference, we cannot determine if Theophilus is referring to a psychological Trinity, in which one God hosts Word and Wisdom, or if he is referring to a tripersonal Trinity, in which God, Word, and Wisdom correlate to Father, Son, and Holy Spirit as individual centers of consciousness. However, since *trias* can legitimately be translated as "triad," we can cautiously infer a tripersonal interpretation.[13]

Two later developments strengthened the foundation for tripersonal Trinitarianism. The first was a willingness to refer to the Father, Son, and Holy Spirit as distinct persons. Tertullian, writing in the early 200s, was the first Latin father to use the word *Trinity (trinitas).* More importantly, he distinguishes the Father, Son, and Holy Spirit: "The connection of the Father in the Son, and of the Son in the Paraclete [Holy Spirit], produces three coherent Persons (*personae*), who are yet distinct One

11. Schwartz, *Christology*, 137–60.

12. Theophilus, "Apology to Autolycus," 2.15.

13. A. Williams, "Trinity and Time," 71–72.

from Another. These Three are one essence, not one Person (*persona*), as it is said, I and my Father are One (John 10:30) in respect of unity of substance not singularity of number."[14]

Tertullian's use of the Latin *persona* does not directly imply the contemporary English "person." Latin *persona* derived from *per-sonare*, "to sound through," a reference to the masks that actors wore to fulfill their roles on stage. Since one actor could wear different masks, thereby assuming different personalities, the term *persona* alone, as applied to the Father, Son, and Holy Spirit, does not necessitate tripersonal Trinitarianism. Although Tertullian insists that the Father, Son, and Holy Spirit are "other" (*alium*) to each other,[15] one God could be speaking through three distinct masks. Indeed, Tertullian enables this interpretation when he provides an analogy for the Trinity as sun, ray, and point of light.[16] This analogy suggests one underlying reality expressed three ways, or a masked unitarianism. To anticipate Trinitarianism, distinction must produce unity, not vice versa.[17]

The Cappadocians, early church theologians located in contemporary Turkey, advocate true distinction within unity by conceptualizing God as three distinct *selves*. Writing in Greek in the middle 300s, they assert the basic distinctiveness of the three selves by comparing them—not to one sun manifest in three forms—but to three suns producing one light. Gregory of Nazianzus writes:

> To us there is One God, for the Godhead is One, and all that proceeds from Him is referred to One, though we believe in Three Persons (*hypostases*). For one is not more and another less God; nor is One before and another after; nor are They divided in will or parted in power; nor can you find here any of the qualities of divisible things; but the Godhead is, to speak concisely, undivided in separate Persons; and there is one mingling of Light, as it were of three suns joined to each other.[18]

For both Gregory of Nazianzus and Gregory of Nyssa, the Father, Son, and Holy Spirit are distinct persons within God's being, not superficial modes of God's revelation. The Christian experience of salvation through

14. Tertullian, "Against Praxeas," §25.

15. Tertullian, "Against Praxeas," §9.

16. Tertullian, "Against Praxeas," §8.

17. Tuggy, "Metaphysics and Logic," 3.

18. Gregory of Nazianzus, "Fifth Theological Oration," §14. See also Gregory of Nyssa, "Against Eunomius," §1.36.

three persons is therefore a trustworthy expression of God's deeply interpersonal nature.

But how could the church describe the relationship between the three divine persons producing one God? The tension seemed irresolvable, provoking church theologians to heap paradoxes upon one another. For example, Gregory of Nazianzus writes: "They are divided without division, if I may so say; and they are united in division. For the Godhead is one in three, and the three are one, in whom the Godhead is, or to speak more accurately, Who are the Godhead. Excesses and defects we will omit, neither making the Unity a confusion, nor the division a separation."[19]

While mystics frequently utilize paradox to convey the divine transcendence, Trinitarian theology needed more precise language to avoid accusations of anti-rationalism. Fortunately for early Christian theologians, the preexisting Stoic tradition offered a relational metaphysic declaring distinction-in-fusion. The Stoics advanced the concept of "total mixture" (*krasis di holon*) to describe the inseparable relationship between soul and body, spirit and matter, life and death.[20] Recognizing the utility of this concept, and noting the Stoics' frequent use of the word *khoreo* (to go, move, flow), Gregory of Nazianzus translates it into the verbal form *perikhoreo* (from *peri*, "around," and *khoreo*), as well as the noun form *perikhoresis* (perichoresis). He applies these neologisms to the relationship between the divine and human natures within Christ.[21] But eventually, Nazianzus's invention became the most prominent descriptor, not just for the relationship between the divine and human natures in Christ, but for the Trinitarian relations generally, for the spiritual movement of the three persons within, through, and around one another.[22]

The later theologian Pseudo-Cyril first applies the term *perichoresis* to the fullness of the Trinity.[23] But it is John of Damascus (675–749) who most thoroughly develops the Trinitarian applications of this powerful new concept:

> The hypostases dwell and are established firmly in one another. For They are inseparable and cannot depart from one another, having unconfused mutual circumincession [*perichoresis*] into

19. Gregory of Nazianzus, "Fifth Theological Oration," §14.

20. Lapidge, "Stoic Cosmology," 170–71.

21. Gregory of Nazianzus, "To Cledonius," §4.

22. Moltmann, *Trinity and the Kingdom*, 174–76.

23. Artemi, "Term *Perichoresis*," 23.

one another without any coalescing or mingling, but cleaving to each other. For the Son is in the Father and in the Spirit, and the Spirit is in the Father and in the Son: and the Father is in the Son and in the Spirit, but there is no coalescence or commingling or confusion. And there is one and the same motion, for there is one impulse and one motion of the three hypostases, which is not to be observed in any created nature.[24]

According to John of Damascus, three and one are both essential to the divine being through an interpersonal concept of the Godhead. God is three persons perfectly open to each other in a joyful movement of love. Some contemporary theologians translate perichoresis very technically as "circumincession," "co-inherence," "mutual indwelling," or "compenetration." But other theologians, such as Catherine Mowry LaCugna, noting the similarity between *khoreo* and *choreia* (the root of "choreography"), prefer the less literal but more poetic translation "dance."[25]

Trinamics
(sculpture by Scotty Utz, photograph by Katherine Brooks)

24. John of Damascus, "Exposition of Orthodox Faith," §1.14.
25. LaCugna, *God for Us*, 270–78.

Although hints of the tripersonal Trinity appeared in the early church, concerns about tritheism (that Christians were worshiping three separate gods) undermined any exhaustive pursuit of this idea.[26] Nevertheless, in the twelfth century, the Scottish mystic Richard of St. Victor insisted that differentiated persons are internal to the unified deity. His ideas achieved a certain prominence for several centuries, but then waned as the doctrine of the Trinity drifted to the outskirts of Western theology.[27]

Partly through the influence of Karl Barth, Trinitarian thought made a dramatic return in the twentieth century. While Barth's doctrine continued the Augustinian and Calvinist traditions, which emphasized the one over the three, other theologians began to seriously reconsider the *social* Trinity—the belief that God is three persons united through love into one perfect community. In the late twentieth century, Trinitarian theologians such as Jürgen Moltmann, Catherine Mowry LaCugna, Leonardo Boff, and John Zizioulas began to explore the doctrine's promise and found a range of opportunities open before them. Excited by the possibilities, they asked: If the Trinity is three persons perfectly united by love, and we are made in the image of God, then what does this mean for human community? How could this doctrine change our most basic understanding of reality, the understanding that influences everything we think, feel, and do? Like them, we will now consider the transformative potential these thinkers find in Trinitarian thought.

The Doctrine of the Trinity Shifts Our Most Basic Conception of Reality from Substance to Communion

"Substance" is an important, and overly dominant, concept in Western philosophy and theology. The French philosopher Rene Descartes defines substance as a "thing that exists in such a way that it doesn't depend on anything else for its existence," noting that only God possesses such independent existence. Descartes then defines worldly substances as "things that don't depend for their existence on anything except God."[28] This definition asserts the *dependence* of all things on God, but also asserts their essential *independence* from each other. Descartes's vision unites all reality to God, then fragments that very same reality. Such a

26. Olson and Hall, *Trinity*, 36–38.
27. Olson and Hall, *Trinity*, 57–60.
28. Descartes, *Selected Philosophical Writings*, 177.

substantialist ontology implies, intentionally or accidentally, separation from our neighbors. If God has created us to be metaphysically separate from one another, then what motivates us toward unity? *If, on the other hand, our sustaining God is being-toward-another, and we have received the imprint of our Sustainer, then we are dependent not only on God, but on one another as well.* This mutualistic interpretation of life implies universal communion, thereby rejecting all forms of estrangement, domination, and hierarchy.

This relational metaphysic may disorient us, since we (in the West especially) are more accustomed to the belief that things and people possess an underlying essence that grants them a stable identity. But contemporary physics calls into question the existence of any unchanging substances. Quarks, for example, are the most basic units of protons and neutrons. According to quantum physicists, quarks have neither parts nor dimension, nor can they exist independently of one another—there is no such thing as a "free" quark. Yet, quarks combine to produce the atomic nuclei that grant the cosmos weight and solidity.[29] Metaphorically, we could say that quarks function only in communion.

According to John D. Zizioulas, this social doctrine of the Trinity renders *communion the most fundamental metaphysical concept in Christianity.*[30] God does not *have* relations; God *is* relations. Or, as Peter Phan writes, "In God relation is pure *esse ad*, facing-each-other, pure being-oriented-toward-each-other, pure self-giving-and-receiving-another."[31] Within the Trinity, each divine person possesses a centrifugal nature that seeks fulfillment in their neighbor. God invites humans into the same metaphysical extraversion.

As a reinterpretation of our most basic reality, the Trinity forces us to reconceptualize our relationship to God, one another, and the cosmos. If reality is most basically communion, then to be real is to be in communion, and to be separated is to be less real. Division diminishes being. Prior to relation, in the eternal nothingness that is the absence of relationality, any isolated being is a nonbeing. A solitary being is a nonbeing that yearns to be yet can receive its being only through another. By divine decision, *without relationship there is nothing, even for God.*

---

29. Kohl, "Buddhism and Quantum Physics," 78–79.

30. Zizioulas, *Being as Communion*, 101.

31. Phan, "Relations, Trinitarian," 12:46.

The Trinity Completes the Personal Concept of God as an Interpersonal Concept of God

Catherine Mowry LaCugna writes, "The identity and unique reality of a person emerges entirely in relation to another person."[32] The Bible has always insisted that God is personal, not abstract. Hence, you are not a glorious accident of cosmological evolution; you are a divinely intended gift, given by means of cosmological evolution. Within and beyond the universe is an unending desire for your well-being: "I alone know my purpose for you, says YHWH, my purpose for you to thrive, and my purpose not to harm you, my purpose to give you a future with hope. At that time you will call upon me and come and pray to me, and I will listen to you. You will seek me and find me when you seek me wholeheartedly" (Jer 29:11–13a).

In the biblical view, unrelated personhood is unfulfilled personhood: "It is not good for [someone] to be alone" (Gen 2:18 DRA [gender neutralized]). We can observe this truth today: newborns denied physical contact develop reactive attachment disorders, inmates left in solitary confinement go insane, lonely people become depressed. Without other persons, personality is lost, because personality is fulfilled only through *inter-personality*. The doctrine of the Trinity expresses this theological insight by insisting that God is more than personal; God is *interpersonal*, and lovingly so. Since humans are made in the image of God, the more we love the more joy we receive. Since we cannot deny to God our richest personal experiences, we ascribe to God their consummation. Perfect love and its correlate, pure joy, both belong to God, who invites us into their union.

Critics of social Trinitarianism argue that, if the Trinity implies three unique centers of consciousness, then Christianity has rejected monotheism and adopted polytheism or, more specifically, *tritheism* (the worship of three gods rather than one God in three persons). But Trinitarianism is not tritheism. One way to distinguish the triune God from three gods is by contrasting the Christian Trinity with the Greek troika of Zeus, Poseidon, and Hades. These three gods are separate: ruling separate realms, marrying separate women, and pursuing separate lovers. They are ranked in power, over which they argue and for which they compete. They distrust one another; when their desires clash, they clash. Their

---

32. LaCugna, *God for Us*, 89.

disordered intentions produce a disordered world, as each wields power against the others in support of their arbitrary favorites.[33]

In the Trojan war, for example, Zeus favors the Trojans, but Poseidon favors the Achaeans. When Zeus's sexual attraction toward Aphrodite distracts him from the war, Zeus's wife Hera advises Poseidon of this development, and Poseidon seizes the opportunity to strengthen his side. Later, upset by Poseidon's intervention, Zeus sends him a message:

> Go on your way now, swift Iris, to the lord Poseidon, and give him all this message nor be a false messenger. Tell him that he must now quit the war and the fighting, and go back among the generations of gods, or into the bright sea. And if he will not obey my words, or thinks nothing of them, then let him consider in his heart and his spirit that he might not, strong though he is, be able to stand up to my attack; since I say I am far greater than he is in strength, and elder born; yet his inward heart shrinks not from calling himself the equal of me, though others shudder before me.[34]

Zeus, Poseidon, and Hades rule the cosmos but threaten chaos. Hades lusts after Zeus's daughter Persephone and abducts her, with Zeus's permission. Her mother Demeter, goddess of agriculture, threatens to destroy the harvest and starve humankind, and thereby deny the gods their sacrifices. Zeus must plead with Hades for Persephone's return. Even the natural order is not safe from these three gods' cravings.[35] Zeus, Poseidon, and Hades are three gods, and in no way one God. They exemplify tritheism, and in the worst way.

Many things are triune, both three and one, in which the three are distinguishable but inseparable. A triangle is three unique sides that make up one triangle. The French flag is three different colors that make up one flag. Hydrogen cyanide is three different atoms (HCN) that compose one molecule. Deuterium is three different particles—proton, neutron, and electron—united into one atom. To assert that any of these examples is one but not three, or three but not one, is foolish. Likewise, the Trinity is three persons united through love into one God, both three and one, hence *triune*.

33. Homer, *Iliad*, §13.1.

34. Homer, *Iliad*, §§15.158–67.

35. Hesiod, "Hymn 2."

The Doctrine of the Trinity Celebrates Difference as the Ongoing Source of All Being

Zeus, Poseidon, and Hades are certainly different from one another, but not in a good way. The mismanagement of their differences may produce a desire for pure unity, one perfect God who holds all power and makes all decisions, thereby avoiding all conflict. But there is a better way to negotiate difference that unites the many, rather than replacing them with the one. Too often, even the Christian tradition has shied away from this option. Indeed, in its concern to avoid tritheism while advancing Trinitarianism, the Christian tradition has frequently advanced a slightly triune monotheism. When the three are mentioned, they sometimes become identical triplets with little distinction. Gregory of Nyssa, for example, asserts that the only difference between the three persons of the Trinity is their order of being: the Son is begotten of the Father and the Holy Spirit proceeds from the Father; otherwise they are indistinguishable.[36] But if integration necessitates sameness and difference threatens unity, then a homogeneous God offers our diverse world little hope.

Moreover, if the three are virtually indistinguishable from one another, then there is no reason for them to be three. All conversation would become monologue, offering as much novelty as talking to yourself. Difference, on the other hand, invigorates community and stimulates creativity by provoking sameness out of its torpor. Sameness is static, but difference is kinetic. Sameness roots us to the present, but difference opens us to the future.

Charles Hartshorne argues that the intensity of aesthetic experience depends on *contrast*. Artists fill a blank canvas with color, recognizing that diversity integrated is beauty. And great diversity, perfectly unified, produces the most intense beauty.[37] Jürgen Moltmann places this aesthetic insight within the very heart of God. For Moltmann, the three persons of the Trinity are truly *different* persons of the Trinity, throbbing with communicable life.[38] We have already argued that if God is a self-identical subject (a single person), then God cannot be love, because love implies relatedness. Now, we argue further that *vitality implies difference*.

36. Gregory of Nyssa, "On 'Not Three Gods.'"
37. Hartshorne, *Creative Synthesis*, 303.
38. Bermejo, "Circumincession," 1:742.

Hence, the superabundant creativity of the Trinity implies difference within God.[39]

Moltmann expresses this insight by asserting the true uniqueness of the divine persons, who differ from one another in function, experience, and memory.[40] Functionally, the Spirit inspires the prophets whom the Father sustains and the Son perfects. Experientially, the Son suffers death and (the feeling of) abandonment by the Father, while the Father laments his Son's suffering. At the ascension, the Son relinquishes physical presence to the church so that the Spirit can animate its ministry. In the Christian scheme of salvation, God prefers cooperation over mere operation. Different functions produce different perspectives, which produce different experiences, which produce different memories, all of which distinguish the Trinitarian persons. Hence, the persons of the Trinity are in no way interchangeable. As distinct centers of subjective experience, they are true persons, with a strong sense of self that they place at one another's service. These three persons, characterized by *perfect internal presence and perfect external openness*, are by their very nature equals.

God is uniqueness loving uniqueness, difference loving difference: creation, incarnation, and inspiration are not the sequential activities of one person in three different historical guises, as suggested by Sabellius's modalism. Nor is God a primary substance hosting secondary difference. Instead, *distinct persons generate divinity through love*. Interpersonal uniqueness energizes the divine community, such that unity-in-difference is the very source of all reality. In contrast, if we predicate uniformity as our sacred ideal, then intolerance becomes our sacred mission. If unity necessitates sameness, then ethnic cleansing is a necessary precursor to national community, churches are right to practice racial exclusion, and the spirit is best conjured by homogeneity.[41] A truly Trinitarian faith, on the other hand, will enthusiastically embrace diversity.

The Doctrine of the Trinity Celebrates Freedom

The difference embedded within God—the uniqueness of the divine persons—grants their relations freedom and consequence. They respond to each other in different ways, at different times, for different reasons. The

39. Moltmann, *Trinity and the Kingdom*, 57.
40. Moltmann, *Trinity and the Kingdom*, 81.
41. Moltmann, *Trinity and the Kingdom*, 81.

various combinations of such uniqueness, amplified by an openness to time, offer inexhaustible possibilities for interaction. Within God, history never repeats itself, nor does it echo.

Such an understanding challenges the traditional interpretation of *aseity*. Aseity means "self-causing," that God is the source of God's own being, that God has no cause other than God's self. Early Christian theologians borrowed the concept from Greco-Roman thought. Believing that religious ultimacy demands metaphysical independence, they insisted that transcendence excludes relationship. In this view, God needs no one and relies on no one for his being or satisfaction. Creation is thus an utterly gracious act, meeting no need of God's, who generously grants us life in this beautiful universe.[42]

Feminist theologians have argued that the ascription of self-sufficiency to God improperly exalts traditionally masculine qualities like emotional invulnerability, thoughtless self-assertion, and condescending paternalism. Societies who worship such a self-sustaining God will also exalt lone wolf males who act unhindered by any concern for the broader society. According to this critique, the doctrine of aseity does not provide insight into God so much as it reinforces male privilege while stunting male psychology.[43]

We are reinterpreting the doctrine of aseity by asserting that, while God is uncaused, the three persons who constitute God are co-originating. That is, the Trinity does not depend on an external source for its existence. Yet simultaneously, the persons within the Trinity are interdependent. God has invited creation into that interdependence. If God ever had the capacity for perfect self-satisfaction, then God has forsaken that capacity *for us*. Rejecting isolated self-sufficiency, God instead chooses *increase-through-relation*. Each person in the Trinity says, "I am because you are," to the other persons. Eternal self-sufficiency makes a bold choice for everlasting relationship and all that relationship entails—vulnerability, exultation, despair, joy, suffering, and love.

The capacity for choice implies that God has no nature. God is free, unconstrained by a cause or an essence or a universal law or even goodness itself. *God is decision before attribute or being.* God asserts this divine freedom in Exod 3:14. If we translate the Hebrew verb *'ehyeh* in the future tense, then God states, "I will be who I will be." God *is choosing* to become

42. Hampson, "Theological Implications," 36.
43. Rea, "Gender as Divine Attribute," 106–8.

who God is, and God is love. That choice is absolute, so that God's love becomes spontaneous. This spontaneity makes the divine love *appear* natural, since that love penetrates to and emanates from the divine core. Nevertheless, it is a continuously chosen identity. God could very well choose otherwise, but will not, because God has also chosen to be *ḥesed*. *Ḥesed* is the Hebrew word for loving-kindness, steadfast faithfulness, and great mercy (Pss 86:5; 107:43; etc.). As the covenantal love and loyalty that God shows to us, and the covenantal love and loyalty that we *should* show to one another, *ḥesed* is the ideal of relationship. *Ḥesed* keeps its promises, even at great personal cost.

God is trustworthy because God has chosen to be trustworthy, not because God is constrained by an unchangeable nature.[44] If God did not have this freedom to choose, if God were constrained by an essence, then God would not be a *person*. Reality would be defined by the nature that precedes God, not God's choice for communion. And the most basic substrate of the universe would be an impersonal force, analogous to gravity, rather than a personal God sustaining relationship with and between persons.[45]

The Doctrine of the Trinity Embeds Feelings and Emotions within God

Interpersonal relations within God, coupled with God's openness to creation, generate a complex of feelings and emotions within the divine. God does not just feel; God feels absolutely. Moreover, negative emotions such as fear cannot diminish the divine capacity for feeling because God is love, and love casts out all fear (1 John 4:18). Hence, the feelings and emotions offered to us by the universe are holy. They are not to be overcome; they are to be celebrated. Indeed, *increasing openness to feelings and emotions is part of our theosis, or divinization.*

God feels, and God feels absolutely. But God also feels *perfectly*. That is, God's emotions are always appropriate to the situation. We human beings, on the other hand, may have unhelpful responses to certain situations. We may feel a tinge of celebration at the suffering of a friend because we are aware of our own suffering but doubt the reality of others', and their obvious suffering reassures us within our hidden suffering. We may feel envy at the *success* of a friend due to deep-seated doubts

44. Zizioulas, *Being as Communion*, 44.

45. Zizioulas, *Being as Communion*, 18–19.

about the value of our own contribution. Insecure and desiring prestige, we may seek power over rather than service of. When these feelings arise, they are grounded in a sense of separation that God abhors.

But God is empty of any excluding, occluding self.[46] All separation is illusion and God, as all-knowing, is not deluded. As a result of God's perfect wisdom God feels perfectly, which is to love perfectly. In other words, *God feels what should be felt as deeply as it can be felt.*[47] Within God there is no capacity for celebrating another's pain or envying another's success, because God is perfect. "Perfect" does not mean unchanging, but changing perfectly. This concept of God transforms our interpretation of human life. Now, the source of every human affect (our deepest emotions) is the divine affection. And for every sacred affect there is a sacred season, a time to laugh and a time to cry, a time to dance and a time to mourn (Eccl 3:1–8).

Our experience of Jesus as the Son of God affirms these sentiments. If God doesn't feel anything, if God is *impassible* (as Christian theology has so often asserted), then why does Jesus the Son of God feel so much? A detached God would be incarnated as an aloof automaton, but Jesus was an emotional prophet. A self-sufficient God would be incarnated as a reclusive hermit, but Jesus wasn't a loner. He was social, passionate, and vital. For the Parent, for the Child, for the Spirit, and by way of consequence, for all beings, to live vividly we must love dangerously. Love risks life, and God as love lures the universe into this risk, into the fullness of being.[48]

When God Chose to Be Love, God Chose to Be Time

My parents raised me in a moderate, mainstream church outside Richmond, Virginia. At Tuckahoe Presbyterian, almost everybody accepted Darwin's theory of evolution, no one expected Jesus to come back next week, and nobody talked about other religions going to hell. The community was loving, not controlling. Yet one teaching bothered me. In conversations, prayers, hymns, and sermons, I learned that God resided in eternity, but humans resided in time. I wasn't exactly sure what eternity was, but I could tell that it was *other* than time, and it was *better* than

---

46. Cobb and Griffin, *Process Theology*, 142.
47. McDougall, *Pilgrimage of Love*, 51.
48. Cobb and Griffin, *Process Theology*, 26.

time. Fortunately, I was reassured that one day, after I died, I would be in eternity with God and everybody else I loved who had died before me.

Even as a child I found this teaching confusing, and it made me feel a little resentful toward God. If God loves us, and if God is in eternity, and if eternity is better than time, then why did God put us in time? I felt like God sent us from the palace out to the woodshed before we'd even done anything wrong. Sure, the woodshed is better than the woods, but why aren't we in the palace with God? God's creation of the universe, and placement of creatures therein, seemed inhospitable.

I wish that I could blame my childhood dismay on an undeveloped feeling for language. But in English, "eternity" is too often associated with "timelessness." The *Oxford English Dictionary* defines eternity as "in expressed or implied opposition to time," "existence with reference to which the relation of succession has no application," or most simply, "timelessness." It provides an example from an 1853 theological essay: "Eternity, in relation to God, has nothing to do with time or duration." The *Oxford English Dictionary* even explicitly associates "eternity" with the afterlife: "Opposed to 'time' in its restricted sense of duration measured by the succession of physical phenomena. Hence, the condition into which the soul enters at death; the future life." It then provides an example from Shakespeare's *Hamlet*: "All that lives must die, Passing through nature to eternitie."

As an adult I still believe that contrasting God in eternity with humankind in time is harmful, so harmful that we should reject the definition of eternity as timelessness. If we are on earth and God is in heaven, then God is elsewhere. And if we are in time and God is in a timeless "eternity," then God is elsewhen. Too often, traditional theology worships a God twice removed—not in our place, and not in our time.[49]

Yet, given our knowledge of God as God has revealed Godself to us, such separation is not God's mode of operating. The Creator of the universe who enters the universe as a person—who clothes divinity in matter, who locates divinity in space, who moves divinity through time—that is not the type of Creator who would reside in a more privileged state than creation. That is not the Creator who would choose *incarnation*.

To relate to one another is to both cause and influence one another. Without this change there is no relatedness, and without relatedness there is no personhood. Hence, when we assert that God is loving relationality,

49. Oord, *Pluriform Love*, 115–17.

we are also asserting that God is internally timeful, since persons can interact only through time. Relatedness and time are as inseparable as two sides of the same coin.[50] Hence, when God chose to be love, God chose to be time.

In this view, God is not *being* itself; God is *becoming* itself.[51] But asserting that God is timeful does not imply that God exists within the history of *this* universe, within our own space-time, as it were. God is present to us here and now, but God is not limited to *our* here and now.[52] As noted earlier, since Einstein's theory of general relativity, we have lost belief in absolute time. Multiple different times characterize our universe—gravity and velocity both dilate time—so time here may be quite different from time there. How fast would time proceed for God, and which time would be God's? Instead, in asserting that God is timeful we are asserting that *change characterizes God's internal existence*, which is an interpersonal existence. God is related, within God's self and to our selves and to our universe. The medium of relationship is time. Hence, God is timeful.[53]

For a relationship to be real, it must be open—open to the free action of the other, open to the risk that vulnerability entails, and open to the future that no one person controls. It must be open to change, hence open to time.[54] Being timeful does not render God fickle. God remains everlastingly characterized by *ḥesed*. God's character never changes, but God's character expresses itself in various ways due to the changes that occur within time.[55] Confronted with injustice, *ḥesed* expresses itself as anger. Confronted with justice, *ḥesed* expresses itself as approval. Confronted with moral evil, *ḥesed* expresses itself as condemnation. Confronted with contrition, *ḥesed* expresses itself as mercy.

50. Rice, "Trinity, Temporality," 322–24.

51. Thatamanil, *Immanent Divine*, 196.

52. Brunner, *Christian Doctrine of God*, 266–71.

53. Barbour, *Religion and Science*, 234.

54. Pinnock, "Systematic Theology," 108.

55. Hartshorne, "Dipolar Conception of Deity," 279–83.

The Trinity Is not an Abstract Concept; the Trinity Is a Potential Experience

Trinitarian thought produces Trinitarian action, which produces the Trinitarian experience of graced time. The Greeks called graced time *kairos*. We can call it "eternity," so long as we define eternity to be time-as-blessing. In our experience, thinking, acting, and feeling are themselves triune. Each influences the others, as each is influenced by the others. And these three are entirely relational. The entirety of each is affected by the entirety of the others. Thinking, acting, and feeling are conceptually separable yet experientially united, distinguishable from yet perfectly open to their counterparts.

At the risk of self-congratulations, for which I apologize, I would like to share a Trinitarian experience. My church was on a mission trip to northern New York one summer, to do rural rehab on houses in an impoverished area of the country with brutal winters. I was partnered with Keith, a high school student who knew ten times more about construction than I did. At one of the houses we worked on, a small hole in the roof leaked water directly onto the bed of the six-year-old girl below. Any time it rained in the middle of the night, she would wake up sopping wet. At this point in our workweek, we had completed our main project on the house and had only one day left for projects. We could fix the girl's roof only if we could do it in eight hours. We decided to try.

The program had galvanized steel panels available for a metal roof. The problem was their slipperiness. Keith and I needed to drill screws through the tin into the rafters, but we would slip while doing so and risk falling over the edge. The ground, mind you, was a perilous six feet below. So, Keith and I figured out a system: standing next to each other, we grabbed the peak of the roof with our outside hands to keep from sliding. Then I held the screw with my inside hand while he held the drill with his inside hand. In this way we were able to attach the metal to the beams without falling off the roof.

Our activity was meaningful, purposeful, and united. I disappeared into the flow of the action so that, even though I was acting, the action felt effortless. Such was the coordination of our activity that Keith and I seemed to act as one, although the job could be achieved only by two. Time itself—the medium through which our activity occurred—flowed as gracious opportunity. Temporarily freed from the burden of our egos through the synthesis of our egos, we found that relationship—to the person you act *with* and the person you act *for*, the little girl below, watching us—can render time eternal.

Love is vulnerability, and within God, this vulnerability is absolute. It penetrates to the core of each divine person's being, flows through that core, then surfaces again, unceasingly. The persons of the Trinity do not possess any independent, preceding identity that then enters into relationship with the other persons. Every person depends, has always depended, and will always depend, on every other person for their divine being. If God is anything in itself, then God is relationship itself, *infinite relatedness expressed as interpersonal love mediated by time.* When we participate in this divine reality, when we manifest God on earth, we may discover a Holy Spirit—an undertow of grace that bears us to our goal—God's beloved community.

3

Joy in the Earth

I think it pisses God off if you walk by the color purple in a field somewhere and don't notice it. People think pleasing God is all God cares about. But any fool living in the world can see it always trying to please us back.

—ALICE WALKER[1]

Why Is There Something Instead of Nothing?

THIS QUESTION IS THE most basic of all the unanswerable questions that we must answer. By "unanswerable," I mean "cannot be answered with certainty," unless that certainty is manufactured by the answerer. By "must answer," I mean that we answer the question with our very lives: how we interpret them, feel them, and think them through. We inevitably choose. For this reason, we should choose consciously.

Science cannot make the decision for us. Fundamentalists may insist on a literal reading of Scripture and claim that Genesis is perfectly accurate as a historical and scientific text. In so doing, they reject scientific claims about the origins of the cosmos. But other Christians accept our powers of observation and reason as divine gifts. For these Christians,

1. Walker, *Color Purple*, 195.

64

science is a sacred practice. At this point the Big Bang seems to be the best explanation for the origin of our universe, but we still have a hard time explaining what produced the Big Bang. In attempting to explain the origin of the universe, we end up in an infinite regress: If the multiverse produced our universe, then what produced the multiverse? What produced the physical laws that govern the multiverse? Eventually, our powers of inference reach their limit. Theists stop the infinite regress by positing God, both as Creator and Sustainer of the unceasing process. Science can neither prove nor disprove this claim, leaving us, as rational beings, with the freedom, necessity, and consequence of choosing our religious orientation.

For many people the question "Why is there something instead of nothing?" begins a spiritual search. The question invites us to consider the very real possibility that there could be nothing instead of something, and this nothingness would be absolute. Instead of this vibrant, pulsing universe, and our living experience of it, there could be naught but a cold, dark silence, with no one to lament its emptiness. But even the words cold, dark, and silent are only metaphorical descriptors of this desolation, which cannot be thought or spoken. Absolute nothingness lies beneath all qualities and beyond the reach of language. It is the tomb of being, and it is a very real possibility. We, and this cosmos that we inhabit, might never have been. At any moment, we could *not be*, were it not for our Creator and Sustainer.

Our Creator Is Our Divine Parent

In keeping with the warmest strains of his own religious tradition, Jesus calls God the Creator "Abba," Aramaic for "Father" or, more warmly, "Dad." In Jesus's Bible, Hosea provides one of the most affectionate descriptions of God as Abba, writing in Abba's own words:

> When Israel was a youth, I loved them dearly, and out of Egypt I called my children. . . . I taught Ephraim to walk, taking them by the arm—but they don't acknowledge that I was the one who made them whole. I led them on a leash of human kindness, with bonds of caring. I was to them like those who lift infants to their cheeks; I bent down to them and fed them. (Hos 11:1–4)

Abba is not cold, distant, or unfeeling; Abba is present, compassionate, and attentive. In choosing the symbol of YHWH as Father, Jesus is declaring that the Creator and Sustainer of the cosmos cares for each individual. The full attention of the ever-increasing infinite is directed at us, personally. Thus, Abba is omnipresent in two ways: Abba is everywhere, and Abba is undistracted. We may feel forgotten in the numberless masses, but we are precious in the sight of Abba.

According to both Hosea and Jesus, YHWH the Father God (Abba) is compassionate. In the Hebrew Bible, compassion is something you feel in your womb (*rechem* or *beten*). Scholars translate the Hebrew words *rechem* and *beten* as "womb," "bowels," or "heart" when referring to the body, and as "mercy" or "compassion" when referring to a feeling. Both *rechem* and *beten* provide *maternal* imagery for God. When Babylon conquered Israel and took its leading citizens from Jerusalem into exile, many Jews felt forgotten by their God. But the prophet Isaiah (or his followers in the Isaiah school), writing in the voice of God, assures them:

> Can a woman forget her nursing child
> > or show no compassion [*rechem*] for the child of her womb [*beten*]?
> Even these might forget,
> > yet I will not forget you. (Isa 49:15 NRSV)

And, sensitive to the yearning of the exiled for home, Isaiah also writes, again in the voice of God: "As a mother comforts her child, so I will comfort you" (Isa 66:13).

Sometimes, the Hebrews' maternal imagery for God is explicit birth imagery. Frustrated that Israel so quickly rushes to other gods, Deuteronomy accuses: "You deserted the Rock who gave you life; you forgot the God who bore you" (Deut 32:18). And God declares to Job, "Has the rain a father, or who has fathered the drops of dew? From whose womb did the ice come forth, and who has given birth to the hoarfrost of heaven?" (Job 38:28–29 NRSV). And there is substantial evidence to justify translating El Shaddai, traditionally "the Almighty," as "the Breasted One."[2] Such passages deny YHWH any *single* gender with which to identify, explicitly declaring YHWH/Abba to be *omni-gendered* or *nonbinary*.

Jesus continues this Jewish tradition, revealing the intimacy of Abba through the imagery of father *and* mother. Jesus had innumerable Hebrew images for Abba to choose from: Creator (Gens 1:1), King (Ps 99:1), Lawgiver (Exod 20:2–17), Judge (Ps 7:8–11), Lord (Exod 4:10), Jealous (Exod 34:14; "Jealous" is capitalized as a proper name), Fire (1 Kgs 18:38; Exod 13:21), Warrior (Exod 15:3), Potter (Isa 24:8), Rock (Ps 31:1–8),

---

2. Biale, "God with Breasts."

Shepherd (Ps 23:1), etc. But in his own teaching, Jesus chose imagery of warmth and care: God as Father (Luke 11:22; following Mal 2:10) and God as Mother (Luke 15:8–10; following Deut 32:18).

In contemporary English, persons who identify with both genders, or are nonbinary, use the pronouns they/them. In keeping with this development of language, for the remainder of this book we shall assign the pronouns they/them to Abba. We do so for several reasons. Historically, the church has always recognized that God the Creator is beyond all gender categories. *The Catechism of the Catholic Church* summarizes this long tradition: "We ought therefore to recall that God transcends the human distinction between the sexes. He is neither man nor woman: he is God."[3] Problematically, historical language for God has been exclusively male: God the Creator is a "he," God the Christ is a "he," God the Spirit is a "he," and God the Trinity, those three persons as one God, is a "he." Exclusively male language for a gender transcending God misrepresents the divine nature; hence, it is theologically inaccurate.

Moreover, exclusively male language for God misrepresents males as more divine than females and nonbinary persons. But everyone is made in the image of God, no matter their gender identity. Therefore, our language for God should allow everyone to see themselves in God. Referring to Abba, God the Creator, as "they" corrects this imbalance, allowing nonbinary persons, so often excluded both socially and theologically, to understand themselves as manifestations of divinity. (Later in the book, we will introduce the Holy Spirit as Sophia, who is metaphorically female, thereby providing a gender-inclusive image of God the Trinity.)

For the rest of this book our primary term for God the Creator and Sustainer will be Abba rather than the customary terms such as Creator, Sustainer, God, or Father. As noted above, Abba is the Aramaic term of endearment for Father, although (as noted above) it conveys more affection and closeness than its English counterpart. Jesus spoke Aramaic and used the term explicitly in his prayer life: when pleading to be freed from the pain of crucifixion, Jesus prays to "Abba, Father" (Mark 14:36). This usage continued in the early church. The apostle Paul promises that, because Christ refers to the Creator as Abba, Christians can do so as well: "Those who are led by the Spirit of God are the children of God. . . . Through the Spirit, God has adopted you as children, and by that Spirit we cry out, 'Abba!'" (Rom 8:15b–16a). Today, many Jewish children in

---

3. United States Catholic Conference, *Catechism* (1994), §239.

families familiar with Hebrew will call their father Abba, which is more readily translated as "Dad," "Daddy," or "Papa."

Not only is the term *Abba* entirely biblical and appropriately intimate, it offers several additional advantages. Relative to the word *God*, Abba suggests the warmth of a person to whom we can relate rather than an abstraction that we ponder. Relative to the word *Father*, Abba suggests less formality and greater familiarity. And relative to the words *Creator* or *Sustainer*, Abba refers to the whole person rather than a function thereof.

Regarding gender, the Aramaic word is clearly a masculine noun. Fortunately, for our purposes, it has the advantage of ending in the letter *a*, which provides it with a feminine tone in many European languages: for example, Maria and Antonia are feminine; Mario and Antonio are masculine. This fortuitous ambiguity in the word provides it with some flexibility as we try to develop a gender-inclusive concept of God.

Finally, since we will call God the Creator Abba, for the rest of this book the term *God* itself will refer primarily to God the Trinity, the community of persons—Creator, Christ, and Spirit—united through love into one living divinity. These references will not be perfectly consistent. Theological language should be sufficiently precise so as not to confuse, but sufficiently elastic so as not to obstruct the divine plenitude. When writing about faith, there is always a tension between precision and transparency, logic and metaphor, reason and imagination. Moreover, the perfect cooperation of the three deeply involves them in one another's work; even though they have distinct responsibilities, they fulfill their distinct responsibilities alongside one another. This co-involvement consolidates their activity, rendering it distinguishable but inseparable. From the perspective of theological language, God the Sustainer, God the Christ, and God the Spirit together form God the Trinity, granting the word *God* an indefiniteness appropriate to divinity's overflowing nature.

Why Does Abba Create and Sustain the Universe?

Abba, our Mother and Father, rolls the stone away from the tomb of being, freeing us to emerge from nothingness. Here, within the divinely sustained creation, we participate in the interplay of cold and warmth, of darkness and light, of silence and sound, of all the mutually amplifying contrasts that grant life its passion. Abba continually overcomes nonbeing to grant us, not just being, but *becoming*—diversity and difference transforming one another through time. Everything that *is*, is *of God*, including *us*: "I lie down and sleep; I wake again, for the Lord sustains me" (Ps 3:5 NRSV). But this claim raises the question: Why does Abba create and sustain the universe at all, especially with its suffering? Why doesn't Abba just retreat into blissful divinity?

Unlike us, God chooses God's nature, and God has chosen dynamic, interpersonal love as the divine core. This love is superabundant. It will overflow our concepts, overflow our language, and even overflow itself. Traditionally, Christianity has deemed God to be infinite. We will deem God to be an *ever-increasing infinity*.[4]

We may deny infinity the capacity to increase. Infinity is, after all, infinite. But first, the divine majesty cannot be limited by our human logic. Second, work by mathematicians on infinity suggests that it *can* increase. In the 1920s, David Hilbert pointed out that if you had an infinite hotel with an infinite number of rooms, and the hotel was full, then it could still accommodate one more guest, if each guest simply moved one room number up (1 to 2, 2 to 3, 3 to 4, etc.), thereby leaving the first room open for the new guest. So, infinity can increase by one, *so long as there is movement*. But he also points out that infinity can increase by infinity. That is, if a hotel with an infinite number of rooms, all full, were to be visited by an infinitely long bus of new guests, then the hotel could accommodate all of them by having each current guest move from their room number n to room number $2n$ (1 to 2, 2 to 4, 3 to 6, etc.), thereby leaving an infinite number of rooms free for the infinite number of new guests, *so long as there is movement*. Hilbert then went on to prove that any infinite hotel could accommodate an infinite number of buses with an infinite number of new guests, but that math is over my head.[5]

Infinity is capacious and always increasing in capacity.[6] But again we ask, if infinity is infinite, then why is it not infinitely pleased with itself? Why isn't God self-satisfied? Christian theologians, following Plato, have insisted that since only imperfect things can develop or increase, and God is perfect, then God cannot develop or increase.[7] Divine development would imply divine imperfection. For this reason, creation can add nothing to the being of God, who is already perfect and not in need of

4. Edwards, "Axiological Reflections," 25.

5. Gamow, *One, Two, Three—Infinity*, 17–18.

6. Ramanuja, *Vedartha Sangraha*, 38, §43.

7. Plato, *Republic*, §381.a–c.

development. Therefore, God's creation of this universe is an act of sheer grace, doing nothing for God but everything for us.

We have shown that infinity can increase. Now, we argue that *if infinity can increase, then the divine perfection demands that infinity increase infinitely, forever.* Because God's choice is to continually overflow God's self, God is by nature creative. In fact, God is infinitely creative, ever increasing, and ceaselessly self-surpassing, without depletion or dilution. This concept of divine development does not suggest that God is deficient in love, wisdom, or joy, always grasping for more. Instead, this concept insists that God is superabundant, overflowing with all three, in everlasting self-donation.

God's creativity is deeply tied to God's interpersonal nature. In the Christian view, God had already decided to be interpersonal relationship, three persons as one God, "prior" to creation. This "prior" does not refer to priority in time, but to priority of being. Abba creates and sustains our time from Abba's own time, which the Greeks called *kairos*, time-as-blessing. God is the one for whom the blessedness of time always abides. We call this blessedness eternity.

According to the Christian tradition, God has chosen *not* to be a perfectly self-satisfied unity, a blissful One without a second. Instead, God has chosen to be love, and to overflow as love. But love gains reality only when it is concrete. God could not be content with an abstract love for abstract persons in an abstract place, so the ideal sought expression in the actual, the universal sought expression in the particular. This desire for particularity, for definite form in a specific location, necessitates *limitation*.[8] For love to flow, those who are beloved must be somewhere rather than everywhere and someone rather than everyone. Differentiation allows agape to *move*: from here to there, from now to then, from me to you, from us to them. Because limitation coupled with time puts love in motion, it is better to be limited than unlimited. Limitations are the means of God's grace, because they permit completion through one another; they permit love. Our inabilities are completed by their abilities, while their inabilities are completed by our abilities. Through interanimation we find completion. Paul asks, "If the body were all eye, what would happen to our hearing? If it were all ear, what would happen to our sense of smell?" (1 Cor 12:17).

---

8. Whitehead, *Religion in the Making*, 152.

Abba also creates to share the divine beauty: "I was a hidden treasure, wishing to be enjoyed, so I created the world that I might become
enjoyed."[9] Now, the act of creation is a gift from Abba to us. Again, God
is *evermore*: evermore beauty creating evermore beauty to be enjoyed by
evermore perceivers. Crucially, Abba participates in this enjoyment, because Abba creates, sustains, and resides within the enjoyers (us), feeling
what we feel. God is both the beauty that is enjoyed and the enjoyment of
that beauty. This process is continual: we are the isthmus between Creator
and creation, fully participating in creation while ever growing in awareness of the Creator.[10] Because our potential is never actualized, we can
forever progress in our awareness, forever drawing closer to God, forever
bringing pleasure to God, "for whom and through whom all things exist"
(Heb 2:10). We are the conduit through which God's infinite mystery is
everlastingly revealed to itself.

Completion by another is better than self-contained perfection. The
universe is not designed for independent self-sufficiency. It is designed
for deep relationality because continual increase is better than unchanging completion. Mutual influence and related freedom produce ongoing
novelty, rendering time everlastingly new.[11]

How Does Abba Create and Sustain the Universe?

Most human beings experience awe at the beauty of nature. Whether it
be a sunset over the ocean, majestic mountain view, or campfire dancing
against the night, the magnificence of the natural world enchants us. This
enchantment runs so deep that some people experience nature itself as
holy. American naturalist John Muir writes:

> Long, blue, spiky-edged shadows crept out across the snow-
> fields. . . . This was the alpenglow, to me the most impressive
> of all the terrestrial manifestations of God. At the touch of this
> divine light, the mountains seemed to kindle to a rapt, religious
> consciousness, and stood hushed like devout worshippers wait-
> ing to be blessed.[12]

---

9. Ali, "Islam and the Unity," 112.
10. Ali, "Islam and the Unity," 112.
11. Buber, *I and Thou*, 66.
12. Muir, *Wild Muir*, 87–88.

The beauty of nature overwhelms Muir, to the point that he deems it divine. For him, natural beauty is not merely a pleasing arrangement of objects; it is an expression of God. Serving God-in-nature, Muir campaigned to protect America's wilderness, eventually inspiring Teddy Roosevelt to establish America's national park system.

Tragically, although Muir's experience of God in nature was beautiful and produced beneficial change, the weight of the Christian tradition would deem it heretical. Traditional Christianity insists that God is above the world, not within it. This perspective is concerned that, if some people experience matter as holy, they will lose their sense of a personal God. Scholars of religion call the limitation of God to nature *pantheism*. Pantheism is constructed from the Greek roots *pan* (all) and *theos* (God): all is God. According to pantheists, the material universe is sacred, but there is no transcendent Creator in heaven. Prominent atheist Daniel Dennett observes:

> Is this Tree of Life a God one could worship? Pray to? Fear? Probably not. But it did make the ivy twine and the sky so blue, so perhaps the song I love tells a truth after all. The Tree of Life is neither perfect nor infinite in space or time, but it is actual, and if it is not Anselm's "Being greater than which nothing can be conceived," it is surely a being that is greater than anything any of us will ever conceive of in detail worthy of its detail. Is something sacred? Yes, say I with Nietzsche. I could not pray to it, but I can stand in affirmation of its magnificence. This world is sacred.[13]

Dennett's vision appeals to atheists because it denies deity but preserves awe. It avoids the constraints of stifling religion, while celebrating science as aesthetic pleasure. Unbound from God, we are fascinated by nature. And in that fascination, we find new meaning and purpose.

This (non)religious, pantheistic vision is so attractive that traditional monotheists feel compelled to argue against it. Fearful that recognizing the divinity of nature will result in the elimination of God, these dualistic theists, who emphasize the Creator-creation distinction, *exclude* God from nature. They insist that God is utterly transcendent and in no way immanent, beyond but not within. Anglican theologian N. T. Wright argues:

> Biblical theology [makes] the case that the one living God created a world that is other than himself, not contained within

13. Dennett, *Darwin's Dangerous Idea*, 94.

himself. Creation was from the beginning an act of love, of affirming the goodness of the other. God saw all that he had made, and it was very good; but it was not itself divine. . . . Collapsing this distinction means taking a large step toward pantheism.[14]

For Wright, the divine presence within matter threatens to annihilate the divine presence in heaven. This concern is legitimate, as we have seen with Dennett's declaration that nature is sacred but impersonal. Pantheism also risks decaying into mere materialism, the firm belief in matter's existence coupled with a denial of all religious realities. But Wright doesn't merely critique pantheism; he also implicitly critiques pan*en*theism. Panentheism is constructed from the Greek roots: *pan* (all)—*en* (in)—*theos* (God). All is *in* God, even as God exceeds that all. Thus, panentheism is the belief that God emanates the universe from God's very own being, such that the universe *participates* in divinity. Panentheism recognizes nature as sacred, while also preserving the personal God of theism.

The Trinity Is the Soul of the Universe

But how can God reside in the cosmos while exceeding it? Panentheist theologians have objected that classical, dualistic theism divides the world (matter) from God (spirit), thereby dimming the brilliance of creation. As a correction, they assert the presence of God within the world through a soul-body analogy: the Trinity is the soul of the universe, just as the universe is the body of the Trinity. The soul-body analogy allows us to sense God within the universe even as God exceeds the universe, just as the soul resides within the body even as it exceeds the body.[15]

(Here, from a systematic perspective, "God" refers to either God the Sustainer [Abba] or God the Trinity, or both at the same time. Since Abba's openness to Christ and Spirit is perfect, Abba's soul is Trinitarian—living, open, and dynamic. Abba bears primary responsibility for creating and sustaining the universe, but Abba's support thereof is inherently Trinitarian.)

The soul-body analogy articulates our experience of God as both immanent and transcendent, both within and beyond. It ascribes the holiness of the universe to a source beyond, thereby celebrating the divinity

14. Wright, *Surprised by Hope*, 94.
15. McFague, *Models of God*, 76–77.

of all reality, while preserving the personhood of God.[16] The soul-body analogy also implies that God *feels* the universe, just as we feel our own bodies. God the Sustainer, God the Participant, and God the Celebrant are all God the Open, affected by creation just as creation is affected by God. Therefore, the divine sustenance of the universe is a continuous process that permeates the very *being* of God, rendering it the *becoming* of God.[17]

We find warrant for this belief in Scripture. Even as the Hebrews visualized God on a heavenly throne, they were careful not to limit God's presence to that throne. The Chronicler proclaims: "Who can build a house for God, whom heaven itself, even the highest heavens, cannot contain?" (2 Chr 2:6). But not only does God's *personality* fill the universe, God's very *being* fills it as well. God is *within* all things, even as God *exceeds* all things. The book of Sirach states:

> It is by God's plan that each of these fulfills its own purpose;
>> by the word of YHWH, they are held together.
> No matter how much we say, our words are inadequate.
>> In the end, God is everything. (Sir 43:26–28)

And in the Christian Scriptures, the apostle Paul takes up this sentiment multiple times: "Who has given God anything to deserve something in return? For all things are from God and through God and for God" (Rom 11:36); "There is one God and Creator of all, who is over all, who works through all and is within all" (Eph. 4:6); "In [God] we live and move and have our being" (Acts 17:28). God is in all things, but not contained within them; and separate from all things, but not isolated from them.[18]

From a Trinitarian perspective, the act of creation includes all three persons: the Bible describes the cosmos as created through Christ, in whom the fullness of God was pleased to dwell, and in whom all things hold together (Col 1:15–20). Likewise, the Hebrew Scriptures describe Wisdom, whom Christians would later identify with the Holy Spirit, as a manifestation of God, pervading all things, more active than all active things (Wis 7:22b–25 DRA). The Sustainer creates through both Christ and Spirit.

---

16. Ramanuja, *Vedartha Sangraha*, 16, §13.

17. Barbour, *Religion and Science*, 322–25.

18. Ali, "Islam and the Unity," 113.

Abba's Intellect Pervades and Structures the Universe

Indeed, we can encounter the *mind* of Abba in the universe, in the form of mathematics. Historically, mathematicians have generated frameworks and theories that were later applied to astronomy, physics, and engineering. For example, the Greek mathematician Apollonius of Perga analyzed conic sections—the circle, ellipse, parabola, hyperbola, etc. His analyses later proved useful to astronomers studying the motion of celestial objects. Kepler, for example, discovered that the planets travel in ellipses around the sun, not circles, and relied on Apollonius's preexisting analyses to work out his mathematical physics.[19] Thomas Malthus applied Leonard Euler's preexisting geometric growth tables to demographic studies, noting that the resulting overpopulation would produce an intense struggle for survival. Charles Darwin read Malthus and generated his evolutionary theory of natural selection. Einstein could not have developed his general theory of relativity, which predicated the curvature of space, without reference to Bernhard Riemann's preexisting theories of differential geometry.[20]

Given the outstanding power of mathematical reason to make sense of the physical universe, many mathematicians regard its practice as more than an intellectual exercise. Pythagoras legendarily endorsed mathematical endeavor as a religious practice. For Pythagoras, to understand the universe was to understand its divine source. Hence, scientific investigation was spiritual development, and vice versa. Correlating the number one to a point, the number two to a line, the number three to a plane, and the number four to a cube (the three-dimensional space in which we live), the Pythagoreans concluded that the universe is composed of numbers. When they discovered that musical intervals are based on numerical ratios, they proceeded to combine mathematics with mysticism.[21] The Christian tradition absorbed the Pythagoreans' mathematical mysticism and deemed the cosmic order an expression of the mind of Abba. According to this interpretation, the Divine Architect expresses the orderly, divine mind within the orderly, material universe. Hence, to study nature is to study God.

19. Baravalle, "Conic Sections," 101.

20. Kragh, "Anthropic Myth," 723.

21. Guthrie, "Pythagoras and Pythagoreanism," 8:182–83.

God the Geometer, **from the** ***Bible Moralisée*** **(thirteenth century)**

These insights cohere with the Jewish and Christian Bibles, which find the sustaining mind of the Creator in creation. Of course, neither tradition makes specific reference to mathematical mysticism. Yet both traditions express awe at the divine reason expressed through the cosmic order. In the Hebrew tradition, the psalmist exclaims, "YHWH, what variety you have created, arranging everything so wisely! The earth is filled with your creativity!" (Ps 104:24a). Jeremiah writes, "The earth was created by God's power. God's wisdom fixed the earth in place and God's knowledge unfurled the skies" (Jer 10:12). And Proverbs declares, "For it was through [Wisdom] that God laid the earth's foundation; through her that the heavens were set in place" (Prov 3:19–20).

Early Christians found this divine wisdom in both Jesus of Naza-reth and the Holy Spirit. They identified Jesus with the logos—the sacred reason, creative principle, or divine order—through which the universe was made:

> In the beginning there was the Word [*logos*]; and the Word was in God's presence, and the Word was God. The Word was pres-ent to God from the beginning. Through the Word all things came into being, and apart from the Word nothing came into being. . . . And the Word became flesh and stayed for a little while among us; we saw the Word's glory—the favor and posi-tion a parent gives an only child—filled with grace, filled with truth. (John 1:1–3, 14)

The logos permeates the universe and permeates our minds, granting us the capacity to reason, to better understand the universe and to better understand God.

Language about God Is Iconic

As we discuss the nature of God, we have ascribed certain qualities to God such as community, infinity, love, joy, increase, and omnipresence. We created these words to describe this universe and our own feelings within it. Since they are products of the cosmos for the cosmos, they can apply only metaphorically or poetically to God. God—Sustainer, Par-ticipant, and Perfecter—lies well beyond the reach of our this-worldly language. Therefore, anytime we speak of God, *we should recognize that the words we use are more dissimilar to God than similar, that they are more inaccurate than accurate.* They should never be taken exhaustively or literally.

Instead, language about God is *iconic*.[22] An icon is a depiction of a divinity or saint appropriate for contemplation and meditation. Although the painters of icons are accomplished artists capable of three dimen-sional portraiture, icons have a two dimensional presentation. They look flat, but this flatness is purposeful: it reminds the viewer that they are not looking so much *at* the icon as *through* it, into the sacred space beyond. It reminds the viewer that they are not meditating on the object, but on what the object represents.[23]

---

22. Farrugia, "Iconic Character," 3–5.
23. Ouspensky, *Theology of the Icon*, 1:472.

Many centuries before Christian icons came into existence, the Buddha issued a similar caution. He did not want his followers to become attached to his teachings, so he told them that, if someone points at the moon, then you should look at the moon, not the person's finger. In other words, you should look to the goal of the Buddha's teachings, not the teachings themselves.[24] Similarly, iconic language points beyond itself, to God. Optimally, God flows through the language, as God flows through the icon. But God remains always beyond.

We issue these caveats here because our language is about to break down. We have spoken of God as a community of persons, which is a real attribute that tells us something real about God. But it is also false, and in a good way. That is because we, as persons, must be careful not to spread ourselves too thin. We have limited time and limited attention; if we pay too much attention to our work, then we neglect our relationships. If we pay too much attention to our relationships, then we neglect ourselves. We must find that ever-elusive balance. But God becomes disanalogous to us here. God is an ever increasing infinity who does not get spread thin. God's omnipresence cannot be diluted in any way: "God is an infinite sphere whose center is everywhere and whose circumference is nowhere," runs an ancient metaphor.[25] Wherever we are, there the fullness of God dwells. Or, in the words of the Upanishads: "That is fullness. This is fullness. From fullness comes fullness. When fullness is taken from fullness, fullness remains."[26]

God is an infinitely overflowing plenitude, and that plenitude is here and now. But it must hold itself in reserve or we would be constantly overwhelmed. For our relationship with God to be mutual, God must conceal some of Godself, that we might be granted the freedom to respond. Although working with a unitarian concept of God, the Jewish tradition of Chabad Hassidism embeds mutuality within God through the doctrine of *tzimtzum*, "contraction." God limits the divine being to make room for creation, so that creation is not overwhelmed by its source. Consider an analogy: If the Sun and Earth were too close, then the Sun would burn Earth away. But the contraction of the Sun to the center of the solar system allows it to illuminate Earth without destroying it. Without the Sun, Earth would be a frozen wasteland. Without

24. Rounds and Epstein, *Śūraṅgama Sūtra*, §2.61.

25. Copenhaver, *Greek "Corpus Hermeticum*," xlvii.

26. See Brihadaranyaka Upanishad, in Mascaro, *Upanishads*, 5.1.1.

the Sun's contraction, Earth would be a burning hell. Hence, the Sun's self-limitation generates a relationship through which we come alive.[27] Similarly, God's self-limitation grants us the freedom to become who we are, *in relation to God*. God doesn't drown us in divinity but allows us to swim in the currents of the sacred.

Abba's Creation of the Universe Is Continual

As noted previously, God prefers cooperation to mere operation. The three persons of the Trinity have different functions, which provide them with different experiences and different memories. They are truly unique, truly three while truly one. One of those functions is creation. I have often referred to the Creator, the member primarily responsible for the existence of the universe, as Sustainer, because our experience of Abba as the soul of the cosmos implies *ongoing support* as well as ancient establishment.[28]

Theologians call the belief that Abba sustains the universe at every moment of its being *continuous creation*. Interpreting Abba as Creator alone runs the risk of *deism*. Deists believe that God created the universe, much like a clockmaker, then set it on a shelf to run of its own accord. From this perspective, the universe is divinely established but no longer divinely supported. God is remote and indifferent. In contrast, we are arguing that Abba is more like a singer than a clockmaker. Abba continually sings the universe into being; if the singer stops, then the song stops.[29]

By interpreting Abba as Sustainer, we argue that Abba is continually loving the universe into being. We experience that love in the beauty of the cosmos, the majesty of its expanse, the grandeur of its design, the intricacy of its details, the delicacy of its formulation, and the mathematical perfection of its physics. Above, we argued that God is ever more. Now, we also argue that God is *ever creating*. Through trust of the ever creating evermore, the moment-by-moment progression of time becomes the grace-by-grace gift of God.[30]

27. Margalit, *Pearl and the Flame*, 142.

28. Schleiermacher, *Christian Faith*, 1:214–15, §38.2.

29. McCabe, *God, Christ, and Us*, 103.

30. Bowman, "God for Us," 18–20.

Divine Interdependence Sustains
Cosmic Interdependence

"The universe is God's self-portrait," writes Octavia Butler, who interprets our kaleidoscopic cosmos as a revelation of unity-without-uniformity, or what we are calling agapic nondualism.[31] Nothing is separate from anything, and all differences are related. Expressing that openness, all aspects of material reality are effected and affected, originated and influenced, by the rest. In the language of contemporary physics, the universe is not made of solitary objects that bounce off each other; it is made up of waves and fields that flow into one another. Just as God is not God without any one person of the Trinity, nothing in the universe is what it is without the rest of the universe. And just as the persons of the Trinity are neither identical nor separate, but united, so the things of the universe are neither identical nor separate, but united. This union does not eradicate difference; this union joins difference. Unifying love is the lifeblood of the universe, and *love expresses itself through matter as nonduality*. For this reason, we best live in the world when we most love the world.[32] Any attempt to claim something for yourself, to separate it from the whole, is a sin. Sin is separation: vice tears, virtue mends, and apathy watches.

The elements of the cosmos are much like the pieces that make a stained glass window. Each piece contributes its own quality, while all the qualities together create the overall effect. As all the pieces influence each other, no piece is separate from the rest, and every piece finds its realization within the whole. Alone, it is a shard. With others, it is art. But this beauty relies on difference. If all the glass and iron were assimilated, melted down and stirred so that it became One and only One, devoid of difference—then it would be an ugly brown blob. But if the part retains its difference within the whole, and offers that difference to the whole, and is *open* to the difference of others as well, then the different qualities together produce beauty. The individual pieces of glass, like the elements of the universe, are *open-with-qualities*.

The color red, for example, feels one way when bordered by black and white. It feels another way when bordered by pink and light blue. Our experience of redness is determined by its relationship to other colors. But what if something is just red, without any adjacent color? Then, isn't it just redness itself, its own unique expression without corruption

31. O. Butler, *Parable of the Sower*, 315.
32. Tagore, *Stray Birds*, 72, §279.

or distortion? But red in relation to red is different from red in relation to green. And even a pure, red field will produce different experiences in different people. Red means one thing to a communist and another to an anti-communist, one thing on Chinese New Year and another in the red-light district of Paris, one thing to a battlefield medic and another to a hemophiliac dependent on blood transfusions. In the universe of human experience—which is the only universe we occupy—red does not exist uninterpreted, and its interpretation is always determined by its relations. Nothing exists unrelatedly.

Various Christian theologians have found the relational imprint of the divine on the cosmos. The apostle Paul writes: "Though invisible to the eye, God's eternal power and divinity have been seen since the creation of the universe, understood and clearly visible in all of nature" (Rom 1:20a). According to Paul, *creation is an icon of God.* Athanasios of Alexandria (ca. 298–373) retrieved the Stoic notion of the *logoi spermatikoi* (seeds of divine reason) and affirmed that every aspect of reality carries an imprint of the divine.[33] Augustine (354–430) called this imprint the *vestigia Trinitatis*, or traces of the Trinity, and he scoured the world for triads that reflected their Trinitarian source. Augustine noted that love implies a lover, a beloved, and the love itself, hence a triad; and that the mind, its love for itself, and its awareness of itself also constitute a triad.[34] The constituents of these triads are inseparable from one another, inextricably related, yet of one substance. Hence, they are analogous to the relations between the persons of the Trinity.

We find the imprint of the Trinity in the interdependence of the elements of the cosmos. This diversity-in-harmony implies four truths, according to Bin Song: 1) each thing is unique, 2) each thing is related to and inseparable from other things, 3) each thing accommodates the being of other things without losing its own integrity, and finally, 4) all things change and evolve together.[35] Simple physics suggests the truth of this interdependence. Philosopher Sydney Shoemaker notes that physics cannot define any aspect of the universe according to its *intrinsic* properties. Instead, everything is defined through its relationships. For example, mass is the property of matter that measures its resistance to acceleration, while matter is anything that has mass and takes up space. An atom is the basic unit of a chemical element, while a chemical element

33. Cattoi, "Response to 'Buddhist Musings,'" 83.
34. Augustine, *On the Trinity*, 26–30, §§9.2–4.
35. Song, "Ru Theology of Nondualism," 251–52.

is composed of atoms with an identical number of protons. An electron is a stable subatomic particle with a negative charge, while a negative charge characterizes an atom that has gained an electron. All definitions rely on *extrinsic*, dispositional properties (how *x* relates to *y*), because *x* doesn't possess any intrinsic properties by which it can be defined.[36]

We experience the nonduality of the different elements of reality as *contingency*. Things are either contingent or necessary. If they are contingent, then they may or may not exist. If they are necessary, then they must exist. In other words, a contingent thing *can* be, but a necessary thing *must* be. Theologians have generally argued that only God is necessary; God must, by nature, "exist." We have argued earlier that the persons of the Trinity are contingent on one another since they co-originate one another, and this co-origination through love is glorious. As Gregory Boyd argues, "Contingency is one of God's eternal perfections, not a defect."[37]

But the Trinity itself, the communion of persons, is necessary, existing by its very nature. The universe, in contrast, is contingent on God's sustaining grace. The universe could very well *not* exist. Nondualism goes one step further and argues that, by divine design, the elements of the universe are all contingent on one another. This *horizontal* contingency allows our continuous co-creation of one another by the grace of God. As the persons who are God—Sustainer, Christ, Spirit—arise through their relations, so the elements of the universe arise through their relations.[38]

God Mediates All Blessings through Time

The doctrine of the Trinity celebrates one of the most basic aspects of human existence: becoming through time. As temporal beings, we will find fulfillment only in being as becoming. Time is a blessing because time allows change. Without change nothing new could arise and nothing old could cease.[39] We could not elicit potential, act with consequence, create with inspiration, or develop beyond our current self. We could not be moral, self-surpassing beings, nor could we be moral, self-surpassing societies. We could never *increase*.[40]

---

36. Shoemaker, *Identity, Cause, and Mind*, 210–11.

37. Zizioulas, *Being as Communion*, 18–19.

38. Gunton, *One, Three and Many*, 170.

39. Siderits and Katsura, *Nagarjuna's Middle Way*, 287.

40. Cobb and Griffin, *Process Theology*, 83.

We may fear time, because within time all things eventually wither and die: "The grass withers and the flower wilts when the breath of YHWH blows upon them. How the people are like grass!" (Isa 40:7). We find ourselves in a universe of growth and decay, of birth and death, of creation and destruction, in which our personal demise is assured. Alas, our tendency to fixate on decay, decline, and death tricks us into a thirst for changelessness, which we hallow as timeless eternity. We then place God there, beyond the destruction to which we are subject. But to assert that divinity lies beyond change, in changelessness, is to derogate the timeful creation and, by implication, its Creator.

The solution lies in recognizing the blessedness of existence within time. Human existence is, by divine design, the unity of time with being.[41] God made us in God's own image, for loving self-donation expressed as conversation, singing, dance, touch, laughter, and weeping. These divine blessings can take place only within the flow of time. Since we are love, we are time.

Love through time allows plurality to become unity. For the sake of simplicity, let us consider the example of a mechanical engine. An engine is composed of interrelated parts creating a whole. The parts unite to perform one function. None of them could perform this function on its own. Separated, they are inert chunks of metal unworthy of any common designation. Assembled, they become a motor with the potential to propel itself.[42] But the interrelatedness of the parts, their creation of the whole, and the successful performance of their function can manifest only through changing relations—through time. Separate parts that move in coordination through time are *many* things operating harmoniously as *one* thing. They are both many and one, simultaneously.

Since things relate to one another by changing in relationship to one another, changelessness is unrelatedness, a state of being impossible for a Trinitarian God. Any thing that does not change must be isolated. From the perspective of our interconnected universe, a separate thing is no thing since it rests outside the churning, relational nexus that grants reality its being.

Within time nothing is permanent and all things are changeable, so all activity is consequential. The past need not determine the future, which is free. In a dynamic universe sustained by a timeful God, our

41. Katagiri, *Each Moment Is Universe*, 104.
42. Haines, "From Organicist," 65.

creativity, responsibility, and promise are vast. Indeed, impermanence grants freedom because it denies any unchanging essence. If everything is related to everything else, and everything is continually changing, then nothing has a permanent nature. The potential within our timeful, ever increasing God becomes the potential within our timeful, ever increasing universe, such that Jesus declares, "With God, all things are possible" (Mark 10:27 KJV).

Our ascription of permanence to things, what the Buddhists consider the main source of our suffering, is caused by the pace at which we experience time. In our own life, for example, we may live near a boulder that seems unchanging. But if we were to accelerate time, then all illusion of permanence would vanish. From the Big Bang to the end of the universe, however it might end, we would see stars arise and cease, galaxies form and collide, elements created and destroyed. We might even see a boulder turned to sand by wind and rain. In this accelerated perception of the universe, impermanence would be immediately apparent.

Someone might protest that the boulder is permanent from the perspective of one short human lifespan. In a purely physical perspective, an eighty-year life may seem quite brief relative to a ten-million-year-old boulder. But even if the boulder *seems* permanent, our *experience* of it will not be. It will be a source of self-esteem when we climb it in childhood; a source of anxiety when our own children climb it years later. It will be a symbol of solidity on first impression; a symbol of inevitable decay when we notice the winter ice enlarging its fissures. Human life is littered with these experiences, in which we assign intense value to a thing, then find that value changing. People are elated to have the winning lottery ticket, until Uncle Joe shows up at their door bemoaning his financial state and pleading for help. The aspiring actor pursues fame, until she can't go to a restaurant without being mobbed. The young soldier seeks glory in combat, then returns home traumatized. The delicious dessert gives us indigestion. Our evaluation of everything, even the most seemingly desirable things, changes.

The Taoists tell a story about our inability to ascribe a firm value to things or events. There was a farmer whose horse, upon whom the farmer was reliant, ran away. His neighbors exclaimed, "What a pity!" But the farmer replied, "We'll see." The next day, the horse returned with another horse it had met in the wild, and the neighbors exclaimed, "What a blessing!" But the farmer replied, "We'll see." The next day, the farmer's son was gentling the wild horse when he fell off and broke his leg. His neighbors exclaimed, "What a pity!" But the farmer replied, "We'll see." Then an army came through the village conscripting soldiers, but the farmer's son was safe due to his broken leg. The neighbors exclaimed, "What a blessing!" But the farmer replied, "We'll see." The farmer recognized that the churning flux prevents us from knowing for certain what is good and what is bad. Recognizing this incapacity helps us respond to events calmly. The farmer never ceases to farm, care for his family, or speak with his neighbors. He still acts and prepares for the future, but with wisdom. The impermanent nature of things doesn't cause him anxiety; it grants him peace.

We can also reflect on the nature of time by slowing it down until things seem to be unchanging. But even then, the astute observer would note the slight changes taking place and the almost imperceptible interrelatedness of all things and would conclude that everything will eventually change everything else. The only way to stop this process would be to stop time. In that case, everything would be locked in place. There would be no cause, no effect, and no succession of events. In that case, and only in that case, objects would have an unchanging *essence*, but only because they had no time through which to change each other. Time grants relationship, while the absence of time imposes separation. For this reason, to ascribe an essence to things is to assert their separation from one another.[43]

We are proposing an ultimate reality "understood entirely as activity rather than as substance."[44] As noted above, God is the singer and the universe is the song. Melody needs motion, movement from tone to tone in a rhythm that generates beauty. Melody is constantly becoming, never "being," never standing still. Music can't reside in an eternal timelessness, because without time there is no music. Likewise, the universe itself "becomes" continually; it is divinity singing.[45] The gifts that we receive within it, like music itself, are more events than things, more verbs than nouns, something to enjoy, but not something to possess.[46]

43. Barnard, "Postmodern Understanding of Separatism," 621–22.

44. Thatamanil, *Immanent Divine*, 173.

45. Streng, *Emptiness*, 37.

46. Primavesi, *Gaia and Climate Change*, 4.

Abba Embeds Beauty within the Universe

Having discussed the relational nature of the universe, and the reliance of relationality upon time for its expression, we will now explore a peak experience of relationship, the experience of beauty. Crucially, I have chosen to discuss beauty while discussing the cosmos, before we have discussed humankind. This placement is an assertion. If we discuss beauty when discussing human experience, then we implicitly assert that beauty arises from our *perception* of the universe and does not preexist that perception. Beauty would have no being independent of us. But if we discuss beauty *before* we discuss humanity, then we implicitly assert that beauty preexists us in the universe and was always there, waiting to be perceived. The Bible suggests that beauty, as an enjoyable quality of the universe, preexists us.

In the first chapter of Genesis, after each day of work but before the creation of humankind, Abba declares the result "good" (Hebrew: *tov*). Abba already enjoys the cosmos, even before humans join it. Yet, after Abba creates humans, Abba declares the universe "very good" (Hebrew: *tov meod*), because now humans can *join Abba in that enjoyment*. We can see the goodness that Abba sees, share that experience with one another, and praise Abba "in the beauty of holiness" (Ps 29:2b KJV).

But if the beauty of the cosmos is a gift, why is anything "achingly beautiful"? This experience is so common that writing programs identify "achingly beautiful" as a cliché. Why isn't the experience of beauty an unalloyed pleasure? Sin is separation—from God, one another, and the cosmos. Beauty is salt in that wound because beauty reminds us of our separation. The universe and its inhabitants are emanations of Abba, unique expressions of the divine nature. Just as the Sun produces light and heat, so Abba produces spirit and matter. Abba created us for awareness of this primordial unity, but our capacity to perceive it has been lost, and our intuition tells us that *we lost it*.

When we ache for beauty, we are aching for reunion. We sense the infinite within the finite and yearn for what we cannot fully receive. Sometimes, in a state of agitation, we may want to possess beauty for ourselves. But we cannot extract anything from everything because it is all of a piece. Like clouds reflected in a stream, the object of desire cannot be extricated from its environs. We will come back empty handed and frustrated until we learn to revel in beauty, without possessiveness.

Cosmic Evolution Fosters the Experience of Beauty

Among the three persons of the Trinity, Christ is Truth, Spirit is Wisdom, and Abba is Law. Although this may seem a restrictive designation for Abba, those who have known lawlessness best know the blessing of law. The opposite of law is chaos, and the correlate of law is cosmos. Abba, as the Architect of cosmos, has blessed the universe with physical laws that govern the interaction of mass, energy, space, and time. Discerning these physical laws is like discerning the rules of a game that we are watching people play. We can't see the rules themselves, but we see that the game is ordered, we infer the rules that provide that order, and we thank the Author of those rules.[47]

In the human quest for understanding, the natural sciences seek to understand these physical laws. Over time, scientists have developed numerous symbol systems by which to analyze them—chemical notation, nuclear notation, gene nomenclature, mathematical physics, etc. Faith also calls us to study natural law, for within the cosmic order we encounter the mind of Abba. Hence, there should be no conflict between science and faith. They are twin aspects of one underlying quest for knowledge.

The physical laws of the universe foster increasing complexity through time. According to physicists, the process of *cosmic evolution* began with the Big Bang, when an extremely dense bundle of energy suddenly expanded, producing space, time, and the four fundamental forces of the universe with it. After 370,000 years, the universe was homogeneous, a diffuse cloud of hydrogen with some helium and traces of lithium. This universe would have been quite boring, unless you really, really loved hydrogen. Fortunately, this pervasive *simplicity* possessed a disposition to *complexity*, an innate tendency to become more differentiated through time. *Stellar evolution* began when gravity condensed the hydrogen, helium, and lithium into stars. The gravitational pressure of those stars fused the hydrogen, sequentially, into helium, carbon, oxygen, neon, magnesium, etc., culminating in iron.

Once iron was formed, stars of a certain mass collapsed, exploding as supernovas. These explosions produced (most of) the periodic table of elements, which began to combine in complex ways, initiating *chemical evolution*. On Earth, about 3.5 billion years ago, some of these chemicals began to adapt to their environments, utilize energy for growth, and replicate themselves. Life appeared, and the process of *biological evolution*

47. Feynman, *Finding Things Out*, 13.

began. Living organisms developed increasingly sophisticated ways of sensing their environment, becoming responsive to hot and cold, light and dark, safety and danger, prey and predator. Eventually, the process of *neurological evolution* produced an expansive knowledge of the environment. But something surprising happened when organisms became aware, not only of their environment, but of *themselves*. Even more mysteriously, at the height of neurological evolution, organisms became *aware of their awareness of themselves*. The cosmic evolution that began from a unitary seed of hyper-concentrated energy has resulted in living beings who can contemplate their own existence, discern the origins of the universe, and commemorate the processes that brought them into being. Cosmic evolution has resulted in something radically *new*. Cosmic evolution has resulted in *us*.

Paradoxically, in a universe that tends to disorder, complexity has *emerged* from simplicity. The concept of *emergence* arose in the late nineteenth century.[48] Emergence argues that several things can combine to produce a new thing that is qualitatively different from its constituent parts. The classic example is water. Pure hydrogen at forty degrees Celsius at sea level is a flammable gas. Pure oxygen at forty degrees Celsius at sea level is a flammable gas. But if you combine them into their most stable form, you get water, which at forty degrees Celsius at sea level is a nonflammable liquid. We breathe oxygen, burn hydrogen, and drink water.

Water cannot be properly understood as the sum of oxygen and hydrogen because the properties of water are so different from those of oxygen and hydrogen. Combination is not addition; combination is transformation. For this reason, to understand water you must study water itself. Anyone trying to study water by studying oxygen and hydrogen separately, then predicting the properties of their union, would fail. Emergence is unpredictable because emergence is truly new. The whole is not only *greater* than the sum of the parts; the whole is *other than* the sum of the parts.

The human mind is an emergent property of matter. As such, it perceives beauty, which is an emergent property of the universe. At this dizzying height of evolutionary experience, a door opens into "ecstasy" or *ex stasis*: stepping "outside of oneself" into the teeming expanse of the universe. Swept up into the rapture of this cosmic perspective, we gain a

---

48. Baylis, "Philosophic Functions of Emergence," 373–75.

glimpse into the mind of Abba the Artist, into their overwhelming intelligence and excruciating patience.

Natural Law Is Unbreakable to Foster Human Community

In 1991, a vibrant eleven-year-old named Rossi was rehearsing for his school play in Virginia Beach. More spirited than prudent, he decided to work his way across the support beam that hung twenty feet above the stage. He fell and landed on his head. They rushed him to the hospital, and his community prayed, and his doctors struggled, but on the third day, Rossi died.

Many members of the boy's church believed that Rossi's death was the will of God, but their minister disagreed. He thought that it was a tragic accident, over which God weeps with us. According to this minister, the purpose of physical law—the inescapable law of the physical universe—is the creation of freedom, consequence, and community. Physical law creates freedom because, within a cosmic order, we can (partially) anticipate the outcome of our actions, so that *it matters what we do*. Chaos would assign a random outcome to any action we took and deny significance to our activity. But physical law creates one shared backdrop against which all persons act out the cosmic drama.[49] Without this cosmic reliability, reason could not be rational, virtue would have no virtuous outcome, and chaos would deny consequence. Without physical law there could be no individual freedom or functioning community.

Physical law governs *reality*, not an illusion. We experience a real universe sustained by a real God to be experienced by real persons. Because it is real, it is important. We cannot dismiss the suffering and injustice in our world as inconsequential. We must take upon ourselves the concreteness of our lives, both individual and social, and work to improve them. Our interpretation of reality may distort it, projecting our own illusions and addictions onto its willing screen. But these too can be cleansed, partially and effortlessly, in community and over time. Reality gives us a truth to approach, just as physical law and the gift of reason grant us the means to approach it.

Yet, if physical law is so essential to our well-being, then why do we fantasize about escaping it? Why do we thirst for a magical universe in

49. Buber, *I and Thou*, 165.

which we—the individual superhero, the powerful wizard—bear greater power than the actual universe would ever afford us? Certainly, we love stories and the occasional escape. But such thirst also suggests our own selfish desire to be unbound by that which binds us all. We want to break the divine law that provides for our common good. We want to rule as monarch rather than cooperate as partner.

Or maybe we want the laws to bend, just a little, to save the life of a beautiful eleven-year-old boy. Rossi's pastor, Rev. Dr. Clement A. Sydnor III, my father, wrote:

> You might be thinking, as I have thought, "If only God had suspended, only for a second, natural law, the law of gravity, we would still have Rossi with us. His mother and brother and uncle and we who love him so, would not be hurting as we are." . . . But God does not suspend the laws that God has established. If God suspended those laws, then our universe would no longer be dependable and predictable. Anxiety and anarchy, confusion and chaos would mark our world and characterize our relationships.[50]

Order is the precondition for harmonious relationality.[51] It is not a prison of predictability. It makes any activity consequential, hence meaningful, and frees us from the randomness that would make all relationships impossible. The will to power may crave freedom from the community-creating order, and compassion may even want to bend the law on occasion, but (in the end) love accepts that order as the blessing it is.

Moral Law Is Breakable to Allow Human Freedom

In addition to *unbreakable* physical law, Abba has also infused the universe with *breakable* moral law. Moral law is that manner of conduct that grants us our greatest fulfillment, both as individuals and societies. *The moral law is love.* Christ came to give us abundant life (John 10:10). Therefore, the purpose of the moral law is not to restrict our actions but to increase our vitality. We can flourish only together: as individuals, we come to the fullness of life through love; as communities, our joy increases as the cosmos evolves toward the divine pattern within it.

50. C. Sydnor, "Trust and Tragedy," paras. 8–9.
51. Cobb and Griffin, *Process Theology*, 166.

Yet, unlike natural law, the moral law is entirely breakable. Instead of loving God or neighbor, we can hate both. Indeed, we can *hurt* both. We can choose evil. The inviolability of physical law makes our choices consequential, while the violability of moral law makes them free. If the moral law was unbreakable, then we would be puppets, but God has no desire to be a puppeteer. The persons within the Trinity act freely and consequentially toward one another, as do we, who are made in the image of God.

We Are in Nature, and Nature Is in Us

Regarding the natural environment, human beings have too long acted greedily, as if nature were a resource external to us. Such an interpretation insists that human beings are separate from nature and that nature exists to serve humanity's desires. If so, then it has no intrinsic value. Our current practices suggest an *economistic* ontology that reduces all things to their economic utility, rendering the world around us dead and subordinate. We see dirt, not nature.

For theists, to produce a theistic environmental ethic we must first generate a sound theology of nature—an interpretation of the world as it relates to the divine. This theology of nature will propose what the world is and, by way of consequence, how we should act toward it. Since God transcends nature and assigns nature its value, this cosmology is more than a natural theology—an interpretation of religion that reduces all spiritual phenomena to a material cause. This cosmology is a *theology of nature*—an interpretation of nature as sustained and ensouled by Abba, hence alive, sacred, and intrinsically valuable.[52]

Environmental ethics were not a pressing concern when the Bible was written. The total human population probably numbered one hundred million. Wilderness still covered most of the earth. Rivers were free of industrial pollutants and landfills were uniformly biodegradable. But people were in constant danger from wild animals, disease, and starvation. The biblical environment was threatening, not threatened. For this reason, we can extract no explicit environmental ethic from the Bible. Yet we can ground a twenty-first-century environmental ethic on its theology of nature, which carries rich implications for human behavior toward the world.

52. Ramanuja, *Vedartha Sangraha*, 41, §47.

First and foremost, because the universe is the body of Abba, and Abba is the soul of the universe, whatever we do to our environment, we do to Abba. To use another metaphor, Abba is the Architect, and creation is Abba's cathedral, within which Abba dwells. We may forget this truth, but nature does not: "Turn to the animals, and let them teach you; the birds of the air will tell you the truth. Listen to the plants of the earth, and learn from them; let the fish of the sea become your teachers. Who among all these does not know that the hand of YHWH has done this?" (Job 12:7–9). Certainly, nature can be enjoyed—just as it is proper to enjoy our own bodies as expressions of God, so we can enjoy nature as an expression of God. Indeed, our love of God will facilitate our enjoyment of the world. If we try to make it serve us, we will be frustrated because that is not its purpose. But if we enjoy the world in service to God then we will know true satisfaction, for both we and the world will be fulfilling our function.

Second, we must recognize that our relationship with nature is one of *mutual immanence*. We are in nature, and nature is in us. Exploitation implies dualism and separation, the belief that whatever is good for us must be good for nature. But our intensifying environmental crisis insists that what is good for nature is good for us, because our relationship with nature is *nondual*. If we truly knew God, and God-in-nature, then we would meet our needs in a way respectful of the environment. Instead, we poison our own well: "How much longer must our land lay parched and the grass in the fields wither? No birds or animals remain in it, for its people are corrupt, saying, 'God can't see what we do'" (Jer 12:4).

Human life is potentially rich, so rich that it might be called blessed. We have the grace-given ability to integrate God and world into one sentient, conscious experience until we can *feel* St. Patrick's blessing: "God beneath you, God in front of you, God behind you, God above you, God within you."[53] God and world do not compete within human experience in a zero-sum game. Indeed, the most abundant life is that which perfectly combines the experience of God, self, and world. This combination does not produce a pantheistic fusion, an indistinct mass of divinity, ego, and matter. Instead, it produces a *triune* experience of God, self, and nature as distinguishable yet inseparable, cooperating to render life holy.

---

53. St. Patrick; quoted in Rohr, *Everything Belongs*, 55.

4

The Abundance of Life

[Human beings] are a part of the whole called by us universe, a part
limited in time and space. [We experience ourselves, our] thoughts
and feelings as something separated from the rest, a kind of optical
delusion of our consciousness. This delusion is a kind of prison for us,
restricting us to our personal desires and to affection for a few persons
nearest to us. Our task must be to free ourselves from this prison by
widening our circle of compassion to embrace all living creatures and
the whole of nature in its beauty.

—ALBERT EINSTEIN[1]

What Are People For?

TO LIVE A GOOD life, we must consider what life is for. Certain forces
in our culture may not want us to experience the depth of life. To serve
their own purposes, these powers and principalities need to keep us distracted so that we will toil, consume, obey, or hate. And to ensure our
conformity, these forces will spread a *metaphysical sickness*—a diseased
interpretation of life.

1. Pritscher, *Re-Opening Einstein's Thought*, 14 (edited for gender inclusivity).

Often, this mass-marketed spiritual disease promotes comparison between persons, assigning them higher and lower status. Such ranking produces anxiety about place, an obsessive concern with our relative worth. Trapped in a zero-sum universe, we compete for power and prestige. Tragically, we "accept praise from one another, yet don't seek the praise that comes from the One God" (John 5:44b).

The endless agitation caused by this struggle exhausts us. Are we more or less important than they are? How can we know for sure? One way to convince ourselves of our value is to acquire symbols of success, cultural expressions of our superiority. But someone else always has a superior expression of relative worth. And so the cycle continues.

No benevolent God would create such a cutthroat mess. This anxious, hierarchical arrangement arises from elsewhere. A benevolent God could invite us only into abundant coexistence. Below, I will provide an alternative understanding of life, grounded in the conviction that unity is our natural state. Religious charlatans and spiritual pickpockets may present God as a mere assistant in the cutthroat game, but honest religion frees us from our insecure ego, thereby revealing our true importance within the sacred whole.[2] To experience this divinely granted importance, we must know why we are, and who we are.

God Makes Human Beings for Unity with God

To briefly review the arguments of our first three chapters: Human existence is not a glorious accident; it is a divine gift. The giver is the Trinity—three persons united through love into one perfect community, pulsing with life. Lamenting our nonbeing, the Infinite overflowed itself, thereby granting us being through creation. By the grace of God, we are delivered from nothingness into fullness. And this process has not ended: Infinity overflows itself continually, *for us*. We reside in the abundance of God. Everywhere we look we see divinity—in nature, in neighbor, even in the mirror. All reality is sacred; in response, we are to celebrate all reality—including our self—as sacrament.

God loved us before we became aware of ourselves, knows us better than we know ourselves, and pervades us like heat pervades fire. "In God we live, move, and have our being," Paul asserts (Acts 17:28), because God is everywhere: within and beyond, immanent and transcendent. For

2. Simpson, *Days of Heaven*, 17.

this reason, Augustine declares that God is "more intimately present to me than my innermost being, and higher than the highest peak of my spirit."[3] To the extent that we *open* ourselves to this inner wellspring, to that extent we cultivate our *true* self. To the extent that we *close* ourselves to this inner wellspring, to that extent we cultivate our *false* self. The abundant life demands that the false self die to the true self (Mark 8:35).

The first Christians called this process *theosis*. This Greek term has been translated as divinization, although that translation is a bit misleading since we will never become God. But we can become more *godlike*— more loving, generous, and open. The Bible makes this possibility clear. In the Gospel of John, Jesus himself declares, "As you, Abba, are in me and I in you; I pray that they may be one in us, so that the world may believe that you sent me" (John 17:21). Peter agrees that we are invited to "become participants in the divine nature" (2 Pet 1:4). And Paul promises, "We, who with unveiled faces reflect our God's glory, grow brighter and brighter as we are being transformed into the image we reflect" (2 Cor 3:18a). If divinization is the process of becoming more *loving*, then demonization is the process of becoming more *hateful*. Love treats the other as a blessing who deserves life, just like we do. Fear treats the other as a threat that endangers our own being. In the eye of faith, every person is a second universe who offers to challenge and enrich our own.

In a triumph of imperialism over mysticism, the Western Church repressed this invitation to *theosis*: transformation into the image of God within us. They feared that followers would claim to *be* God, rather than to be unified *with* God. Such divine-human unity would threaten the status of God as transcendent. By analogy to human affairs, an accessible divinity would threaten the status of an exalted emperor, the monarch on high who maintains social order. Therefore, according to imperial logic, the celestial ruler must be separate from the ruled, just as the earthly ruler must be separate from the ruled: power must be held by objective authorities uncorrupted by emotion, personally invulnerable, politically distant, and (all too frequently) willingly violent.

In contrast to the god of empire, Jesus had preached a warm, accessible concept of God as Abba: "Father" or "Dad" (Luke 11:2–4). Astoundingly, Jesus's church became the official religious institution of the Roman Empire, which had executed Jesus only three hundred

---

3. Augustine, *Confessions*, 83.

years earlier. Unfortunately, Jesus's nurturing divinity did not serve the religiopolitical needs of the imperium.[4]

Today, there is a Christian movement returning to the affectionate God preached by Jesus. This God is our father (Mark 14:36) and our mother (Luke 15:8–10) who deeply desires our well-being. Feeling insignificant, we may doubt this love and ask, with the psalmist: "When I behold your heavens, the work of your fingers, the moon, and the stars which you set in place—what is humanity that you should be mindful of us? Who are we that you should care for us?" (Ps 8:3–4). But Jesus assures us of God's intimate concern: "Aren't five sparrows sold for a few pennies? Yet not one of them is neglected by God. In fact, even the hairs on your head are counted! Don't be afraid; you are worth more than a whole flock of sparrows" (Luke 12:6–7). No matter how limitless the universe, no matter how infinite the stretch of time, no matter how countless the teeming beings, God loves you—personally, infinitely, and exhaustively.

Those who are parents can attest: having a second child does not dilute their love and delight in the first child. The Krishna-worshiping tradition within Hinduism powerfully illustrates this divine delight. Their vision of salvation is to play, especially dance, with Krishna in the gardens of Vrindavan. But Krishna's devotees need not wait or take turns. Instead, Krishna multiplies himself endlessly, that he might dance with each devotee individually, devoting his full attention—spiritual, emotional, and physical—to his partner. For Krishna worshipers, the inexhaustible God is absolutely present to every devotee: no matter how numberless the dancers, God will partner individually with each.[5]

We are each God's own dancing partner. Every lover wants to give to their beloved. Recognizing this truth, every lover must be willing to *receive* from their beloved. Love is either reciprocal or twisted. God, who invites us into divine love, blesses our self-giving and laments our self-withholding. According to Charles Hartshorne, if God is invulnerable to us, if we cannot move God to celebration or lament, then God is not love and the Bible is untrue.[6]

---

4. Kreitzer, "Apotheosis of Roman Emperor," 216.

5. Schweig, *Dance of Divine Love*, 270–72.

6. Hartshorne, *Divine Relativity*, 55.

God Makes Human Beings for Unity with the Cosmos

Marcion of Sinope was a second-century Christian theologian. We know him only through his detractors, but the consistency of their account suggests some reliability. His thought was eventually rejected by the church because Marcion was a *dualist*—he interpreted reality as characterized by opposing poles, and he preferred one pole over against the other. So thoroughgoing was his dualism that he even posited two gods: an Old Testament god of matter, who subjects humankind to unjust, contradictory, and brutal laws; and a New Testament god of spirit, who frees us from law into a new disposition of mercy and grace. Hence, the loving Father of Jesus is not to be confused with the stern Lawgiver of Moses, and Christianity would only be corrupted by any association with Judaism or its Scriptures.[7]

Recognizing that Jesus was a Jew whose teachings derived from his Hebrew faith and its Scriptures, and whose arguments were primarily with other Jews about Judaism, the church eventually declared both the Hebrew Bible (the "Old Testament") and the Newer Testament (the "New Testament") canonical and authoritative. Through this choice, the church made a historical decision for the *unity of reality*. The Creator is benevolent, creation is real, and salvation occurs *within* the world; it does not take us *out of* the world. Matter and spirit, body and soul, time and eternity were to be united, not divided. Although the term would have been unfamiliar at the time, the church chose *nondualism*.

According to nondualism, nothing exists except through its relationships to other things. Our world is wholly related, produced by relations and dependent upon relations. Every part is open to every other part, to its core, so that every part belongs entirely to the whole. Made in the image of the related God within the related universe, our calling is to feel, think, and enact this relationality. To fulfill the divine intention for creation, *to experience joy*, the universe needs faith—a deep trust in the fundamental unity of being.

Faith does not free us from matter, nor does faith oppose material existence. Instead, faith *completes* material existence, imbuing it with meaning, purpose, and beauty. The Bible makes this argument: in Gen 2, God makes Adam from *adamah*, the ground. Being of the ground, Adam (literally: "red") is red, like the clay from which he was born. Even the life force within us, our blood (Hebrew: *dam*), bespeaks our earthly ties.

7. Stephenson, "Marcion."

Adam is an earthling, quite literally, as are we. This status is not a limitation; it is our original blessing. We are dust quickened by God.[8]

We have argued above that the universe is the body of God, and God is the soul of the universe. To honor our God-given unity with the universe, and our divinely granted souls, we need bodies. Our bodies are our means of relationship with friends, family, and lovers. Without the clear and distinct sense experience offered by our bodies, we would drift about in an existential ether. Relations would be dilute, personality would be vague, and uniqueness would be trivial. We would be abstractions, and as abstractions relating to abstractions, our interpersonal exchanges would be impoverished. But the particularity granted by our bodies grants our experience definition and signification. Hence, the body as a means of relation is a blessing.

Because we are embodied souls in a cosmos, and because body, soul, and cosmos are all inseparable, our richest experiences will unite spirit and matter. We can find innumerable examples of such experiences, when the border between self and universe disappears. Norman Maclean, in his memoir *A River Runs through It*, writes of fly-fishing along the rivers of western Montana. For Maclean, fly-fishing was more than sport. It was a gateway to the unity of all things and his own participation in that unity: "On the river the heat mirages danced with each other and then they danced through each other and then they joined hands and danced around each other. Eventually the watcher joined the river, and there was only one of us. I believe it was the river."[9]

Religious mystics have always insisted on the unity of humankind and the cosmos within God. As a result of this unity, we can never be satisfied with either a Godless world or a worldless God; we need our souls to be filled with both.[10] Certainly, we can wonder why the universe is so astoundingly huge and why we are as nothing within its endless expanse. Yet, if we erase the false boundary between ourselves and the universe, if we let the inside out and the outside in, then we become expansive indeed. How much do you contain? The answer to this question is determined by how open you are. If absolutely open, then you can contain the whole universe. If absolutely closed, then you contain naught but your empty self. You are as full as you are empty. You are as empty as you are full.

8. Almalech, "Cultural Unit Red," §3.1.4.

9. Maclean, *River Runs through It*, 61.

10. Fackenheim, *Religious Dimension*, 200.

Mysteriously, such unification with the material cosmos may even make us more capable. Hector Cole, a master of traditional sword making, observes the unity of self and object that is necessary to his trade: "When you put the sword into the fire, your mind enters the fire with it. Otherwise, the endeavor will fail."[11] The dancer Maria Tallchief describes this disappearance of self into cosmos and cosmos into self as the very height of artistic expression: "From your first plié you are learning to become an artist. In every sense of the word, you are poetry in motion. And if you are fortunate enough . . . you are actually the music."[12]

God Unites Body and Soul for Human Flourishing

The body does not compete with the soul; it unites with the soul to produce embodied, soulful experience.[13] Embodied experience feeds the soul, while the soul informs embodied experience. Meaning arises from this union: embodiment allows loving relationship, materiality allows intense sensation, and decisions within time produce moral consequence. Soul and body are as inseparable for vitality as light and heat are for fire.

Despite the church's rejection of Marcion, who preferred spirit over matter and soul over body, early Christianity sometimes wavered in its commitment to embodiment as blessed. The church arose within the context of Greek philosophy and Jewish asceticism that sometimes devalued material existence, and the church sometimes absorbed these influences. For example, in the fourth century Athanasius wrote an influential biography of Anthony of Egypt, considered the father of Christian monasticism. According to Athanasius, Anthony "used to eat and sleep, and go about all other bodily necessities with shame when he thought of the spiritual faculties of the soul. . . . It behooved a man to give all his time to his soul rather than his body."[14] In the *Philokalia*, an anthology of early Christian monastic writings, St. Neilos the Ascetic marvels at Moses's courage: "These holy men achieved such things because they had resolved to live for the soul alone, turning away from the body and its wants."[15] In the centuries that

11. Nash, "Barbarian Battle Tech," 4:5–13.
12. Tallchief with Wells, *Tallchief*, 14.
13. Ramanuja, *Vedartha Sangraha*, 90, §116.
14. Athanasius, "Life of St. Anthony," §45.
15. Nikodimos and Markario, *Philokalia*, 1:212.

followed, flagellants punished their bodies, gnostics escaped their bodies, and women were seen as excessively embodied.

Given the above, the term *soul* has a problematic history, and some theologians have rejected the concept as inevitably anti-body. Yet soulless bodies may prove as unsatisfactory as disembodied souls, especially as we develop concerns about the "soulless" culture in which we live. The *Oxford English Dictionary* defines *soulless* as heartless, cold, and mechanical, lacking in warmth and feeling. By way of consequence, soulless culture is passionless, dull, and uninteresting, and a soulless place lacks character, uniqueness, and distinction.

By way of extension, a soulless economy reduces human persons to units of production and consumption. Its marketers study our depths to control us, while advertisers manipulate our insecurities, politicians target our identity group, and elementary school students are defined by their test scores. Meanwhile, imperial accountancy translates everything and everyone into a dollar value. Threatened by an ever-encroaching *thingness*, a universe of hollow surfaces, we yearn for the abundance of life that surely exists somewhere, but certainly not here.

The body alone is ill suited to resist its own objectification. Indeed, separated from any *inherent* value or meaning, it becomes a vulnerability. Girls and boys are shown computer-altered images of "ideal" types and made to feel insecure. Anxious adults compete in the placement of their bodies, struggling to be seen at the right restaurant on the right vacation with the right people. After this calculated onslaught, we may doubt if we are in the right body.

Cunningly, these bodily insecurities are then offered the topical anesthetic of consumption. Clothes, protein powders, makeup, cars, jewelry, liquor, and "exclusive memberships" all promise to free us from our externally inculcated self-loathing. By design, these offer only a brief numbness from which the pain of insecurity will arise again—and the need for an anesthetic. So continues the cycle of anxiety-driven consumption upon which our economy is based, much of which is founded on our own doubts about our own appearance and worth. We do not experience this system as disembodied. We experience it as soulless.

In this modern day context, we yearn for *soulful* culture. The *Oxford English Dictionary* defines *soulful* as "full of soul or feeling; of a highly emotional, spiritual, or aesthetic nature; expressing or evoking deep emotion. "Soulful" can be used as a noun: "As much as a soul can hold or contain," as in "she got her soulful of tenderness from the community."

In these examples, "soul" becomes a synonym for kindness, warmth, and depth, a cipher for our most human sentiments. We sense that our authentic self is at best neglected, at worst endangered, by our soulless culture.

So existentially useful is the concept of soul that the most prominent atheist in the Western tradition, Friedrich Nietzsche, utilized it extensively, even as he attempted to reconstruct a culture in which God had died. Fearing an encroaching descent into triviality, Nietzsche elevated the soul to remind his readers of their most noble aspirations and prevent a descent into the Last Man:

> The soul that has the longest ladder and reaches down deepest—the most comprehensive soul, which can run and stray and roam farthest within itself; the most necessary soul that plunges joyously into chance; the soul that, having being, dives into becoming; the soul that has, but wants to want and will; the soul that flees itself and catches up with itself in the widest circles; the wisest soul that folly exhorts most sweetly; the soul that loves itself most, in which all things have their sweep and countersweep and ebb and flood. . . . But that is the concept of Dionysus himself.[16]

According to Nietzsche, we need the soul to create soulful life in a soulless culture. Yet he insists that the soul must *fulfill* the body, not compete with it.

The concept of the soul has also been criticized due to its association with reward and punishment. In individualist religion, the soul bears the record of our deeds, like a secret police file. Based on this record, God judges the individual soul, sending it to either heaven or hell. But in this account the soul has no inherent relationality. Its function is exclusively *eschatological*—bearing our eternal destiny. The threat of punishment polices individuals, but does not indicate our basic call to community. For this reason, such legalistic concepts of the soul are inadequate to persons made in the image of the Trinitarian God.

How could we reconceptualize the soul as interdependent rather than isolated? Any concept of the soul that is faithful to the Trinity must invite us to live *for one another*. We can recall our previous definition of God as "an infinite sphere whose center is everywhere and whose circumference is nowhere."[17] Applying this geometric concept to humankind, we can define the soul as *a point with an infinite number of radii, of infinite*

16. Nietzsche, *Ecce Homo*, 306.

17. Copenhaver, Greek *"Corpus Hermeticum*," xlvii.

length, lacking any circumference. By their very nature, our souls radiate outward and seek connection, and connection grants us expansiveness.

Euclid, the founder of geometry, initiated this *relational* way of conceptualizing the universe. The most basic unit in his philosophy is the point. Euclid defines a point as that which has no parts or magnitude, thus has no existence in and of itself. Instead, points are *granted* existence by the pattern of relations in which they dwell, combining with other points to form a line, plane, cube, sphere, etc. By itself, the point is an abstraction. United to others, it constitutes reality.[18]

The soul is nothing in itself. Only through its relationship to other souls does the soul come into being, connected and open. It becomes everything, even while retaining its own location, perspective, and identity. The soul can then offer its uniqueness to all other souls, thereby granting them their own uniqueness, a gift that they have already reciprocated. In this conception, the soul becomes a boundless horizon that we wall off only to our own detriment.

God Makes Human Beings for Unity with the Self

"You shall love your neighbor as yourself," declares Jesus, quoting his own Hebrew Bible (Lev 19:18; Mark 12:31). Frequently, the Christian tradition has interpreted this statement to mean: "You shall now love your neighbor as you *already* love yourself." But this interpretation errs twice: it assumes self-love, then it bases neighbor love on that assumed self-love. Jesus was far too insightful to assume self-love within his followers. The residents of Roman-occupied Judaea were conquered, humiliated, taxed, and impoverished. Branded as inferior to their occupiers, they were taught to hate themselves. Even today, healthy self-love is rare. As a teacher with profound insight into the human situation, Jesus was not *assuming* self-love; Jesus was *counseling* self-love.

God-love grounds both self-love and neighbor love. These three loves are woven together; they are *triune.* How we treat others is linked to how we treat ourselves because, within God, we are members of one another (Eph 4:25). If love is the balm, then we must apply it universally, to both self and neighbor. But this practice creates an ambiguous situation. We are invited to self-donation, an openness to others that gives life to all. But in certain circumstances, self-donation can result in self-destruction.

18. Dyson, *Infinite in All Directions*, 17.

Parents can be controlling, lovers abusive, neighbors contemptuous, and bosses narcissistic. The love of God may call us to suffer *creatively* for others, but it does not call us to suffer *destructively* for others. For this reason, we must reject any uncritical altruism, any concern for others that eclipses all concern for self. *Self-donation never justifies self-erasure.* Instead, the self from which we donate should be rich, so that we can donate much.[19] In the contemporary language of psychology, we are called to interdependence, not codependence. We do not approach one another out of lack, but out of confidence, because "God did not give us a spirit of timidity, but one of power, love, and self-discipline (2 Tim 1:7 ISV).

The psalmist assures us of our internal riches and God-given value: "You created my inmost being and stitched me together in my mother's womb. For all these mysteries I thank you—for the wonder of myself, for the wonder of your works—my soul knows it well (Ps 139:14). The prophet Malachi asks, "Are we not all the children of God? Has not one God created us?" (Mal 2:10). Our status as children of God, revealed to the Hebrews as true for all humanity, is the sure foundation for our self-love. This status is indubitable, running from Deut 14:1a ("You are children of the Lord") to 2 Cor 6:18 ("'I will be your father, and you shall be my children,' says the Lord Almighty"). This status is universal, since Abba is the maker of all. Amy-Jill Levine notes, "In Israel's Scriptures, God's concern is not restricted to insiders: it extends to strangers, to slaves, to women, and to any who are oppressed, for we are all children of God."[20]

Baptism is the ritual through which Christians observe humankind's universal status as God's beloved. Every Christian baptism recapitulates Christ's baptism: "When all the people were baptized, Jesus also came to be baptized. And while Jesus was praying, the skies opened and the Holy Spirit descended on the Anointed One in visible form, like a dove. A voice from heaven said, 'You are my Own, my Beloved. On you my favor rests'" (Luke 3:21–22). Whenever we baptize, we declare the baptized person to be a beloved child of God, on whom God's favor rests.

Christian baptism is the particular rite that celebrates the universal truth of divine love. We can declare this fact at any age, whether the recipient is one day old or one hundred years old. Some churches baptize infants because, quite factually, God's love precedes our capacity to

---

19. Bacon, "'Thinking' the Trinity," 460.
20. Levine, *Light of the World*, 62.

respond. It is waiting for us to become aware of it and always inviting us into that awareness. So, the local church promises, for the universal church, to make God's love known to the child. In speech and action, in all that it does, the church will declare, "See what love God has for us, that we should be called the children of God. And so we are!" (1 John 3:1).

Baptism protects no one from the difficulties of life, but it can inoculate the baptized against the misery that accompanies a misinterpretation of suffering. *Suffering is not inflicted by God as punishment, nor is it a test of faith, nor is it the result of any ancestral stain.* The origin of suffering is mysterious, but our status within suffering is assured: we are baptized, we are beloved, and we shall overcome with the support of our community and the love of God.

Self-love is sacred, but it is also necessary because our interior lives are not simple. Our capacity for self-love and self-hatred, for self-doubt and self-absorption, implies *internal differentiation*. Augustine muses, "I have become a question to myself," because a person is more like a society of persons than a single person.[21] We can be both the person who loses their temper and the person who struggles *not* to lose their temper. We can be the person who hates herself and the person who wants to love herself. We can carry on an internal dialogue with ourselves, giving ourselves pep speeches or putting ourselves down. If you get angry with yourself, then you are the angry person, you are the target of the anger, and you are the observer who realizes that all this anger is useless.

We are made in the image of God, for loving self-relationship. But how is that image expressed through our interior complexity? Following Greek philosophy, Christian theology has traditionally asserted the absolute *simplicity* of God, an unfortunate theological move. Theologians such as Anselm of Canterbury argue that God's self-being, self-reliance, and independence necessitate simplicity. Any composite object—like a chariot—is made of its parts. The being of the chariot *depends* on the being of the wheel, axle, carriage, draft pole, and yoke. If any of those are missing, then the chariot is incomplete and is not even a chariot. By way of analogy, since God cannot *depend* on anything for God's existence, God cannot be composite; God must be simple. As Anselm writes, "Whatever is composed of parts is not completely one. It is in some sense a plurality and not identical with itself, and it can be broken up either in

---

21. Augustine, *Confessions*, §10.33.

fact or at least in the understanding. But such characteristics are foreign to you [God], than whom nothing better can be thought."[22]

If God is simple, and human beings are made in the image of God, then human beings should also be simple. Faced with any tensive aspects of our being, like reason and emotion, simplicity demands that we prefer one and annihilate the other. Reason must be pure, unsullied by emotion. The spirit must transcend rather than sublimate matter. The soul must be freed from its earthly prison, the body. By deeming one aspect of ourselves an absolute good and the other a contaminating evil, we try to free ourselves from the tension between the two—and our own interior riches. By reducing complex reality to simplistic fantasy, we hope to end all internal contest.

For millennia we have attempted to understand through simplification, to our detriment. Seeing kaleidoscopic reality as a black-and-white still life may grant us cognitive control but only produces shallow misinterpretations, clumsy decisions, and continual confusion. The Bible, in contrast, values the person as a *unity* of body and soul, matter and spirit, reason and emotion. The Bible sanctifies human complexity—spiritual, intellectual, and moral.

The Bible also asserts *divine* complexity. For example, in the Bible God *converses*. Sometimes, the conversation even changes God's mind (Exod 32:14). When we humans converse, there is a part of us that is conversing and part of us that observes the conversation. One part participates, and the other evaluates. The evaluating part makes sure the conversation is going well, avoids pitfalls, regrets mistakes, and redirects when necessary. For any skilled negotiator or counselor, this evaluative part must be highly developed. It is also helpful at large family dinners.

Human cognition is expansive, which grants us *consciousness of.* We feel, and we know that we feel. We think, and we know that we think. Would we deny to God this basic human facility? When God spoke with Moses, was God pure participant, unaware that a conversation was going on? Is God so simple as to lack any mechanism for conversational evaluation? When we think of God, we think of infinite capacity, not inferior capacity. If our internal differentiation reflects superior mental capability, then God must possess this capability infinitely. Hence, God cannot be simple; God must be complex. And not just complex, but infinitely complex.[23]

---

22. Anselm, *Basic Writings*, 92.
23. Ramanuja, *Vedartha Sangraha*, 20, §19.

The beauty of God's infinite complexity lies in its perfect harmony. God's internal complexity is symphonic. The divine mind is like an orchestra, not a soloist. Being made in the image of God, we are made for the union of complexity and harmony. *Love harmonizes complexity.* Within the Trinity, the perfect love of each person for the other produces splendid harmony, which is divinity. Within any human, self-love unites internal diversity into healthy personality. Self-hatred, on the other hand, produces a fractured person who suffers—and spreads that suffering to others.

God Makes Human Beings for Unity with One Another

Made in the image of God, we are not made to be alone. Self-sufficiency is abhorrent to the human condition. Today, medical science is asserting that loneliness can be lethal.[24] The Bible declares this truth in the beginning: the Garden of Eden meets all of Adam's material needs, grants him safety and security, and provides him with meaningful work. He even has God to talk to. Nevertheless, Abba discerns that Adam needs a partner. Adam needs to do more than just work and live; he needs to work *with* and live *with*. For Adam, and all humankind, self-sufficiency is insufficient. There is more. The soul (like God) seeks relationship *not* through a sense of lack, but from a feeling of potential, the intuition that openness to another offers increase. We are pulled by promise, not pushed by need.

The original Hebrew reveals the intensity of this desire. Recognizing Adam's heartache, Abba creates for Adam an *ezer*. This term has often been translated as "helper," but *ezer* implies much more. The Hebrew Bible applies *ezer* three times to nations that Israel, under threat, sought military aid from (Isa 30:5; Ezek 12:14; Dan 11:34). And it applies the term sixteen times to Abba/YHWH as Israel's defender, protector, or guardian (Exod 18:4; Deut 33:7, 26, 29; Ps 20:2; 33:20; 70:5; 115:9–11; 121:1–2; 124:8; 146:5; Hos 13:9; etc.). The term can be translated various ways: the NIV translates *ezer* as "strength" in Ps 89:19, for example. So, Eve is no mere assistant; she is Adam's rescue from emotional desolation; she is his deliverance from existential impoverishment.[25]

Two caveats are necessary here. First, *Eve's status as Adam's deliverer does not mean that all women are spiritually superior to all men.* Abba

24. Rico-Uribe et al, "Association of Loneliness," 16.
25. Freeman, "Woman, a Power Equal," 19–20.

could have made Eve first, and she could have needed Adam, in which case Adam would have been Eve's deliverer. The order of creation is accidental, not essential. Adam and Eve's status is interdependent and equal. They rescue *each other*—had Adam not already been there, Eve would have been equally desolate. Second, Adam's desire for Eve does not establish a heterosexual norm for all humankind for all eternity. Their love for each other symbolizes *all* human love, not merely *erotic* human love. Like all of us, they need an ally, companion, friend, coworker, conversation partner, counselor, *and* lover. These relationships, including erotic ones, occur across an array of genders. *The depth of our love determines the quality of our relationships, regardless of gender.*

Genesis insists that we are not made for isolation; we are made for each other. Contemporary science endorses this religious insight. Psychiatry declares any mental condition that separates us emotionally from others to be an illness.[26] The prime example of such illness is narcissism. For narcissists, self-love is exclusive love. Narcissism plucks the narcissist from the interpersonal web of life and confines them within themselves, depriving them of the reciprocating affection that is our lifeblood. Equally painful, the self-love of the narcissist is unrequited. They love themselves, but they hate themselves back for it. Their self-relationship is abusive; their internal diversity is a cacophony.[27] Tragically, the part of the narcissist that must die so that the narcissist might live is the part that makes the decision. Love threatens the narcissistic self because love invites the relational self into being. In an act of masochistic self-preservation, the narcissist must reject love and any hope of prospering with others. Narcissism is no mere personality disorder; it is a tear in the fabric of being.

God does not make humans to *be*. God makes humans to *be with*. Human being is *being with* others. The capacity for solitude is healthy, and the need for retreat is real, but enduring isolation sickens the soul. Any interpretation of human being must acknowledge our interpersonal nature, with our constitution by self, and other, and God. This melded life begins on the day we are born. We realize instinctively that our survival rests outside of us, that our destiny depends on our caregivers.

Theologian John Mbiti articulates this truth through his interpretation of *ubuntu*, an African concept of humanity: "Whatever happens to the individual happens to the whole group, and whatever happens to the

26. American Psychiatric Association, *DSM-5*, 265.
27. W. K. Campbell and Miller, "Narcissism," 5:369.

whole group happens to the individual. The individual can only say: I am, because we are; and since we are, therefore I am."[28] According to Mbiti, the individual is inseparable from society, just as society is inseparable from the individual. So, there is no conflict between the two—only a just society achieves flourishing individuals, precisely because it recognizes their freedom, nurtures their potential, and encourages their cooperation. Unjust societies that deny equal opportunity are inherently *against* the individuals that compose them. Too frequently, those who extol "individualism" are only masking their privilege behind the rhetoric of virtue, through which they separate themselves from others. In the words of Barack Obama, "We can only achieve ourselves by sharing ourselves."[29]

Our celebration of community does not subject the virtuous individual to any vicious crowd. What we are proposing here is a *nondual* understanding of humanity based on divine agape. Because we are fully individual and fully social, influence flows both ways. Nevertheless, as fully individual, we cannot participate in any identity fusion in which our personhood is lost to the mob: "Thou shalt not follow a crowd to do evil" (Exod 23:2 WEB). At times, the individual must resist the society for the sake of the society, as did Harriet Tubman, Sophie Scholl, Bayard Rustin, and the "Tank Man" of Tiananmen Square.

Interpersonal Love Manifests God in Human Community

My student, Torrey Joyner, was a brilliant academic, excellent basketball player, and campus leader at Emmanuel College in Boston. After graduation, he was teaching and coaching in a middle school in Connecticut when he caught a virus. The virus itself was relatively harmless, but his body's immune system overreacted and attacked his spinal column, leaving him partially paralyzed from the waist down. Throughout the ordeal, he was supported by friends, family, and his girlfriend Andrea. Several years later, he and Andrea were married. Torrey, now in a wheelchair, wanted to stand to take his vows, so that he could look Andrea in the eye while giving them. He worked hard at physical therapy, but also relied on the support of his friends. When the time came to take his vows, two of his groomsmen brought him a walker, then helped him to stand. They

---

28. Mbiti, *African Religions & Philosophy*, 106.

29. Obama, "Remarks by President Obama," para. 11.

removed the wheelchair. Torrey looked Andrea in the eye, supporting himself, but also supported by his best man, who stood behind him with his hand on Torrey's back. The first groomsman supported the best man, and the next groomsman supported that groomsman, on down the line, five men linked together in support of one, so that he could support himself and declare his love for the woman who supported him and whom he would support.

"No one has ever seen God," writes John. But his assertion does not mean that God is completely invisible: "Yet if we love one another, God dwells in us, and God's love is brought to perfection in us" (1 John 4:12). According to John, we see God by loving one another. At Torrey's wedding, we saw the invisible God. This experience should not surprise us, since God is love, and we are made in the image of God. But God as Trinity is not an *independent* self. God as Trinity is a community of *interdependent* selves who support one another. Likewise we, who are made in the image of God, are made to support one another. For this reason, notes Mark Heim, "The personal bonds humans form with each other are the repositories of the deepest fulfillment most of us know."[30]

I am not, nor can I be, a separate whole. *I am interrelatedness.* You might ask yourself: *Where* is your unrelated self? *When* was your unrelated self? The newborn's first attunement is to its mother, not itself. Contemplation reveals that there is no I without You, no self without community. We are all located, and we are all integrated. This flow of locality into locality, of uniqueness into uniqueness, generates a pulsing cosmos. Residing in a universe sustained by an internally differentiated and perfectly energetic God, we cannot flourish without difference. For this reason, the other—the one who is different from me, who does not conform to my established mode of interpretation, who renders the obvious suddenly unfamiliar—comes to me not as threat but as opportunity, as a symbol of God, as an "infinity from on high." *The other is the life-granting neighbor whom God invites us to love.*

Because we are made for one another, peak experience will be unified experience. One example of unified experience is flowing conversation. Flowing conversation erases the boundary between self and other. When you are in a conversation, and your conversation partner's words are affecting you, and your words are affecting your conversation partner, where is the dividing line between you? Through language my thoughts

30. Heim, *Depth of the Riches*, 56.

become your thoughts and yours become mine. We exchange feelings and laugh together and cry together. We enter the conversation in one state and depart it in a different state—comforted, enraged, saddened, encouraged, or enlightened.

But in such a flowing conversation, we do not change each other. Instead, *we are both changed by the conversation.* The conversation becomes, through our openness to one another, a third entity, an emergent reality, within which your thoughts and mine combine, but are not confused. Yes, our thoughts constitute the conversation, but from those thoughts arises a new thing with its own activity and its own becoming, an unexpected and abundant manifestation that discloses the mysterious potential resident within relationship.[31]

Made in the image of God, we are made for flowing love.[32] There is no part of us that is cut off from the rest of the universe. The isolated, pure, rational consciousness does not exist, has not existed, and will not exist. Indeed, it cannot exist, because the mind cannot be separated from the body, reason cannot be separated from the senses, and the self cannot be separated from others. According to our Trinitarian understanding of humankind, Descartes's project—his quest for certain knowledge through rigorous introspection—was wrongheaded. Thirsting for epistemological certainty, for perfectly reliable knowledge, he reduced himself to pure rationality. There, alone in his mind, he discovered God, the infinite cause of his *concept* of an infinite God.[33] Being perfect, this God was not deceptive, so Descartes decided that he could trust his knowledge. Sensory experience was of real objects and reason was competent to analyze it.

Such confirmation would suffice a robot, but it is inadequate to human understanding, because we are more than robots. We not only sense and think; we also *feel.* Most gloriously, we feel *love.* But in his *Meditations* at least, Descartes had received no knowledge of love. How could he have, as an isolated consciousness? Love does not grant us certainty. Rather, love casts us into all the complexities and ambiguities of this-worldly existence and its attendant emotions. Love demands risk; love demands *incarnation.*

This understanding of humankind as relational endorses a *centrifugal* self. We are invited to expand more deeply into God, the world, neighbor, and self. Our nature is not to be fixed; our nature is to change,

31. Gadamer, *Truth and Method*, 383.
32. Voss Roberts, *Dualities*, 39–40.
33. Descartes, *Meditations on First Philosophy*, §3.7.

to increase, and to surpass ourselves, both as individuals and as societies. Through this process, we embrace reality ever more wholeheartedly. The great currents of life lie within and without, awaiting our participation. In contrast, petty egoism is impoverished.

Divine Love Assures Human Freedom

"When Christ freed us, we were meant to remain free" Paul declares (Gal 5:1). Curiously, the Christian tradition has too often denied human freedom, asserting that God foreordains every thought and every action of every person. In one way, such a view must be reassuring. Everything that happens is the will of God. We need not understand; we need only trust that this course of events is divinely ordained, no matter how seemingly horrible to our human eyes. Regarding our own actions, given that we don't know what God has ordained, we can act *as if* we decide, *as if* our decisions matter, *as if* we are free. But all the time, a power and wisdom greater than ourselves is in control, acting in our own best interest, even if we cannot recognize the beneficence.

We can make multiple critiques of this theology. First, it opens religion to Freudian calls for atheism. Freud asserts that religion arrests human development by replacing the biological father figure with a psychological god figure. The Father God provides comfort but leaves the believer in a state of permanent childhood.[34] To mature, Freud insisted, we must overthrow this father figure, both biological and psychological, and assume full responsibility for our lives:

> I must contradict you when you go on to argue that men are completely unable to do without the consolation of the religious illusion, that without it they could not bear the troubles of life and the cruelties of reality. . . . They will, it is true, find themselves in a difficult situation. They will have to admit to themselves the full extent of their helplessness and their insignificance in the machinery of the universe; they can no longer be the center of creation, no longer the object of tender care on the part of a beneficent Providence. They will be in the same position as a child who has left the parental house where he was so warm and comfortable. But surely infantilism is destined to be surmounted. Men cannot remain children forever.[35]

34. Freud, *Totem and Taboo*, 183.
35. Freud, *Future of an Illusion*, 72.

According to Freud, religion is an escape mechanism by which humankind flees from reality into fantasy, generating an illusory universe that
stunts human development. Reason and observation, in the form of psy-
choanalysis, can free us from the illusion, but only for the courageous
individual willing to risk the true terror of life.

Second, theistic determinism—the belief that everything happens
in accord with the will of God—approximates *nihilism*. Nihilism is the
belief in nothingness. This belief can bring comfort since, if nothing matters, then there is nothing to worry about and nothing we do matters. But
the same can be said for worship of an all-controlling God since this God
rejects all human value. Again, nothing we do matters. All our reasoning,
no matter how exacting, is farcical since every decision is predetermined.
All our actions, no matter how loving, are meaningless since they do not
emerge from a free self.[36]

Finally, the assertion that all things happen according to the will of
God is not biblical. If everything happens according to the will of God,
then why did God inspire the prophets to preach social justice? If the
world is always perfectly in accord with the will of God, then nothing
could happen contrary to the will of God, and there would be no need
to change anything. Yet God constantly speaks through the prophets,
admonishing Israel to return to the covenant, to the way of compassion:

> You hate the arbiter who sits at the city gate, and detest the one
> who speaks the truth. Rest assured: since you trampled on the
> poor, extorting inhumane taxes on their grain, those houses you
> built of hewn stone—you will never live in them; and those pre-
> cious vineyards you planted—you will never drink their wine.
> For I have noted your many atrocities, and your countless sins,
> you persecutors of the righteous, you bribe-takers, you who
> deny justice to the needy at the city gate! (Amos 5:10–12)

If ancient Hebrew society had been *already* ordered in accord with the
will of God, and the prophets knew this, then they would have had to
adjust their rhetoric. They might have said: "Everything happens according to the will of God, so everything is as it should be, and we shouldn't
change anything. But to give us some make-work, God is asking us to
improve our society, so that we can all pretend to make a difference. And
whether we do that make-work or not is up to God, so now let's pretend
to decide."

---

36. Cottrell-Boyce, "Soteriological Uncertainty," 14–15.

Jesus, who worked in the tradition of the prophets, also recognized the glaring gap between God's will and human practice, teaching his disciples to pray, "Thy [Abba's] will be done." But if it is already being done, then why do Christians pray for it to be done? And who is supposed to do it? Jesus prays for the will of Abba to be done because it is not being done. The will of Abba is a world in which generosity is universal, power is honest, prosperity is shared, and fear is renounced. This world did not exist for the prophets, it did not exist for Jesus, and it does not exist today. For this reason, Jesus invites us to enact the divine will, to become the hands of God on earth, to redeem society with justice.[37]

For the prophets and for Christ, hence for Christians, *theism is a humanism*—a deep faith in the importance of human well-being. God is the most humanizing concept we have. Christ is God *as* humankind, just as Christ preached a God *for* humankind. To live out this preaching, Jesus prioritizes love over all else. Since Christ is a humanist, Christian thought must be humanistic. And given our inherent need for a feeling of agency, to experience ourselves as active participants in our own lives as well as the unfolding of history, humanistic thought must recognize human freedom.

This *vertical* relationship between God and humankind, characterized by freedom and love, translates into the *horizontal* relationship between humans. That is, we are called to love one another as God loves us. We each possess an interior region of being particular to ourselves but available to others through communication. This uniquely personal area allows us to contrast with one another, and through this contrast we jar one another out of the prison of self-identity. Hence, others are not called to be who we want them to be; they are called to be who they are. You are not my need and certainly not my neediness. You are you. And if I truly understand *us*, then I will recognize that I need you to be you if I truly want to become myself. Because if you are you, then you are surprise, you are unexpected, you are grace.[38]

By God's declaration, we are free (John 8:36). God wants free persons to whom God can relate, not puppets that God can control. Some people assert that we are not free because we are born with characteristics we did not choose, into an environment we did not create. Since we choose neither our nature or nurture, and we are constructed by both, we

---

37. Oord, *Uncontrolling Love of God*, 62–64.
38. Murdoch, *Sovereignty of Good*, 66.

are not free. But this argument makes an impossible demand of freedom. To be free, you must be completely *uninfluenced*. In this view, all influence is control. But such freedom would demand that we be born as a characterless nothingness into an empty expanse, like placing an actor on stage with no set, no cast, no audience, and no script. The actor would be absolutely free of constraint, but also devoid of potential. The actor would have nothing to do, nothing to say, and no decisions to make. The actor could create, but how much? To what end? For which people?

There is no absolute freedom, only relational freedom, even for God. Any thought otherwise is a destructive fantasy. We may find the relationships we are born into cumbersome and the world that we inherit distressing. But what would it be like to be unencumbered? The only way to be unencumbered is to be a vapor in a void. *There is no effective freedom without moral significance, and no moral significance without inherited context.* Catherine Keller observes, "We are indelibly marked by our past. We cannot escape the process of being influenced and of influencing. But we may exercise creative freedom within it."[39] Hence, context is the gift through which we express our free personhood.

To be free is not to be *uninfluenced*; to be free is to be *uncoerced*.[40] Our freedom to influence and be influenced, coupled with freedom from coercion, makes us moral agents. We cannot choose our personal characteristics, family values, or national culture, but we can come to awareness of them and choose our response to them. Jesus, for example, could have joined those who hated Samaritans or he could have joined those who loved across religious difference. He chose the latter. He could have devoted his genius and charisma to personal enrichment, but instead devoted it to the exploited. Like Jesus, within our personhood and context, we can choose. We can emphasize self or community, power or service, fear or love, greed or generosity.

In this Trinitarian view, freedom is not characterized by pure autonomy, or freedom *from*. Autonomy frees us from external coercion, but this is only a preliminary step on the way to ideal sociality. The next step, which is dependent on but supersedes autonomy, is *mutuality*. Autonomy grants us freedom from the coercive other, but leaves us in fragmented isolation. The isolation produced by autonomy must become the mutuality produced by interdependence. Thus, freedom *from* best expresses

---

39. Keller, *On the Mystery*, 22.

40. Oord, *Uncontrolling Love of God*, 183.

itself as freedom *for*. The end of subjection allows the beginning of community.[41] Therefore, the purpose of our own freedom is to maximize the freedom of others.

Made in the image of the ever-increasing God, we are capable of self-surpassing. Our actual self is laden with potential selves, so that we are in constant self-creation. But wisdom realizes that fullness of self is only found in the fullness of relation—in love. From love derive meaning, purpose, and joy. The more expansive the love, the greater the joy. Without love, all these godsends shrivel in the claustrophobic space of the self. With love, they flourish and grow along the branches of our relationships.

Since permanence is an illusion, we must seek disillusionment. We are not static; we are dynamic. We are not limited to who we *are*; we are enabled by who we can *become*.[42] Our powers of imagination and creation allow self-expansion through time in the image of our infinite God. Consider Karla Faye Tucker of Houston, Texas. In 1973, Tucker's mother led her, at age fourteen, into a life of prostitution and drug use. At age twenty-one, in a drug-induced haze, Tucker broke into an apartment with her boyfriend, Danny Garrett, to "case the joint." They murdered the two occupants with a pickax. Between committing the crime and her arrest five weeks later, Tucker bragged that each swing of the pickax gave her pleasure.

Tucker was arrested and convicted of murder. While awaiting sentencing, she read the Bible and had a powerful conversion experience. At sentencing, she was sentenced to death. Over the next fourteen years, as her case worked its way through the court systems, she became a model prisoner, married her chaplain, Rev. Dana Brown, and refused to commit violence even when attacked. She sought to have her sentence commuted from execution to life in prison. As her execution date approached, numerous people petitioned for clemency, including Pope John Paul II, the World Council of Churches, and the brother of one of her murder victims. The warden of her prison testified that, based on her long-term behavior, she had in all likelihood been reformed. But all appeals were rejected and, on the order of Governor George W. Bush, Texas executed Karla Faye Tucker on February 3, 1998.

Prior to her execution, Karla Faye appeared on the Larry King Show on CNN, in which they discussed her crimes and her faith:

41. McDougall, *Pilgrimage of Joy*, 188.
42. Westerhoff, *Nāgārjuna's Madhyamaka*, 163–64.

KING: Let's go back. You're a very attractive young girl. You're smart. What went wrong? What happened 14 years ago?

TUCKER: Bad choices, drugs . . . a lot of drugs, a lot of anger and confusion, no real guidance, I was just out of hand, and had no guidance at a certain point in my life when I was most impressionable and probably could have been steered the right way. There wasn't anybody there to steer me.

KING: Where were mother and father?

TUCKER: My mother was doing drugs, and she lived a very wild life. My father had tried up to a certain point, but he had no control. My mother had him under a threat that if he laid a hand on us or did anything to us, she'd have him put in jail.

KING: What happened on that terrible day?

TUCKER: The details of what happened that night, I don't share. I mean, that's the worst night of my life, and I don't—with how I feel now, I don't relive that night.

KING: Do you think it was another person?

TUCKER: Yes, it was definitely.

KING: How, to yourself, do you explain that? I know you don't want to—so forgetting the details, how do you explain it to yourself that I was involved in a violent slaying?

TUCKER: I can't—I can't make sense out of it. I don't know how to make sense out of it except that the choices that I made to do drugs, to buckle to peer pressure and everything else—it was inevitable that something like that was going to happen in my life.

KING: Did you enjoy the violence?

TUCKER: I said I did. I was—at that time in my life, I was very excited about doing different crazy, violent things, yes. It was a part of me that was used to fit in with the crowd that I was hanging around to be accepted.

KING: How do we know, as a lot of people would ask who don't know you, that this isn't a jailhouse conversion?

TUCKER: I don't try and convince people of that. For me, if you can't look at me and see it then nothing I can say to you is going to convince you. I just live it every day and I reach out to people and it's up to them to receive from the Lord the same way I did when somebody came to me. . . . There is evidence, consistent evidence, in a person's life.[43]

43. L. King, "Karla Faye Tucker," lines 15–98.

Karla Faye Tucker's radical change in personality, which was denied by those who celebrated her execution, suggests the impermanence of the self and the potential for transformation that this impermanence confers.

Our dynamic concept of the soul denies any permanent self, thereby allowing us to "outwit identity." It also cautions the brittle self. This self becomes so invested in certain beliefs and identities that it refuses to change. Such stubbornness is not based on evidence, reason, or compassion, but on an attachment to current convictions. Debate teams at White colleges didn't want to debate teams from Black colleges, because the encounter would disabuse them of their comforting racial mythology. Likewise, we can convince ourselves that only our religion is true, or only our race is pure, or only our nation is virtuous. Then, when we meet a fact that doesn't fit, or we're presented with a well-reasoned argument against these convictions, our inflexible self will respond with anger—its last line of defense. Identity addiction turns the living self into a dead tree, dried out and inflexible, that splinters in the winds of change.[44]

Our concept of the soul, on the other hand, rejects self-absorption. God frees us from placing ourselves at the center of the universe. Since the universe invariably contradicts this placement, the narcissist suffers continual disappointment and frustration. All narcissists are unhappy, no matter how rich or powerful, because the universe does not orbit them. None of us are the universe's center of gravity; God frees us from that fixed position so we can participate in the flow. The Trinity *Sustains* that flow, *Participates* in that flow, and *Enchants* that flow.

Any Flight from Freedom
Denies Our God-Given Personhood

We fear freedom like the nestling fears flight. So, we flee from our God-given freedom in various ways. We have already discussed the temptation to declare every event the will of God, a declaration which is neither healthy nor biblical. Another way is to render ourselves automata by subjecting every decision to a divinely given algorithm. In this way, we need not decide because God has already decided for us. The controlling God tells us how to worship, what to wear, what to eat, what to read, whom to marry, and where to live. Such automaticity meets certain needs: fearing

44. Lao Tzu, *Tao Te Ching*, 182, §76.

accountability, we avoid all decision. Fearing the expanse, we stay on the narrowest of narrow paths.

The retreat into automatized activity deprives us of choice. But this retreat is broken backed. No flow chart, no matter how ancient or intricate, can negotiate this infinite universe. Our cosmos purposefully overflows all efforts at intellectual control. We cannot be an automaton within an algorithm, or a puppet under a puppeteer, because God doesn't want us to. God wants us to think, choose, act, and accept responsibility for our actions. God wants us to be persons to whom God can relate. And for us to be persons, God must deny us any automatic decision-making process within which we could hide our personhood. *God must deny us certainty and grant us ambiguity.*

The algorithm-defying infinity of the cosmos also forbids us any resort to pure instinct—reflexive, predetermined, unexamined responses to situations. Instinct works for ants but not for people. The world simply presents our brain with too much information to immediately know the most profitable course of action. Instead, we must deliberate: gather missing information, consider our principles, imagine different outcomes, evaluate which outcomes are desirable, solicit the advice and insight of others, and finally, always prematurely, decide. So complex is this process that our brains have evolved the best tool for such analysis—consciousness. Recognizing the danger of simplistic instinct in a hypercomplex world, consciousness interrupts our automaticity. It allows us to survey an expanse of options and think before we act. Through this demanding process we can make the better decision, which is almost never the first instinct.

There is no freedom *with* certainty, and no freedom *without* ambiguity. The reflexive certainty provided by strict legalism or brute instinct would deprive us of both freedom and consciousness. Tragically, our thirst for certainty is a thirst for escape from our God-given condition, which was always intended as a gift. We find evidence for this gift in the very directability of the universe, our capacity to create the future. The present is contingent. The worst historical tragedies could have been prevented by more noble human efforts. And the future is unwritten because we co-author the cosmic drama with God. We are both the playwrights and the actors, and we perform best when we understand that God is love.

5

To Marry Heaven and Earth

This doctrine of the Kingdom of Heaven, which was the main teaching of Jesus, and which plays so small a part in the Christian creeds, is certainly one of the most revolutionary doctrines that ever stirred and changed human thought. It is small wonder if the world of that time failed to grasp its full significance and recoiled in dismay from even a half apprehension of its tremendous challenges to the established habits and institutions of [humankind]. It is small wonder if the hesitating convert and disciple presently went back to the old familiar ideas of temple and altar, of fierce deity and propitiatory observance, of consecrated priest and magic blessing, and these things being attended to reverted then to the dear old habitual life of hates and profits and competition and pride. For the doctrine of the Kingdom of Heaven, as Jesus seems to have preached it, was no less than a bold and uncompromising demand for a complete change and cleansing of the life of our struggling species, an utter cleansing, without and within.

—H. G. WELLS[1]

---

1. Wells, *Outline of History*, 8. Edited for gender inclusivity.

No Concept of Christ Can Cage the Person of Jesus

EDWINA SANDYS, GRANDDAUGHTER OF Winston Churchill, sculpted Christa "to portray the suffering of women."[2] Christa was a statue of Christ crucified, but as a woman, femininity hanging naked on the cross. Christa's initial revelation, in 1984 at St. John the Divine in New York City, produced a theological storm. Those offended insisted that Jesus was a man and should stay a man and that involving Christ in gender play harmed the faith. Episcopalian Bishop Walter Dennis accused the cathedral dean, the Very Rev. James Park Morton, of "desecrating our symbols"[3] and insisted that the display was "theologically and historically indefensible."[4] Apparently, we are saved not just by the Messiah, but by a *male* Messiah specifically. Hence, to toy with the masculinity of Christ was to toy with salvation, a dangerous and unnecessary game.

But other followers of Jesus found the statue stimulating, even liberating. Did Jesus have to be a man? Or could a woman have gotten the job done? Or a nonbinary person? For some, Jesus's male gender was necessary for salvation. For others, it was an accidental quality of the Christ, assigned at random. Or maybe it was a concession God made to our sexism; the Christ *could* have been a woman, but we just wouldn't have listened to a woman back then. Would we listen to a woman now?[5]

Certainly, the debates revealed much about the debaters. Some seemed to worship maleness as much as Christ, some saw themselves in the beaten woman, some seemed hungry for a female savior, and some wondered if nonbinary persons would ever be seen, if a still-binary Christ was causing this much of an uproar. Everyone saw Christa as unsettling. Either she was blasphemous, unsettling the ordained order; or she was empowering, unsettling an oppressive patriarchy. The difference lay in whether the viewer sought to be unsettled or not, whether they wanted to preserve the inherited or create the new.

"Who do you say that I am?" asks Jesus (Matt 16:15). Over two millennia, his followers have given many different answers to this question. The church has called councils to dispute Jesus's identity, issued statements of faith providing definitive answers, and enforced those answers in sometimes brutal fashion. Yet Jesus always outwits our definition of

2. Frank, "30 Years Later," para. 6.
3. New York Times, "Bishop Attacks Display," para. 2.
4. New York Times, "Bishop Attacks Display," para. 3.
5. Vasko, "Redeeming Beauty," 199–200.

him, like a trickster slipping his chains. Although at times the Christian tradition has interpreted Jesus as a wrathful judge or tribal warlord, Jesus himself interprets his message as good news for *all* (Mark 13:10), rebuking his disciples: "You do not know what spirit you are of, for I have not come to destroy people's lives but to save them" (Luke 9:56). According to Jesus, his appearance is an opportunity for divine joy to enter human hearts, that we might have abundant life (John 10:10; 15:11). For this reason, when he approaches the disciples Jesus assures them, "Take heart, it is I; do not be afraid" (Matt 14:27 NRSV). Accepting the appearance of Jesus as good news, in this chapter we will provide a life-giving interpretation of Jesus that accords with his own.

Jesus Is the Earthly Expression of the Heavenly Christ

We have argued previously that creation is continuously sustained by the Trinity, three persons united through love into one God. Those three persons prefer cooperation to mere operation, so they divide their responsibilities between them, assigning priority even as they share responsibility. Of the three, one Sustains, one Participates, and one Celebrates. Jesus is the Participant, the one charged with coming to us concretely, in our time and our space. Hence, Jesus is the Christ.

To argue that Jesus expresses a divine person coheres with our Trinitarian position, which honors both relationality and particularity. Jesus is a particular expression of a particular person of the Trinity, designated to relate directly to humankind. As such, he is Emmanuel, "God with us," both fully human and fully divine.

This sentiment appears in the earliest biblical writings. Paul argues for the preexistence of Jesus as the Christ and the participation of Christ in creation:

> Christ is the image of the unseen God and the firstborn of all creation, for in Christ were created all things in heaven and on earth: everything visible and invisible, thrones, dominions, sovereignties, powers—all things were created through Christ and for Christ. Before anything was created, Christ existed, and all things hold together in Christ. (Col 1:15–17)

In Paul's understanding, Jesus of Nazareth is the Cosmic Christ, present at creation, grounding creation in communion, and then expressing that

communion within creation.[6] The cosmos itself groans for consummation, as do we (Rom 8:22–23), and Jesus is the image of this fulfillment.[7]
He is not just a wise teacher or inspired prophet; he is the human manifestation of Abba's purpose for the universe.

Jesus's resonance with the cosmos is so profound that, when the
authorities insist his disciples quiet down, Jesus replies, "I tell you, if they
were to keep silent, the very stones would cry out!" (Luke 19:40). Stones
can sing because the appearance of Christ in the cosmos "christifies" all
reality, revealing the interior illumination with which it has always been
charged. As participants in the Christ event, we are now invited to see
God shining through this diaphanous universe, to see the divine beauty
within everything and everyone.[8]

The Centrifugal Love of God Leads to the Incarnation

The divine community is centrifugal, not centripetal. Because they abhor
exclusion, they could never be satisfied with love curved in on itself, with
love of like for like, of Parent for Son and Daughter. The divine community seeks out, by its chosen nature, love of other. According to medieval
theologian John Duns Scotus, the creation of the world is the inevitable
act of a divinity who loves yet always desires to love more. Participation
in creation, vulnerability to it, is the inevitable expression of creative love.
It was planned from the beginning, without reference to the history of the
world, even as it makes that history sacred.[9]

The incarnation, as a superabundant event, ratifies this-worldly
existence in all its particularity. It testifies that we are unique because it
is good to be unique. We are someone somewhere, not everyone everywhere, because it is better to be concrete than abstract. And Jesus testifies
that life, even with its intense suffering, is worth its passion. After the incarnation we need not ascend to God, because God has descended to us,
expressing the divine preference for finite particularity over any infinite
absolute.[10] Given the above, the incarnation is not a remedy for sin, nor is
it a judicious adjustment to an unintended fall. Instead, the incarnation is

---

6. Moltmann, *Trinity and the Kingdom*, 112.

7. Boff, *Trinity and Society*, 186–87.

8. Delio, *Hunger for Wholeness*, 45.

9. Duns Scotus, *Four Questions on Mary*, 23–24.

10. Rohr, *Wondrous Encounters*, 122–24.

an unconditional celebration of creation *as creation*. Incarnation follows creation like celebration follows birth.[11]

In other words, having created the cosmos, God couldn't stay away from it. God doesn't love at a distance, but as a presence, even if that presence involves great risk. We, who are made in the image of God, may not want to see that image in all its perfection, to see how we have missed the mark. Distorted humanity, craving and grasping and clinging, fears the perfecting mirror and may very well shatter it upon meeting.

American photographer Lewis Hine (1874–1940) held up one such mirror. Hine was a trained sociologist who left a teaching position to work for the National Child Labor Committee in 1908. The NCLC was working against the child labor practices of the day. At the time, children younger than ten years old were working, bleeding, and dying in factories across America. Initially hired to research and write about their conditions, Hine also began taking pictures. Their publication led to threats of violence against him by factories' security forces, who didn't want the world to see the truth of working children's suffering. To get access to the factories, Hine had to sneak in, like a thief in the night (1 Thess 5:2), masquerading as a traveling salesman, public official, specialized mechanic, and others. Over time his images took over the movement. Hine noted, "If I could tell the story in words, I wouldn't need to lug around a camera."[12]

Through the efforts of Hine and many more, the federal government outlawed child labor in 1938. Hine's images changed America because images transform us, more so than abstract ideas. Hence, God came to us as a person, so that we might see the divine image (Heb 1:3). Jesus, as the perfect image of God, reveals both our hidden suffering and our hidden potential.

The nondual nature of the incarnation opens us to paradox. We tend to consider spiritual dualities as repelling one another, like two ends of magnets with the same charge. The closer they approach, the more intensely they resist. But Christ came to marry heaven and earth, God and humankind, spirit and matter, body and soul. In Jesus, "God accepts limits to dissolve the limits that made it seem as if God and humans were opposites. The great wonder of the Incarnation is that we're not."[13]

The great statement of this unification came at the Council of Chalcedon in 451 CE, which declared that Christ is fully human and fully

11. Boff, *Trinity and Society*, 186.

12. Sampsell-Willmann, *Lewis Hine*, 121.

13. Luti, "Divinized," para. 5.

divine, the reunion of false binaries, the one in whom matter is spirit and spirit is matter. Jesus expresses these paradoxes through the manner of his incarnation. God as Christ was born an impoverished Jew in an occupied land. At the nativity, the wealth of God comes to us in poverty, the power of God comes to us in powerlessness, and the help of God comes to us in helplessness.

Jesus Reveals the Intimacy of God

"YHWH is close to the brokenhearted and rescues those whose spirits are crushed," declares the psalmist (Ps 34:18). Jesus is the fulfillment of this assurance. In Jesus, we see that love draws near.

This divine intimacy refutes the traditional Christian doctrine of divine impassibility—the belief that God is incapable of feeling either pain or pleasure, suffering or joy. Impassibility argues that God's being is unaffected by our lives. Once again, this belief derives from philosophy, not Scripture. Plato, for example, notes that the healthiest body is the most resistant to disease, the strongest plant is the most resistant to drought, the sturdiest house stands strongest against the storm, and the wisest soul is the most impervious to events. Since excellent things resist external influence, and God is most excellent, God must resist all external influence. Therefore, we do not affect God. Moreover, anything that is perfectly excellent cannot be improved and has no need for change. Therefore, God is unchanging.[14]

This concept of God was picked up by Christian theologians and became standard in Christian theology, but it never fit with the biblical portrayal of God. In the Hebrew Scriptures, God is emotional: "YHWH saw the great wickedness of the people of the earth, that the thoughts in their hearts fashioned nothing but evil. YHWH was sorry that humankind had been created on earth; *it pained God's heart*" (Gen 6:5–6 [emphasis added]). The doctrine of impassibility ignores numerous biblical texts in which God is interactive, even conversational (Exod 33:11). The Bible ascribes qualities to God that imply divine feeling, such as compassion (Exod 22:27). God even changes God's mind when presented with a convincing argument (Num 14:13–25; Amos 7:3, 6). Impassibility implies

---

14. Plato, *Republic*, §§380–81.

that God is a majestic citadel, but the Bible claims that God is an ocean of feeling, open to the breadth of experience that God continually sustains.[15]

What does the adjective *impassible* do to our concept of God? The word *impassible* is closely related to its cousin, impassive. The thesaurus offers first-order synonyms for impassive such as emotionless, reticent, taciturn, and apathetic. More alarmingly, it offers second-order synonyms for impassive such as cold-blooded, hardened, heartless, and indifferent. None of these terms describe the biblical God, whom Jesus reveals to be a vulnerable God, one of forgiveness and mercy.

God's openness opens us to God: "God is the most irresistible of influences precisely because he is himself the most open to influence," states Charles Hartshorne.[16] God is true relationship, and true relationship changes both poles of the relationship. There is no absolute beyond the related, no escape hatch into which the Creator retreats from creation. God is *ḥesed*, loving-kindness, hence always fully present—undistracted, undisturbed, and undismayed.

Jesus Reveals That Abba Is Personal

For Jesus, Abba is a person who cares about us as persons, and this love is what really matters. God offers no promise that life will be easy, but an absolute promise that God will be with us in all things. Hence, there is nothing to fear, for nothing can separate us from the love of God (Rom 8:31–39).

Some people reject the concept of a personal God as trivial. Certainly, it can become so. The personal God can become like Santa Claus, the gift giver who plays favorites. For those who place a high premium on social order, God can become lawgiver, police officer, prosecutor, judge, and jailer all in one, ensuring punishment of those we deem deserving. For the bigoted, God becomes a projection screen onto which we cast our biases, assigning them to God in a covert act of self-deification. For the tribal, those who bitterly demarcate an in-group and out-group, God hates who we hate and loves who we love.

The capacity for a concept, such as that of a personal God, to be abused does not warrant its dismissal. Human cleverness can always turn good into evil. The majority can use democracy to oppress a minority,

---

15. Hartshorne, *Divine Relativity*, xvi.

16. Hartshorne, *Divine Relativity*, xv.

but that abuse incriminates the majority, not democracy itself. Political power uses beauty, in the form of propaganda and pageantry, to legitimate its rule, but that abuse incriminates power, not beauty. Prosperity preachers apprentice God to their greed, but that abuse incriminates the preacher, not God. In such a crafty world, impersonal notions of God as first cause, ultimate reality, truth, or The One may seem more attractive than any analogy to our mercenary humanity.

But the cost of such abstraction is too high. These concepts overlook the blessing of personality, the crowning achievement of the cosmos. Billions of years of cosmological evolution have produced us—thinking, feeling, conscious beings with agency who not only exist, but celebrate our existence. We are the universe coming to awareness of itself, and we exult in that awareness. Science recognizes the source of this process as the physical laws governing the universe (or multiverse). But what is the source of those laws? Could it be a joyful community of persons who wish to produce joyful communities of persons? Faith trusts that our personal God invites us into the fullness of personality by means of a person-creating universe.

Jesus Reveals That the Personal God Is a Compassionate God

According to Jesus, Abba our Parent is *compassionate*. In the story of the prodigal son, the father *runs* to welcome the prodigal home, because he was filled with compassion (Greek: *esplanchnisthē*). Jesus himself, as a manifestation of God, displays the same care and concern for those he meets. When he sees the crowd of weary outcasts waiting to hear him preach, he is filled with compassion (Matt 9:36; Greek: *esplanchnisthē*). In another instance, noting the hunger of the crowd and their need for food, Jesus states, "I am moved with compassion" (Matt 15:32; Greek: *splagchnizomai*). The Greek word for compassion derives from *splagchnon*, which means bowels or gut. Compassion is not some abstract ethical demand; compassion is something you feel in your "heart" (which is a frequent translation of *splagchnon* into English).

For Jesus, our compassionate Parent is a unifying symbol. Following Jürgen Moltmann, we can contrast it with the image of lord. The lord is distinct from the servant, above the servant, of a different class and family from the servant. But a good Parent unites their children into one family.

The lord may care for his servants but does not concern himself with the ups and downs of their daily lives, while Jesus's Parent is emotionally vulnerable and unconditionally available. The lord's estate is a hierarchy, but the family is a unit. Hence, the lord separates, but the Parent unites. Thus, in describing God as Parent, as both Mother and Father, Jesus is inviting his followers to become one household.[17]

Given the omni-gendered Hebraic concept of God, and the Christian interpretation of Jesus as the Child of God, we shouldn't be surprised that, in 1984, Jesus came to us as Christa. Jesus uses explicitly feminine metaphors for God, such as the story of the woman with the lost coin (Luke 15:8–10), in which the woman symbolizes God in her desire for reunion with the wayward. Jesus refers to himself as a mother hen, gathering her brood under her wings (Luke 13:34). And seeing the image of God in his poor, exhausted followers, Jesus commands them, "Be compassionate [Greek: *oiktirmōn*, another term for visceral sympathy] just as your Father is compassionate" (Luke 6:36 CEB).

Jesus Reveals the Divine Vulnerability

A good mother or father is emotionally vulnerable to their children, even the most wayward. The word *vulnerable* derives from the Lain *vulnus*, which means "wound." In the incarnation, God risks woundedness. We have already argued that the incarnation was planned from the beginning, prior to history, as a divine celebration and ratification of creaturely existence. But we have also noted the freedom that God grants us, freedom for kindness and freedom for cruelty. God's perfect openness allows God to feel more deeply than we do, to participate fully in the life-producing contrasts of pain and pleasure, grief and celebration, sorrow and joy. Given this capacity, our cruelty must have tempted God to abandon the plan, to remain in the safety of heaven. But God has also chosen to be *ḥesed*, loving faithfulness, and *ḥesed* always fulfills its promises. So God draws close to us, close enough to be killed.

Infant Jesus reveals our inhospitality to divine vulnerability. He was not allowed to be born in his hometown; empire forced his parents to Bethlehem. Once there, he was not allowed to be born in a house; social strictures forced them into a barn. Once born, there was no crib for him to sleep in, so they laid him in a feeding trough. Then he was forced to

---

17. Moltmann, *Trinity and the Kingdom*, 70.

flee from his homeland into Egypt, to escape the murderous soldiers of a mad king.

Cross Distortion
(sculpture by Scotty Utz, photograph by Katherine Brooks)

The rejection of God in the birth narrative only foreshadows the rejection of God in the crucifixion, yet still God comes, revealing the danger that God hazards *for us*. If God is to celebrate creation, then God must do so unconditionally. God must become *fully* human, open to the prodigious expanse of events, sensations, emotions, and thoughts that God loves into being. God, having chosen to amplify joy through suffering and pleasure through pain, affirms this decision by subjecting divinity to the very contrasts that divinity created. God must delight, and God must sorrow.[18]

Crucially, the Hebrew Scriptures testify to Emmanuel, "God with us" (Isa 7:8; 8:7). The incarnation of God in Christ is the flawless consequence of this sentiment. Jesus acknowledges our exposure to the soaring and searing spectrum of experience that God sustains by subjecting himself to the same range of events and their resultant passions. Entirely open to the ebb and flow of earthly life, Jesus will turn water into wine at a wedding (John 2:1–11) and weep over the death of a friend (John 11:35). He participates fully, he commends full participation to his followers, and he laments the guardedness of his contemporaries: "We piped you a tune, but you wouldn't dance. We sang you a dirge, but you wouldn't mourn" (Matt 11:17).

Jesus Reveals the Universal, Unconditional Love of God

Through his teaching and actions, Jesus reveals the universal love of God for all humankind. According to the psalmist, Abba knit together each person in their mothers' wombs (Ps 139:13), hence is the Creator and Sustainer of all. Since each person is beloved by Abba, each person should be beloved by us, including those whom society deems vile.

This religious insight appears early in the Jewish Scriptures. Roman philosophers like Tacitus believed that "the gods are on the side of the stronger."[19] In contrast, Exodus proclaims that the heart of God is on the side of the weaker—the powerless, oppressed, enslaved Israelites who are struggling to obtain their freedom. In this struggle, the Pharaoh and his advisors represent the gods as they were usually understood in the ancient world, as siding with the powerful hierarchy of the unjust state.[20]

God's special concern is not for the mighty and the successful, but for the lowly and the downtrodden, for the stranger and the poor, for the widow and the orphan. The most defenseless people in the ancient world were those who did not have a powerful community to protect them. With no effective or impartial justice system, safety derived from family or tribe, which would punish anyone who harmed a member. Hence, to

18. Wolterstorff, *Lament for a Son*, 89–90.
19. Tacitus, in Ratcliffe, *Oxford Treasury*, 439.
20. Natan Margalit, email to author, Aug. 30, 2023.

be without family or tribe was dangerous. For this reason, the Jewish law expressed special concern for the orphan, widow, foreigner, and poor, none of whom had sufficient protection.

The Jewish law did not simply insist on deference to the vulnerable; the Jewish law placed a special concern for the vulnerable into the vulnerable heart of God, *who assumes the role of their father, hence protector* (Ps 68:5). Deuteronomy declares:

> For YHWH is the God of gods, the Sovereign of sovereigns, the great God, powerful and awe-inspiring, who has no favorites and cannot be bribed; who brings justice to the orphan and the widowed, and who befriends the foreigner among you with food and clothing. In the same way, you too must befriend the foreigner, for you were once foreigners yourselves in the land of Egypt. (Deut 10:17–19)

According to the prophets, the call to care for the poor is not a suggestion. It's a command with consequences, and the consequences are brutal. The prophet Ezekiel interprets God's destruction of Sodom as a direct consequence of their neglect for the poor: "This was the guilt of your sister Sodom: she and her daughters were arrogant; they had abundant food and not a care in the world, but she refused to help the poor and needy" (Ezek 16:49–50). God is not an impassive observer of social structures; God condemns social stratification and advocates for those whom society ignores.

Jesus places himself within this prophetic tradition. When he begins his ministry, he is selected to read the prophet Isaiah to his synagogue. Jesus reads:

> "The Spirit of our God is upon me: because the Most High has anointed me to bring Good News to those who are poor. God has sent me to proclaim liberty to those held captive, recovery of sight to those who are blind, and release to those in prison—to proclaim the year of our God's favor." Rolling up the scroll, Jesus gave it back to the attendant and sat down. The eyes of all in the synagogue were fixed on him. Then he said to them, "Today, in your hearing, this scripture passage is fulfilled" (Luke 4:18–24; from Isa 61:1–2).

Jesus then begins his ministry as *includer of the excluded*, enacting unifying love in a segregated world. His inclusion is so radical as to offend his listeners: "Should anyone press you into service for one mile, go two miles," he instructs (Matt 5:41b). Jesus's audience would have known that this teaching referred to Roman soldiers, the hated occupiers, who could force any Jew to carry their gear for one standard mile. Jesus says to carry it for two, thereby fostering an audacious vision of reconciliation. But Jesus isn't all talk; he expresses this love by healing the servant of a Roman centurion (Luke 7:1–10), showing love for the occupier, in imitation of the universal God who sends rain on both the righteous and the unrighteous.

Samaritans were loathed by many, accused of using the wrong Torah with the wrong tenth commandment, worshiping on the wrong mountain (Gerizim instead of Jerusalem), and intermixing with Greeks and Persians. Jesus visited and asked to stay in a Samaritan village, but they refused to host him since he was on his way to worship in Jerusalem. His disciples wanted to rain fire on the village, but Jesus rebuked them (Luke 9:51–56). Then, he went on to make a Samaritan the hero of his most famous story (Luke 10:25–37).

When he did interact with the hated religious other, he did so charitably. Jesus met a Samaritan woman at a well. She had gone through five husbands and was currently living with another man out of wedlock. In the eyes of the ancient world, she was impure, of the wrong gender and the wrong religion with a stained past. So outcast was she that she was drawing water at noon, in the heat of the day. Most women drew water together, communally, in the morning and evening. This gathering was an important opportunity to talk, share news, and build community. If the woman was at the well alone, then she was shunned, and anyone interacting with her would be contaminated.

Exhausted from his labors, Jesus asked her to draw water for him. In a world of strict dietary laws, this request was a particularly intimate act of transgression, an invitation to the uninvited. In exchange for the well water, he offered her living water. In the Jewish tradition, Abba is the Source of living water (Jer 2:13; 17:13), "Source" here being the Hebrew word *maqor*: fountain, spring, or womb (Lev 12:7; 20:18).[21] Thus, in offering her living water, Jesus is offering her God.

For the Samaritan woman, was living water a symbol for inclusion, community, self-acceptance, respect, value? However she interpreted Jesus's promise, she willingly accepted his offer of new life, to the great dismay of the disciples, who were still stuck in a purity mindset (John

---

21. Natan Margalit, email to author, Aug. 30, 2023.

4:7–30). In a final display of compassion, Jesus never asked the troubled woman to leave her current partner because he knew that, in such a brutally patriarchal society, she would be defenseless without a man.

Jesus also displayed God's universalism through his practice of table fellowship. Much like dinner tables today, dinner tables in Jesus's day were segregated. Jew ate with Jew, Roman with Roman, rich with rich, poor with poor, healthy with healthy, and sick with sick. Some of these divisions were the result of social conventions, others were the result of religious structures. All of them were designed to protect one group from contamination by another, especially during a meal, that most intimate of times when something that is outside of us enters us and becomes us. During a meal, we cannot allow those who are other to us to enter our household. We cannot allow *them* to pollute *us*.

Jesus preaches against this segregation: "Whenever you give a lunch or dinner, don't invite your friends or colleagues or relatives or wealthy neighbors. They might invite you in return and thus repay you. No, when you have a reception, invite those who are poor or have physical infirmities or are blind" (Luke 14:12–13). In the ancient world, poverty and sickness were frequently considered divine punishment; hence, outcasts deserved to be cast out. Those who cast out the outcasts were simply enforcing the divine will. By insisting on hospitality toward outcasts, Jesus is communicating the universal divine compassion. And he insists that God's embrace of the rejected, as symbolized through Jesus's inclusive ministry, will be consummated in the coming kingdom, in which "people will come from the East and the West, from the North and the South, and will take their places at the feast in the Kingdom of God" (Luke 13:29). Over against any elitist conceits of purity and contamination, Jesus proposes the joy of open hospitality, joy that erases all social divisions and unites everyone into one family at one table sharing one meal.

In making this pronouncement, Jesus is not rejecting his religious tradition; Jesus is extolling the openness of his religious tradition. For example, Jose ben Jochanan, chief justice of the Sanhedrin in the second century BCE, had already declared, "Let your home be open wide and let the poor be members of your household."[22] To this day, many Jews declare at the Passover meal, "Let all who are hungry come and eat, all who need, come eat the Passover with us."[23] We cannot know if Jesus

---

22. Katz, *Babylonian Exile*, 297, §1:5.

23. Avery-Peck and Neusner, *Routledge Dictionary of Judaism*, "Passover," 111.

encountered these teachings or not, but we can know that Jesus's teaching was continuous with his tradition, even as he emphasized selected strains within it.

Jesus practices what he preaches by dining with the unclean, those whom his society hated, and not without reason. For instance, he eats with tax collectors such as Levi, Matthew, and Zacchaeus. Tax collectors were the quislings of their day, Jewish agents of the Roman Empire, backed by the violence of empire as they extorted money from their fellow Jews. Their greed sullied anyone associated with them, yet Jesus invites them into his new world in an intimate way.

God touches untouchables in the person of Jesus. He dines in the house of Simon the leper (Matt 26:6), breaking bread with the rejected. Asked to be healed by another leper, Jesus heals through touch, thereby returning him to the community, both physically and socially (Matt 8:3). As Jesus is walking through a crowd, a woman with a twelve-year flow reaches out to touch the fringe of his cloak and is immediately healed. Jesus feels power flow out of him and demands to know who has touched him. The woman identifies herself, trembling in fear, undoubtedly aware of the taboo she has just violated, but Jesus simply responds, "My daughter, your faith has saved you; go in peace and be free of your affliction" (Mark 5:25–34).

Jesus endangers himself to reveal the agapic love of God. A crowd brought a woman "caught in the very act of committing adultery" before Jesus, asking him what they should do. They wanted to challenge his preference for mercy over punishment when almost every male present would have supported stoning her as well as, in all likelihood, anyone defending her.[24] (The passage insists that she was "caught in the very act of committing adultery" to reassure readers that she had not been framed by a jealous husband who didn't want the expense of divorce and saw a lynch mob as the most expedient solution to his problem. Still, it might have been a setup.) But Jesus goes on the rhetorical offensive, instructing the mob, "Let the person among you who is without sin throw the first stone." After his challenge, the defeated men slowly shuffle away. Then Jesus says to the woman, "Where did they go? Has no one condemned you?" And she replies, "No one, Teacher." To which Jesus replies, "I don't condemn you either" (John 8:1–11a).

24. Baloyi, "Re-Reading of John 8:1–11," 4–5.

Jesus Overturns the Social Hierarchy

We compete for place, acquiring more power so that we can acquire more money so that we can consume more resources. The origin and outcome of this competition is ceaseless comparison that produces either envy or pride. Jesus saves us from ourselves by preaching and practicing a celebratory *egalitarianism*, a recognition that all are *equally* loved in the eyes of God, so no one can be worth more than anyone else, because *all possess infinite value.*

Those at the center often deny the value of those at the margins, but God prefers to work through the margins, in a divine challenge to the perceived center. Jesus himself comes from the margins—poverty, Judaism, Galilee—and propagates the truth of their value until he is killed by those at the center. His genealogy anticipates his marginalization (Matt 1:1–17). It lists Tamar, who had to disguise herself as a prostitute to become impregnated by her reluctant patron, Judah (Gen 38). It lists Rahab, an actual prostitute who helped the Israelites conquer Jericho (Josh 2). It lists Ruth, a Moabite widow who chooses to join an Israelite family (book of Ruth). And it lists Uriah's wife Bathsheba, who was "seduced" and impregnated by King David, who then had her husband killed in battle (2 Sam 11). We may look to the center for salvation, but God sends it from the margins. As the revelation of God, Jesus becomes the new, "decentering center," the center who denies us any boundary.

The margins have the clearest perspective. The margins see the hypocrisy in hierarchy and realize that "what is prized by humans is an abomination in the sight of God" (Luke 16:15a). If God loves us all equally, which is absolutely, then there is no need to claw for priority of place. Christianity is an equality gospel, not a prosperity gospel. Jesus sees through the deceitfulness and pretense of those who cherish places of honor in public while "devouring widow's houses" behind the scenes (Luke 20:47). He condemns those who give ostentatiously, out of their abundance, praising instead the poor widow who gives even out of her poverty (Luke 21:1–4). We seek eminence, but God wants charity; we seek gain, but God wants justice. For this reason, Jesus warns his disciples, "All who exalt themselves will be humbled, and all who humble themselves will be exalted" (Luke 14:11).

Jesus inverts the social order in his practice as well as his preaching. When the disciples argue about who among them is the most important, Jesus reprimands them, pointing out that "I am among you as the one who serves you" (Luke 22:27b). In the Gospel of John, Jesus emphasizes this life of service by washing his disciples' feet. Travelers' feet were dirty and sore and always in need of attention, but only servants washed other people's feet. It was a job for the lowly. Peter was so uncomfortable with this awkward act of intimacy that he protested and initially refused Jesus's ministrations, but Jesus prevailed:

> After washing their feet, Jesus put his clothes back on and re- turned to the table. He said to them, "Do you understand what I have done for you? You call me "Teacher," and "Sovereign"—and rightly, for so I am. If I, then—your Teacher and Sovereign— have washed your feet, you should wash each other's feet. I have given you an example, that you should do as I have done for you. (John 13:12–15)

Oddly, although Jesus explicitly commands his disciples to "do as I have done for you," foot washing never became a sacrament in the mainstream Christian denominations, perhaps because it was just too upside down and intimate for any institution to bear.

Jesus Preaches the Kingdom of God

"Possibility is not a luxury; it is as crucial as bread," observes Judith Butler.[25] The Bible agrees: "Without a vision the people perish" (Prov 29:18). We tend to call artists, musicians, and poets "creatives," and limit "creativity" to this category of persons. In fact, we are all creators in every moment of our lives, by both what we do and don't do, by both how we conceptualize ourselves and how we conceptualize others. We may not be able to draw, but every time we interact with a stranger we create emo- tions in that stranger by treating them respectfully or disrespectfully. We may not be able to sing, but our decision to feed hungry children creates one world and our decision not to creates another. We may not be able to write poetry, but whether we let the other driver in or crowd them out affects that driver as well as the overall traffic pattern on that day. Because we exist through time, to be is to become, and to become is to create.

The Creator created us in the image of God, to be creative. Thus, we are *homo creator*, the species that creates and is free in what it creates. As creativity involves risk, it is an act of courage, like unto God.

25. J. Butler, *Undoing Gender*, 29.

For our creativity to be constructive, for it to go somewhere, it needs a goal. This goal interprets our times, directs our decisions, and energizes our activity. If freely chosen, it turns an aimless life into a purposeful journey. And with this purpose comes meaning, because inspiration accompanies aspiration.

Jesus received from his Jewish tradition a vision in which "the Lord will become king over all the earth" (Zech 14:9a). This kingdom is good news for the generous but bad news for the greedy. Isaiah writes:

> Woe to you who make unjust policies
>   and draft oppressive legislation,
> who deprive the powerless of justice
>   and rob poor people—my people—of their rights,
> who prey upon the widowed
>   and rob orphans! (Isa 10:1–2)

Isaiah's God is not warm and fuzzy. Isaiah's God cares deeply for the downtrodden. Their oppression—*and their oppressors*—anger God. This anger is resolute and consequential, provoking God to act. Speaking for God, Isaiah issues a threat: God will subject Judah to conquest and captivity for breaking the divine covenant through their dismissive cruelty toward the poor.

But Isaiah also issues a promise, a road map to redemption. Judah's repentance, expressed as care for all and neglect of none, will avert God's punishment. After criticizing his fellow Jews for religious fasting even as they oppress their workers, (Isa 58:3b), Isaiah continues:

> This is the sort of fast that pleases me:
>   Remove the chains of injustice!
> Undo the ropes of the yoke!
>   Let those who are oppressed go free,
>   and break every yoke you encounter!
> Share your bread with those who are hungry,.
>   and shelter homeless poor people!
> Clothe those who are naked,
>   and don't ignore the needs of your own flesh and blood! (Isa 58:6–7)

To this day, Isa 58 is the haftarah, the liturgical reading from the Prophets on Yom Kippur or the Day of Atonement.[26] God's blessing, according to Isaiah, does not result from individual virtue, rigorous legalism, or ritual

---

26. Natan Margalit, email to author, Aug. 30, 2023.

purity. *God's blessing arises from the practice of charity as you work for justice.* Religiosity that neglects mercy only angers God.

The Hebrew Scriptures demand kindness toward the outcast and reveal God's active concern that this kindness be shown. Jesus intensifies this urgent concern for justice in his preaching of the imminent kingdom of God, also known as the kingdom of heaven. The kingdom of heaven is God's disruption of human history, redirecting it from injustice toward justice. Jesus, the herald of this new way of living, begins his ministry by declaring, "The time is fulfilled, and the Kingdom of God has come near; repent, and believe in the good news" (Mark 1:15).

Jesus's characterization of his preaching as "good news" (*euangelion*) seems a bit exclusive, because it does not sound like good news for everyone. The Newer Testament records Jesus's Beatitudes ("Blessings") in both Matthew (the Sermon on the Mount) and Luke (the Sermon on the Plain). Most Christians have heard of the Sermon on the Mount, but fewer have heard of the Sermon on the Plain, and not without reason. The Sermon on the Plain is explicitly economic: while Luke declares, "Blessed are you who are poor" (Luke 6:20a), Matthew hedges, "Blessed are the poor in spirit" (Matt 5:3a). Moreover, Luke couples each of Matthew's blessings with a corresponding woe, a move that most likely gave rise to the church's preference for Matthew over Luke:

> Then [Jesus] looked at his disciples and said:
> "You who are poor are blessed,
>   for the reign of God is yours.
> You who hunger now are blessed,
>   for you will be filled.
> You who weep now are blessed,
>   for you will laugh.
> You are blessed when people hate you,
>   when they scorn and insult you
>   and spurn your name as evil
>   because of the Chosen One.
> On the day they do so,
>   rejoice and be glad:
>   your reward will be great in heaven,
>   for their ancestors treated the prophets the same way.
>
> "But woe to you rich,
>   for you are now receiving your comfort in full.
> Woe to you who are full,
>   for you will go hungry.

Woe to you who laugh now,
　　for you will weep in your grief.
Woe to you when all speak well of you,
　　for their ancestors treated the false prophets in the same way."
　　(Luke 6:20–26)

Why does Jesus characterize a preaching that explicitly threatens the rich and powerful as "good news"? Perhaps because they (at least some of them, I hedge, because Jesus didn't qualify his statements) need to be rescued from themselves . . . Perhaps because I (from a global perspective, I am quite wealthy) need to be rescued from myself. Self-satisfaction in a world of poverty demands hardness of heart. To waste what others need, to consume ostentatiously while others starve, distorts the soul and diminishes our capacity for joy. It requires removing ourselves from the human family, separating ourselves from those with whom God created us to be in communion. God, who *is* relationship, creates us in the image of God, to be *in* relationship, not with some but with all, because all are God's creatures. God is joy because God is love, and we shall become joy to the extent that we become love.

For this reason Jesus preaches, "Don't judge, or you yourself will be judged. Your judgment on others will be the judgment you receive. The measure you use will be used to measure you" (Matt 7:1–2). He warns against the emotional distancing techniques that we use to dismiss the suffering of others. From a place of comfort, we assure ourselves that they are poor because they are lazy, or they are sick because they have bad habits, or they are sad because they never learned to think positively. Thus we render our neighbor, whom Jesus calls us to love, *no one of concern*. Fearing guilt instead of anticipating joy, we separate ourselves from those to whom we are connected. But this judgment of others judges our self; we have to change our selves to feel *less*; we have to become what we are not, preferring moral convenience to fullness of life.

Jesus's uncompromising universalism is good news to all, because it restores the communion that all have lost. This loss is an open wound. We have lost the easy friendship of childhood to the complicated politics of adulthood. We have lost the dreams of the young to the disappointments of the aged. We see the perfect harmony of the cosmos, then look at ourselves and find chaos within and without. Jesus preaches to restore what we have lost, not by going backward, but by going forward into the kingdom of God.

What is the kingdom of God like? Jesus's vision is not something that we could have imagined, any more than we could have imagined a new color. It has only one constitution, and that is the law of love: "I give you a new commandment: Love one another. And you're to love one another the way I have loved you" (John 13:34). This law binds us together, uniting fragments into wholeness, like the scattered pieces of a puzzle finally arranged to create their beauty.

Wholeness is holistic and leaves nothing out. Therefore, the love that unites reality will unite those aspects of reality that we may deem irredeemable, beyond the reach of salvation, everlastingly separate from ourselves. But Jesus challenges us to include those whom we most deeply desire to exclude, to love those whom we would hate:

> You have heard it said, "Love your neighbor—but hate your enemy." But I tell you, love your enemies and pray for your persecutors. This will prove that you are children of God. For God makes the sun rise on bad and good alike; God's rain falls on the just and the unjust. If you love those who love you, what merit is there in that? Don't tax collectors do as much? And if you greet only your sisters and brothers, what is so praiseworthy about that? Don't Gentiles do as much? Therefore be perfect, as Abba God in heaven is perfect. (Matt 5:43–48)

Once again, Jesus has selected the most agapic passages from his own Scripture and updated them for his audience. Proverbs 25:21 admonishes, "If your enemies are hungry, give them bread to eat; and if they are thirsty, give them water to drink" (NRSV). Jesus sees the healing potential in this commandment, which opens the door into a new reality, a reality that we will finally recognize as home.

Jesus declares that such a homecoming is immeasurably valuable, like treasure hidden in a field or a pearl of great value—if you find it, you would sell all that you have to buy the field or the pearl (Matt 13:44–46). Perhaps our realism—the very same realism that constricts our imagination—tells us that this kingdom can't be built, or that the treasure doesn't actually exist. But Jesus counsels patience through imagery familiar to his audience: the kingdom of God is like a tiny mustard seed that becomes a large mustard plant (Matt 13:31–32), or a pinch of yeast that leavens the whole loaf (Matt 13:33). Small beginnings produce great change, even today.

Jesus also declares that the kingdom of God is a spiritual reality, not an objective reality. It does not come in a way that can be observed or pointed out. Instead, "the Kingdom of God is among [Greek: *entos*] you"

(Luke 17:20–21). The Greek *entos* can also mean "within," so many older translations of this verse read "the kingdom of God is within you." Translators of the Bible must choose one and footnote the other, but our both/and strategy of interpretation allows us to choose both: the kingdom of God is a spiritual reality that we feel *within* us as affection grows *among* us. It grows in both places at once because we are inseparable from one another. We are agapic; we are nondual.

Jesus exemplifies the "creative passion for the possible" that gives time a new direction.[27] Our past is dark, full of warfare, brutality, misogyny, slavery, heterosexism, racism, ableism, and poverty. Jesus imagines a better world, one of equality, openness, and invitation. For Christians, this vision is our new cause. It is the cause for which we work, but also an actual cause, of which our activity is the effect. That is, *we are to be caused by the brilliance of the future, not the darkness of the past.* An architect imagines a building, then draws up plans for it, and those plans structure the activity of the people working to build it, thereby creating the future imagined by the architect. Likewise, Jesus is the architect of the kingdom of God, and his followers actualize his blueprint for its construction. Time has become advent, a "coming toward" that also leaves behind. But this leaving behind does not counsel amnesia: the past still *informs* us, but it no longer *determines* us.

Jesus's Healing Powers Threatened the World's Political Powers

After the exodus, in the desert, when the Jews were threatened by the wilderness, God declares to them, "I am YHWH, who heals you" (Exod 15:26b). Based on this divine self-description, the Jews gave a new name to God: YHWH Rapha, the Lord who heals. God's healing activity occurs throughout the Hebrew Scriptures, both as promise and as activity: God heals infertility (Gen 21:1–7), diseases (Ps 103:3), wounds (Jer 30:17), and broken hearts (Ps 147:3). God heals Zion specifically because they are outcast (Jer 30:17 again).

Jesus, as a touching manifestation of God, does all these things, so "the people all tried to touch Jesus, because power was coming out of him and healing them all" (Luke 6:19). But problems arise when Jesus tries to heal *society*. Many people don't want healing, even of physical illness.

27. Moltmann, *Trinity and the Kingdom*, 217.

We can grow comfortable with the way things are. This truth especially applies to social ills, to which we can become addicted.

The Roman occupiers didn't like charismatic healers out in the countryside attracting followers. This tension came to a head when Jesus visited the temple. Like many from the countryside, he may have had an idealized image of the temple's function. When Jesus confronted the reality of temple life, its hawkers and mongers and lenders and commerce and barter, he was deeply offended, for he had expected the house of prayer promised by Isaiah (56:7), without traders as promised by Zechariah (14:21). Instead, he saw firsthand the den of thieves condemned by Jeremiah (7:11). Zeal for God consumed him, so he began to flip tables, spilling money on the ground, driving out the money lenders, and driving out the sacrificial animals for sale, so that people could finally make offerings in righteousness (Mal 3:3b).

"Nothing is more perilous than truth in a world that lies," writes Nawal El Saadawi, an Egyptian political activist imprisoned for her work.[28] Jesus disturbed the economic, political, and religious power that had aligned in occupied Judea. The Galilean carpenter became a revolutionary agitator and undesirable citizen. Given the appearance of love in a world of hate, crucifixion was inevitable. In the end, the rejection of Christ by humankind symbolizes the rejection of God by humankind. We prefer the miserable and familiar to the promising and new. And so, very soon after Jesus's visit to the temple, disturbed power conspired to put down its disturbance.

The Crucifixion Reveals God's Self-Risk *for Us*

At great risk, truth became enfleshed in Jesus of Nazareth. After ministering in northern Judea for some time, Jesus went to Jerusalem. He went there in the service of life, knowing he would die:

> Christ, though in the image of God, didn't deem equality with God something to be clung to—but instead became completely empty and took on the image of oppressed humankind: born into the human condition, found in the likeness of a human being. Jesus was thus humbled—obediently accepting death, even death on a cross! (Phil 2:6–8)

---

28. El Saadawi, *Memoirs from Women's Prison*, 203.

As the Author of life, Abba determines that intensity depends on contrast. Light has more existence in relationship to darkness; warmth has more existence in relationship to cold. Recognizing this, Abba creates a universe of contrasts, including the contrasts of pleasure and pain, joy and suffering, celebration and grief. Christ, emissary of the Trinity, then ratifies this decision and expresses sympathy for the world by entering the human situation, as Jesus of Nazareth. Tragically, having granted us the freedom to reject truth, Jesus's ministry leads to the passion and crucifixion.

By defining Jesus as truth (John 1:14), the Bible denies truth any heavy, inert characteristics. Like a good cut that a carpenter would call *true*, Jesus is perfectly plumb with reality. He is truth, so truth becomes a way of being in the world rather than an unchanging thing to possess. *Truth is more verb than noun*: "They who *do the truth* come to the light, that their works may be revealed, that their works have been done in God" (John 3:21 WEB [emphasis added]). Recognizing that truth is an activity, early Christians sometimes referred to their faith as *the Way* (Acts 19:9). This reference made sense, because the first Christians were Jews and practitioners of halakah, the totality of laws, ordinances, customs, and practices that structure Jewish life to this day. The term *halakah* derives from the root *halakh*, which means "to walk" or "to go." For this reason, halakah is usually translated as "the Way." It is *not* an inert mass of unchanging rules. It is a way to go through life well, as community.

The way we go through life must constantly adapt to the way things are. In Judaism, this need has produced a long tradition of debate and argumentation. Jesus participated in these debates, producing his own interpretation of halakah, which his followers eventually came to call the evangelion, gospel, or "good news." According to Jesus, *the Way expresses itself through time in loving activity*. In this view, an act of kindness is just as true as a skilled carpenter's cut, balanced mathematical equation, or logically demonstrated argument.[29]

Alas, being the Way is dangerous. Prophets are always in danger: to the patriots, they seem pernicious; to the pious multitude, blasphemous; to those in authority, seditious.[30] According to the Gospel of Luke, after a last supper with his disciples Jesus retreated to the Mount of Olives and prayed, "Abba, if it's your will, take this cup from me; yet not my will but

---

29. Zizioulas, *Being as Communion*, 73–74.
30. Heschel, *Prophets*, 23.

yours be done" (Luke 22:42). The cup would not be removed. Later in the night a crowd, led by Jesus's disciple Judas, approached Jesus to arrest him. Infuriated, one disciple swung a sword and cut off a man's ear, but Jesus rebuked him and healed the man (Luke 22:51). Then Jesus was led away to die.

Over the next few days, Jesus was mocked, beaten, crowned with thorns, and flogged. Then, the Romans drove nails into his hands and feet and hung him on a cross, naked and humiliated before the world, until he suffocated to death. As he was dying, Jesus prayed, "Abba, forgive them. They don't know what they are doing" (Luke 23:34a).

Crucifixion is an incomprehensibly "grotesque and gratuitous" act invented by the Romans to terrorize subjugated peoples. This torturous execution was public, political, and prolonged, reducing the victim to a scarred sign of the Empire's power. In this instance, it also reveals the ab-solute participation of God in human history, in the person of Jesus. Jesus, God's fleshly form, is meek. Jesus is not the *master* of embodied life; he is *subject* to embodied life. He inhabits what we inhabit—the plain fact of hu-man suffering, the mysterious joy of religious community, and the intimat-ed assurance of a loving God. He symbolizes divine openness to the agony and the ecstasy, but also to the unresolvable paradox of faith: "My God, my God, why have you forsaken me?" Jesus cries from the cross (Mark 15:34). He simultaneously acknowledges the presence of God and the absence of God. He accuses God of abandonment, demands of God a defense, yet dies before receiving one. Perhaps God has no adequate answer.

Theologically, the crucifixion of Jesus testifies to the unholy within the universe, useless suffering that freedom produces but God abhors. From the gift of freedom, something emerges in creation that is alien to Godself. God did not intend the unholy, but God allows it out of respect for our autonomy and moral consequence. Crucially, God suffers from this demonic fault in reality. God in Christ undergoes alienation from God through crucifixion.[31] In other words, freedom is of God, but the results of freedom may not be. Faced with a choice between freedom and insignificance, God has chosen to preserve freedom and allow suffering. We may wish it otherwise, but God prioritizes vitality over security.[32]

Yet, God does not make these choices at a distance. In the incarna-tion, we see that God has entered creation as unconditional celebrant. On

31. Moltmann, *Crucified God*, 270–74.
32. Schleiermacher, *Christian Faith*, 1:292, §51.2.

the cross, we see that God has entered creation as absolute participant. No part of the divine person is protected from the dangers of embodiment. God in Jesus is perfectly open to the mutually amplifying contrasts of embodied life, and God is perfectly subject to the grotesque and gratuitous suffering that God rejects but freedom allows. God is completely here; God is fully human, even unto death. For the cosmic Artist in a position of creative responsibility, authentic love necessarily results in vulnerable suffering. Creation necessitates incarnation, and incarnation results in crucifixion.

The Resurrection Reveals
God's Choice for Love and Joy

God is love that experiences hatred but remains love. If Jesus's story ended with the crucifixion, it would be an abject tragedy: hate would have defeated love, suffering would have defeated joy, cruelty would have defeated mercy. All the powers of darkness would reign victorious on earth. Instead, God announces the divine decision for life over death through the resurrection:

> On the first day of the week, at the first sign of dawn, the women came to the tomb bringing the spices they had prepared. They found the stone rolled back from the tomb, but when they entered, they did not find the body of Jesus. While they were still at a loss over what to think two figures in dazzling garments stood beside them. Terrified, the women bowed to the ground. The two said to them, "Why do you search for the Living One among the dead? Jesus is not here; Christ has risen!" (Luke 24:1–5a)

Existential vitality demands experiential texture, and the choice of the living God is to be absolutely alive. Made in God's image, we are offered God's vitality. Since God elects life over death, joy over suffering, and hope over despair, the crucifixion must yield to the resurrection. Crucifixion alone would repudiate the divine will. Crucifixion offends God, who responds by raising us to life, just as a mother lifts her infant to the breast (Isa 49:15). Human suffering invokes divine healing. So, Jesus was raised from the dead by love that defeats hatred. His resurrection was not the act of an individual; it was communion celebrating itself and declaring its victory over division.[33]

---

33. Zizioulas, *Being as Communion*, 113.

The crucifixion acknowledges that suffering *is*; the resurrection promises that joy *will be*. As the soul of the universe, God feels all that the universe feels, but unclouded by fear or despair, because God has ensured that *every* crucifixion will be defeated by its very own resurrection. Julian of Norwich (c. 1343–c. 1416) was an English theologian and mystic. As a female in the Middle Ages, she knew suffering, having lived through the Black Death, the Peasants' Revolt, and a life-threatening illness. During this illness she received visions of Christ. In one vision, on the brink of death, Jesus assures her, "Since I have brought good out of the worst-ever evil, I want you to know by this; that I shall bring good out of all lesser evils, too."[34] In this revelation to Julian, the crucifixion and resurrection are not distant historical events; they are the deep pattern within creation, an ever present promise that illness will yield to health, woundedness will yield to healing, and death will yield to life.

The Incarnation, Ministry, Crucifixion, and Resurrection Tell a Sacred Story

Humans have the freedom to live with the grain of the universe or against it. When choosing greed, hatred, and domination instead of generosity, love, and community, we choose against God and create suffering for ourselves and others. The crucifixion exposes the ongoing horror of our choice *against* God. In the crucifixion, corrupt power believed that it could defeat divine truth, but the spirit *of* the universe could not be defeated by the spirit *against* the universe.[35] Even Roman nails cannot tear the divine fabric.

In this narrative, Christ became human as God always intended. From the moment that the Trinity *conceives* creation, Christ chooses to *enter* creation. The Artists must celebrate their art; the Playwrights must perform their play.[36] Yet these Creatives are not smarmy, shallow romantics. Instead, they acknowledge our exposure to the soaring and searing spectrum of experience that they sustain. They know that we are susceptible to an inexhaustible range of events and their resultant

---

34. Julian of Norwich, *In Love Enclosed*, 49; from *Revelations of Divine Love*, §13.29.

35. Zizioulas, *Being as Communion*, 108.

36. Moltmann, *Creating a Just Future*, 84.

feelings, yet they affirm the varieties of embodied experience by undergoing embodied experience.[37]

Through his love of life, Jesus exemplifies the human call to enjoy God forever, a call that opens us to the world. Since God is loving everything into being at every moment, awareness of God broadens our love to all things in all times. To see what this love looks like, we look to Jesus who is all that a human can be. Christ's life is communion itself, while Christ's preaching resists those forces that impede communion. Christ heals, restoring the soul's communion with the body. Christ loves, exemplifying interpersonal communion. Christ preaches, demanding that society become communion. Christ includes, broadening our practice of communion. Christ speaks truth, those words that invite our minds into communion. And in preaching the kingdom of God Christ offers hope, which is communion with time. Christ reveals the fundamental harmony from which we come, within which we live, and to which we will return. For this reason, he is the Alpha and Omega, the beginning and the end, the first and the last (Rev 22:13).

Jesus Reveals the Fullness of Divinity as the Fullness of Humanity

Jesus always outwits identity.[38] Like the plus symbol in LGBTQ+, Jesus's meaning is never defined, hence always open to expansion. Jesus becomes new things in new places for new people, so that he can always be healing anew. Over the ages, Jesus has been rabbi, rebel, messiah, prophet, martyr, dissident, friend, healer, preacher, philosopher, ancestor, guru, peasant, spirit, liberator, feminist, womanist, Dalit, Black, White, Asian, African, et al. The meaning of Jesus changes in every context, so that Jesus is always becoming more, always surpassing himself, always transforming in new ways. Our concept of Jesus must overflow conceptualization the way Jesus overflows being, because Jesus is always *more than*.

For this reason, as the early Christians began to reflect on Jesus and the impact he had on them, they increasingly came to see him as more than they had thought. In his lifetime, they recognized him as a prophet, rabbi, Son of God, and even Son of Man. But more reflection produced ever higher estimations. The earliest writings of the church interpret him

37. Annan, *After Shock*, 56–57.
38. Loughlin, "What Is Queer," 149.

as "the reflection of God's glory, the exact representation of God's very being" (Heb 1:3), the one in whom "all the fullness of God was pleased to dwell" (Col 1:19), the "image of the unseen God" (Col 1:15) who, like the Father, has "life in himself" (John 5:26).

Why was the church's concept of Jesus ever increasing? Jesus is a superabundant person, absolutely free, perfectly present, and radically open. According to Revelation, he is the great Amen, the one who says yes to life in its entirety (Rev 3:14). Jesus personifies a spontaneous resonance with the living God, and he offers that resonance to us, through him, as one prong of a tuning fork animates the other. The encounter with Jesus offers more than a perfect example of human life, more than an opportunity to *imitate*, by force of will. Instead, *Jesus's activity activates us because Jesus's Spirit activates our spirits.* Jesus is not an external ideal that we copy; Jesus is an internal power that we receive. For this reason, Jesus is not just Friend, Teacher, and Healer. Jesus is Savior. Jesus is the Christ.

6

Sophia, the Animating
Power of Wisdom

There is a vitality, a life force, an energy, a quickening that is translated through you into action, and because there is only one of you in all of time, this expression is unique. And if you block it, it will never exist through any other medium and it will be lost. The world will not have it. It is not your business to determine how good it is nor how valuable nor how it compares with other expressions. It is your business to keep it yours clearly and directly, to keep the channel open. You do not even have to believe in yourself or your work. You have to keep yourself open and aware to the urges that motivate you. Keep the channel open. . . . No artist is pleased. [There is] no satisfaction whatever at any time. There is only a queer divine dissatisfaction, a blessed unrest that keeps us marching and makes us more alive than the others.

—Martha Graham[1]

1. De Mille, *Martha*, 264.

I Was a Very Confused Young Man

IN JANUARY 1996, I became interim codirector of Programa Nogalhillos, a Presbyterian Border Ministry site based in Nogales, Arizona. The purpose of the program was to foster cooperation between the Presbyterian Church (USA) and the National Presbyterian Church in Mexico, that country's second largest Protestant denomination. Each site had two codirectors, one Mexican and one American. I was a returned Peace Corps volunteer who had never been to Mexico, hadn't spoken Spanish in three years, and had no theological training. I liked challenges. This would be a challenge.

The previous American codirector of the program had brought some Pentecostal (Holy Spirit–centered) pastors into the program and was trying to integrate them into the more staid Presbyterian system. The integration presented certain difficulties, as the Pentecostals had a few practices that the Presbyterians were suspicious of, like exorcisms. My Mexican codirector was a traditional Presbyterian and licensed medical doctor who had taken up a second career in ministry. He considered mental illness to be a medical problem that should be treated by a psychiatrist while the church provided love and support. The Pentecostals believed mental illness to be caused by demon possession.

This disagreement was fairly minor until one of my codirector's parishioners began to struggle with mental illness. My codirector referred him to a psychiatrist and offered him pastoral support, but the parishioner believed himself to be possessed. His family called the Pentecostals, two of whom traveled down to Hermosillo to exorcise the demon. They told me about the exorcism beforehand, without telling me that it was my codirector's parishioner. I must have gotten a look of wild-eyed excitement when I heard about a potential exorcism, because they gently declined to invite me: "When the demon leaves the body, it looks for someone weak in their faith to possess," they explained. "It would be dangerous for you to be there."

They performed the exorcism, which was successful—for a while. Unfortunately, the parishioner got repossessed during the next Sunday's worship service and began throwing chairs around their little church, causing a bit of a disturbance among the rest of the congregation. My codirector found out that the Pentecostals had performed the exorcism and drove six hours from Hermosillo to Nogales to confront them. He asked me to moderate, since I had come to know them quite well.

What ensued was one of the most fascinating conversations I have ever been involved in. By "involved in" I mean "listened to in a state of uncertainty and dread." It covered the relationship between science and religion, with my codirector arguing that mental illness was a brain disease that required medical treatment and the Pentecostals arguing it was a spiritual curse that required exorcism. It covered the theology of the Holy Spirit, with my codirector arguing that Christians couldn't be possessed by evil spirits because they were already filled by the Holy Spirit and the Pentecostals arguing that evil spirits were more attracted to Christians because they wanted to drive out the Holy Spirit. As the conversation continued, I had the startling realization that I was completely out of my depth.

To be honest, I wasn't even sure what the Holy Spirit did. The Father created and the Son saved, but what did the Holy Spirit do? I knew that it was part of the Trinity, and that it came to the church on Pentecost, and that it was supposed to be in all Christians, but I still didn't really know why it was necessary or important. I had the vague feeling that it made you feel good. My Presbyterian tradition valued doing things decently and in order, so an uncontrollable Holy Spirit placed a distant third to the Creator and Savior.

Over the years, I have come to see the Holy Spirit as a life-giving power, coequal within the Trinity. I still believe that mental illness is a medical problem, and I remain suspicious of exorcisms. But the Holy Spirit has a distinct and necessary role to play in faith. I will share my interpretation of her work below.

The Holy Spirit Is a Divine Promise

"Is it possible to live on this earth with a generosity, abundance, fearlessness, and beauty that mirror Divine Being itself?" asks Cynthia Bourgeault.[2] Her implicit answer is that we can, if imperfectly. As the perfectly living person, Jesus of Nazareth is the portal through which divine communion flows into the world. Jesus runs *with* the grain of the universe and teaches us how that grain runs. In so doing, Jesus lets loose a new Spirit in the world, an enlivening Spirit who quickens us toward abundance. Hence, we do not become Christlike by imitation but by empowerment, not by will but by inspiration.

---

2. Bourgeault, *Wisdom Jesus*, 24.

Pierre Teilhard de Chardin, an evolutionary scientist and Jesuit priest, observes, "There is something afoot in the universe, something that looks like gestation and birth."[3] To him, the universe isn't a collection of surprisingly well-organized, dead matter. The universe is a womb for religious consciousness. Every evolution—the evolution of stars into elements, of elements into chemistry, of chemistry into biology, and of biology into consciousness—every evolution has led to increased complexity and increased capacity, culminating in the twin blessings of self-awareness and God-consciousness. We can interpret this sprawling, magnificent process as a glorious accident that inexplicably produced us, or we can interpret it as a divine gift that begs gratitude toward the Giver. If there is a Giver, then our evolution into ever increasing enjoyment is no accident. It is God's plan, mediated by matter. Evolution has instilled in us a great metaphysical hunger, a hunger that can be satisfied only by the Good, the True, and the Beautiful, a hunger that can be satisfied only by God. *The universe is an invitation, and the Holy Spirit is the host.*

We Yearn for the Spirit Like We Yearn for Fulfillment

When the Hebrews fled Egypt, they found themselves alone in the wilderness, no longer under Egyptian law. Societies need law to function, so God provided the Israelites with a new legal code governing both social and religious life. This new law code was remarkably egalitarian for the time, if also occasionally severe. Even though the law is interpreted differently by different Jewish denominations, some of which favor evolving religion and some of which favor tradition, it structures Jewish life to this day. Ideally, habitual observance of the law transforms the practitioner, so that fulfillment of the law becomes spontaneous rather than forced.

This ethical spontaneity had long been a dream of the Jewish people, a dream that God shared. According to the Hebrew Scriptures, God doesn't want automatons obeying an external code; God wants persons animated by God's own compassion:

> For this Law that I give to you today is not too difficult for you,
> nor is it beyond your reach. It is not up in heaven, so that you
> need to ask yourselves, "Who will go up to heaven for us and
> bring it down to us, so that we may hear it and keep it?" Nor is
> it beyond the seas, so that you need to wonder, "Who will cross

---

3. Teilhard de Chardin, *Making of a Mind*, 57.

> the seas for us and bring it back to us, so that we may hear it and
> keep it?" No, the word [*dabar*] of God is very near to you; it is
> in your mouth, and in your heart, so that you can keep it. (Deut
> 30:11–14)

The Jews had experienced the law within, not as a set of rules but as an
internal guide. This moral calling always competed with everyday fears,
practical expediency, and mundane advantage. But having glimpsed the
warmth that social life could offer, and the spiritual abundance that God
intended, they ached for its realization.

In response, their prophets promised this realization, but as an act
of God rather than an act of the people. Jeremiah, writing in the voice of
God, declares:

> Behold, the days are coming, says YHWH, when I will establish
> a new covenant with the house of Israel and the house of Judah.
> It will not be like the covenant I made with their ancestors when
> I took them by the hand to bring them up out of the land of
> Egypt—a covenant they broke, though I was their spouse, says
> YHWH. But this is the covenant I will make with the house of
> Israel after those days, says YHWH: I will put my Law in their
> minds and on their hearts. I will be their God, and they will be
> my people. (Jer 31:31–33)

Jeremiah's promise is extravagant—an innate knowledge of God so perfect that religious education is unnecessary. This transformation would
make everyone a prophet, someone who discerns God's hope for humankind and cannot help but to act out that hope, leading society into the
fullness of social life.

Jeremiah's vision began with Moses, who lamented, "If only all of
God's people were prophets! If only YHWH would bestow the Spirit
[*ruach*] on them all!" (Num 11:29b). In Hebrew grammar, *ruach* is a
feminine noun. To Moses and the Israelites, the spirit of God (*ruach
Elohim*) was a grammatically feminine, spiritually animating presence.
It motivated the prophets, but only long enough for them to complete
their mission, at which point it departed. They yearned for a day when
the spirit of God would permanently inhabit and inspire all Jews, or all
people, depending on interpretation. In contrast to later Christian interpretation, the spirit was not a unique person within a tripersonal God.
Instead, it was one aspect of a unitary God, like the charisma of a skillful
leader or the intelligence of a noted genius. For this reason, most Jewish
translations of the biblical *ruach* leave it in the lowercase (spirit) while

most Christian translations put it in the uppercase (Spirit), in anticipation of the Holy Spirit of the Christian Trinity.

The term *Holy Spirit* (*ruach ha'kodesh*) itself occurs three times in
the Hebrew Bible, once in Ps 51 and twice in Isa 63. Still, from a Hebraic
perspective, even this term refers to an aspect of the one God, not to a
person within the Trinity. Both traditions agree on the effective power
of the spirit, which God would pour out onto all (Isa 44:3), replacing
their hearts of stone with hearts of flesh, empowering them to walk in
the ways of God (Ezek 36:26–27). According to some prophets, this inspiration will not be limited to the Jewish people, but will transform *all*
humankind:

> I will pour out my Spirit on all humankind.
>   Your daughters and sons will prophesy,
> your elders will have prophetic dreams,
>   and your young people will see visions.
> In those days, I will pour out my Spirit
>   even on those in servitude,
>   women and men alike. (Joel 3:1–2)

Around 30 CE, in occupied Judea, the followers of an itinerant rabbi crucified by the Romans experienced this outpouring.

The Disciples Received the Holy Spirit from Jesus

Jesus, the itinerant rabbi, was a Jewish prophet inhabited by the Holy
Spirit of God, like all Jewish prophets. According to the Christian tradition, Jesus is unique in transferring this Spirit to his disciples, thereby fulfilling the Hebrew prophecies. In Acts, certain detractors had insinuated
that the spirited behavior of the rabbi's followers was caused by spirits—
alcoholic spirits. But Peter defended them: "These people are not drunk,
as you think, for it is only nine o'clock in the morning!" (Acts 2:15). He
then went on to quote the above passage from Joel and argued that this
new inspiration was the fulfillment of Joel's prophecy.

Peter's argument was continuous with the teachings of Jesus. Jesus
had predicted his own death and resurrection, as well as his assumption
into heaven afterward. Naturally, his disciples wanted him to stay with
them forever, to continue his teaching and healing ministry, to save them
from the pain of bereavement. But Jesus denied them the comfort of his
ministry, instead calling them to become his ministers: "Peace be with

you. As Abba God sent me, so I am sending you," declares the resurrected Jesus to his disciples (John 20:21), indicating their impending promotion into the role he had once played alone.

We can only imagine the mixed emotions the disciples felt on receiving this charge. Their charismatic leader, the one they experienced as the Son of God, the preacher who drew crowds and the healer who worked miracles, told them that they would do what he had done and more, for in fact they would do "greater works than these" (John 14:12). In case they felt a flush of pride, they had to remember his pre-passion question, which he posed to them as they competed for pride of place: "Can you drink the cup that I am going to drink?" (Matt 20:22), to which they had enthusiastically replied in the affirmative. He assured them that they would indeed drink from his cup, then he was flogged and tortured to death on a cross.

For the transfer of power from Jesus to the disciples to occur, Jesus had to depart. Just as the Spirit had animated Jesus's body on earth, empowering him to teach, heal, and prophesy, that same Spirit would animate the disciples, making them the body of Christ and empowering them to continue his mission. But the Spirit would not only *ratify* Jesus's message; the Spirit would *expand* upon it, revealing to the disciples what they had not yet been ready to hear, guiding them from truth into all truth (John 16:12-13), teaching them everything (John 14:25-26).

The Holy Spirit arrived fifty days after Passover, on Pentecost:

> When the day of Pentecost arrived, they all met in one room. Suddenly they heard what sounded like a violent, rushing wind from heaven; the noise filled the entire house in which they were sitting. Something appeared to them that seemed like tongues of fire; these separated and came to rest on the head of each one. They were all filled with the Holy Spirit and began to speak in other languages as she enabled them. (Acts 2:2–4)

Previously, Jesus had been the light of the world (John 9:5). Now, the disciples were called upon to be the light of the world, a tall task for a motley crew of peasants, widows, fishermen, marginal women, and tax collectors. These disciples would become the church. Over two millennia, the church has spectacularly succeeded and miserably failed in its mission, making peace and waging wars, feeding the poor and groveling to the rich, expanding scientific knowledge and perpetuating superstition.

The Trinity Possesses a Capacity for Sympathetic Joy

"If you have two people in a room, you have a conversation. If you have three people, you have politics," an old lawyer once said to me. In my experience, this statement has proven itself true many times. This validation reveals something problematic about human nature, but it also reveals the audacity of Trinitarian theology. As mentioned earlier, the Jewish tradition interprets the spirit of God as an *aspect* of God, not as a *person*, not even as a functionary in the heavenly court. But the energized Jewish community centered around the risen Jesus experienced this Spirit as a unique power that was inextricably related to the Creator and Jesus, but also distinct from them. In a way, this interpretation continues the Hebrew tradition, because the Hebrew Scriptures do not assert that Wisdom receives her knowledge and power from elsewhere, from any male figure; she has it of herself.[4] She is her own person, and strong.

Problematically, Christian theology has rarely treated the Holy Spirit as an actual person, but rather as an impersonal force binding the two other persons together. In our argument, the Holy Spirit must be personal because a third person suggests the divine capacity for *sympathetic joy*. Sympathetic joy is the ability to experience someone else's joy as our own. God's capacity for sympathetic joy is also a human possibility, present in humanity because preexisting in God, of whom humankind is the earthly expression.

Historically, Christians have sometimes designated the Holy Spirit as the third person of the Trinity, implying rank between the persons, but such inequality is impossible within divinity. The presence of *three* persons is imminently consequential, but it doesn't make any particular person the *third*. Instead, *each person is third to the other two*. This status is important because it exemplifies the openness of divine love.[5]

The meaning of the third person of the Trinity struck me one day while driving my two young sons to school. They were in the back seat playing with each other, tickling each other, laughing, giggling, and singing. I listened to them, occasionally glancing in the mirror to watch, and was flooded with joy at their love for each other. I then became aware of the ecstatic power of my third party, sympathetic joy. There was a buoyancy to it that came from observation without participation. This delight accompanied a willing selflessness that celebrated their love without envy

4. Schüssler Fiorenza, *Jesus*, 157.
5. J. P. Sydnor, "Dance of Emptiness," 41.

or jealousy. I did not want to interrupt their relationship or even *join* their relationship at that moment. I simply wanted to revel in it—in my perception of it, as third party—more fully.

A cliché description of human purpose claims that we are "to love and be loved." This description is inadequate because it does not recognize our call to celebrate love that is not our own, nor does it recognize the potential riches implicit in that call. Free of ego investment, third-person love offers a kind of spiritual weightlessness. It is a love that we do not participate in yet celebrate wholeheartedly. Thus, the third person of the Trinity symbolizes the infinite openness of the sacred. The Trinity revels in *all* relatedness, not just their *particular* relatedness. They consecrate *universal* interdependence, not just their own network of interdependence.

The third person of the Trinity, as third person, is the symbolic window through which the light of infinite relatedness flows. As C. S. Lewis notes, if John, Mary, and Pat are friends, and Pat dies, then Mary has not just lost Pat. She has also lost how Pat relates to John, and all the aspects of John that Pat brought out of him that Mary couldn't.[6] We are multifaceted, and different people bring out different aspects of each other. If we want to see the whole person, then we need to relate to them *with others*. Someone else may bring out their quirky humor, or oddball interests, or rambunctious adventurousness. If we are not jealous, then we can enjoy these facets of our friends that we cannot elicit, but our other friends can. If we are jealous, then we will know less of the person we seek to control. The larger our circle of friendship, the deeper our knowledge of one another will be. Heaven is other people.

Love overflows, always seeking to draw more participants into its community. It rejects all exclusive, tribal love. Were tribal love divine love, were God a nationalist god, then the Christian symbol of God would be a closed love that excludes the other.[7] We have all known lovers who loved each other and no one else. They treat one another ethically and support one another, but do not extend that treatment to anyone outside their closed system. Their ethics are *particular* (for each other) rather than *universal* (for all). In their worldview, only *they* can be the victims of injustice, because outsiders do not deserve to be treated justly. Such

---

6. Lewis, *Four Loves*, 61–62.
7. Boff, *Trinity and Society*, 43.

exclusive love is capable only of self-righteousness and indignation. It locks others out and locks us in.

To love the outsider implies a love of difference. Such love is a godsend, because difference amplifies love. If love within homogeneity sufficed, then the same could simply practice self-love and find satisfaction there. For love to be Trinitarian, *difference* must be loved. As love unifying difference, the Trinity is a great symbol of hope. Power can repress the frictions of difference, creating a superficial peace by force, but true unity is achieved only when difference *voluntarily* unites. In this Trinitarian worldview, the human rejection of difference is morally wrong because it is ontologically askew—it rejects the diverse reality that God sustains and celebrates.

All worldviews that exalt uniformity and control create an artificial chasm between human and human, a chasm that fills with disgust and fear. Unity cannot just *tolerate* diversity; unity must *sanctify* diversity, including gender diversity, as an expression of God's differentiated, relational being.[8] To sanctify gender diversity, all aspects of gender must be expressed in God—those at the ends of the spectrum, those in the middle, and those not on the spectrum at all. To sanctify this diversity, we have referred to Abba, God our Mother and God our Father, as "they."

The Holy Spirit Embeds Femininity within God

The Bible ascribes multiple characteristics to the Holy Spirit, linking her to the Sustainer and the Christ while ascribing to her a particular function. The baptism of Jesus, in which the Holy Spirit descends in the form of a dove and Abba endorses Jesus's ministry, conveys the uniqueness and harmony of each person within the Trinity (Luke 3:21–32). In this passage, each divine person is in a unique location with a unique perspective and a unique role to play, while their activity is perfectly harmonized for the coming story of salvation.

We can also note that the Greek word for dove, *peristera*, the symbol of the Holy Spirit, is a feminine noun (see also John 1:32). Indeed, the Spirit is frequently associated with feminine aspects of the divine. For example, the Spirit is associated with the wisdom that God (read: the collective activity of the Trinity) grants us. She is a Spirit of Wisdom (Deut 34:9). In the book of Proverbs, Wisdom (her name, a proper noun, hence

---

8. Coakley, *God, Sexuality, and Self*, 54.

capitalized) is a character who acts and speaks, raising her voice in the open squares and declaring: "Surely I will pour out my spirit [*ruach*] on you; I will make my words known to you" (Prov 1:20–23 NKJV). The prophet Isaiah says that the spirit of God will rest on the coming Messiah, enabling him to rule with wisdom and justice (Isa 11:2). And after Pentecost, the early church felt empowered by the wisdom of the Spirit, which allowed them to preach boldly and argue skillfully (Acts 6:9–10).

The Hebrew word for wisdom is *hokmah*, a feminine noun. For this reason, the Hebrew Scriptures most often refer to Wisdom in the feminine gender: "Grow in discernment! Grow in Wisdom! Don't you give up on her, and she will never give up on you; if you love her, she will protect you. Wisdom is supreme—so acquire Wisdom!" (Prov 4:5–7). Proverbs, a collection of Hebrew wisdom sayings, may have been collected in the eighth century BCE. Approximately seven hundred years later, the book of Wisdom, written in Greek, states: "I called for help and the spirit of Wisdom [Greek: *Sophia*] came to my aid. I valued Her above even my throne and scepter and all my great wealth was nothing next to Her. I held no precious jewel to be Her equal, because all the gold in the world was just a handful of sand compared to Her" (Wis 7:7–8). That author goes on to associate Wisdom with Spirit again, declaring: "In Wisdom there is a spirit of intelligence and holiness that is unique and unmistakable . . . pervading every intelligent, pure, and most subtle spirit" (Wis 7:22b–23). Finally, the author asks, "But who has ever mapped out the ways of heaven? Who has ever discerned your intentions unless you have given them Wisdom and sent your Holy Spirit from heaven on high? It was because of Her that we on earth were set on the right path, that we mortals were taught what pleases you and were kept safe under Her protection" (Wis 9:17–18).

The grammatically feminine Hebrew Wisdom figure continued into the Greek and Latin translations of the Bible. In the Greek translation (the Septuagint), *hokmah* was translated as *sophia*, a feminine noun and the root of the contemporary English word *philosophy* (*philos*: love, *sophia*: wisdom; the love of wisdom). In the Latin translation (the Vulgate), *hokmah* was translated as *sapientia*, a feminine noun and the root of the contemporary scientific classification for humankind, *homo sapiens* (*homo*: human, *sapiens*: wise; wise humans, a somewhat generous appellation).

We have already discussed the maternal imagery for God in the Bible, citing such Hebrew texts as: "You deserted the Rock who gave you life; you forgot the God who bore you" (Deut 32:18), "From whose womb did the ice come forth, and who has given birth to the hoarfrost of heaven?" (Job 38:29 NRSV), and "Can a woman forget her nursing child, or show no compassion for the child of her womb? Even these may forget, yet I will not forget you" (Isa 49:15 NRSV). This imagery continues in the writings of the early church: "Like newborn babies, be hungry for nothing but milk—the pure milk of the word that will make you grow into salvation, now that you have tasted that our God is good" (1 Pet 2:2–3). And one of the most defining texts of the Newer Testament, 1 John 4:8b, asserts that God is love (*Theos agapē estin*). In this passage, *Theos* is a masculine noun and *agapē* is a feminine verb, a grammatical fusion that shatters any gender essence and places the omnipresent God everywhere on the gender spectrum.

All such gender imagery is metaphorical yet consequential. Exclusively masculine imagery for the divine divinizes masculinity and profanes femininity. Moreover, the false binary itself marginalizes nonbinary persons. Nevertheless, the Western Christian tradition has generally used exclusively masculine language for all three persons of the Trinity as well as the Trinity itself. This exclusivity was always patriarchal, never biblical, and begs correction.

Thankfully, the feminine metaphors for God in the Bible, plus the uniquely Christian doctrine of the Trinity, present an opportunity to embed gender diversity in God. This theological move will allow us to divinize gender difference. At the same time, we can transfer the inherent divine equality to society. Made in the image of God, we are called to gender equality and the celebration of all gender difference. Although never *literal*, these gender diverse metaphors are *powerful* because they find their source in their prototype, the all-encompassing nature of God.[9]

To embed femininity within God, to celebrate the Wisdom of God, and to recognize the personality of the Holy Spirit, *we will henceforth refer to the Holy Spirit as Sophia and assign her a feminine pronoun.*[10] Many traditionalists, accustomed to an exclusively male God, may reject any insinuation of the female into the divine as heretical. But the association of Sophia with the Holy Spirit is not an innovation; it is a retrieval of tradition. The early church was rich in feminine imagery for the Spirit. For example, the lost Gospel of the Hebrews was an early second-century account of Jesus produced by Jewish Christians (Jewish followers of Jesus

---

9. Johnson, *She Who Is*, 113–20.

10. Johnson, "Redeeming the Name," 120–23.

who retained their Jewish customs). In that Gospel, Jesus refers to the Holy Spirit as his Mother: "My Mother (*mētēr*), the Holy Spirit, took me just now by one of my hairs and carried me off to the great Mount Tabor," he states.[11]

The noncanonical Apocryphon of John refers to the blessed One as Mother-Father[12] and states, "I shall praise and glorify . . . the three: the Father, the Mother, and the Son, the perfect power."[13] Likewise, as John wanders grief stricken after the crucifixion, the Trinity appears to him and says, "Why do you doubt, or why do you fear? . . . I am the One who is with you always: I am the Father; I am the Mother; I am the Son."[14] In the noncanonical Gospel of Philip, the author declares that Mary could not have been impregnated by the Holy Spirit, because "when did a woman ever conceive with a woman?"[15]

Around 340 CE the Syriac theologian Aphrahat writes: "As long as a man has not taken a wife, he loves and reveres God his Father and the Holy Spirit his Mother, and he has no other love." The early church theologian Jerome (c. 347–c. 419), in his commentary on Isaiah, writes:

> [In the text] "like the eyes of a maid look to the hand of her mistress" [Ps 123:2], the maid is the soul and the mistress (*dominam*) is the Holy Spirit. . . . Nobody should be offended by this, for among the Hebrews the Spirit is said to be of the feminine gender (*genere feminino*), although in our language [Latin: *spiritus*] it is called to be of masculine gender and in the Greek language neuter.[16]

And in the early fourth century, the Syriac theologian Ephrem writes of Jesus's double birth from two wombs, that of divinity and that of humanity:

> If anyone seeks Your hidden nature,
>   Behold it is in heaven in the great womb of Divinity.
> And if anyone seeks your revealed body,
>   Behold it rests and looks out from the small womb of Mary.[17]

11. Van Oort, "Holy Spirit as Feminine," 22.
12. Wisse, *Apocryphon of John*, 109.
13. Wisse, *Apocryphon of John*, 103.
14. Pagels, "God the Mother," 296. See also Wisse, *Apocryphon of John*, 99.
15. Isenberg, "Gospel of Philip," 134.
16. Van Oort, "Holy Spirit as Feminine," 22–23.
17. Ephrem the Syrian, *Hymns*, 138.

In the later fourth century, an Egyptian preacher (perhaps Symeon, whose writings were falsely ascribed to the monk Makarios) writes about "the grace of the Spirit, the Mother (*mētēr*) of the holy."[18]

Patriarchy erased the tradition of calling the Holy Spirit "Sophia" and assigning her a female gender.[19] We retrieve it as metaphor. Sophia is a metaphorically female *person*. Because she is the Spirit who animated Jesus, she cannot be reduced to the presence of Christ. She is full of Christ, just as Christ is full of her, because Truth expresses Wisdom just as Wisdom expresses Truth. But she is not an adjunct of Christ any more than Christ is her adjunct. They are unique and equal persons, offering unique and equal gifts to the story of salvation. In other words, the persons of the Trinity have unique functions, but these functions overlap due to the perfection of their cooperation. The Creator creates *through* Christ and Sophia, while Sophia is the Holy Spirit *of* the Creator and Christ, and Jesus serves as an emissary *from* Abba and Sophia. Just as the double helix of our DNA produces one person, so the triple helix of Abba, Jesus, and Sophia produces one deliverance.[20]

Now, with one further move, we can have a gender-balanced Trinity. Jesus is male, Sophia is female, and Abba the Creator and Sustainer is nonbinary, nondual, gender inclusive, transgender, or omni-gendered. In this way, God expresses the full spectrum of gender identities that God creates, sustains, and loves. Again, traditionalists may deem this move to be innovative or heretical, but tradition has already declared that the Creator transcends gender. We have considered biblical depictions of God as Father and Mother. God is also associated with nongendered metaphors like a rock (Ps 18:2), the sun, a shield (both in Ps 84:11), the One (Deut 6:4), and light (1 John 1:5). Again, we are retrieving a gender-inclusive tradition that patriarchy erased. Henceforth in this book, whenever discussing the Trinity in constructive, creative terms, we will utilize gender-balanced or gender-neutral language for God (the Trinity) and the three persons who compose the one God. Often, when discussing the Trinity historically or biblically, we will use the old masculine language for the sake of clarity. But whenever proposing how we can think about the Trinity today, we will use omni-gendered language.

---

18. Pseudo-Macarius, *Fifty Spiritual Homilies*, 176.

19. Schüssler Fiorenza, *Jesus*, 144.

20. Johnson, *She Who Is*, 222.

This theological transition necessitates new language. Different formulations can emphasize different perspectives on the healing work of God that traditional terminology has overlooked. For example, alternative Trinitarian formulations might include Parent-Son-Daughter, gender neutralizing the Creator/Sustainer and preserving the male gender of Jesus, while ascribing a female gender to the Holy Spirit. We could refer to YHWH-Jesus-Sophia, emphasizing the proper name, hence personality, of each person. We could refer to the Trinity as Fidelity-Love-Power, which emphasizes the steadfast faithfulness of the Sustainer, the powerful love of the Redeemer, and the vivifying energy of the Spirit. The formulation Sustainer-Participant-Celebrant highlights the ongoing activity of the Creator, the continual participation with risk of the Christ, and the consummating lure of the Spirit. These formulations are gender neutral, hence gender inclusive. Each formulation provides a different insight into our tripersonal salvation, thereby expanding our understanding of the work of God for us. Although these formulations may prove disorienting at first, they are worth the intellectual effort since they expand our understanding of God's ongoing activity. Trinitarian language should be an arena of playful experimentation, not dogmatic restriction, as churches search for language that best communicates the ever-unfolding love of God and the exuberant creativity of God in our multicolor universe.

Sophia Is Active throughout Time and throughout the Cosmos

Although the Sustainer is the person of the Trinity most responsible for creation, all three persons create and sustain together so the cosmos may bear the imprint of agapic love. For this reason, we find Bible passages that describe the participation of each person in creation. Here, we will concern ourselves with the contribution of Sophia.

Reading the Trinity into the Hebrew Scriptures, we find Sophia present in the very beginning: "In the beginning God created the heaven and the earth. And the earth was without form, and void; and darkness was upon the face of the deep. And the Spirit of God moved upon the face of the waters" (Gen 1:2 KJV; see also Prov 3:19–20; 8:22–31; Ps 104:30). At the outset, God intended the universe to be more than dead matter. God intended the universe to be full of Spirit, which is to be full of Life. For Spirit to be present, not just *at* the beginning, but *in* the beginning, embeds Spirit within every aspect of the universe, revealing the divine commitment to richness of experience. Self-organizing matter isn't enough; there must be a great expanse of feelings, desires, dreams, and decisions.[21]

Sophia fulfills matter by lifting it into the heights of Spirit. She does not neglect material existence; she consummates it. In so doing, she rejects any language that implies existence is "nothing but" matter. We hear such language frequently: love is "nothing but" the neurotransmitter oxytocin, consciousness is "nothing but" a neurological illusion, morality is "nothing but" an evolutionary adaptation of social animals. To materialist assertions that "spirit is nothing but matter," Sophia replies, "Yes, spirit is matter . . . *and more*. Spirit is abundance."

We can discern this abundant quality within the universe: "God's Spirit adorns the heavens," states Job (26:13a). Due to this adornment, things are not mere things; they are ensouled, they are sacred, they are beautiful.[22] Sophia as Spirit is the superfluous boon in the universe, the net positive that we never earned but always enjoy. She is embedded in reality as its source of significance, weaving meaning into being and turning life into instruction. Sophia's presence is the presence of grace itself. For this reason, knowing Sophia is a gift: "Happy are you when you find Wisdom, when you develop discernment. For she is more profitable than silver and brings yields greater even than gold. . . . Her paths are pleasant ones, and all her roads lead to peace" (Prov 3:13, 17).

Sophia's specific divine charge is the unification, harmonization, and enchantment of our interior life or subjectivity. "Subjectivity" is a philosophical term that refers to our private thoughts, feelings, memories, and desires, to which only we have direct access, but which we can share through various forms of communication. Our subjectivity finds its precedent in the subjectivity of each Trinitarian person, just as our intersubjectivity finds its precedent in the Trinity itself.

God is the ground of being, and not just physical being, but all being—emotional, moral, spiritual, rational, aesthetic, mathematical, etc. God is maker of all things, visible and invisible, and God embraces all that God has made. We, made in the image of God, are made for fullness of being, to embrace all that God has made. We are matter and spirit,

21. Johnson, *Women, Earth, and Creator*, 60.
22. Ramanuja, *Vedartha Sangraha*, 70–71, §87.

body and soul, brain and mind. To neglect any aspect of ourselves diminishes our personhood.

Sophia neglects nothing. She sees beneath appearances and teaches us to do the same, granting us interior awareness, helping us to recognize the interior awareness of others, then connecting everything to generate a living communion. Through this unceasing process, she frees us from the impoverishing illusion that we are the only thing alive. She connects depth of self to depth of self, soul to soul, bringing to experience what was always true and helping us to live plumb with creation as intended. "The glory of God is a human being, fully alive," writes Irenaeus,[23] and Sophia within us secures this glory.

As our inhabitant, Sophia empowers the process of *theosis*, through which we draw ever closer to God, taking on God's nature (John 10:34; following Ps 82:6). Sophia transforms us according to the likeness of God (Eph 4:24) and clothes us in Christ, granting us adoption as the children of God (Gal 3:26–27). We are humans who are becoming increasingly divine. Through this process, our petty egotism dies to the fullness of Christ, which is the fullness of life. We cease to be hovels of the self, becoming instead temples of the Spirit (1 Cor 6:19). Such internal transformation changes everything around us, placing us in a new cosmos, more beautiful and promising than the previous. We are becoming one with ourselves, one with God, and one with the cosmos. Through Sophia we are becoming agapic, hence nondual.

Jesus's revelation of agapic love is limited by his sheer humanity—the finitude of his this-worldly work. One human life, even a divine human life, cannot exhaustively reveal the infinitude of divine potential. The inherent limitations of Jesus's teachings, their limitation to one culture and one language in one time, coupled with the imperially enforced brevity of his ministry, leave space for us to learn more.[24] Sophia teaches us more. As the Spirit of the universe, Sophia acts throughout the universe. Jesus the Christ plays the role of absolute participant, acting in a particular time and particular place with particular people. Sophia acts everywhere so that Jesus can act somewhere; Sophia acts in all times so that Jesus can act in one time. Hence, Sophia continues revelation, infusing agapic love into all times and all places through inspired people, guiding the cosmos toward the divine love that Jesus so perfectly revealed.

---

23. Irenaeus of Lyons, "Against Heresies," §7: *Gloria enim Dei vivens homo.* Literally: "For the glory of God is the living person."

24. Dupuis, *Toward a Christian Theology*, 299–300.

Sophia Enhances Life

"Whoever finds me finds life," declares divine Wisdom (Prov 8:35a). In making this declaration, Sophia tells us what to look for in religion: good religion does not *suppress* life; good religion *intensifies* it. Religion does not remove us from everyday events; religion places us deeper within them. In Betty Smith's *A Tree Grows in Brooklyn*, the character Francie Nolan aptly prays:

> Dear God . . . let me be something every minute of every hour of my life. Let me be gay; let me be sad. Let me be cold; let me be warm. Let me be hungry . . . have too much to eat. Let me be ragged or well dressed. Let me be sincere—be deceitful. Let me be truthful; let me be a liar. Let me be honorable and let me sin. Only let me be something every blessed minute. And when I sleep, let me dream all the time so that not one little piece of living is ever lost.[25]

Francie lives in a poverty-stricken neighborhood in a poverty-stricken borough, but no matter. Sophia enchants everyday life, rendering the ordinary extraordinary. She grants us that sudden insight and ongoing awareness that makes us more alive to life and more grateful for living. While she can produce mountaintop experiences, she does not rely on them, preferring instead to beautify the plains where most people live most of the time. Through her awareness, we become aware of the holiness of everyday experience—of chores and relaxation, work and vacation, dishes and meals, babies and diapers. Abba sustains every moment of our lives, Jesus participates in life with us, and Sophia brings life to its abundance, helping us recognize that each moment is sacred, even if each moment seems indistinguishable from every other moment in the long series of moments that constitute a life.

"The Spirit, then, is what interrupts the fallen worldly order and infuses it with the divine question, the divine lure, the divine life," writes Sarah Coakley.[26] The divine life is a life of awe—awe at being itself, awe that there is something rather than nothing. Awe grants us eyes to see the grandeur of the universe and the generosity of God (Isa 29:23), who gave before we could deserve. Such accurate perception allows us to feast on life instead of nibbling around the edges.

---

25. B. Smith, *Tree Grows in Brooklyn*, 421.
26. Coakley, *God, Sexuality, and Self*, 56.

An openness to the experience of awe may risk spiritual hedonism, a self-centered craving for religious pleasure. In individualistic religion, spiritual pleasure produces private enjoyment but no intensified concern for neighbor. Such hedonism is insufficient to faith. The gift of awe, if accepted deeply, never stops at personal gratification. Instead, awe transforms us. The giftedness of the universe, with all its superfluous beauty, opens us to God's generosity, then fills us with that same generosity. The other becomes our neighbor when we realize that all God's creatures are also God's beloved, and the gift is also for them. Now, having achieved a community of awe, we can share what Abraham Joshua Heschel calls *radical amazement*, celebrating together the knowledge that "just to be is a blessing. Just to live is holy."[27]

Awe also heightens our ability to perceive beauty, both that of the creation and that of God. The Christian tradition speaks too little about divine beauty, even though the Bible declares it to be worthy of desire:

> One thing I ask of you, YHWH:
>   one thing I seek:
> that I may dwell in your house
>   all the days of my life,
> to gaze on your beauty [*noam*]
>   and to meditate in your temple. (Ps 27:4)

The beauty of God is something to appreciate, not to possess. After its vision we let it go. Nevertheless, it leaves behind a charged universe. Sophia teaches us that creation, as divinely sustained, is not value neutral. God is beautiful, and the universe that God sustains bears this beauty: "It is delight that constitutes creation, and so only delight can comprehend it, see it aright, understand its grammar. Only in loving creation's beauty—only in seeing that creation truly *is* beauty—does one apprehend what creation is."[28] Saturated in beauty, the universe is not merely a collection of objects with varying degrees of utility. It is a work of art, an intricate fabric woven by the Trinity, ever pulsing with kaleidoscopic patterns. Things are good *in themselves*, not for what they can do for us. The universe is here for us to behold and love; indifference is blind.[29]

Because beauty has divine power, it can be put to demonic purposes. At the Nuremberg rallies, Hitler's Nazis used beauty to intoxicate

27. Heschel, *Moral Grandeur*, 264.

28. Hart, *Beauty of the Infinite*, 252.

29. Farley, *Eros for the Other*, 80–81.

Germans with racial hatred and a thirst for power over. To make sure the intoxication didn't wear off, Leni Riefenstahl documented the 1934 rally in her groundbreakingly manipulative *Triumph of the Will*, shown throughout the Reich. The film begins with Hitler flying to Nuremberg, his shining airplane piercing the clouds, then descending to earth like the chariot of a Norse god. As he preaches from his Germanic temple's rostrum, his manic disciples worship him as savior, forgetting that the antichrist always pretends to Christhood. They had been forewarned: well-organized, calculating evil can use any aspect of human culture— science, religion, education, beauty—to hateful ends, as Hitler and Rief-enstahl proved. Culture divorced from love is divorced from God, to its own inevitable destruction.

Beauty coupled with love, on the other hand, draws us out of our greed by forcing us to recognize that value lies *outside* us, as well as *inside* us. The exteriority of beauty invites us to acknowledge the significance of something besides ourselves, freeing the self from itself, uniting our hearts to the cosmos.[30] This state endures because love perpetually re-freshes beauty, allowing reality to always give more of itself, "like a stream pouring out of an infinite source." The thing that is beautiful overflows our categories of containment and control; it is always *more than* our concept of it.[31] Hence, boredom never infects accurate perception; God never gets bored.

Beauty is a good in itself, but it also opens us to truth. We sometimes prefer self-deceiving lies to unadorned reality, always to our own detri-ment. But if God is trustworthy, and God sustains a trustworthy universe, then we should trust reality as it is, without the embellishments of ego. We should be honest with ourselves and with others, *especially* when such honesty will produce the promising pain of growth. Jesus declares, "I am the way and the truth and the life" (John 14:6a), thereby associating the practice of love (the way) with the acceptance of truth and birth into new life. According to Jesus's own teaching, he only began this process, leaving it to Sophia to bring to completion: "I have much more to tell you, but you can't bear it now. When the Spirit of truth comes, she will guide you into all truth" (John 16:12–13a). Sophia empowers us to accept the truth about ourselves, because Sophia already knows this truth and loves us more than we will ever love ourselves. By accepting Sophia's truth, we

---

30. Murdoch, *Sovereignty of Good*, 59.

31. Farley, *Eros for the Other*, 82.

also accept her love for us *as we are*, and her invitation to become *who we might be*.

Sophia Grants Us Holy Desire

Desire quickens us, providing energy for activity. Desire can get a bad rap, because so much desire is unrequited. Whether we desire perfect love, or effortless money, or a just society, to desire is to experience frustration. For this reason, some wisdom teachers have advocated the complete transcendence of desire. Even if that is possible, it is not natural to the Christian tradition, based on the life and teachings of Jesus, who desired the inclusion of the excluded, reconciliation between enemies, and justice in society. Certainly, we can become consumed by petty desires for power, prestige, and recognition, but Sophia instills in us the holy desire for *more*—more love, more beauty, more peace, more hope, more justice, more faith, and more joy—so that we might be caught up into the life of God.[32]

The Greek word for desire is *eros*. Here, "erotic" is used in the broadest sense of the term, derived from the Greek *eros*, as the pervasive desire that animates the cosmos. Desire provides a goal, then bequeaths the energy needed to attain that goal. Desire thereby pulls us forward through time, granting life direction and purpose. Without desire there would be no frustration, but no motivation either. Without desire there would be none of the vitality evinced by Jesus of Nazareth, whose life was eros for the kingdom of God.

Unfortunately, in English, eros has become associated solely with sexual desire, or the erotic. Here, we are defining eros as the desire that animates the cosmos, including but not limited to sexual desire. Eros and desire are aspects of love, upon which the universe is founded.[33] Faith should bless eros rather than denigrate or ignore it, because eros is most basically the desire for relationship, the desire not just to *be*, but to *be with*. Eros is the attraction of one entity toward another and their movement into ever-deepening bonds.[34] As relational and attractive, eros expresses, resonates with, and lures us toward the interpersonal love within the Trinity.[35]

---

32. Coakley, *God, Sexuality, and Self*, 111.

33. Coakley, *God, Sexuality, and Self*, 8.

34. Coakley, *God, Sexuality, and Self*, 316.

35. Coakley, *God, Sexuality, and Self*, 10.

When we recognize divine creation as desirable, we reap an affection toward reality itself. This affection is *mystical*. The mystic feels fondly toward existence. Hence, mysticism is the opposite of aversion. It marvels at life, seeks unity with life, and plunges deeper into life. As always, our embodiment will complicate this intensification; even the greatest of saints will prefer the smell of flowers. But recognizing that all contrasts originate in God, and that God is benevolent, grants us an openness to the spectrum of experience even as we prefer some aspects to others. In this way we appreciate the warmth that follows the cold, just as we appreciate the divine healing that will follow all wounds.

Eros invites us to feel intimate with all things. To feel intimate with all things is to feel open to them, to participate in them and they in you, to derive energy from their energy and to grant them your own in an open process of mutual increase. If we are open, then we are capable of being intimate with the universe. If we are closed, then we separate ourselves from its magnificence. Through intimacy, we find ourselves alive in a world that is itself alive. At this point, observes Thomas Merton, "The gate of heaven is everywhere."[36]

Eros inevitably produces frustration. To desire God is to oscillate between absence and presence, disappointment and fulfillment, yearning and satisfaction. But this oscillation itself frees us from our spiritual inertia by granting us a foretaste of the more that is available. Through holy desire we are offered unending spiritual discovery. Paul writes:

> It's not that I have reached it yet, or have already finished my course; but I'm running the race to grab hold of the prize if possible, since Christ Jesus has grabbed hold of me. Sisters and brothers, I don't think of myself as having reached the finish line. I give no thought to what lies behind, but I push on [*epekteinomenos*] to what is ahead. My entire attention is on the finish line as I run toward the prize—the high calling of God in Christ Jesus. (Phil 3:12–13)

For Paul, salvation is not an event but a process within which one "presses on" and "strains toward." Since the process is never ending, our development is never ending as well.

Gregory of Nyssa called Paul's concept of "pushing on" *epektasis*. *Epektasis* is the perpetual progress of the finite toward the infinite, drawn by the beauty of infinity itself. This process denies any resolution or satiety

---

36. Merton, *Spiritual Master*, 146.

since the soul can never fully encompass God. We can stretch forever into the limitless, placing us in an everlasting paradox of frustration and advance, thirst and celebration. In this schema, God is not *unknowable*; God is endlessly *more knowable*. Sin is complacency and virtue is thirst: "Let anyone who is thirsty come to me, and let the one who believes in me drink," declares Jesus, promising his followers that the Spirit would flow out of their hearts like living water (John 7:37–39).[37] Faith begins in discontent yet ends in joy. Along the way, it shatters all the idols that pretend to ultimacy, that declare themselves triumphant, that craftily lure us into spiritual stasis.

Sophia Grants Us Freedom

"Now our God is the Spirit, and where the Spirit of our God is, there is freedom," declares Paul (2 Cor 3:17). God is a God of abundance, not of scarcity, so the Spirit of God inspires us to live lives of abundant freedom. With Sophia, we do not need strict rules and regulations that keep us on the narrow path in a dangerous world (Gal 5:18). Instead, we need the Trinity, through whom we Create in Love with Wisdom. This Trinitarian charge, to Create in Love with Wisdom, is our most basic calling as it fulfills Jesus's commandment to love God and neighbor. For this reason, Augustine interpreted love as the root of freedom: "Love, and do what you will: whether you hold your peace, through love hold your peace; whether you cry out, through love cry out; whether you correct, through love correct; whether you spare, through love do you spare: let the root of love be within, of this root can nothing spring but what is good."[38]

Sophia does not *displace* our personhood or will; she *fulfills* our personhood and will. Sophia reasons *with* us, acts *with* us, and bears consequences *with* us. Our transformation is like that of a person transformed by a book, or someone who recovers from childhood trauma, or who overcomes an addiction; we feel that the *new* self is our more authentic self, and when we look back upon our *old* self, we are thankful for self-surpassing. Sophia, as the power of the ever-increasing Trinity, is the Holy Spirit of self-surpassing. She grants us the discontentment we need to begin the journey, the energy we need to continue the journey, and gratitude that we are on the journey.

37. Blowers, "Maximus the Confessor," 151–53.
38. Augustine, "Homily 7," para. 8.

We are entering an age of increased receptivity to Sophia, in which we seek the alignment of our inner life and outer conduct. Previous generations were expected to power through, to endure rather than heal, to fulfill their duties no matter how scrambled they felt on the inside. Combat veterans came home after seeing their best friends shredded by shrapnel and were expected to be "strong," not "weak." So, they repressed their trauma, held down jobs, and started families; only their wives knew they woke up in the middle of the night screaming. Badly matched couples met their responsibilities to one another in loveless marriages, having been pressured into such by their elders. The children of farmers inherited and worked the farm even though they hated farming.

Increased freedom and awareness produce increased flourishing, and Sophia increases freedom and awareness. Therapy matches the wounded with the wise to produce healing, a variety of talking cures having replaced the obligation to suffer in silence. Marriages are expected to be fulfilling, not just functional; assistance is available to make them so. And a panoply of vocations allows young people to match their calling to the world's needs.

In the past, religious people may have been satisfied with indoctrination, with being told what *their* religion thinks, which is so much better than what the *other* religion thinks. If our tribe is good and their tribe is evil, then certainly our creed is holy and theirs is demonic. But this contrast simply reduces theology to ideology, a belief system that unites us *against* an enemy rather than uniting us *with* God.

Today, people don't want to be told what to think. They want to feel the enriching truth of faith. They want thinking, feeling, and acting to be triune, three aspects of one united person. Religious people today want to be whole. Sophia, as the harmonizing power within personality, works to grant this wholeness.

Sophia Is a Spirit of Love, Power, and Justice

We are continually transformed "because God's love [*agapē*] has been poured into our hearts through the Holy Spirit, who has been given to us," writes Paul (Rom 5:3b). Some critics of the Christian emphasis on love, disturbed by how unloving some Christians can be, have dismissed it as *luff*. This wordplay associates love with fluff, an airy insubstantiality that does nothing. We fluff up a pillow to make the stuffing take up more space; we fluff up an argument because we have three pages written and need to hand in a six-page paper. Fluffy love produces words about words and activity that enacts nothing. In sailing, the useless flapping of a sail in the wind is also called luff. Hollow words deny the church purpose and direction; luff denies the pilot all power of navigation. The boat with luffing sails drifts with the current. The pilot must immediately trim the sails to get rid of the luff and regain control of the boat.

To the extent that Christian love is luff, it is not agape. Agape is not fluffy, trivial, or useless. Agape changes everything, and Sophia grants the agapic love that empowers us to become agents of change. She is not meek; she is determined. Sophia herself declares: "I have good counsel and sound judgment; I have understanding and power as well" (Prov 8:14).

Through our inhabitation by Sophia we see with God's eyes, hear with God's ears, and act as God's hands. Now, we see what was previously rendered invisible and irrelevant. We see starving children so we can feed them, we see unhoused persons so we can shelter them, we see exploited workers so we can advocate for them, we see persecuted minorities so we can involve them. Just as God heard the Israelites' cry and freed them from Egypt, so we now hear the world's cry and liberate it from injustice: "Only they who hear with the ears of others can speak with the mouth of God," observes German theologian Dorothee Soelle.[39]

Sophia's work does not begin on Pentecost, with the foundation of the church. She, like Christ, is active *at* the beginning and *from* the beginning, in creation. Her inspirational work occurs in *all* times and places so that Jesus's continuing ministry of presence can occur in a *particular* time and place. For this reason, we can discern her activity before Christ, in Christ, and after Christ, especially in the work of the prophets, through whom God reveals the divine vision to humankind: "Prophecy never comes through an act of human will, but comes as people have spoken for God under the power of the Holy Spirit" (2 Pet 1:21).

Because Sophia acts in all times and all places, we can find her activity throughout the world, wherever people have worked for an expansion of love. Sophia's activity places within humankind a general knowledge of the good and the freedom to choose, for good or evil, so our lives are filled with moral consequence. We see the activity of Sophia wherever we see the activity of love. Simone Weil writes, "Every time that someone has, with a pure heart, called upon Osiris, Dionysus, Buddha, the Tao,

39. Soelle, *Silent Cry,* 293. See also 283–84.

etc., the Son of God has answered him by sending the Holy Spirit. And the Holy Spirit has acted upon his soul, not by inciting him to abandon his religious tradition, but by bestowing upon him light—and in the best of cases the fullness of light—in the heart of that same religious tradition."[40] According to Weil, where there is love, there is God, not in any *one* religious tradition, but in *all* religious traditions, so long as they are inspired by the "woman clothed with the sun" (Rev 12:1).

The most superficial acquaintance with human history reveals a tenacious darkness in our collective soul. Ours is a long history of cruelty, murder, lies, domination, exploitation, hoarding, arrogance, and scorn. Yet we can always find resistance as well, those saints who have worked to increase joy and reduce suffering, who have advocated compassion and rejected cruelty, who prefer truth to lies, who voluntarily and generously give more than they receive. Pockets of this resistance are everywhere, consisting of every race and gender and nation, formed by people of all religions and no religion, persevering despite the dangers of perseverance, acting in hope when reason counsels despair. This resistance, so apparently diverse, constitutes one holy family, "for all who are led by the Spirit of God are children of God" (Rom 8:14).

Sophia Is the Spirit of Rest and Peace

At this point, life with Sophia may sound exhausting. She is active and engaged, growing and changing, always loving dangerously and never abandoning hope. We may want to take a break *from* her, but instead we can take a break *with* her, because God too enjoys rest. After creating the cosmos, "The heavens and the earth and all their array were completed. On the seventh day God had finished all the work of creation, and so, on that seventh day, God rested. God blessed the seventh day and called it sacred, because on it God rested from all the work of creation" (Gen 2:1–3). On each previous day of creation, surveying the work of the divine hands, God had declared that work "good." But after the creation of humankind on the sixth day, God had declared creation "very good," because God has the company of persons made in the divine image. God has someone to enjoy that good work *with*. So lovely is this sharing that God decides to forever dedicate time to undistracted co-celebration. God

40. Weil, *Letter to a Priest*, 15.

creates the Sabbath, dedicating one day of the week to rest instead of work, to enjoyment instead of production, to being instead of becoming.

We should all be more like God, celebrating time as sacred. Perhaps we consider ourselves more energetic than God, not in need of rest and recreation. Perhaps we are driven by the need for recognition because we fail to recognize our full recognition in the eyes of God. Perhaps the pressure to produce comes from outside forces that threaten reprisal if we fail them. In any event, the need for productivity *and* enjoyment is woven into our being, because it is woven into God's being, from which our being derives.

Jesus, God as human, rested a lot, most often to pray (Luke 5:15–16; see also Mark 1:35; Mark 6:46; Luke 4:42; Luke 6:12; etc.). He worked hard teaching, healing, prophesying, traveling, surrounded by crowds, arguing for kindness in a cruel world, trying to turn our endemic hard-heartedness into compassion. Recognizing his human limitations, he remembered to love himself as he loved his neighbors and took time to recuperate, trusting God's promise: "My Presence will go with you, and I will give you rest" (Exod 33:14).

Jesus, being a good leader, wanted the same rest for his disciples that he himself needed. They traveled with him, worked with him, and became exhausted with him, much like those inspired by and working to implement his teachings today. After sending them into the countryside to minister, Jesus gathered them in again and, noting their weariness, advised them to escape to a deserted place, by themselves, to rest a while (Mark 6:31a). Today, he invites us to do the same: "Come to me, all you who labor and carry heavy burdens, and I will give you rest. Take my yoke upon your shoulders, for I am gentle and humble of heart. Here you will find rest for your souls, for my yoke is easy and my burden is light" (Matt 11:28–30).

Sunday as Sabbath has disappeared from modern culture, and regular rest has disappeared with it. Economists once predicted that, as per worker productivity improved, we would be able to work less. Instead, we are working more. No one knows exactly why. We consume more; our houses and cars are bigger and our lives filled with more gadgets. Medical care can save lives that would have been lost half a century ago, but is very expensive. Increasing population on a finite planet makes resources more expensive. Whatever the cause, it feels as if life is perpetually accelerating, like an out-of-control treadmill threatening to exhaust then discard us. We don't have time, but time has us.

This loss is significant. Stopping and resting helps us notice the beauty that we otherwise overlook. Finding that the world continues without our effort frees us from the anxiety produced by self-importance. Sabbath reminds us that, *without our effort*, the waves still lap the shore, the wind still rustles the leaves, the stream still makes its way to the sea. The Sabbath clarifies our spiritual vision, making a temple out of time, helping us to see God's activity by ceasing our own. Within this temple we find surprising abundance, an abundance that puts the lie to our scarcity mindset.[41] The Sabbath is Spirit as time, and the first step to perceiving her work is to see time as sanctuary.[42] We may doubt the availability of such experience in our age of busyness and distraction, but there is "still a rest reserved for God's people—the Sabbath rest. For all those who enter God's rest also rest from their own work, just as God did. Therefore, let us strive to enter into that rest" (Heb 4:9–11a).

Sophia hallows time because Sophia is a Spirit of peace and joy (Rom 14:17). Indeed, Jesus associates her arrival with the arrival of peace: "The Paraclete, the Holy Spirit whom Abba God will send in my name, will instruct you in everything, and she will remind you of all that I told you. Peace I leave with you; my peace I give to you; but the kind of peace I give you is not like the world's peace. Don't let your hearts be distressed; don't be fearful" (John 14:26–27). The arrival of Sophia, after the ascension of Jesus, is the arrival of Wisdom *and* the arrival of Peace, because Sophia is the Inner Reminder that God's covenant of peace cannot be removed (Isa 54:10). Secure in steadfast love, we can cast all our anxieties on God, in the confidence that God cares for us (1 Pet 5:7).

Sophia does not resolve the ambiguities of life for us. She is the Spirit of activity and rest, celebration and lament, freedom and responsibility, desire and satisfaction. Seeking certainty, we may want these tensions resolved in favor of an absolute—annihilating one pole of the relationship to create an artificial and unreliable simplicity. But Sophia denies us this resolution because she is the Spirit of life, and life thrives within generative tensions. God is not pure simplicity; God is perfectly harmonious, maximal complexity. We are made in the image of God, for balance and harmony, to which Sophia leads us. As our inner guide, she is the uncreated grace of life, the great compassion who is sensitive to our deepest longings. At Pentecost, she enters the church like fire, granting

41. Heschel, *Sabbath*, xviii.
42. Heschel, *Sabbath*, 70.

the fledgling community a seething desire for justice, the courage to speak truth, and the hope needed to manifest God's vision. Today, as we exert ourselves against humanity's stubborn tendency to self-destruction, even as we are tempted to despair in our efforts, Sophia assures God's co-creators of our inherent victory, whispering, "The kingdom will come."

7

Suffering, Love, and Joy

Soyen Shaku walked past a house where he heard much crying because
the master of the house lay dead. He entered, being well known in
the locality, sat down, and cried with them. Said one of those present,
"Master, how can you cry? Surely you are beyond such things?" Soyen
Shaku answered gently, "It is this which puts me beyond such things."

—Douglas John Hall[1]

Love Suffers, Celebrates, and Questions

"Is the whole universe worth the tears of one tortured child?" asks
Dostoevsky in *The Brothers Karamazov*.[2] He raises the perennial question: If God is love, then why do we suffer so much? This question burns
through the Bible, from Genesis to Revelation. Theologians call attempts
to answer this question *theodicy*, from the Greek *theos* (God) and *dikē*
(justice), or a "vindication of divine justice."

There are some topics that wise theologians avoid, humbly heeding
the psalmist: "YHWH, my heart has no lofty ambitions, my eyes don't

1. Hall, *God and Human Suffering*, 11.
2. Fyodor Dostoevsky; quoted in Fiddes, "Suffering in Theology," 178.

look too high. I am not concerned with great affairs or marvels beyond my scope" (Ps 131:1). We, being imprudent, shall indeed concern ourselves with great affairs and marvels beyond our scope. We aim too high when we attempt to reconcile human suffering with a loving God. Our answers will fail us, but that failure is necessary, because the struggle to answer is a spiritual discipline. Our failure will form us.

The goal is not a definitive solution; the goal is a strengthened soul. And thinking about God with others, freely and openly, strengthens the soul. This exercise is roughly analogous to the Zen practice of meditating on a koan. A *koan* is an unsolvable riddle: "What is the sound of one hand clapping?" The practitioner watches their mind search frantically for a solution, trapped in its addiction to definitive answers and firm truths. Eventually, the meditator realizes the futility of the search, but this realization does not produce defeat. Instead, it opens the meditator to the presence of a truth beyond language, accessed in a sudden flash of insight, or *satori*.

Likewise, with regard to theodicy, our conversation may not produce conclusions, but it can produce transformation. Such transformation is not rational (produced by reason and reducible to reason) nor is it irrational (in violation of reason). Instead, it is transrational, beyond reason, like the beauty of a melody or painting. And like beauty, such transformation can produce reliable truths that then inform all reasoning.

Theodicy is only for those who are *not* currently suffering, at least not any more than usual. For those in anguish, we can offer only our own tears: "Weep with the weeping," Paul advises (Rom 12:15). Those who are suffering will interpret any justification of God as an intellectual evasion of compassion. To speak of theodicy when your neighbor is suffering curses them with deeper loneliness; theodicy is incompatible with a ministry of presence.

Theodicy is for those who want to make sense of life and are willing to fail. Wrestling with theodicy *now* will at least save us from beginning the process—distraught, frantic, and desperate—when suffering strikes us later.

The book of Genesis offers a strange and powerful story. On the night before Jacob crosses the Jabbok to reconcile with his brother Esau, a stranger approaches him. They wrestle throughout the night until daybreak when the man, unable to defeat Jacob, injures Jacob's hip. Jacob eventually gains the upper hand, and the man demands to be let go. "Not until you give me a blessing," replies Jacob. In response, the man renames

Jacob Israel, or "he struggles with God." Jacob demands to know the man's name, but the man refuses to give it and departs. The injured Jacob then names the place Peniel, or "the face of God," because there he had seen the face of God and lived.

The story is remarkably honest, denying easy answers or hollow exhortations. To be in relationship with God is to wrestle, to triumph, to be injured, and to be blessed. The Hebrews could have been named those favored by God, those blessed by God, or those protected by God, but they were named "Israel," those who struggle with God. Today, we too are Israel because we too struggle with God.

We should not—yet must—attempt theodicy. We should not attempt theodicy because it does not help the suffering and may even harm them. We cannot succeed at theodicy because the answers never suffice. Yet we must offer a theodicy because human beings are the species that persistently, sometimes obsessively, asks why. This bold questioning is one of our greatest glories. We dare to ask questions that we cannot answer. Incessantly asking "Why does that happen?" has produced science—and knowledge of the universe down to the smallest quanta. It has produced philosophy, asking, "Why are we here?" It has produced psychology, asking, "Why do we act the way we do?" And it has produced theology, asking, "Why do we sense a God within and beyond our trying universe?" Because human beings are the species that asks why, we must ask why this loving God sustains such a trying universe. Embarking upon theodicy, we implicitly ask if our universe is comprehensible and risk the possibility that it may not be.

If we fail in our search for a final understanding of the *spiritual* universe, then we are not alone. The *physical* universe currently presents a similar opacity. Approximately 85 percent of the matter in the universe is dark matter of an unknown nature, approximately 68 percent of the energy in the universe is dark energy of an unknown nature, and physicists increasingly turn to an unobservable multiverse to explain their observations. Theists are no more obligated to cease their search for understanding than cosmologists. The current, and perhaps permanent, incompletion of the project does not render it worthless since progress occurs through the search itself. Perhaps, for both theology and cosmology, reconciliation will be ever approached though never achieved.

The most appropriate response to suffering will always be ethical, not intellectual. It will focus on what we *do*, not what we *think*. In a "perfect" world, we could never be heroic or sacrificially loving. But in this broken world we can work to heal. Love becomes the trademark practice of faith in a suffering world. Through the practice of love, we increase. This dangerous abundance blesses human thought, feeling, and action with so much significance that we call it holiness. To be holy is to bear both beauty and consequence. Given our status as a^ctive agents in an active world, our primary question should not be "Why is there suffering?" Our primary questions should be "How can we alleviate suffering? And how can we alleviate it *together*?"

To Alleviate Suffering, We Must Recognize That Different Wounds Require Different Balms

My wife, Abby Henrich, is a pastor. Over two decades of ministry, she has supported, counselled, prayed with, and prayed for numerous parishioners with numerous challenges. Almost all these challenges were different in some way. Parishioners have struggled to recover from childhood trauma, sexual abuse, substance abuse disorders, and mental illness. Parishioners have gone through divorce, unemployment, and unexpected bereavement. Some have had trouble conceiving children, suffered miscarriages, and developed postpartum depression. Others have died after long, painful battles with cancer. Youth have come out as LGBTQ+ and worried about the reaction of their peers. Our entire community has struggled with the vexing grief of suicide.

Each difficulty and each individual require a different pastoral response. People with addictions need strength, divorcees need hope, abuse survivors need healing, youth need love, the unemployed need advice, and the terminally ill need courage. There is no one-size-fits-all response to suffering, no if-then algorithm to prescribe the perfect response to every situation, no single balm that heals every wound. Human problems are manifold, and our responses to them must be manifold as well, if we wish to heal. Pastors—as well as parishioners themselves, because they are also involved in healing—must be flexible, wise, and present.

Jesus was a pastor who healed in manifold ways. He healed spiritually, revealing the perfect love of God for all and the infinite value of each. He healed socially, erasing the artificial boundaries that segregationists had manufactured. He healed ethically, demanding the practice of love in a world riven by hate. He healed physically, curing people of disease.

He even turned water into wine at a wedding, to make sure the dancing wouldn't stop.

YHWH, Abba, God as Architect, designs and sustains a world that privileges dynamic growth over static ease, because the greatest gift we can receive is that of an enlarging soul. God recognizes the inevitable injury that will befall us as our souls confront the challenges that enlarge them. Jesus, God as Sojourner, enters creation to ratify the divine decision, validate our struggle, and reveal the fullness of life available within the difficulty of life. Sophia, God as Wisdom, continues the multiform healing ministry of Jesus, *through our activity*, inspiring humankind toward the love, justice, and wholeness that characterize the kingdom of God.

Consequently, the Trinity acts *for* us, but the Trinity also acts *with* us. We become who we are by acting *with* the Trinity, by becoming Trinitarian. *Faith fulfills our Trinitarian nature.* Faith is an existential possibility, an option for living, the experiential *more* for which we have hungered and for which there is satisfaction. To savor this abundance is to savor God.[3]

Alas, the abundance is often obscured by loneliness, conflict, anxiety, bereavement, anger, self-hatred, other-hatred, regret, guilt, shame, addiction, poverty, illness (sometimes terminal), depression, meaninglessness, and more. The range of human suffering is as deep and broad as human brokenness itself. Jesus is a physician (Mark 2:17), and every physician knows that different diseases require different treatments. There is no panacea, physical or spiritual.

For this reason, the love of Abba, Jesus, and Sophia is as diverse as human needs and takes as many forms as there are human difficulties. *Any interpretation of their cooperative work must recognize the many healings that they offer and not reduce that multiplicity to one limited story.* The theological approach to human suffering must be pluralistic, utilizing a variety of approaches to heal a variety of ills. Thus, in this chapter, we will not discuss the *one* way that the Trinity heals; we will discuss the *many* ways that the Trinity heals.

Trinitarian healing is no opiate. Recognizing the challenges of life, Trinitarian faith seeks to *heal* the pain, not *dull* the pain. It offers transformation, not symptom relief. And, like the healing of a this-worldly physician, spiritual healing happens here and now, not in some lofty metaphysical realm or far-flung future.

3. Boff, *Trinity and Society*, 175.

The Trinity Heals by Offering Us Full Personhood

The triune God is the source of all personality, the esteemer of each and every person, and the quickening ground of interpersonal relationships. God makes true personhood possible. But if true personhood is possible, and if we are created for fullness of life, then this state begs the question: How true am I as a person? How closely do I follow the grain of the divinely sustained universe? How much do I cut across that grain, rendering my own journey—and that of those around me—more difficult?

Jesus reveals the abundant life available to us as embodied souls, as expanses of feeling resident within material bodies. Jesus jars us out of our existential slumber into new life pervaded by possibility. Faith trusts that this new life is possible because faith trusts that God has not created us absolutely different from God, but has created us in God's own image, to participate in the life of God. Indeed, we are so like God that one of *us*, Jesus, can be called the Child of God.

Jesus is the picture of divine life, the earthly manifestation of the Trinitarian relationality that lies within, beneath, and beyond the fabric of the universe. He exemplifies humanity as a perfect expression of openness and vulnerability. He is communion itself; in Jesus we see love perfectly expressed through human activity. We experience him as fully human and fully divine, and we sense our own invitation to become fully human, which is to become love.

Sin Is Separation

If love unifies, then sin separates. Instead of reaching out to others, we coil into ourselves. We do this as individuals, sacrificing the common good to our petty selfishness. We do it as groups, looking for that negative reference group that our in-group can organize itself *against*. Such separation defies the intention of God, who has joined all things together. All reality is nondual, united in agape. Separation *itself*—separation from the environment so that we can exploit it, separation from our neighbors so that we can use them, separation from other religions so that we can condemn them—separation itself is sin, a tear in the fabric of being that demands mending.[4]

---

4. Habito, *Living Zen, Loving God*, 36–37.

Sin alienates us from one another, then helps us come to terms with that alienation through the ruse of *pride*. Pride interprets the self as separate from and higher than others. In a bid to mend the fabric of being, Jesus declares, "The last will be first, and the first will be last" (Matt 20:16). He is trying to save us from ourselves, condemning our prideful- ness, counseling the participation of an open self in an open community. The strength of this community is predicated on the strength *and open- ness* of the selves that constitute it.

Jesus also tries to save us from self-trivialization. Everyone has a sense for the transcendent woven into the universe. Everyone senses that mere matter cannot exhaustively explain the beauty and power coursing through experience. Sophia is present, within and without, inviting us to overcome. We fear difficulty, but ease and comfort are the real dangers. Returning home after spending World War II in a Japanese POW camp, Ernest Gordon wrote:

> [After the war,] everyone spoke of seeking security. But what did security mean but animal comfort, anaesthetized souls, closed minds, and cold hearts? It meant a return to the cacophonous cocktail party as a substitute for fellowship, where, with glass in hand, people would touch each other but never meet. They would speak, but nothing would be said and nothing heard. They would look at their partners, but would not see them. With glassy eyes they would stare past them into nothingness.[5]

Riskless life pains the living God, who offers us more. Since vitality is God's desire for us, triviality is sinful. Hell might very well be air-conditioned.

The Trinity Delivers Us beyond Eden

Given the intransigence of our self-inflicted misery, we may be tempted to sigh for Eden. A return to innocence, simplicity, and unstudied spon- taneity can prove attractive to anyone struggling through the inevitable complexities and disappointments of adulthood. But the fullness of life lies beyond Eden, not in a return to Eden. Could God's purpose for us have been fulfilled by running around naked in a garden for all time? Such a life would not have fulfilled the image of God within us, an image that includes the capacity for reason, the ability to create, and the necessity of choosing between good and evil. To fulfill the image of God within us, we

5. E. Gordon, *To End All Wars*, 223.

had to become more than naked innocence. We had to become experience, and not just any experience, but experience that transcends itself.

If experience surpasses innocence, then we should thank God that Eve ate the fruit. It may have been God's plan all along. Every child who learns the Adam and Eve story asks why God put the serpent in the garden, as well as the tree itself. If the goal was perpetual ignorance, then why not just leave them out? Of course, God also told Adam (not Eve, at least not directly) not to eat of the fruit. But Paul notes the tendency of any law to cause its own disobedience: "Does it follow that the Law is sin? Of course not! Yet I wouldn't have known what sin was except for the Law. And I didn't know what 'to covet' meant until I read, 'Do not covet.' But sin, seizing the opportunity afforded by the commandment, produced in me every kind of covetousness" (Rom 7:7).

Eden was a setup. God put the tree in the garden and said, "Don't eat from that tree." Then, God put a serpent in the garden as well. We mistakenly associate the serpent with Satan, an association foreign to ancient Jewish symbolism. Serpents were associated with intelligence, not evil, as the story itself suggests: "Now the serpent was more crafty [*arum*] than any of the wild animals the Lord God had made" (Gen 3:1a NIV). The Hebrew word *arum*, as applied to the serpent, has been translated as "crafty," "cunning," "clever," "subtle," "shrewd," and "intelligent." But when applied to a person, as in Prov 14:8, it can be translated as "prudent" or "sensible." Jesus himself says, "Be wise as serpents" (Matt 10:16b).

Eve admired this quality of the serpent, then aspired to it: "And when the woman saw that the tree was good for food, and that it was pleasant to the eyes, and a tree to be desired to make one wise, she took of the fruit thereof, and did eat, and gave also unto her husband with her; and he did eat" (Gen 3:6 KJV). Western Christianity has called this event the fall. We will take a contrary approach.

Eve does not cause the fall; Eve causes the rise. God needed a hero to cooperate with the divine plan and set humankind on the trying path of *theosis*, or divinization, that process through which we draw ever closer to the unreachable God. God needed a hero to lift humankind from preconsciousness to consciousness, a hero who could grant us the freedom within which we can relate to one another meaningfully. Eve is that hero. As the founder of culture, she leads us into understanding. Genesis itself records this rise, as it remembers the first generations: "Adah gave birth to Jabal, the ancestor of those who live in tents and raise livestock. His brother was Jubal, the ancestor of all those who play the harp and the flute. Zillah gave birth to Tubal-Cain, the forebear of blacksmiths and coppersmiths" (Gen 4:20–22a). Through Eve's decision, humanity's "eyes were opened." We have gained unimaginable abilities, discerning the tiniest elements of nature, observing the farthest reaches of space, visiting the darkest depths of the sea, and the journey continues.

Alas, awareness is painful. Adam and Eve, like toddlers becoming children, realized that they were naked. Ashamed, they made clothes for themselves. Then they took these clothes off to make babies, the brothers Cain and Abel, who grew into strong young men. And so the violence began. Our freedom to participate in moral judgment, to choose between good and evil, results in Cain's murder of Abel. We became free, but we used that freedom to initiate violence against the innocent. Even if we did not *initiate* the violence, we became free to respond in a disproportionate, retaliatory manner. Cain's descendant Lamech declares: "Adah and Zillah, listen to my voice, spouses of Lamech, hear what I say: I killed a man who wounded me—a youth who merely struck me! If Cain's deed will be avenged sevenfold, then Lamech's will be avenged seventy-seven times!" (Gen 4:23–24) Lamech's berserk vengefulness anticipates eons of human violence. We have been immersed in needless brutality like fish immersed in poisoned water, too accustomed to the situation to realize that anything is wrong.

We cannot undo Eve's decision. Although some of us may sigh for Eden, there will be no return to innocence: "So YHWH drove them from the garden of Eden, and sent them to till the soil from which they had been taken. Once they were banished, winged sphinxes with fiery, ever-turning swords were placed at the entrance to the garden of Eden to guard the way to the Tree of Life" (Gen 3:23–24). Genesis declares that our expulsion from innocence to experience is permanent. We cannot go back, and we should not want to. Instead, we must go forward. If abundant life is to be found, then we will find it east of Eden, where joy and suffering entwine.

The Play of Contrasts Generates Meaning

Our eventual wholeness must place us beyond our starting point, beyond naivete. Just as no child in the womb can anticipate what life will be like outside the womb, Adam and Eve could not anticipate what life would be like outside Eden. In all probability, they feared the agony but could not anticipate the ecstasy.

God places us within the play of contrasts, such as agony and ec-stasy, to grant us significance. Beings and events reveal their fullness only in relation to their opposite which, through its opposition, brings them to completion. Hence, they are not opposites; they are *mutually amplifying contrasts*. The gnostic Gospel of Philip declares: "Light and darkness, life and death, right and left, are siblings of one another. They are inseparable."[6] The Gospel asserts that reality, like God, is dialectical—giving, receiving, changing, growing.

Therefore, we should be unsurprised by our own movement through contrasts. God creates both the light and the darkness (Gen 1:1–5), that the light might shine in the darkness (John 1:5), because there it shines most brightly. Thus, the meeting places of contrasts are not borders; they are areas of exchange where each flows into and out of the other. Partici-pation in this process makes us larger, freer, and more compassionate.[7]

Compassion is not easy. At some point, exhausted by the flux of life and doubtful of the good God, we will all join in Job's lament: "Who con-tinues to bruise someone when they're broken and screaming for help? In the past didn't I weep for the troubled? Didn't I grieve for the oppressed? But when I expected good, evil came; when I waited for the light, dark-ness came" (Job 30:24–26). Love in a dangerous universe requires cour-age. To be in deep relationship with someone is to be vulnerable, not just to that person, but to all that might happen to them. For this reason, many retreat from dangerous relation into safer isolation, where the suf-ferings of others cannot reach them.

Why counsel compassion in a suffering world? Prudence suggests that compassion is too costly. But mysteriously, compassion grants us more joy, more hope, and more peace. These blessings seem to arise from relationality itself, from our human love which serves as a conduit of divine love. Compared with the safety of isolation, the risk of love now seems alive.

I myself have resisted love. When our first child, Josiah, was born, it was a thrill to watch him develop. His first smile, his first giggle, his lurching attempts to crawl, his drunken stumbling as he learned how to walk, the music as he exclaimed "Dada!" or "Mama!" were all gifts. Yet what I found was that, as Josiah grew, I began to love him more than I had anticipated. I began to experience a terrifying tenderness, and that

6. Isenberg, "Gospel of Philip," 142.
7. Steindl-Rast, *Deeper than Words*, 39.

scared me, because Josiah is mortal. I had no God-given assurance that everything in my life and in my children's lives would pan out the way I wanted it to. As my love for Josiah grew, my fear grew along with it. What if something went wrong? What if there was a car accident?

We mute the song of the universe with fearful, cautious earplugs. We must risk grief to live life well.[8] My own advocacy of relationality and vulnerability rightfully opens me to criticisms of socioeconomic privilege. My own vulnerability is much less dangerous than the vulnerability of workers in the developing world, women in misogynistic societies, sexual minorities under fundamentalist regimes, and ethnic minorities under nationalist governments. It might be arrogant to prescribe vulnerability from my safe suburban home. To address this legitimate concern, I will turn to the assistance of Toni Morrison.

Toni Morrison's *Beloved* is a novel about American Blacks living during the time of slavery. As such, it grants us a literary example of human openness under conditions of horrific suffering. In the novel, two characters disagree about the extent to which a human being should love in a racist, violent world. The maternal character, Sethe, is willing to risk love, while her lover Paul D recoils from such vulnerability: "Risky, thought Paul D, very risky. For a used-to-be-slave woman to love anything that much was dangerous, especially if it was her children she had settled on to love. The best thing, he knew, was to love just a little bit, so when they broke its back, or shoved it in a croaker sack, well, maybe you'd have a little love left over for the next one."[9]

Paul D, understandably, wants to protect his self from the cruelties of White enslavers. To protect his self, he must not love too much. The invulnerability that he pursues leaves him with enough self to survive loss, even the horrible losses experienced by Blacks in mid-nineteenth-century America. But Sethe disagrees; she *must* love: "That's the way it is, Paul D. I can't explain it to you no better than that, but that's the way it is. If I have to choose—well, it's not even a choice."[10]

Why would Sethe, placed in a horribly dangerous situation, assent to love others who are subject to the very same danger? Because she has discovered that love cannot be separated from life without loss of life. In Sethe's condition, her only power is the superabundant love that prudence demands she resist. She realizes that this love, in this situation,

8. J. Butler, *Frames of War*, 15.

9. Morrison, *Beloved*, 45.

10. Morrison, *Beloved*, 45.

will necessitate her suffering. Yet she chooses it as an expression of her passion for life. The enslavers may steal her body, her sex, and her labor, and they may try to steal her children, but they cannot steal her love.

Sethe exemplifies the dangerous love that lies at the heart of God. If God is three persons united into one community through love, then vulnerability belongs to God. Therefore, God cannot be apathetic, unfeeling, or unchanging. Instead, God is passionate and emotional. To correct millennia of theological discourse about the unfeeling God, we now need theology that extols the openness of God to the world in all its glory and suffering. God no longer *transcends* human emotionality. Instead, God is the *depth and source* of human emotionality.

The Unifying Love of God Strengthens Us

God has chosen to be a "plenitude of longing love," writes Sarah Coakley, who invites us into "full and ecstatic participation in the divine, Trinitarian life."[11] Life arises when we *love God back* and participate in the archetypal Love of which all worldly love is an expression. Paul prays that:

> God, out of the riches of divine glory, will strengthen you inwardly with power through the working of the Spirit. May Christ dwell in your hearts through faith, so that you, being rooted and grounded in love, will be able to grasp fully the breadth, length, height, and depth of Christ's love and, with all God's holy ones, experience this love that surpasses all understanding, *so that you may be filled with all the fullness of God.* (Eph 3:16–19 [emphasis added])

To be filled with the fullness of God is to live according to the intention of Abba, as exemplified by Jesus, as inspired by Sophia. Together, the Trinitarian persons elevate us out of our selves into their selves.

Our parishioner Nicole Lawless had a very powerful experience of this elevation. Struggling as an adolescent with a potentially lethal illness, she received concrete intervention from God:

> I went through so much growing up—it was some tough stuff. I also had a severe eating disorder. In bed one night—I thought I would die—for real. I swear that God, Jesus, the Holy Ghost came to me—told me to get up and go eat a piece of bread. I was to think of myself as a separate person—step outside myself and

11. Coakley, *God, Sexuality, and Self*, 10.

see myself as a child and take care of her. This was God's will for me. No one was going to take care of me, but it was an insult to God for me to disrespect myself. This is God's child, I heard, I felt or sensed. I think of that a lot. It's tough love, but it works for me whenever I want to give up. God says no—I made you—I want you to keep trying. And when you learn how your pain can help others, then there is hope, there are reasons to stay open to life's challenges.[12]

The psalms refer to God as "our refuge and strength, a very present help in times of trouble" (Ps 46:1). For Nicole, this passage offers a concrete description of God's activity, not an abstract idea about the divine nature. God will help us to do what we can't.

Jesus, the Child of God, had a very strong sense of self that he placed in service of others. The authorities feared him because he was strong, not because he was weak. Even more dangerously, he shared his strength with others. The powerful, sensing an increase in power among the powerless, responded with violence. They do the same today because tyrants want us to have a weak sense of self. Unsure people are easily controlled, while confident people can disrupt the tyrants' systems of privilege.

Healthy self-love is distinct from pathological self-love because healthy self-love opens us up to the other—divine or human—while pathological self-love closes us off. The true self wants to live and give life, and it does so by giving and receiving love: "We know that we have passed from death to life because we love our sisters and brothers; if we refuse to love we are still dead," writes John (1 John 3:14). Too often we fear the wrong death. We fear the death of the old self for the new because we *are* the old self, and we are attached to ourselves as we are. To avoid transformation, we restrict ourselves to a love that we can manage. We are like caterpillars that are perfectly comfortable with their familiar tree branch and resolve never to fly.

Who are we called to love? An expert in the Jewish law poses this question to Jesus:

> "Teacher, what must I do to inherit everlasting life?" Jesus answered, "What is written in the law? How do you read it?" The expert on the law replied: "You must love the Most High God with all your heart, with all your soul, with all your strength, and with all your mind, and your neighbor as yourself." Jesus said, "You have answered correctly. Do this and you'll live." But the

12. Nicole Lawless, email to author, Apr. 3, 2022.

expert on the law, seeking self-justification, pressed Jesus further: "And just who is my neighbor?" Jesus replied, "There was a traveler going down from Jerusalem to Jericho, who fell prey to robbers. The traveler was beaten, stripped naked, and left half-dead. A priest happened to be going down the same road; the priest saw the traveler lying beside the road, but passed by on the other side. Likewise there was a Levite who came the same way; this one, too, saw the afflicted traveler and passed by on the other side. But a Samaritan, who was taking the same road, also came upon the traveler and, filled with compassion, approached the traveler and dressed the wounds, pouring on oil and wine. Then the Samaritan put the wounded person on a donkey, went straight to an inn and there took care of the injured one. The next day the Samaritan took out two silver pieces and gave them to the innkeeper with the request, 'Look after this person, and if there is any further expense, I'll repay you on the way back.' Which of these three, in your opinion, was the neighbor to the traveler who fell in with the robbers?" The answer came, "The one who showed compassion." Jesus replied, "Then go and do the same." (Luke 10:25–37)

The expert in the law wants Jesus to provide him with a categorical grid, a map of humanity that will tell him who is an ally and who is an enemy, who is in and who is out. Jesus, the preacher of the cosmic Creator who loves all their children, turns the question on its head. For the protagonist of the story, he selects a despised Samaritan, a resident of Judaea to whom many in his audience would have denied the status of neighbor, yet who acts neighborly. The villains of the story are the indifferent priest and Levite who are too rich, important, and busy to dirty their hands helping the unfortunate man. Jesus's atypical cast of characters obliterates the questioner's preexisting categorical grid and denies him the usual markers of ethnicity, religion, and social status by which to determine human value.

But Jesus isn't simply trying to transform the man's categorical grid. Jesus is trying to transform *the man himself* by inviting him into the mind of the universal Mother and Father who deem all humanity their children, who want us to treat one another, not just as neighbors, but as family. John sums up the teaching rather bluntly: "If you say you love God but hate your sibling, you are a liar. For you cannot love God, whom you have not seen, if you hate your neighbor, whom you have seen. If we love God, we should love our siblings as well; we have this commandment from God" (1 John 4:20–21).

As the symbol of God, Jesus loves those whom society deems un-lovable, thereby restoring the unloved to society. At the same time, he frees society from its anxiety-producing stratifications and exclusions. Jesus heals through touch (John 9:2–3; Matt 8:1–3), erasing the false boundaries of inclusion and exclusion that have no place in the Vision of God, placing everyone at the center of a new commonwealth that has no boundaries.

To be clear: in his healing, Jesus is not condemning disability. Jesus is condemning our rejection of the disabled. Jesus heals, not to show that these persons should be accepted *now*, but to show that their exclusion was *always wrong*. First and foremost, it is the self-righteous judgmental-ism of the abled that Jesus is treating in these stories.[13]

Love Will Sacrifice for Justice

The love of Jesus reveals the love of God as *active*. Love is much more than a feeling or a thing—love is something you do (1 John 3:16–18). To participate in love is to participate in God; to refuse to participate in love is to refuse to participate in God. Too often, faced with exploita-tion, oppression, and injustice—with an insufficiently loving and unjust society—we do nothing. We adopt a stance of apathy to protect ourselves from their suffering while we continue to profit from their suffering through cheap food, cheap products, and cheap services.

Faith understands the hungry to be our family whom we allow to starve.[14] It also recognizes that, by God's own choice, God has no other hands than ours.[15] But becoming the hands of God will not grant us the kind of life we tend to fantasize about, a life of ease, recognition, and money. Instead, to become the hands of God involves sacrifice. This sac-rifice is not *to* God, in order to placate the divine wrath. This sacrifice is *for* God, in order to create a more compassionate world and increase the divine joy. To use more technical language, the sacrifice that God val-ues is not *propitiatory*—it does not attempt to appease God or atone for sin. Instead, the sacrifice is *creative*—it participates in God by repairing

---

13. Voss Roberts, *Body Parts*, 33–35.

14. Soelle, *Inward Road*, 26.

15. Soelle, *Suffering*, 149.

society, sometimes at great personal risk. To challenge injustice is to pick up the cross.[16]

Creative suffering that overcomes injustice reduces the needless suffering caused by injustice. One example of unjust, needless suffering is the countless animals that have been killed over the millennia as sacrifices to appease wrathful deities. Like most early religions, ancient Judaism practiced animal sacrifice to purify the nation of its sins, thus making atonement with God:

> [Aaron] shall slaughter the goat of the purification offering that is for the people and bring its blood inside the curtain and do with its blood as he did with the blood of the bull, sprinkling it upon the cover and before the cover. Thus he shall make atonement for the sanctuary, because of the uncleannesses of the Israelites and because of their transgressions, all their sins . . . When he has finished atoning for the holy place and the tent of meeting and the altar, he shall present the live goat. Then Aaron shall lay both his hands on the head of the live goat and confess over it all the iniquities of the Israelites, and all their transgressions, all their sins, putting them on the head of the goat and sending it away into the wilderness by means of someone designated for the task. The goat shall bear on itself all their iniquities to a barren region, and the goat shall be set free in the wilderness. (Lev 16:15–22 NRSV)

Our modern minds have several reactions to this passage that ancient minds would not. First, we may note that neither the goat that was killed nor the goat that was driven into the wilderness had done anything morally wrong, they being goats. Like the legendary whipping boys of medieval Europe, they bore the sins of another, though innocent themselves. The scapegoating ritual reiterates one of Adam and Eve's first abuses of their moral freedom: blame externalization. When Abba asks why they are clothed and if they had eaten fruit from the tree of the knowledge of good and evil, Adam blames Eve and Eve blames the serpent. This instinct to assign responsibility for our own transgressions to others continues in the religiously sanctioned ritual slaughter of animals.

Prior to the prescription of ritual slaughter, Abba had already revealed themselves to the Israelites as merciful and forgiving: "I AM! I am God, YHWH, compassionate and gracious, slow to anger, abundant in kindness and faithfulness; faithful to the thousandth generation, forgiving

16. Soelle, *Thinking about God*, 133.

injustice, rebellion, and sin" (Exod 34:6–7a). Today, one wonders why the ritualists ever thought that a God who identifies as merciful and forgiving would be propitiated by the slaughter of the innocent.

We may also wonder why the ritualists thought that God *needed* sacrifice, or any kind of transactional relationship with humanity, as if God had an empty belly that only priests could fill. But this idea of exchange between humanity and divinity, of a mutual relationship based on mutual need, permeated the ancient world. During sacrifices in Roman religion, the priest would pray, *Do ut des*, or "I give so that you may give." The sponsor of the sacrifice did not give out of gratitude or generosity; the sponsor of the sacrifice gave to get. The ritual presumed that the gods would materially benefit from the sacrifice and respond with material benefits to the sponsor of the sacrifice. The ritual presumed a divine-human ledger sheet.[17]

God is an overflowing fountain of life, not a bartering merchant. The Hebrew psalmists recognized the inadequacy of such a petty, transactional god and encouraged the practice of gratitude instead of propitiatory sacrifice. Writing in the voice of God, Ps 50 declares:

> I don't need oxen from your stall,
>   or goats from your folds,
> since every beast of the forest is mine already;
>   I have cattle on a thousand hills! . . .
> Do I eat the flesh of oxen, or drink the blood of goats?
>   Offer me a sacrifice of thanksgiving instead,
>   and fulfill the vow you make to me! (Ps 50:9–10, 13–14)

The uselessness of sacrificial animals' suffering is not an insight of the modern animal rights movement. Anyone with an adequate concept of God as beyond neediness would see the needlessness of ritualized animal slaughter, as did Isaiah thousands of years ago: "Slaughtering an ox is like murdering a person; sacrificing a lamb is like breaking a dog's neck" (Isa 66:3).

Apparently, God rejects human sacrifice as well as animal sacrifice. The progenitor of the Israelites, Abraham, had come within a hair's breadth of sacrificing his son, Isaac, to YHWH. This story reassured the Israelites that they were as devoted to YHWH as their religious neighbors were to Molech and Baal, even though their religious neighbors (according to Hebrew testimony) offered human sacrifices. The Israelites, on

17. Watson, *State, Law, and Religion*, 41.

the other hand, had been forbidden from offering human sacrifices to
YHWH (see Deut 12:31; Lev 18:21; etc.) Nevertheless, it appears that,
overawed by the ritual devotion of human sacrifice, some Israelites suc-
cumbed to temptation and practiced it.

The prophets and historians of Judaism roundly condemn these actions. Ezekiel laments, writing in the voice of God, "You slaughtered my
children and sacrificed them to the idols" (Ezek 16:21). Jeremiah repeatedly condemns the Israelites for child sacrifice. Writing in the voice of
God, three times he laments their backsliding into an abomination which
God did not command or decree, a crime so foul it could never have
entered the divine mind (Jer 7:31; 19:5; 32:35). According to the biblical
historians, both Ahaz and Manasseh, kings of Judah, sacrificed their sons
in the fire and were punished by YHWH for doing so (2 Kgs 16:1–4;
21:1–6; see also 1 Sam 15:22–23). All agree that *human sinfulness is not
reduced by inflicting useless suffering; it is increased.*

Jesus Prioritizes Agapic Love over against Propitiatory Sacrifice

In the ongoing debate between legal rigorists and the prophets of justice,
Jesus specifically identifies with the prophets. His mother may have had
something to do with this, since she herself seems to prefer the God of
the prophets to the God of the hierarchs. Upon learning that she would
bear the Christ child, Mary offers the first meditation on the meaning of
Christ, which makes her the first Christian theologian. In so doing, she
reiterates many of the social inversion themes of the prophets such as
Hannah (1 Sam 2:8), in which Abba promises to correct the cruel stratifications of society:

> My soul proclaims your greatness, O God,
>   and my spirit rejoices in you, my Savior. . . .
> You have shown strength with your arm;
>   you have scattered the proud in their conceit;
> you have deposed the mighty from their throne,
>   and raised the lowly to high places.
> You have filled the hungry with good things,
>   while you have sent the rich away empty.
>   (Luke 1:46–47, 51–53)

According to Mary, God actively rejects distorted values that deem persons to be worth more than or less than others, a distortion that God never intended for one human family.

In keeping with Mary's prophecy, Jesus explicitly identifies himself with the prophetic lineage when he begins his ministry. Anticipating his intense focus on the universal, unconditional love of God for all, especially those unloved by society, he quotes Isa 61, which declares good news to the poor and release to the captives. This emphasis on love and justice continues throughout Jesus's ministry, both explicitly and implicitly. When Jesus is criticized for dining with tax collectors and sinners, he instructs his critics to "go and learn what this means, 'I desire mercy, not sacrifice'" (Matt 9:9–13; see also Matt 12:7). Here, he is quoting another Hebrew prophet of justice, Hosea. Writing in the voice of God, Hosea had declared, "For I desire kindness toward others, not sacrifice; acknowledgement of God, not burnt offerings" (Hos 6:6).

When an expert in Jewish law asks Jesus which commandment is the most important, Jesus points to love of God and love of neighbor. The lawyer approves of Jesus's emphasis on love, declaring that "this is much more important than all burnt offerings and sacrifices," to which Jesus replies, "You are not far from the kingdom of God" (Mark 12:28–43a). Elsewhere, Jesus condemns those who legalistically give a tenth of their income to the temple but neglect justice, mercy, and faithfulness (Matt 23:23). And Hebrews has Jesus quote Ps 40: "You [YHWH, Abba] who wanted no sacrifice or oblation prepared a body for me, in burnt offerings or sacrifices for sin you took no pleasure" (Heb 10:5–6; Ps 40:6).

Jesus's rejection of propitiatory sacrifice determines our interpretation of his crucifixion. Jesus did not die to satisfy the wrath of an angry God *against* us. Jesus died because he had revealed the love of a forgiving God *for us.* When he went to Jerusalem with the disciples, he attempted to worship in the temple but never made it past the courtyard, so enraged was he by the commerce taking place. He cleansed the temple, driving out the merchants, overturning the tables of the money changers, and chasing away those selling sacrificial animals (Mark 11:15–18).

Because temple commerce was so important to the Jerusalem economy, Jesus's actions enraged the power elite to the point of murder. When evening came, he and the disciples left Jerusalem. I wonder if that night, realizing how much he had upset a cruel hierarchy, realizing that their vengeance was at hand, Jesus said to his disciples (and here I'm paraphrasing): "Like anybody, I would like to live a long life—longevity has its place.

But I'm not concerned about that now. I just want to do God's will. . . . And so I'm happy tonight; I'm not worried about anything; I'm not fearing any man. Mine eyes have seen the glory of the coming of the Lord."[18]

Martin Luther King was murdered the day after giving that speech. He was murdered for attempting to repair relations between Blacks and Whites, and between the rich and the poor, to the benefit of all. Two thousand years earlier, Jesus attempted to repair relations through his teaching and actions, at the cost of his life. Repairing the world will bring both great joy and great suffering. Being love to souls in separation, who have grown accustomed to that separation, who are miserable but used to it, is dangerous. Monica Coleman asks, "Do you want to be made well? I like this question for all that's behind it. The healers are asking: Are you willing to have a new experience? You know sickness, but you don't know wellness. You've learned how to manage what you do know. You know it like the back of your hand."[19]

The Crucifixion Does not Produce Salvation

Too many people have been alienated from Christ by Christian theology. One of the most alienating doctrines is the sacrificial atonement theory, the belief that Jesus died as a propitiatory sacrifice for our sins, having taken our sinfulness onto himself to save us from eternal damnation. A close relative is substitutionary atonement theory, Anselm's belief that, since finite humankind has sinned against an infinite God, and cannot re-pay its infinite debt, God sent Jesus as an infinite, divine-human substitute to expiate our guilt for us, thereby restoring right relationship. Despite Jesus's own prophetic privileging of social justice over propitiatory sacrifice, these "atonement theories" came to dominance in the Western Church.

According to these legalistic theologies, God is one lawgiver giving one law, promising one reward (heaven) or one punishment (hell). Be-cause no one follows that law perfectly, all are deserving of hell. But Jesus frees us from that fate by taking our punishment onto himself, balancing the scales of infinite justice, thereby granting us entrance into heaven. Salvation is largely pushed into the afterlife, affecting this life primarily by anticipation. Since all human conduct is reprobate, selfish, and displeas-ing to God, ethics becomes a theoretical exercise, at least with regard

18. M. King, *Call to Conscience*, 222–23.
19. Coleman, *Not Alone*, 125.

to the God-human relationship. This model of justice is retributive, demanding an eye for an eye and rejecting any possibility of spontaneous, unconditional forgiveness—or grace.[20]

Numerous criticisms of these doctrines have been made over the centuries. First and foremost, the concept of God as a vengeful autocrat who can be appeased only through death by torture does not cohere with Jesus's revelation of Abba as a loving Parent. Loving parents are not inflexible disciplinarians, and skillful parents frequently forgo their wayward children's punishment. Jesus denies that Abba is an agent of legalistic wrath. Certainly, our horrific cruelty to one another over the millennia has pained God, but one more act of horrific cruelty, the crucifixion, did not end that pain, it just exacerbated it. Jesus rejects any "underlying image of God as an angry, bloodthirsty, violent, and sadistic father, reflecting the very worst kind of male behavior," writes Elizabeth Johnson.[21]

The God of Jesus could not be the god of any violent atonement theory, because the teachings of Jesus are incompatible with redemption through violence, and the ethics of Jesus seek to propel humankind beyond its addiction to domination through violence. Any schoolchild, upon learning that God needed Jesus's death to be appeased, will naturally ask why God didn't just forgive us outright, without demanding the brutal death of an innocent man. Frequently, the answer will have something to do with Adam and Eve's "original sin," which separated humankind from God and needed reparation. But Jesus had never heard of "original sin," nor did his Jewish tradition interpret Adam and Eve's story the say way Augustine would four hundred years later. Judaism did not then (and does not now) teach that all humans inherit the guilt of Adam and Eve's disobedience and therefore need collective forgiveness. Rather than collective guilt, Judaism taught and teaches that each individual is responsible for their own actions and can resist their evil inclinations, with great difficulty, thereby choosing the good.

Anselm's substitutionary atonement theory, in which Jesus substitutes himself for the punishment due to us, is based on the medieval feudal system in which it arose. The lord of an estate was the source of order, protection, and development for all residents, so the preservation of the lord's honor—the source of his authority—was paramount. Any lord who had been offended by a serf had to punish that offense, for the good of all.

20. Johnson, *Creation and the Cross*, 5–6.
21. Johnson, "Redeeming the Name," 124.

Without that honor preserved, the social order would descend into chaos and everyone would suffer. In this way of thinking, Jesus is the lord's son who takes the serfs' offenses onto himself, thereby preserving the honor of the lord, the order of the estate, and the lives of the serfs.

The theory has a certain attractiveness as it renders the crucifixion an action by God for us, but it is insufficient to the life and teachings of Jesus. Jesus preaches repentance so that people will enter into loving community. He wants them to *change*: to forgive, reconcile, include, be generous, be kind, be humble. In Anselm's theory, the serfs do nothing. Theoretically, they watch the exchange, feel gratitude, and are transformed by that gratitude. But they aren't characters in the story. They're just spectators. To Jesus, his audience were active participants in an unfolding story, and he invited them to decide what role they would play in that story.

Anselm's theory also prioritizes justice over mercy, but Jesus teaches, "Blessed are those who show mercy to others, for they will be shown mercy" (Matt 5:7). In the story of the prodigal son, Jesus reveals the unconditional forgiveness of God for the wayward child. For Jesus, God is mercy without reference to justice, but according to Anselm's theory, any lord would feel compelled to demand expiation from an offending serf. Indeed, for the lord to demand expiation—to punish through violence—would make that lord like unto God.

Jesus did not punish through violence. Jesus was the innocent victim of violence, which raises another objection to these violent atonement theories: one person should not be punished for the crime of another. Today, this is a universal principle of law that nearly every society sees as reasonable. God, being merciful, just, and rational, could not violate this principle. The use of a whipping boy could never enter the mind of God, because any such use would be abusive. The whipping boys of legend were playmates of young princes who would be punished in the princes' stead. This punishment conformed to Anselm's theory of transformation through spectatorship: theoretically, the prince would feel bad that his friend was being punished and reform his behavior. In reality, the system allowed royals to act with impunity, knowing that someone else would bear the consequences of their actions.

"Jesus Christ died for your sins" is the oft-repeated phrase that summarizes violent atonement theories. Alas, this declaration doesn't stand up to the stress test of pastoral ministry; it doesn't help pastors care for parishioners or parishioners care for each other. For example, a couple finally gets pregnant after years of trying. Five months into the pregnancy, they discover that the fetus's kidneys are developing outside its body. The condition is inoperable and the fetus is terminal, so they have to undergo a dilation and extraction abortion. Should the pastor reassure them, "Jesus Christ died for your sins"? A woman was sexually abused by her father and brothers while she was growing up. Did Jesus Christ die for *her* sins? Did Jesus Christ die for *their* sins? What does that statement even do?

To say "Jesus died for your sins" negates Jesus's message and ministry. It does not heal. It renders us passive. That is, I fear, the point. Jesus preaches a new social order, a universalism and egalitarianism that heartened the humble and threatened the proud. That preaching got him crucified. Then, as a new religion based on Christ arose in the Roman Empire, his teachings got crucified as well. Violent and politically mute atonement theories were substituted for the transformative message of the Christ. The church declared the social implications of the gospel dead and buried, laid them in the tomb, and rolled a rock in front of the entrance.

The Crucifixion Reveals God's Abhorrence of Human-Induced Suffering

The depths of life are unavoidable, and shallow answers to deep questions are like dead weight to a swimmer. Violent atonement theories are shallow answers. As the archetype of useless suffering, the cross speaks to us, but only as a protest against violence. For this reason, placing the locus of salvation in the violence of crucifixion will never make sense. The disciples had already experienced divine empowerment simply from being in the presence of Jesus and sharing his life. Through this religious invigoration, they recognized Jesus as the Messiah (Mark 8:29), the Son of the living God (Matt 16:16), the Savior of the world (John 4:42). Jesus himself implies that his death is not necessary for redemption. When Zacchaeus the tax collector commits to a new life of honesty, the not-yet-crucified Jesus declares, "Today salvation has come to this house!" (Luke 19:9). No one in the fledgling Jesus community wanted or needed him to die.[22]

Then why *did* Jesus die? As mentioned above, the purpose of the incarnation is to express divine solidarity with life. Jesus reveals the

22. Crossan, *Jesus*, 161–62.

empathic participation of God within the life-giving yet sometimes brutal contrasts that characterize the universe. Abba, our Father and Mother,
intends the adversities of embodied life to unite us in their overcoming.
Such overcoming bequeaths our lives meaning and consequence. Sophia
is our guide in this process, but instead of listening to her, we have divided ourselves against one another in our infinite thirst for finite resources.

Despite our choice for division, which is very much a rejection of
Sophia's guidance, Christ incarnated as Jesus, subjecting himself to moral
evil as well as natural challenge. He reveals the divine purpose for us
in the face of difficulty: alliance, helpfulness, generosity, courage, rationality, perseverance, etc. He also provides ethical correction to dispense
with our self-induced misery. His revelation repudiates moral evil, which
acquires power through physical, social, and intellectual violence. In response, moral evil murdered Jesus on the cross.

The cross is the opposite of God. There, the Son of God experienced
God-forsakenness.[23] Divinity itself descended into *protest atheism*,
the cry that there is too much suffering in the world for it to have been
the design of a good God. Long before Rome invented crucifixion, the
psalmist had praised God: "If I go up to the heavens, you are there; if I
make my bed in Death, you're already there" (Ps 139:8). Jesus on the cross
is the historical expression of the psalmist's insight into faith: God is with
us even in the atheism caused by affliction. God is not just *ontologically*
omnipresent; God is *experientially* omnipresent. God is empathically,
emphatically everywhere.

The presence of God in the God-forsakenness of the cross reveals
the suffering of God in every useless sacrifice throughout history. Jesus is,
in the words of John the Revelator, "the Lamb slain from the foundation
of the world" (Rev 13:8 KJV). Priests sacrificed animals to appease an
angry god, centurions crucified rebels to appease a distant emperor, and
overseers flogged serfs to appease a cruel lord. Rather than breaking the
chain, Christian theologians developed violent atonement theories that
made Abba the Sacrificer and Jesus the Sacrifice.[24]

Jesus himself condemned such irreligious violence: "The hour is
coming when anyone who kills you will claim to be serving God. They
will do these things because they know neither Abba God nor me" (John
16:2b-3). Jesus is the power inverter, the murdered scapegoat who

---

23. Moltmann, *Crucified God*, 27.
24. Presbyterian Church (U.S.A.), *Book of Confessions*, Heidelberg Catechism, §31.

declares the violence of ritual sacrifice unholy. He inverts the violent *so-cial* order, rejecting revenge for reconciliation and purity for embrace. He inverts the violent *economic* order, rejecting accumulation for generosity and stratification for equality. He inverts the violent *religious* order, rejecting respectability for justice and rigorism for kindness. In the words of René Girard, "The God of Christianity isn't the violent God of archaic religion, but the nonviolent God who willingly becomes a victim in order to free us from our violence."[25]

Violence and oppression are sinful. If "Jesus died for sinners," then what does his death do for those who are *sinned against*? If Jesus dies for the sins of the oppressors, then how does he die for the sufferings of the oppressed? In truth, Jesus died *for* the oppressed, *as* the oppressed, demanding an end to oppression on the part of all oppressors. The failure of Christian theology to make this point has allowed Christians to gleefully oppress. James Cone points out that racist "Christians" in twentieth-century America could hang Blacks from lynching trees while worshipping Jesus on the cross, without irony.[26]

If the story of Jesus ended with the crucifixion, then the cosmos would be eternal night. The cynics who "know how the world works" would be right: cruelty would be more useful than kindness and any prudent person would prefer power to love. If Roman nails had the last word, then hope would be a lie and faith would be foolish. Meaning and purpose would drain out of the universe to be replaced by calculated opportunism. We could no longer gaze upon the beauty of God. We would instead be condemned to casting furtive, fearful glances over our shoulder. Yet this cursed situation did not arise because, by the power of God, crucifixion yields to resurrection.

25. Girard, *Evolution and Conversion*, 219.
26. Cone, *Cross and Lynching Tree*, 30.

The Lynching Tree
(sculpture by Scotty Utz, photograph by Katherine Brooks)

God's Absolute Rejection of the Crucifixion Expresses Itself in the Resurrection

"There is no greater love than to lay down one's life for one's friends," declares Jesus (John 15:13). In this declaration, Jesus associates love with death because Jesus well knows that love is perilous. Hatred is safer than love, despair is safer than hope, and fear is safer than faith; hence their attractiveness. But Jesus does not call us to safety; Jesus calls us to life. Life is love in the shadow of death, and love in the shadow of death is love that defeats death. For this reason we can find God everywhere, even in the "thick darkness" (Exod 20:21), even in the tomb.

The symbol of love defeating death is the resurrection. Jesus did not *rise* from the dead. Jesus *was raised* from the dead by God, by the agapic communion of three persons. His resurrection was not the act of an individual; it was an act of community. It was communion celebrating itself and declaring its victory over division. To the extent that the "hero" is an individual who acts alone, without need of assistance, Christ is no hero. Were he such, then he would contribute to the forces of individualization and separation. But as the perfectly loving person who was crucified, died, and *was resurrected*, he becomes Savior.[27]

The power of God triumphs by means of the power of God, not by means of the power of this world. The Romans who crucified Jesus believed in the power of this world, which is the power of godless violence. Throughout the empire, many awaited the messiah, christ or "anointed one." Previous recipients of this exalted title were Aaron, the high priest of Israel (Sir 45:15); Saul, the first king of Israel (1 Sam 24:10); and Cyrus, the Persian emperor who allowed the Jews to rebuild their temple (Isa 45:1). Given this pedigree, people naturally expected wealth, power, and conquest of their savior. They wanted a messiah who trafficked in absolutes, who would establish absolute dominion, thereby resolving all the ambiguities of history. They got no such magnificence. Instead, they got an authentic revelation of God as love, the image of all-forgiving meekness who prays for enemies and tormentors.[28] They got reconciliation between persons, which is ultimately reconciliation with God.

God makes a universe that makes itself, that evolves from simplicity to complexity, toward God. Likewise, God makes persons who make themselves. We have the freedom to live plumb with the divinely sustained cosmos or against it. When choosing greed, hatred, and power over generosity, love, and community, we choose against God. The crucifixion symbolizes our freedom to make this choice, a freedom that makes our choice for God meaningful. Through the cross, inhumanity believed that it could permanently defeat humanity, but the spirit *of* the universe could not be defeated by the spirit *against* the universe. Hatred cannot defeat love, and division cannot defeat communion. The will of the godless cannot override the will of God, which is to life in its fullness.

27. Zizioulas, *Being as Communion*, 113.

28. Bulgakov, *Churchly Joy*, 40.

In a context in which suffering is recognized as a universal human constant, the cross is not a scandal but an assurance. Jesus is God among the suffering; hence, Jesus is God among us, especially the poor and lowly. Through the divine identification with our condition, we receive assurance that God is with us in our affliction. Unity within suffering defeats suffering, a defeat symbolized by resurrection. God as love promises resurrection to all the vulnerable ones who have been doubted, denied, betrayed, and crucified. Thus, the suffering of vulnerability is not the final word. Kent Annan writes, "We don't have to minimize either suffering or uncertainty. Our love for truth can help protect us from ourselves and from worshiping an untrue god that can't survive the trial of this world. Let our faith too be nailed regularly to the cross of this world. Any faith that dies there was dead to begin with. What is resurrected is Life."[29]

Resurrection to life leaves us among the tensions of experience. The resurrection does not end suffering, but it reveals that God's finger is on the scale of the universe, tipping it in favor of joy. In the words of John Gilmer:

> Jesus declares: This world is filled with suffering. But take heart! Suffering will not have the last word. Death will not have the last word. Evil will not have the last word. Poverty will not have the last word. Sickness will not have the last word. Failure will not have the last word. War will not have the last word. Sorrow will not have the last word. Oppression will not have the last word. Loneliness and divorce and broken relationships will not have the last word.
>
> Jesus declares: Life will have the last word. Peace will have the last word. Joy will have the last word. Love will have the last word. Victory will have the last word. Justice will have the last word. Beauty will have the last word. Truth will have the last word. Freedom will have the last word. Because I will have the last word.[30]

Jesus's resurrection is the historical expression of God's eternal preference for the good. Jesus is released from the stubborn darkness of the tomb as truth is released from the stubborn lies of the world.

Jesus was resurrected *to* us, not *away* from us. Resurrection is into embodied life, not a spiritual heaven. We can trust that, having tasted death, Jesus savored life all the more. He arose to hear the sounds of

29. Annan, *After Shock*, 37.
30. Gilmer, "Joy in the End," paras. 13–14.

nature, smell life in the soil, and feel the warmth of the sun on his face. All these sensations must have felt wonderfully extravagant after three days in the tomb. He could once again feel the Infinite Creative Benevolence, not as a mountaintop experience, but in the moment-by-moment progression of everyday life.[31]

Resurrection is not just a historical event that we remember; it is an eternal truth that we participate in. That is, the Holy Spirit, Sophia, now invites us to *become resurrection to one another*, in this world. We are to risk entry into one another's lives, as Jesus entered our world. We are to walk in one another's troubles, as Jesus walked in ours. And we are to raise each other up, as God raised Jesus. Such love is laborious, but labor is the height of creativity, and creative love fulfills the image of God within us.

Jesus Is the Sacred Amen within the Cosmos

Active participation in life without fear or dismay is the everlasting and unachievable dream of faith. We seek to practice engagement without anxiety, compassion without disturbance, and presence without agitation, yet somehow we always seem to find ourselves anxious, disturbed, and agitated. We are in good company. The writers of the Gospels were very honest about Jesus's own anxiety, disturbance, and agitation. Jesus slung anger at hypocrites (Matt 23), was troubled by the grief of others (John 11:33), wept over the death of a friend (John 11:35), lamented the impending destruction of Jerusalem (Luke 19:41–44), got tired and needed rest (Mark 6:31), and sweat blood in anticipation of his crucifixion (Luke 22:44). Jesus did not model detached transcendence. He modeled steadfast faithfulness, the *ḥesed* of God.

"It is the propensity of religion to avoid, precisely, suffering: to have light without darkness, vision without trust, hope without an ongoing dialogue with despair—in short, Easter without Good Friday," writes Douglas John Hall.[32] Hall reminds us that Abba did not create, Jesus did not enter, and Sophia has not promised any spiritual absolutes of pure joy, perfect peace, or abiding satisfaction. We may yearn for such a universe, but God denies it to us, because only mutually amplifying contrasts produce existential plentitude; anything that exists independently exists

---

31. Tetlow, *Considering Jesus*, 89.
32. Hall, *God and Human Suffering*, 126.

insufficiently. *Joy, suffering, and love are inseparable; they are triune, like the three points that form a triangle.* Abba declares, "I form light and create darkness, I made peace and create evil; I am YHWH, who does all these things" (Isa 45:7).

Metaphysical difference fosters experiential bounty, even as negative qualities cause tribulation. God prioritizes challenge and development over ease and comfort because God wants our lives to be meaning-laden, not comfort-stultified. Jesus models *ḥesed* within the fluctuating contrasts of existence, revealing that although we are never perfectly safe, we are always absolutely beloved. Now, Sophia invites us into the boldness of the beloved, embracing the multiplicity of existence.

Life is beautiful, difficult, and thrilling. Life asks us how we will respond to its extravagance, and the way we live our lives is the answer. Sophia invites and empowers us to respond in the affirmative, but too often—confused, hurt, or afraid—we say No to the offered bounty.

Historically, Jesus is the inexhaustible Yes to our existential situation, hence the perfect expression of the image of God within the universe. Paul writes:

> Don't think I make my plans with ordinary human motives so that I say "Yes, yes," then in the same breath, "No, no"! As sure as God is faithful, I declare that my word to you is not "yes" one minute and "no" the next. Jesus Christ, whom Silvanus, Timothy and I preached to you as the Only Begotten of God, was not alternately "yes" and "no"; Jesus is never anything but "yes." No matter how many promises God has made, they are "yes" in Christ. (2 Cor 1:17–20a)

Jesus is the Amen, the Yes, because he is the faithful and true witness, the divine participant in creation whose life reverberates with the purpose of creation (Rev 3:14). Jesus fulfills the human calling to say Amen to life *as it is*, to heed the profound whispers of Sophia, to love Abba even in the midst of futility and defeat. To the extent that we can share in Jesus's Yes, to that extent will we find his sacred passion in our own lives.

This Jesus is water to the desert, the faithful one who "lives to live, in absolute spontaneity, in the self-evident meaning of light that shines to shine, clear spring water that gushes to gush, the bird that sings to sing."[33] The example of Jesus, coupled with the inspiration of Sophia, invites us into an existential transformation that we experience viscerally, that

---

33. Boff, *Trinity and Society*, 126–27.

converts the totality of heart, body, and mind. It changes our overall affect, reinterprets our experiences, reorganizes our thinking, and revalues
our values. We do not merely revise our beliefs or tinker with old rituals
or break old habits. We don't just rearrange the furniture; we access a new
way of being alive.[34]

Gratitude Produces Joy

John Makransky aptly describes the experience of life available to us,
which we tend to neglect: "Most of us just haven't learned to pay much
attention to the countless moments of love, kindness, and care that sur-
round us each day: a child at the store reaching for her mother's hand, an
elderly stranger at the park who smiles upon a young family, a grocery
clerk who beams at you as she hands you your change."[35] According to
Makransky, we need unobstructed eyes that see thankfully, eyes that recognize the humbling power of Paul's question: "What do you have that
you didn't receive?" (1 Cor 4:7).

Recognizing God's generosity invites us into the love of reality itself.
We tend to compare the universe as it is with the universe as we would
want it to be. We imagine an easier universe with less suffering, or we
imagine a world in which we are more talented and powerful than we are
in this one. Then we crave that world. Thus, we end up in a transactional
relationship with life, keeping score and analyzing the data according to
our own concept of fairness. Too often, we deem life to be indebted to us.
We've gotten the short end of the stick and God should put things right.
If God doesn't, then we will.

We should not compare the present universe with our fantasies
about a more perfect universe, which is always a universe in which we
are personally better off. Instead, we should compare the present universe with the other real possibility, the true option that God overcame
for us—the option of nothingness itself. Without God there would be
nothing but cold, dark silence. Now, having considered our rescue from
nonexistence, we develop sheer awe at existence itself. We become graced
with gratitude, which frees us from the score-keeping, transactional attitude that always leaves us embittered. Having received eyes to see, we can
finally understand Iris Murdoch's observation that "people from a planet

34. Bazzano, "Deathlife, Lifedeath," 258.
35. Makransky, *Awakening through Love*, 30.

without flowers would think we must be mad with joy the whole time to have such things about us."[36]

Faith recognizes reality as a gift and practices gratitude toward the Giver. *We do not become grateful because we are joyful; we become joyful because we are grateful.* "As I take from the Infinite, so I give infinitely," declares E. Stanley Jones. This statement is surely aspirational. Our resources are finite, and finitude that gives infinitely depletes itself and can help no one. But the sentiment opens our hands, which are cramped from clinging, which have forgotten how to give and receive. Jesus taught that life cannot be hoarded: "Sell what you own and give money to the poor. Make purses for yourselves that do not wear out, unfailing treasures in heaven, where no thief comes and no moth destroys. For wherever your treasure is, that's where your heart will be" (Luke 12:33).

Joy Surpasses Happiness

Unfortunately, in the world of religion, overpromising is more marketable than underpromising. It is also fundamentally dishonest. The Bible, being honest, refuses to overpromise. Paul writes paradoxically of the early Christian communities, "We are afflicted in every way possible, but we are not crushed; we are full of doubts, but we never despair. We are persecuted, but never abandoned; we are struck down, but never destroyed. Continually we carry about in our bodies the death of Jesus, so that in our bodies the life of Jesus may also be revealed" (2 Cor 4:8–10).

Yet even in the midst of these difficulties Paul counsels celebration: "Rejoice in the Savior always. I say it again: Rejoice!" (Phil 4:4). For Paul, the surest sign of spiritual transformation is joy. Joy is not happiness. Joy is an abiding disposition; happiness is a transitory emotion. Joy is what we experience caring for orphans; happiness is what we experience in Disneyland. The two aspects of life are not in competition. We need both, but they are very different. Happiness can be gained without vulnerability. Multimillionaires who compete with one another based on the size of their stock portfolio experience the surge of self that comes with increased riches, prestige, and power. This intoxicating experience is pleasurable and does not necessitate any openness to the larger world's suffering. Indeed, withdrawal into the acquisitive self can render that self immune to the suffering of others. Increased pleasure with decreased

36. Murdoch, *Fairly Honourable Defeat*, 170.

vulnerability can produce superficial happiness. Alas, only toxins produce such intoxication.

Joy is a deeper, more abiding experience that necessitates vulnerability to the world at large. In happiness, the self experiences the pleasures of the self. There is nothing inherently wrong with that because the self too deserves to be cared for. But in joy, the self discerns that the world is fundamentally beautiful and good. Yet, for this beauty and goodness to flow inward the self must become open to the world. The self must put itself at risk. Hence, the experience of joy leaves us at the mercy of tragedy, and tragedy can be merciless—as the crucifixion testifies. Nevertheless, joy senses an underlying grace beneath the play of laughter and tears, and the eventual triumph of laughter—as the resurrection testifies.

Healing Works toward the Kingdom

God is love, and love is something you do. This observation dovetails with our observation that God is activity, more verb than noun, and we are made in the image of God. When we participate in loving activity, we are participating in God:

> What good is it to profess faith without practicing it? Such faith has no power to save. If any need clothes and have no food, and one of you says to them, "Goodbye and good luck. Stay warm and well-fed," without giving them the bare necessities of life, then what good is this? So it is with faith. If good deeds don't go with it, faith is dead. (Jas 2:14–17)

Active love extends our self into the all and allows the all into our self, so that the world's joy and suffering are ours, and will remain so, until we have created the world imagined by Abba, preached by Jesus, and inspired by Sophia, a world of peace with justice—the kingdom of God.[37]

The kingdom of God is not a fantasy. It is the destination that grants our lives destiny. As such, it is the fulfillment of Sophia's promise: "I'll teach you and show you the way you should walk; I will counsel you and keep watch over you" (Ps 32:8). The kingdom of God articulates the divine imagination and moves us into a new realm of possibility. It is not the opposite of reality; it is the purpose of reality, challenging *what is* with *what can be*. It allows us to imagine ourselves and others otherwise, seeing the oppressed liberated from their oppression and the oppressors

---

37. Sobrino, *Jesus the Liberator*, 11.

liberated from their oppressing. By pointing elsewhere, it transforms the here and now.[38] By presenting a vision of deliverance it spurs us to activity, because "when freedom is near the chains begin to chafe."[39]

The universe is an ocean. Shall we leave our spirit a thimble? Our hearts come alive when we create, and our hearts come alive when we love. Hence, the sacred life is creative love. Creative love does not seek out suffering, but it is willing to suffer to reduce suffering. This life offers more abundance than ease. A seven-year-old in a sandbox, playing alone with their toys, can be perfectly happy. But if this state were the best that life offered, then life would be truly tragic. There is more available: commitment, risk, meaning, purpose, challenge, and growth all produce *joy*.

Joy surges up from an unknown depth of self that we share with the unknown depth of other selves, which we all share with the unknown depth of the divine selves. Having this sacred potential, we cannot be satisfied with a superficial happiness that coats the surface of our consciousness. We must become who God has invited us to become or admit that we have denied our own nature. We must risk a generous love, in hope. Thankfully, we do so in the assurance of God's nurturing love, which guides us into new life. Jesus declares: "If you wish to follow me, you must deny yourself, pick up the instrument of your death, and begin to follow in my footsteps. If you would save your life, you will lose it; but if you would lose your life for my sake, you will find it" (Matt 16:24–25).

---

38. J. Butler, *Undoing Gender*, 29.
39. Moltmann, *Crucified God*, 9.

8

Living Community in
a Lonely World

When peoples care for you and cry for you—and love you—they can straighten out your soul.

—LANGSTON HUGHES[1]

Small Miracles Happen Here

WHEN I WAS IN seminary and needed to earn some extra money, I preached regularly at a small Presbyterian church in north Philadelphia. It was a dying White church in a largely Black neighborhood with at most twenty attendees on any given Sunday, mainly elderly. Still, the church conjured religious beauty.

George (named changed for privacy) sang in the church's small choir and performed most solos. As a boy, George had a physically abusive father. To escape the abuse, George joined the army, which sent him into combat in Vietnam. Returning home, he suffered from post-traumatic stress disorder and spent years on the streets of Philadelphia in alcohol addiction. Through Alcoholics Anonymous he achieved sobriety, met a

---

1. Hughes, *Gospel Plays, Operas*, 201.

woman from the church, got married, and became a regular attendee. Together, they never missed a Sunday.

Although he was the church's main soloist, George couldn't sing. At the risk of being disrespectful, for which I apologize: George couldn't carry a tune, and his voice was cracked by years of drinking and smoking. But George didn't know this himself, and he never held back, praising God with full-throated gratitude. His cracked voice reminded the congregation that, in the words of Leonard Cohen, cracks let the light through.[2] The music director kept asking him to sing, and the congregation kept listening, in respectful attention, grateful that he was in recovery, grateful that he had married, grateful that he had found redemption. Their joy in George's joy overwhelmed any discomfort with the performance.

George's years of alcoholism caught up with him, and he was hospitalized with cirrhosis of the liver. Only 10 percent of his liver was still functioning, and the doctors gave him a few months to live. George returned home, weakened, but was asked to sing a solo for the church, of his own choosing. He chose "How Great Thou Art." We gathered one Sunday to watch a frail man, beaten by his father, scarred by war, and poisoned by alcohol, sing from his soul to the glory of God, in joyful rapture. Grace so flooded the sanctuary that, to our ears, he sounded like an angel. George died two weeks later, in the presence of his wife and members of the congregation.

That was a good church. It is closed now. It wouldn't have impressed anyone with its spreadsheets, attendance, or preaching, but it loved Abba, our Parent. Sophia, the Holy Spirit, was active there, flowing through the parishioners, from one to another, inspiring them to be like Jesus and love their neighbor through thick and thin. Some churches promise earth-shattering miracles that defy natural law, but that church kept its eyes open for small miracles, the kind that we too easily overlook. Its openness to small miracles produced them—warmed hearts, settled spirits, and courage in the face of death.

Below, I will provide a doctrine of the church based on agapic nondualism—the unifying love of God that is our source, our sustenance, and our destiny. My presentation will appear idealized, or even naive, since churches can't actually attain these heights. Imperfect persons form imperfect institutions that express the love of God imperfectly. Nevertheless, even in our imperfection, unreachable ideals serve a function. The

2. Cohen, "Anthem."

ideal transforms the real because it gifts us with discontent, spurring us out of complacency and into possibility. The ideal tells us where we are and where we should go. Then, the ideal serves as the mark by which we measure our progress. So, the church described below does not exist in any pure form, but there are many churches of many different stripes that aspire to agapic unity and do much good in the world in pursuit of it, working small miracles like manna from heaven.

Please note: while this chapter will discuss the Christian church, in many ways it could apply to any group whose loyalty to love creates an unnaturally kind community.

In Church, We Fulfill the Image of God within Us

Miroslav Volf argues that "because the Christian God is not a lonely God, but rather a communion of three persons, faith leads human beings into the divine communion." Such communion cannot express itself in solitary life, a private person worshiping a private deity alone. Instead, the divine communion draws us into human communion, into togetherness, into a community that practices love of God and love of neighbor.[3]

God is a way of life, not an abstraction. The Trinitarian life that animates God is *for us*, to be realized in our relationship with God and with each other: "God in us, we in God, all of us in each other."[4] To enter this type of community, a community modeled on the triune God, is an act of faith. Faith is not a moral accomplishment, or rigorous obedience to rigid rules, or stubborn adherence to propositions for which there is no evidence. Faith is openness to the most basic experiential truth of the universe, a way of being that is plumb with reality, the practice of which entails risk.

Jesus ascended to Abba so that Sophia, who had animated Jesus, could now animate his followers. Together, they would continue his ministry as the church. In church God is known not just *in* community, but *as* community, in the freedom of self-communication. This concept of freedom as self-communication and self-gift resists contemporary culture, in which people increasingly delay commitment to preserve what they deem to be freedom: the spontaneity of a life unencumbered by responsibility for others.

3. Volf, *After Our Likeness*, 173.
4. LaCugna, *God for Us*, 228.

Such delayed commitment can lessen the self that it seeks to in-dulge. Self-donation in relationships of mutuality and equality, and in communities of mutuality and equality, is self-fulfillment, not self-re-nunciation. The function of church is to provide communities in which love can be *equitably* given and received. This sacred exchange accesses a new realm of belonging—the domain of Sophia, a gratuitous energy and transformative presence, perpetually reforming and renewing the church. The church experiences Sophia as ever heightening our quality of shared life.[5]

The self finds itself only in community. Hence, to limit self-donation is to limit the self. This statement is not dogmatic; it is empirical and will be ratified by those willing to risk it. Paul writes, "If one member suffers, all the members suffer together with them; if one member is honored, all the members share their joy" (1 Cor 12:26), because "we, who are many, are one body in Christ, and individually we are members of one another" (Rom 12:5 WEB). The phrase "of one another" is one word in Greek, *allēlōn* (ah-LAY-loan). *Allēlōn* and its variations are used one hundred times in the Newer Testament, which repeatedly insists on our insepara-bility from one another.

The church's conviction that we are members of one another ex-presses itself in the doctrine of universal priesthood. Instead of a class of priests who mediate God to the laity, the church believes that there is only one High Priest, Jesus (Heb 4:14–16; 1 Tim 2:5). The sole media-tion of Jesus places all followers on the same spiritual plane. But it does not *lower* their status; it universally *elevates* their status to that of priest. For this reason, Bible passages refer to the fledgling church as a "holy priesthood" (1 Pet 2:5), "royal priesthood" (1 Pet 2:9), and "priests to God" (Rev 1:6; Rev 5:10). In Trinitarian community, our neighbors are portals of God. In older religions, priests offered burnt sacrifices to God to garner goodwill for the people. In contrast, the followers of Jesus are *universally* empowered to offer sacrifices, but of a different sort: "Keep doing good works and sharing resources. These are the sacrifices that please God" (Heb 13:16).

During the Protestant Reformation, leaders such as Martin Luther and John Calvin institutionalized this status by teaching and establishing the *priesthood of all believers*. While certain members of the faith may be educated for and ordained to professional ministry, this did not elevate

---

5. Boff, *Trinity and Society*, 124.

their status over that of other believers; it only assigned them a specific role within the universal priesthood. Pastors ministered through sermons and sacraments, while doctors had a ministry of healing, laborers had a ministry of building, educators had a ministry of teaching, carpenters had a ministry of making, etc. All ministries were equally legitimate, so their (only male, alas) practitioners had equal standing within the democratically governed church.

The priesthood of all believers does *not* mean that each believer is a priest unto themselves with a direct, solo line to God, although this *mis*interpretation has achieved dominance in some denominations. Prayer and Bible study *in isolation*, unchecked by any Christian community, is a dangerous practice, encouraging individuals to confuse their personal spirituality with divine truth. All too often, this practice produces very harmful theology that overconfident enthusiasts propagate with prophetic zeal.

Instead, the priesthood of all believers implies that *we are all mediators of God to one another.*[6] God is always fully present, absolutely attentive, and perfectly solicitous. This presence is what we finite beings receive from the infinite God and what we need most. We may not be present to each other—we may be distracted or disengaged—but God is always fully present to us. In church, we try to make the divine presence real by being fully present to one another. Such presence poses a challenge in this era of technology, when every conversation can be interrupted. We are plagued by the absence of presence. We need to be tended to, and we need to tend, because tending manifests grace.

This conception of the church denies that it is a waiting room for heaven. The function of the church is this-worldly, not next-worldly. God loves us here and now and wants us to thrive here and now, not delay our thriving into some distant future. Certainly, the afterlife is a true consolation for the bereaved, but not at the cost of this life. Because Abba loves us *in this moment*, Jesus's message and Sophia's counsel are both urgent: "After John's arrest, Jesus appeared in Galilee proclaiming the Good News of God: 'This is the time of fulfillment. The reign of God is at hand. Change your hearts and minds, and believe this Good News!'" (Mark 1:14–15).

To take on God's way of being is not possible in isolation. We are spiritually interdependent. Just as we increase culturally through cultural relations, so we increase spiritually through spiritual relations.

6. Ross, "God's Embodiment and Women," 189–90.

Recognizing this truth, Buddhism commends the sangha, Hinduism commends the ashram, Islam commends the ummah, Judaism commends the minyan, and Christianity commends the church. The religions recognize that inertia dooms privatistic, disconnected faith. Individualist salvation, consumerist spirituality, and personalized piety are all deficient because we cannot realize divinized life in isolation. In response, religions create spiritual communities within which lamas, sadhus, imams, prophets, and rabbis jar us out of complacency, from separation to unification, through love. We manifest God's mode of existence by becoming a communion of saints, by forming a spiritual family (Rom 8:29).

Radical Honesty Creates Authentic Community

Jesus is the great Amen of God, the Yes to life in all its agony and ecstasy. Following his example and empowered by the Spirit, the church also says yes to life, to both its joy and its suffering. Suffering wants us to believe that we are alone, but love knows differently. For this reason, the church provides *consolation*. The word *consolation* derives from the Latin *con* or with, and *solus* or lonely. It means "to be with the lonely." Consolation does not take away the pain, but it does lighten it, because pain coupled with loneliness is excruciating. We suffer less when we suffer with others, and we suffer less when we suffer wisely, so we suffer best when we suffer in a wise community.

A thirteen-year-old youth in our church lost a friend who was hit by a truck while riding her bicycle. The Sunday after the accident, the youth came to church and, as her fellow parishioners offered condolences, eventually began weeping. Three matrons of the church, who had known her since she was born, stood up, surrounded her, and just comforted her—undistracted, undisturbed, and undismayed—until she was finished. Did they make her sadness go away? No. Did they explain why this tragedy happened? No. Did they let her know, without words, that life would continue, and become good again? Yes, because they believed in the power of community: "Bear one another's burdens," writes Paul, "and thus fulfill the law of Christ" (Gal 6:2).

Our sharing of sorrows helps us to get real and live authentically, but such sharing occurs only in *backstage* churches. Backstage churches are different from *frontstage* churches. In frontstage churches, everyone puts their best foot forward, showing up well-dressed and clean and all put together. Many frontstage churches believe that God rewards religious virtue with health and wealth. God may test us, on occasion, but if we respond faithfully to the test, then God will reward us with even greater prosperity, as in the utterly shallow, prosaic conclusion to Job. These churches inevitably devolve into the hellhole of *competitive virtue signaling*, in which parishioners compete to see who can appear the most virtuous, hence the most blessed by God.

Worse, if a church believes that God sends suffering as a punishment for vice, then parishioners will have to hide their suffering from each other. We know a woman in a fundamentalist area of the country whose young daughter got cancer. She set up a website to raise money for medical bills and, being a person of faith, she asked for prayers on the website as well. Most comments were kind and supportive, but a large number speculated about how her family had sinned, causing God to punish them. Others suggested ways that they could get right with God so the cancer would go away, or even claimed that their use of modern medicine revealed a lack of faith. The mother had to edit her request for prayer, insisting that the cause of her daughter's cancer was purely medical, and she informed visitors that any comments suggesting otherwise would be deleted.

The belief that human suffering is divine punishment for hidden sin produces frontstage churches and lonely churchgoers, a combination of words that should be oxymoronic. Likewise, the belief that prosperity is a reward for virtue produces pride: "My life is perfect, see how God has blessed me!" This boast is a misery-inducing lie, to oneself and everyone else. It arises from envious insecurity and sinks us deeper within it. It misrepresents God's love as conditional and separates parishioners from one another. Frontstage churches foster rivalry rather than grace and contest rather than community.

"Therefore, let's have no more lies. Speak truthfully to each other, for we are all members of one body," admonishes Paul (Eph 4:25). Because we need to be known, we need to share ourselves with one another. In *backstage* churches, we allow each other to see the inevitable messiness of our lives. Acknowledging the universality of our struggles frees us from envy and recenters us in one another. Sharing life's joys and worries allows us to be loved through both and to love others through both. This love is oxygen for the soul. Acceptance after self-revelation heals, while secrets eat at us like tapeworms.

Transparency Transforms and Transfigures

We have argued that the Trinity is three unique persons united through love into one divine community. Abba, Jesus, and Sophia are specific centers of consciousness, thought, and feeling; hence, each one is a *subject*—a self with a specific identity. An *object* is a thing without consciousness, thought, or feeling, while a subject is a person with consciousness, thought, and feeling. The divine subjects differ from human subjects in their perfect love for, and openness to, one another. What they could hide, they always choose to share. Their subjectivity is *transparent*. Hence, they are not only subjective, they are *intersubjective*—perfectly open and lovingly transparent to one another. *God is intersubjectivity itself.*

By way of consequence, individual uniqueness, and its contribution to the kaleidoscope of difference, is holy. Recognizing our own uniqueness, and our unique value, we desire to be seen. We want the depth of our subjectivity to be known, even if we don't know it ourselves. We want to be acknowledged as a self who possesses a soul. We want to be perceived as consequential, not because we're rich or famous, but because we are of inherent worth. Such co-celebration is what should happen in religious community. The endeavor is sacred, and even partial achievement grants us a foretaste of the kingdom.

As gathering places for the people of God, churches are places of transparency and intersubjectivity. Such openness, in a culture of acceptance, is healing in itself. We can think of participants in an Alcoholics Anonymous meeting who begin by stating their name and their addiction to alcohol, always in full confidence of welcome. Many churches claim to be so welcoming, yet they subtly coerce members into that church's image of what a Christian looks like, encircling them in candy-coated barbed wire. Other churches are truly welcoming, encouraging participants to fully embody the unique image that God created them to be. These churches encourage authenticity, which is confident self-revelation, an external life lived in accord with one's internal self. These churches truly practice Paul's instruction, "Accept one another as Christ accepted us, for the glory of God" (Rom 15:7).

Interdependence
(candelabra by Steve Ferguson, photograph by Jon Paul Sydnor)

The Church Must Celebrate LGBTQ+ Persons as LGBTQ+

Because churches express the interpersonal freedom within God, with which God has gifted us, authentic churches are *low social control* groups. A low social control group respects members' individual freedom and unique contribution, trusting that cohesion will organically emerge from diversity. Some churches betray this nature and become *high social control* groups, subjecting members to shame, guilt, shunning, denial of sacraments, and threats of eternal damnation if they fail to be who the church wants them to be. These churches demand that members subordinate their God-given uniqueness to a church-generated stereotype, hiding their authentic self within a conformist shell. In these churches, where members are opaque to one another, secrets are kept. But, as it is said, where there are secrets, there is shame.

In God-centered community, in which we gather to fulfill the image of God within us, we must trust one another's self-revelation. We must practice intersubjectivity. For decades, most churches have denied the self-revelation of their gay and lesbian members. These members are telling their churches that they can find emotional intimacy only with members of the same sex, they are telling their churches that this disposition cannot be changed, and they are telling their churches that this disposition *does not need* to be changed, that they feel blessed in the loving relationships they are in.

At the same time, most churches are denying the self-revelation of their trans and nonbinary members, who are telling them that they do not identify with the sex they were assigned at birth, that their interior experience is of the opposite gender, or both genders, or no gender, and that they need to live out that identity to live fully. For decades, most churches have told these parishioners that their inner life is unnatural, or unbiblical, or diseased, or in need of repair. Most churches have told these members to conform their *inner* self to their *outer* appearance. In so doing, these churches refuse to see transgendered and nonbinary persons as God sees them: "YHWH does not see as mortals see; mortals see outward appearances but YHWH sees into the heart" (1 Sam 16:7b).

This rejection of their *selves* causes horrific spiritual harm to trans and nonbinary persons. Nevertheless, they persist. They are risking themselves in repeated acts of vulnerability and self-disclosure, like unto God. They are coming out and suffering rejection, yet they continue to reveal themselves until the world sees them the way God sees them. The perseverance of these saints is changing minds, which is changing souls, creating a grace-filled new world. Just as the disciples were allowed to see Jesus transfigured (Mark 9:2–8), LGBTQ+ self-revelation allows the world to see *itself* transfigured, liberated from fear and invited into celebration. This transfiguration is not an act of inclusion on the part of the excluders, with the excluded passively waiting at the gate. No, it is an ongoing act of conversion *by* the excluded, *of* the excluders, *for* the excluders, who continue to suffer behind walls of ignorance. This conversion is for *all*. Like God, it is *for us*; hence, *for all of us*.

For the trans community, external transition to their neurological birth gender is often accompanied by persecution—expulsion from home, loss of job, physical attacks, and worse. Despite this persecution, most record greater life satisfaction *after* choosing to express their internal gender identity.[7] To mark their transition, most trans persons change

---

7. Washington Post Staff, "Nov. 10–Dec. 1, 2022."

their name. Likewise, the Bible frequently renames persons when they undergo a profound change: Abram became Abraham, Sarai became Sarah (Gen 17), Jacob becomes Israel (Gen 32), Simon becomes Peter (Matt 16), and Saul becomes Paul (Acts 13). Associates who reject the transitions of transgendered persons will sometimes express this rejection by "deadnaming" them—calling them by the name given at birth rather than their chosen name. Would these rejectionists also deadname Paul as Saul? Sarah as Sarai? The Bible is about transformation: our potential for it, our call to it, and our invitation to celebrate it. Today we can fulfill that call by supporting LGBTQ+ rights and LGBTQ+ identity, until *everyone* can say, with Alice Walker, "I am an expression of the divine, just like a peach is, just like a fish is. I have a right to be this way."[8]

Bad Theology Produces Suffering

Alice Walker's statement is an act of healing for herself and others. She was wounded by unholy forces that told her she was *not enough*, that she was inherently distorted because she was Black, female, and a lesbian. But she reclaimed her identity as a blessing, then shared that blessing with others, helping them to reclaim their own identities. Tragically, many of the psychic wounds that people receive are from bad theology promulgated in churches. Bad theology threatens believers with this-worldly condemnation and next-worldly damnation, causing "religious trauma syndrome" (RTS)—fear, anxiety, hatred, and self-loathing. This debilitating spirituality is produced by religious ideologies of control.[9] High-control church leaders who want parishioners to be puppets teach that God is a puppeteer and that the leaders are the strings. To disobey is to malfunction. Fearful that freedom will cause people to stray from the straight and narrow path, authoritarian churches erect high walls along that path so parishioners can't peek over the top and see other options for life.

Bad theology is inherently traumatizing. I had a friend in seminary who grew up in rural Texas in the 1980s. In the fifth grade he was at an all-male sleepover party with friends, and they all started looking at pictures of women in underwear in a Sears catalog. They went a few pages past the women's section into the men's section, which my friend was

---

8. Walker, *World Has Changed*, 277.

9. Winell, "Understanding Religious Trauma Syndrome," 23.

much more interested in. He noticed that no one else was interested in the pictures of men in underwear and realized that he was gay. His family went to a fundamentalist Baptist church, and the people there were (otherwise) very nice, but they taught that being gay was sick and sinful, so he thought that he was sick and sinful. He kept his orientation a secret, in shame. I have another friend who was told as a child, by otherwise very nice people, that Jesus was coming back soon and would take all the Christians (Bible believing, born again) to heaven and send everyone else to hell. He went to bed every night in terror, praying for his non-Christian and semi-Christian friends.

And so it continues. Beautiful children are told that they are sinful in the eyes of God. Adolescents are made to feel guilty for the natural sexual drives developing within. Women are told that their gender is responsible for the fall of all "mankind," being morally blamed even as they are linguistically excluded. Suffering church members are asked what they did to offend God to warrant this punishment. Patients on their deathbeds are questioned about their wrongdoings and offered expiation so they won't go to hell. Bad theology obsesses over sin, guilt, purity, and damnation, turning already difficult life into fully accomplished hell by anticipation.

Good Theology Produces Flourishing

Faith reveals that women, men, trans, nonbinary, Black, Brown, White, Asian, able, disabled, rich, poor, middle-class persons and more are all equal. They are equally created by God, infinitely loved by God, and universally called to lives of meaning, purpose, and joy. Recognizing this truth, churches must model *egalitarianism*—equality in thought and practice—to the world. Egalitarian community makes use of *all* members' talents and places them in service of the common good. In contrast, patriarchal and heterosexist communities waste the talents of many members by denying them full access to leadership positions, limiting both personal and institutional flourishing.

As egalitarian, churches are also *universalist*—universally valuing all persons, inside and outside the church, especially those persons devalued by society. *This universalism is the mission of the church.* Since all are children of God and inseparable from one another, ethics becomes universalist—all are treated equally (Matt 5:43–48). Since Abba is the divine mother who births all creation (Job 38:29; Isa 66:7; etc.), and no mother rejects her sinful child, salvation is universal (1 Tim 2:3–4).

In a lethally tribal world, universalism provides the church with a healing mission—resistance to fear, anger, and hatred through the ministry of faith, hope, and love. Assigning the church this mission, Jesus states that his followers should be kind to all, even as God makes it rain on the just and unjust (Matt 5:45). Thus, the church does not prefer Christians to non-Christians, or men to women, or rich to poor. We are all permeated by implicit biases and tribal identities, but joining a church begins a journey of resistance to these traditional loyalties and skewed categorical grids. Through this journey, we learn to value *all* persons, of *every* nationality, race, religion, class, orientation, and gender.

In allegiance to the cosmic God rather than our tribal god, the church replaces natural loyalties with a universal family. Jesus states, "Who is my mother? Who are my kin?" Then, pointing to the disciples, Jesus said, "This is my family. Whoever does the will of Abba God in heaven is my sibling and parent" (Matt 12:48–50).

Egalitarian, universalist churches practice social resurrection, defying accepted norms in witness to the universal God. In the late 1960s, Anne Moody and other civil rights activists tried to racially integrate southern churches. On the Sunday of this action, White churches met the Black activists with armed policemen, paddy wagons, and dogs. A few Whites protested, saying that the Blacks should be let in, but they were outnumbered. Having been rejected from several White churches, Anne and her friend went to pick up two activists who were trying to integrate an Episcopal church. When they got there, the friends were nowhere to be seen, so Anne got nervous. But after circling the church a few times, the thought occurred to her: "What if they got in?"

Anne and her friend walked up the steps to the church, which were miraculously free of armed policemen and dogs. They entered the church, where worship had already started. Two ushers approached them, asking, "May we help you?" "Yes," Anne said, "We would like to worship with you today." "Will you sign the guest list, please, and we will show you to your seats," said the White ushers. Anne and her friend were seated with the other two Black activists, and four Black women worshiped in an all-White church. Anne remembers, "When the services were over the minister invited us to visit again. He said it as if he meant it, and I began to have a little hope."[10]

10. Moody, *Coming of Age*, 309–10.

That was a White church in a White supremacist culture hosting four Black women. Some churches immerse themselves in the gospel but absorb it no better than a rock absorbs water. Other churches immerse themselves in the gospel and absorb it, recognizing that Abba loves all, that Jesus represents the agapic love of God, and that Sophia counsels love without boundaries. These churches practice the gospel to transform society, thereby revealing the universalism of God, rejecting the exclusivism of their society, and implementing Revelation's vision of the saved community, which is a *community of difference*: "After that, I saw before me an immense crowd without number, from every nation, tribe, people, and language. They stood in front of the throne and the Lamb, dressed in long white robes and holding palm branches. And they cried out in a loud voice, 'Salvation is of our God, who sits on the throne, and of the Lamb!'" (Rev 7:9).

The Gospels relate Jesus's radical inclusivity in his story of the prodigal son (inclusion of the sinful), his choice of a Samaritan as hero-protagonist (inclusion of the religious outsider), his decision to dine with Simon the leper (inclusion of the scripturally excluded), his decision to dine with Zacchaeus the tax collector (inclusion of the hated powerful), his decision to converse with the Canaanite woman (inclusion of the marginalized female), and his protection of the woman framed for adultery (inclusion of the socially expendable). In the imitation of Christ, inspired by the Spirit, we are given the vocation of enacting the Sustainer's imagination. This activity is our meaning and purpose.

Churches Should Ordain All Genders to Leadership Positions in the Church

Patriarchy wastes the God-given talents of non-males. All genders should flourish within whatever vocation (calling) God has given them, including the vocation to pastoral ministry. Regarding women specifically, the celebration of women's gifts would be in keeping with the Bible, which deems both men and women to be made in the image of God, to love and be loved and celebrate love (Gen 1:27). Although it was written during times of horrible misogyny and violence, the Bible still repeatedly records women's leadership. Miriam was a prophet (Exod 15:20) who led the exodus along with Moses and Aaron (Mic 6:4). God appointed the prophet Deborah as a judge, leader of the Israelites (Judg 4). When the priests

Hilkiah, Ahikam, Achbor, Shaphan, and Asaiah needed help interpreting a newly discovered religious text, they consulted the prophet Huldah, wife of Shallum (2 Kgs 22:14). Isaiah's wife was likewise a prophet (Isa 8:3). And the prophet Joel predicted that the Holy Spirit would animate both men and women (Joel 2:28–29).

Recognizing the powerful women hailed by his tradition, Jesus chose to celebrate and empower. The Gospel of Luke records that Anna the prophet praised Jesus's arrival at the temple as a boy, making her the third person (after Mary and Simeon) to recognize him as the Messiah (Luke 2:36–38). Once Jesus began his ministry, he defied patriarchy by including women among his disciples; he included among his followers Mary Magdalene, Joanna (the wife of Herod's steward Chuza), Susanna, and many other women who supported Jesus with their own funds (Luke 8:1–3). In the ancient world, women were rarely considered suitable for education, but Jesus invited them to learn (Luke 10:38–42). Matthew records only female disciples being present at the crucifixion (Matt 27:55–56). Luke recounts that women were the first to discover Jesus's resurrection, but when they told the male disciples, none but Peter believed (Luke 24:9–11). Women were Jesus's most faithful disciples, perhaps because Jesus has no fragile male ego to defend.

The early church continued Jesus's liberating praxis. Paul writes that, since all are one in Christ Jesus, there is no longer male and female (Gal 3:28). He acknowledges that women can be prophets (1 Cor 11:5), an acknowledgement ratified in Acts, which deems Philip the evangelist to have four unmarried daughters with the gift of prophecy (Acts 21:8–9). Paul calls Phoebe a deacon of the church (Rom 16:1) and calls Junia an apostle (Rom 16:7). He refers to Euodia and Syntyche as his coworkers (Phil 4:2–3), as well as Prisca, Mary, and Tryphosa (Rom 16:3–12). One of the oldest Christian basilicas in Israel refers to "the Holy Mother Sophronia," while its references to male and female deacons are almost equal in number.[11] Scholars now call this basilica the "Church of the Deaconesses."

Despite this evidence for the historical importance of women's ministry, most churches do not ordain women. They give a variety of "reasons" for their refusal, but there are good reasons to ordain women, who can preach as well as men, perform sacraments as well as men, care for the sick as well as men, interpret the Bible as well as men, and lead as

---

11. David, "Byzantine Basilica."

well as men. These "reasons" cannot justify the ongoing waste of talent and denial of call.

By this time, people are so used to male priests and pastors that they have a hard time imagining otherwise. Given our unholy tendency to divinize the familiar and demonize the unfamiliar, the idea of women's ordination offends many. Nevertheless, those denominations that ordain women generally attract more female than male pastors. The first church that my wife, Abby, and I pastored had a slew of female ministers before we came as co-pastors. When I gave my first sermon, a girl in the congregation exclaimed to her mother, "I didn't know men could preach!" That girl had never felt spiritually excluded, thank God.

By ordaining women and using gender-balanced language for God, we assure girls that they, too, partake in divinity. We inform boys that girls are their spiritual equals and deserving of equally respectful treatment. We encourage women who have been marginalized by their spiritual traditions to feel centered. And we allow men, many of whom have or had emotionally distant relationships with their fathers, to have a closer relationship with their metaphorical Mother-God.

A Church That Follows Jesus Must Work with the Poor to Liberate the Poor

The church is as committed to Christ as it is to the poor. Jesus's identification with the poor is absolute: "The truth is, every time you aided the least of my siblings, you aided me" (Matt 25:40). Despite this statement, the church has more often tried to *convert* the poor than convert *itself to* the poor, allying with the powerful who are rich in resources, to the neglect of the powerless who are poor in resources.

Jesus was powerless and poor in resources. This status enables him to see society the way God sees it, as basic equality distorted by an illusion of rank. We separate ourselves from one another so that we can exploit with indifference. This separation creates injustice: social stratifications that do not cohere with our universal status as children of God. Some social stratification is inevitable, but for certain persons to starve while others waste, for some to live in palaces while others are homeless, for some to consume needless "medical" care while others die from lack of basic medical care, is unholy.

Psychologists and sociologists have accumulated evidence that the rich practice emotional distancing techniques in their relation to the poor. This distancing plays out at crosswalks, for example, where expensive cars are less likely to yield to pedestrians than inexpensive cars.[12] By blaming the poor for their situation, the rich justify their lack of compassion.[13] The Christian tradition calls this practice *sin*. Sin justifies its refusal to love by cultivating separation, then justifies separation by disparaging the objects of its indifference. Sin scorns for the sake of convenience, refusing to see itself in others or others in itself, dehumanizing itself by dehumanizing others, forgetting that others are the sacred mirror in which we see ourselves.[14]

Distorting our perception for self-advantage corrupts our self-perception. Either everyone is cherished, or no one is. Recognizing this truth, the church sees Christ where society sees no one, loving those who have lost the game of success or can't even play it. Through this love we free ourselves from the harsh gaze of judgment, so we can see and be seen with the merciful eyes of God. As Jesus teaches, "Blessed are those who show mercy, for they will be shown mercy" (Matt 5:7).

The practice of charity is a legitimate response to social suffering, but it can also deceive. Being charitable feels good. Some people profit from social suffering by exploiting labor, underpaying workers, denying benefits, and demanding unethical behavior of their employees. Then, these same people get to help the poor, *whose situation they created*, by practicing charity. They get to *be* bad but *feel* good, ensconcing themselves in pretentious self-satisfaction. Because we cannot create a utopia, charity will always be necessary, but it must be practiced alongside social criticism. Charity must ask, "Why is this charity needed? Instead of feeding the hungry, could we eliminate hunger?" In other words, *charity actively seeks to be replaced by justice, the very same justice envisioned in the kingdom of God.*

12. Coughenour et al., "Estimated Car Cost," §3.
13. Lott, "Cognitive and Behavioral Distancing," 102–4.
14. Habito, *Living Zen, Loving God*, 22.

In Their Liberating, Healing Ministry, Churches Co-Create the Kingdom of God with God

Each local church is an incubator of the kingdom of God, where we gather to imagine and disclose what the world should be like. We do so freely, in the confidence that God lets us be us and lets the world be the world, so that both can offer surprise to divinity.

Without freedom there is no community, only coercion and control. Hence, coercive power is expelled from the triune Godhead, and all church doctrines that thirst for *power over* are lies. God is love, which acts upon us in the same way that the beauty of a painting or the magnificence of a symphony acts upon us; that is, by acting *with* us, not *against* us; by *fulfilling* us, not *restricting* us. By co-creating the future with God, we *feel the truth* of Jesus's assurance that "the Kingdom of God is among you" (Luke 17:21), a latent presence among the powers and principalities of the world. The kingdom of God is *ahead* of us as the goal of human progress and *among* us when we deal fairly with one another and work for the universal well-being that God intends.

The Christian tradition teaches that God is unifying love, and the Christian church strives to express the unifying power of God as Abba imagines it, Jesus defines it, and Sophia inspires it. Therefore, to paraphrase Paul, if the church speaks in the tongues of humans and of angels but does not have love, it is a noisy gong or a clanging cymbal. And if the church has prophetic powers and understands all mysteries and all knowledge and if the church has all faith so as to move mountains but does not have love, it is nothing (1 Cor 13:1–2).

God loves people, not the church. Having confused themselves with the kingdom, and the kingdom with themselves, too many churches become committed to self-preservation even when they are no longer involved in kingdom creation. Sexual abuse cases are kept quiet and the abuser is sent elsewhere to abuse again, while the abused is shamed and silenced. The manufacture, concealment, and perpetuation of suffering by an institution created to disseminate the love of God constitutes apostasy.

The Church Is Set Within, not Apart

The church does not preach to the world from afar, in a state of pristine purity. Purity systems create insiders and outsiders, manufacture shame and self-righteousness, and separate us from one another, none of which is of God. God holds the world in being by holding the world to God. God is embrace, and Jesus is God's embrace of the world, an embrace that the church continues to this day. Embrace is the closest relationship possible without absorption, or the disappearance of one party into another. Embrace is nearness that preserves relatedness. Embrace is love.

Practicing embrace in a divided world renders the church countercultural. When humanity has accustomed itself to inhumanity and deemed its inhumanity normal, then the church must behave in an abnormal way. Due to the difficulty of this mission, the temptation to mainstream accommodation will always be there.

Jesus warns that the mainstream leads to a desert. *Our call is to preach agape.* Preaching the universal, unconditional love of God is a pastoral response to vastly powerful cultural forces that tell us we are not good enough, not pretty enough, not muscular enough, not smart enough, not anything enough, but that we can *become* enough if we buy this product or go to this restaurant or drive this car or live in this house. These forces have a hierarchical, comparative, personality-destabilizing metaphysic that they want to inscribe on our minds. The church must actively contest this inscription with an agapic metaphysic.

In so doing, the church will practice the "subversive repetition" described by Judith Butler, which undercuts the repetitions of power, those ceaselessly repeated claims that disfigure our consciousness for the benefit of others.[15] What identity do we want our children to have? Within what culture will we raise our children? What repetitions will they hear? They should be told—persistently, repeatedly, ceaselessly—that they are the children of God, basking in the universal, unconditional love of God for all, a love from which they cannot separate themselves. All of us, including our children, need this assurance, which consumer culture denies us. If the church fails to prophesy, then it fails to love: "Do not be afraid, but speak and do not be silent, for I am with you" (Acts 18:9–10a).

The church is gifted with Sophia, intelligence in context, who serves as our interlocutor with history and culture, the trusted counsel guiding us from misery to flourishing. The church's call is to attend to her counsel, thereby materializing her wisdom in word and deed, until "wisdom is vindicated by her children" (Luke 7:35). It does so through preaching, teaching, protest, prophecy, activism, Bible study, and conversation. Wisdom is consciousness of unity, while ignorance subscribes to separation.

---

15. J. Butler, *Gender Trouble*, 32.

But consciousness of unity cannot arise in isolation, and pride separates us from one another, so the Bible advises us to "be not wise in thine own eyes" (Prov 3:7 KJV). This admonition applies to both individuals and the church itself. God has made foolish the wisdom of the world, cynicism that masquerades as worldliness. This wisdom cannot know God, because to know God is to know *our need for each other.* Vanity is proud of its knowledge, but wisdom recognizes what it does not know. Therefore, the church must seek truth in others, with others, and for others, *including other religions,* in an attempt to develop a common wisdom that will be validated by the flourishing it creates.

The Church Binds the World Together through Prayer

When my father was having quintuple bypass surgery at the age of sixty-three, I told many people about it and generally got one of two responses: "I'll be thinking about you" or "I'll be praying for you." One parishioner, Cay Youngdahl, who was very much a person of prayer, asked me the specific day and time of the surgery. As I told her, she wrote the details down in her calendar and reassured me, "I'll be praying for your dad."

I'm not sure what those prayers did, if they steadied the surgeon's scalpel or strengthened my father's spirits, but they calmed my soul. Through prayers of intercession, people entered my world of concern. They did not leave me stranded or alone; instead, they provided the comfort of community and promised me that, no matter what, they would remain. Under no circumstances, no matter how trying, would I be ghosted.

God *for us* inspires the church in which we are *for each other,* and prayers of petition express this persevering loyalty. Prayer tends to people in a world that is inattentive. Prayer allows us to be intimately present to one another through God, and this presence, in an age of distraction, changes things. It deepens our awareness of one another, thereby revealing our basic unity. It momentarily allows the self to forget the self and all its preoccupations, jettisoning personal anxieties and worries from the center of the universe to the edge, where they belong. Prayer reminds us that the self is not the hub but the spoke of the revolving wheel, shifting our center from self-consciousness to self-surrender.[16] There, the quieted soul can finally hear God's assurance, "You are my beloved."

---

16. Heschel, *Man's Quest for God,* 7.

Prayer expresses our gratitude toward God for the mystery within which we live, which none of us earned yet all of us received. It arises naturally from our astonishment at the inconceivable surprise of living, from our gratitude for being present within the unfolding of time.[17] As gratitude, prayer participates in a boundaryless God who celebrates the whole and wants us to as well: "Prayer, often regarded as a 'means' of reaching God spiritually, can now be seen as the very glory of God and is therefore indistinguishable from the Godself, the once-supposed 'end' of prayer," writes Sam Zhai.[18] In this conception, prayer is more like singing than asking, a joy we are swept into rather than a duty we practice.

Prayer comes naturally to some people but is a struggle for others. An inability to sit and speak with God is not a spiritual weakness; God gives different spiritual gifts to different people so we can fulfill different roles in God's community. Prayer is a spiritual gift, but other spiritual gifts can become prayer, and *prayer alone is never a substitute for action.* When Joan Cheever was fined for feeding the homeless in San Antonio, she explained, "This is how I pray. I pray when I cook. I pray when I serve."[19] Prayer is not a substitute for action; it is our motivation to action, and all action toward the kingdom is prayer.

To Heal One Another Requires Showing Up

Jesus rose with his wounds, which were as real as their healing. If we trust God to heal, then we need not deny our wounds. Acceptance of their reality produces openness to their power, a power that is released in community. In every such act of communal healing, God intimates the new creation. Those receptive to such intimations will naturally gather to express God's grace to one another. During times of great trial, people of faith experience God, and God-centered communities, as helpful. They experience the Creator as loving, even as they experience the creation as enigmatic—beautiful yet tragic, alive yet deadly, providential yet threatening. They choose to live within this paradox because the inhabitation of paradox, the ability to sit peacefully with unanswered questions, offers the most life.[20]

17. Heschel, *Spiritual Grandeur,* 341.
18. Zhai, "Nondualism and Jewish-Christian Relations," 190.
19. McCoy, "What Happened," para. 10.
20. Nouwen, *Wounded Healer,* 93.

Powerful, healing community requires interpersonal loyalty, and interpersonal loyalty requires *being there* for each other. People derive comfort, support, and strength from church, but these benefits depend on regular engagement. Sometimes, people just go to church as needed; hard weeks are followed by church on Sunday, drawing strength from community, and easy weeks are the weeks to take off, because ease fosters the illusion of self-sufficiency. This irregularity may suit the individual, but it doesn't help the community. If we are truly connected, which we truly are, then on bad weeks we should attend church because we need community, and on good weeks we should attend church *because community needs us.*

Paul and Kay Williams, beloved members of a church we served, weren't looking for a church that would meet their needs. They were looking for a church that needed them, because they felt that was where they could best serve God. They had realized that, as mentioned above, every participant in church is a priest, a minister of God, to every other member in a church. The pastor alone is insufficient due to simple time limitations as well as limited life experience. On the Sunday when someone who has lost their job goes to church, they will need other people who have lost their jobs to support them. Parents who are struggling with a child will need other parents, who have struggled with their children, to support them. Those who are grieving need to be loved through their grief, comforted in the truth that grief is a universal experience. The best way to support one another is to *be there* for one another, to attend regularly and live openly.

Love Is Worth the Risk

Having counseled such dangerous vulnerability, we should now consider the real possibility of trauma. Caregivers of traumatized persons run the risk of developing vicarious or secondary traumatization. With vicarious traumatization, the caregiver internalizes the trauma of the cared for and begins to manifest symptoms of the patient's trauma. Vicarious traumatization can produce profound psychiatric disturbances—depression, anxiety, insomnia, etc.

I suffered from this disturbance when I worked as a chaplain in a psychiatric hospital for a year. I counseled patients, led Bible studies and worship services, and prayed and talked with whomever needed company.

To do my job and get to know them better, I read their charts and became acquainted with the horrible suffering so many of them had experienced in childhood, sometimes in utero. Since I was on a ward for patients accused of crimes but found not guilty by reason of insanity, I knew that most of them would never be released from the hospital. After a few months of this chaplaincy, I was watching a movie at home with my wife when I broke down weeping uncontrollably, for no immediately apparent reason.

In the end, my disturbance was relatively slight and my psyche normalized with time, counseling, and professional maturity. I learned to be compassionate with my patients without internalizing their experiences, present to them without absorbing them. Nevertheless, my temporary disturbance raises crucial questions: Should a clinician for the traumatized deliberately restrict their vulnerability to protect themselves from the danger of secondary traumatization? Is self-protection a necessary strategy for successful caregiving? If so, then this agenda seems at odds with the presented theology. God is interpersonal vulnerability, in whose image we are made. Expressing this vulnerability, Christ did not protect himself from incarnation, but joined us in our lives, at great cost. Likewise, caregivers who enter their patients' lives may suffer. If caregivers do not protect themselves, then the resulting psychiatric disturbance might disturb the healthy relationships they do have, as well as impede their ability to care for the traumatized.

How far should a disciple of Christ follow Christ? We live in networks of relationships, with loyalties to family and duties at work and responsibilities to community. We must strike a balance. Jesus had two loyalties, to God and humankind, and those were absolute. We may live in the imitation of Christ, but we are not Christ. Even our call to love dangerously demands critical application and an acceptance of ambiguity, since there are many we are called to love, including ourselves.

Sacraments Nourish Dangerous Love

Close community is nurtured by religious ritual. All religions practice rituals, but religions interpret their rituals differently. Some offer "magical" interpretations of the ritual as a supernatural technology that produces material outcomes. Other religions interpret rituals as meaning-*making* activities, superimposed on life to create order from chaos. In our account, religious rituals are not magic, nor are they meaning-making activities. Instead, they are meaning-*accessing* activities. Religious rituals access a *preexisting* meaning woven into the universe. Because they access the sacred, they are *sacraments*: portals through which the grace that lies within the cosmos flows into our everyday lives. Religious ritual confirms the basic sacramentality of the cosmos. Sacraments use the constituents of the universe—space, time, energy, and matter—as channels of God's grace, revealing them to be possessed of more vividness than common sense alone could explain.

Ritual is a medium of the sacred with transformative power. Indeed, this power may be so transformative that it seems, *perhaps is*, magical, wonder working. Transformation bequeaths knowledge. By way of consequence, ritual is a powerful way of coming to know, of acquiring sound knowledge about human existence in a sacred cosmos. The knowledge that ritual confers is not discursive: it cannot be translated into language, because it is first and finally embodied. The reduction of this embodied knowledge to language, even when necessary, will distort and attenuate it. Therefore, ritual knowledge must remain what it is—embodied, active, and nondiscursive. Below, I will briefly discuss two Christian rituals, baptism and communion. Participating in baptism and communion may lead thought from reason to rumination, and theologians may even translate ritual experience into doctrinal concepts, but all religious ritual resists intellectual mastery because ritual exceeds cognition, just as reality exceeds system.[21] Life is always more than we can think.

Baptism Celebrates Life Itself as Sacred

Despite ritual's resistance to the imperium of words, theology matters. Ritual may not be reducible to theological content, and it may not be translatable into language, but ritual still has cognitive content that language can suggest but not capture. That cognitive content will vary according to the participant, both in depth and meaning: bad interpretations produce impoverished ritual experience, while good interpretations produce enriched ritual experience. And some interpretations of rituals are just plain old inadequate.

My wife and I pastored a local Protestant church for many years. Since it was very much a local church, we ended up baptizing, marrying, and burying many Protestants, practicing or not, in the local community.

21. J. P. Sydnor, "Blessed Transgression," 69.

(In pastoral parlance, we hatched them, matched them, and dispatched them.) Funerals were rarely problematic, but baptisms could get sketchy since, for many of the nonpracticing Protestants, they seemed to be more public performance than sacred rite, more about the after-party than the God of love.

We would meet with parents prior to a child's baptism, talk about the sacrament, and ask what it meant to the parents and extended family. We got a variety of answers, most of which were theologically subpar. Among the most common were: we need to baptize him now, before he gets too old and it looks funny; it's not that big a deal to us, but his grandparents want him baptized; we haven't had a family reunion in a while, and baptisms are more fun than funerals; I'm not sure if I believe this, but my great aunt is concerned that if he dies without being baptized he'll go to hell. Rarely did parents tell us that they wanted to raise their child in the love of God, and they wanted the help of a community in doing so, and baptism would seal that covenant.[22]

At this point Abby or I would have a conversation with the parents. We would talk about baptism and what it means: In the sacrament of baptism, we utilize the everyday element of water to mark the holiness of life, thereby reminding ourselves of the sanctity of both. In baptism, Sophia proclaims that this child is predestined to God's gracious covenant; they are beloved before being capable of love. The congregation, as priests of God to the child, promise to raise the child within the divine love, supporting the child unconditionally as they negotiate a highly conditional world. Thus, baptism begins a journey for all, in the hope that our faith will continue and deepen throughout life, in a community whose purpose, among many, is to discover and enjoy our shared humanity.

This is our theology of baptism, but other communities have different theologies. This divergence came to a head in the archdiocese of Phoenix, where for over twenty years Rev. Andres Arango baptized children by saying, "We baptize you in the name of the Father and of the Son and of the Holy Spirit." The prescribed formula is "I baptize you in the name of the Father and of the Son and of the Holy Spirit." This change in wording caused quite a kerfuffle. The local bishop, Thomas Olmsted, advised parishioners, "If you were baptized using the wrong words, that means your baptism is invalid, and you are not baptized. . . . The issue with using 'We' is that it is not the community that baptizes a person, rather, it is Christ, and Him alone, who presides at all of the sacraments, and so it is Christ Jesus who baptizes." He went on to advise those invalidly baptized by Rev. Arango not to take communion until they had been validly baptized, although he did comfort them, "We can be assured that all who approached God, our Father, in good faith to receive the sacraments did not walk away empty-handed."[23]

Rev. Arango was not the first priest to baptize saying "we" instead of "I." Among some quarters of the Roman Catholic priesthood, a preference had arisen for communitarian liturgy that engaged the whole congregation rather than emphasizing the activity of the priest alone. Enough priests were doing so that the Roman Catholic Church's Congregation for the Doctrine of the Faith issued a prohibition against such communitarian liturgy in June 2020, declaring such baptisms invalid.[24] Earlier, some priests had adapted the baptismal liturgy, baptizing in the name of the Creator, Liberator, and Sustainer, or Creator, Redeemer, and Sanctifier, rather than Father, Son, and Holy Ghost. Theirs was an attempt to use gender-neutral language for God instead of exclusively masculine language for God, an innovation that the Congregation for the Doctrine of the Faith declared invalid in February 2008.[25]

The theology we are developing here dovetails with the communitarian language of Rev. Arango as well as the gender-neutral language of the other priestly reformers. The primary purpose of ritual is *pastoral*—to care for persons in their journey through life. Since pastoral needs change with pastoral circumstances, the performance of ritual need not hew closely to any preexisting pattern. *We must adapt rituals over time,* because the patriarchal formulations of yesteryear may ring oppressive in our egalitarian, universalist minds. Moreover, *the agapic love communicated by the ritual, not the precise wording, makes it effective.* We don't have to "get it right," but we hope that it "works," as does medicine on a disease.[26] The feelings a ritual produces, the understanding it confers, and the activity it encourages render the ritual successful or unsuccessful. The best rituals are indeed communitarian expressions of existential solidarity. These rituals recognize our fundamental unity within a creative power coursing through the universe, whose greatest desire is to accompany us.

23. https://dphx.org/valid-baptisms. Accessed Dec. 29, 2021. Link discontinued.

24. Congregazione per la Dottrina della Fede, "Responsum," "Nota Dottrinale," para. 7.

25. Miralles, "New *Response*," para. 4.

26. Michaels and Sax, "Performance," 305–6.

Because nonbinary persons, women, and men are all equally made in the image of God, hence equally divine, liturgical language should be gender-neutral or gender-inclusive. Exclusively masculine language for God ratifies patriarchy and resists the divinely intended equality. Recognizing that the Bible uses primarily masculine language for God, the church must emphasize those texts that use feminine language for God, thereby advancing feminism—the belief that women and men are equal in talents, rights, and responsibilities. It must also emphasize those texts that refer to a gender-transcendent God, thereby including nonbinary persons within the divine image.

Such inclusiveness is not a dream or even a plan; it is happening already, in many churches around the world. At Grace Community Boston, utilizing the innovation of Rev. James F. Kay for Riverside Church, we baptize "In the name of the Father, the Son, and the Holy Spirit; one God, Mother of us all."[27] We begin the Lord's Prayer with "Our Parent, who art in heaven . . ." And we conceptualize Sophia the Holy Spirit as female in story, liturgy, and song, providing all genders with a feminine divine.[28] Christian theology need not be patriarchal, and Christian liturgy need not be patriarchal.

The Lord's Supper Remembers, Invokes, and Anticipates the Fullness of Communion

Religious ritual either works or it dies. One criterion of effectiveness is the ritual's ability to transform our interaction with the non-ritualized world. If the ritual causes us to interpret and act in ordinary time in accordance with the values expressed in ritual time, then the ritual has succeeded. If the ritual produces no change in our feeling or behavior outside of ritual time, then the ritual has failed.[29] Although ritual practice is introverted, focused on its own space and time, the effect of the ritual practice is extroverted, spilling into and changing everyday space and time. In other words, ritual creates in the present, ritualized space-time what we will strive to create in the future, universal space-time. It enacts a vision of reality and impels action toward that vision.

27. Greene-McCreight, *Feminist Reconstructions*, 126.

28. U. King, *Women and Spirituality*, 206.

29. Jennings, "On Ritual Knowledge," 116.

The Christian vision of reality is the kingdom of God as preached by Jesus and anticipated by the Lord's Supper. The Lord's Supper, or Eucharist, remembers, repeats, and anticipates the communion of saints experienced at table in the presence of Jesus, a communion that will be perfected in the kingdom. By doing so, it breaks down the boundaries between past, present, and future, remembering the past into the present, a present that anticipates our future gathering in the full presence of God. At the same time, it breaks down the boundaries between locales, so we gather at the Jerusalem table of Jesus, the local table of our church, and the future table of the new creation. It unites the work of the divine persons, as we are invited by the same Savior, pervaded by the same Spirit, and giving thanks to the same Creator, thereby communing with the same God.

The invitation to communion is an invitation to community. Since communion is universal, one reality sustained by one God, the community of the table is universal, one gathering at one feast. *An exclusive ritual cannot express inclusive love.* Jesus's teachings and Sophia's intimations both commend a church without boundaries, an "us" without a "them" that fulfills the intentions of Abba.[30] In Jesus's day, those who would pollute a table, those who were to be excluded from table fellowship, were the poor, the maimed, the lame, and the blind, so Jesus says: "When you have a feast, invite the poor, the maimed, the lame, the blind, and you will be blessed" (Luke 14:13–14a). Who are the outcasts today, with whom we would not share a meal? At table, we should exclude only those whom Jesus would exclude, but Jesus included Thomas who would doubt him, Peter who would deny him, and Judas who would betray him. We conclude that Jesus would exclude no one, as do we. *The table must be open.*

Sadly, most invitations to the communion table are exclusive, limiting participation to baptized Christians, or baptized Christians who have been confirmed in their specific faith, or baptized Christians who have been confirmed in their specific faith and are currently in good standing with the church. This limited participation is frequently enforced by religious authorities. Ironically, the authorities of Jesus's day denied the activity of the Holy Spirit within him and would have shunned him from table. It follows that, in our own day, if we deny communion to some, we risk denying communion to Christ.

30. Edmondson, "Opening the Table," 224.

If communion is open to all, then it is open to children. At Grace Community Boston, as soon as a child can digest solid food, they are welcome to be brought forward for communion. This development, which was natural and spontaneous, demanded that we discuss the imagery used for communion. We needed to engage and alter tradition according to our norm: the agapic love of God. Such breaking with tradition is traditional. As Tom Driver notes, rituals change through history. They are created in times and places according to the need of those times and places; as needs change rituals change.[31] A new world will need new rituals, and any community moving toward the kingdom of God strides toward a new world.

Children tend to think literally. The capacity for metaphorical thought develops with age and life experience. Since we were serving communion to very young children, we became concerned that their literal interpretation of eucharistic imagery regarding the body and blood of Christ would make them think that we were all, literally, cannibals.[32] In order to investigate, we asked our parishioners what they remembered about communion from their childhood. The results disturbed us. The body-and-blood language had conjured some gruesome imagery. One parishioner thought that her church had Christ's corpse in the back room, behind the apse, and from this corpse carved up the body and drained out the blood for each week's service. Others had similar memories and were convinced that they were eating and drinking (or their parents were) the literal flesh and blood of Jesus. And they remembered being, let us say, discomfited by this regular occurrence.

Our church believes that all good theology is pastoral theology, so we were more than willing to adapt tradition to this pastoral discovery. While celebrating communion, we began to avoid body-and-blood imagery, emphasizing instead remembrance of Jesus's absolute ethical courage, the presence of Christ among us through table fellowship, and the promised banquet at which all will be filled. Like the early church, and like many contemporary emergent churches, communion became similar to an agape meal or love feast—we replaced wafers with large chunks of fresh-baked bread and goblets of grape juice. Our invitation to table is open, and we have served Hindus, Buddhists, Muslims, agnostics, humanists, and Jews. Utilizing pastorally revised yet biblically grounded

31. Driver, "Transformation," 182.
32. Geary, *I Is an Other*, 158.

language, we began referring to the elements as the "bread of heaven" (John 6:51) and "cup of salvation" (Ps 116:13; see also 1 Cor 10:16). Children partake joyfully and see nothing spooky about the experience.

The Church Itself Is Always Broken and Always Mending

Church is where, ideally, the ultimate truth of the universe—divine love—is granted physical, temporal expression. It is where love is enacted as consistently as possible, felt as deeply as possible, and thought as thoroughly as possible. The church always fails to express love perfectly, but it fails in grace, aware that forgiveness is granted even before the failure occurs.

Jesus tells his disciples that they are "the light of the world" (Matt 5:14), and many times they have been, building orphanages and hospitals, caring for the wounded, making peace, feeding the hungry, visiting the sick, and comforting the bereaved. At other times, the church has been darkness. Any participant in church knows that deep community is dangerous. As Jesus discovered in his relationship to Judas, vulnerability risks betrayal. Nevertheless, the saints persevere (Rev 14:12), striving to embody the unity of the three persons in their own unity and to increase unity on earth. Faith does not guarantee success in this endeavor, nor does it close the gap between human brokenness and the fullness of God. But just as our love is not complete, our failure will not be complete either, and much beauty arises along the way. Sophia promises us that God will complete what God has begun. Given the power of Sophia's activity, the only churches that can't mend are those that don't admit they're broken.

One person who suffered from disillusionment with the church was a young Presbyterian pastor in eastern North Carolina in 1964. Reverend Clement A. Sydnor III, my father, was disappointed to learn that the Beulaville Junior Chamber of Commerce sponsored the Duplin County Agricultural Fair, which oddly had no animals on display but did offer "girlie shows," which were quite a lucrative draw. Many years later, my father told me what these girlie shows entailed. They were not risque southern vaudeville; they were perverse, degrading, and abusive.

My father and four other local pastors began pressing the Junior Chamber of Commerce to stop the girlie shows, and their campaign gathered some momentum. But he was surprised to get pushback from a leading elder in his church, who was also a leading businessman in the community. This parishioner initiated a community-wide controversy, sending slanderous letters to various institutions. In the Presbyterian denomination, when there is significant conflict between a pastor and a prominent church member, the presbytery (local governing body) will step in to resolve the matter.

My father was surprised by the tepid response of the presbytery, which seemed indifferent to the girlie shows and a bit frustrated that a young pastor had created needless headaches by confronting a long-established churchman. Many other young pastors in the presbytery were having similar problems and felt bereft of institutional support. Writing to one of his former professors in seminary, my father explained:

> As you know, this is predominantly a presbytery of young min-isters. The young ministers are getting tired and irritated at the little support and guidance the presbytery as a whole is giving. The turnover is rapid because of this and it will increase in the next two years. . . . If one of us young ministers take something like this to presbytery and bring it up on the floor, we are looked upon with a kind of sympathy because we are young with the zeal of a prophet and pretty soon we will metamorphose into the kind of apostles that all ministers should be—so argue the older and stronger voices of presbytery. The most advice I can get is on how a young minister can be an old minister in one easy step. It is as if God has no use for the prophetic zeal of a young minister and is only tolerating him until he becomes older and wiser. . . . As you can see, I'm pretty disgusted with advice on how to be old at heart, with advice on how not to rock the boat and make waves, and with rolling merrily on to hell.[33]

At the age of twenty-seven, my father left his first pastorate and went to Mount Horeb Presbyterian Church in the Shenandoah Valley, where he had a much better experience. Still, after five years there, he was suf-ficiently disillusioned to leave ministry, earning a doctorate in education and working with the state of Virginia to prevent juvenile delinquency.

He returned to pastoral ministry twelve years later, with his eyes wide open, and pastored several more churches over the next twenty years. These ministries also had their ups and downs, but he loved his calling, and little miracles happened. A family came to his church one Advent season, inquiring about membership. They had a pleasant young son and a vivacious younger daughter with Down's syndrome. They had

33. C. Sydnor, "Letter," paras. 4–5.

been regular attendees at a larger, nearby church, but their daughter had been left out of the Christmas pageant. My dad was appalled, and the girl was immediately named Mary in Bow Creek's pageant, to the family and the church's great joy. That was one of the best Christmas Eve services ever. It was an imperfect church with an imperfect congregation and imperfect pastor, but they worked hard to love like God. And sometimes they hit the mark perfectly, creating the little miracles that sustain us.

9

Agape and Inexhaustible Meaning

Writing and reading decrease our sense of isolation. They deepen and widen and expand our sense of life: they feed the soul. When writers make us shake our heads with the exactness of their prose and their truths, and even make us laugh about ourselves or life, our buoyancy is restored. We are given a shot at dancing with, or at least clapping along with, the absurdity of life, instead of being squashed by it over and over again. It's like singing on a boat during a terrible storm at sea. You can't stop the raging storm, but singing can change the hearts and spirits of the people who are together on that ship.

—ANNE LAMOTT[1]

Bad Interpretation of the Bible
Drives People into Atheism

I TEACH A COURSE on science and religion, and we always discuss Darwin's theory of evolution in class. One semester I was explaining the history of Darwinism and its conflict with those churches that insist on a literal interpretation of Genesis. I also covered those churches that accept

1. Lamott, *Bird by Bird*, 237.

Darwin's theory as a scientific advance, grateful for the powers of observation and reason that God has gifted us.

A student in the back of class was staring at me wide-eyed throughout the lecture. Later, in conversation, I discovered she had been raised
in a fundamentalist church that preached *biblical infallibilism*—the belief
that there can be no mistakes or errors in the Bible. They disavowed Darwin's theory of evolution and insisted on young earth creationism, con-
cluding that Adam and Eve were historical figures, created from scratch,
and that the world was about six thousand years old.

To the members of this church, Genesis was more accurate than any
humanly written science textbook because it was the divinely written word
of God, utterly reliable in all fields of human knowledge, including science
and history. As the word of God, it couldn't be wrong and anything that
disagreed with it couldn't be right. For this community, to reject a literal
interpretation of Genesis due to "scientific discoveries" was the height of
arrogance, a preference for human reason over against faith in God. To
make things worse, her church taught that acceptance of Darwin's theory
of evolution inevitably led to atheism, eugenics, and ultimately, Nazism,
since it assumed cutthroat competition between all parties.

Ironically, my student was a biology major. Biological science con-
siders Darwin's theory of evolution to be foundational, essential for understanding all the subdisciplines within that field. During her college
studies, as the overwhelming evidence for evolution became apparent, she
began to believe that she was an atheist because she had been told that
Darwinism was incompatible with Christian faith. She was being forced
to choose between her intellect and God, and her intellect was winning.

This lecture was the first time she had learned of Christians who
accepted evolution and followed Jesus. She saw that deep faith was compatible with intellectual integrity. She was not, by predilection, an atheist. She trusted God, but didn't have a concept of God that she could
trust. During class, her face expressed the dawning realization that she
could be both a Christian and a scientist, in good conscience, without
compartmentalization.

In this chapter, we will discuss the Bible and its interpretation. What
we understand the Bible to be, and how we interpret it, can draw people
into faith or drive them out of faith. Currently, more people are being
driven out than drawn in. Below, we will propose an understanding and
interpretation of the Bible that accords with how Jesus read his own

Bible—agapically, as an expression of the universal, unconditional love of God for all.

Agapic Interpretation of the Bible Imitates Jesus's Interpretation of the Bible

Jesus was a Jewish rabbi interpreting Jewish Scriptures for his fellow Jews. In respect of his Judaism, I have attempted to avoid *supersessionism* in this book. Supersessionism is the belief that Christianity has *superseded* (surpassed, supplanted, or replaced) Judaism in its covenant with God. It is a form of triumphalism, an assertion that "God likes my religion better than your religion." One thousand five hundred years of persecution, pogroms, and genocide by Christians against Jews should liberate Christians from any *moral* triumphalism, and liberation from moral triumphalism should liberate us from *theological* triumphalism.

One symptom of triumphalism, reaching back to the second century CE, is the use of the terms *Old Testament* and *New Testament*, which imply that God's covenant with the Jews (the "Old" Testament) has been abrogated by God's covenant with the Christians (the "New" Testament). Despite this implication, the church's attitude toward the Jews' "Old" Testament was always ambivalent. On the one hand, the church implied that the Jewish covenant had been superseded. On the other hand, the church utilized it extensively in practice, as had Jesus.

Since we are celebrating Jesus's Judaism, we are also going to celebrate his use of Jewish Scripture. To avoid insinuating that God's covenant with the Jews is abrogated, we have referred to the "Old" Testament as "the Hebrew Bible," "the Jewish Scriptures," and "the Torah." We have referred to the "New" Testament as "the Newer Testament," in keeping with the practice of many contemporary Bible scholars. The term *Newer Testament* is more theologically accurate and less supersessionist. It is also symbolizes Christian repentance for 1500 years of often violent anti-Judaism.

The Church Wrote the Newer Testament

We can now comment on the placement of this chapter in the book, after the chapter on the church. Our consideration of the Bible follows our consideration of the church because *the church wrote the Newer Testament.*

That is why the word *church* (Greek: *ekklēsia*) occurs 114 times, in various forms, in the Newer Testament. The church also decided to include the Hebrew Scriptures in its canon (a *canon* is an accepted list of authoritative writings). This decision was not a foregone conclusion: some early theologians wanted only the Newer Testament to be deemed authoritative, dismissing the Hebrew Scriptures as the archaic revelation of a lesser god. Other theologians, noting Jesus's extensive reliance on the Hebrew Scriptures, wanted to include them in the authoritative canon. This faction won the debate. Even today the Protestant Church disagrees with the Catholic and Orthodox Churches about which Hebrew Scriptures are canonical and which aren't.

The authors of the Newer Testament wrote in much the same way as contemporary Christian authors. They studied Scripture, gathered stories, collected teachings, shared liturgy, read philosophy, debated theology, worshiped regularly, reasoned rigorously, and wrote creatively. They weren't depersonalized automata transmitting words dictated to them by the Holy Spirit. They were human beings, inspired by Sophia, discipled to Jesus, and falling newly in love with Abba.

Christ Was not an Infallibilist, So Christians Should not Be Either

Bad theology manufactures an artificial dilemma between faith and reason, and biblical infallibilism is bad theology. In English, the term *infallibilism* derives from the First Vatican Council's assertion that papal *ex cathedra* (with the full authority of the office) teachings are *infallible*, or without mistakes.[2] A few decades later, American Christian fundamentalists applied it to the Bible, asserting that the Bible is uniformly inspired by the Holy Spirit, should be interpreted as literally as possible, and is applicable to all realms of human life, including history and science.[3]

Similarly, *inerrantism* is the belief that there are no errors in the Bible. Within fundamentalism, the terms *inerrant* and *infallible* hold a spectrum of definitions and ascribe to the Bible varying arenas of authority.[4] We will be using them more or less interchangeably. For a relatively recent, widely distributed, and broadly accepted statement of scriptural

2. Lawlor et al, "Infallibility," 7:448.
3. Gray, "Inspiration of the Bible," §2.
4. Johnston, *Evangelicals at an Impasse*, 36.

authority, consider the Chicago Statement on Biblical Inerrancy (1978). In abbreviation, its authors assert:

> Holy Scripture, as the inspired Word of God witnessing au-
> thoritatively to Jesus Christ, may properly be called infallible
> and inerrant. These negative terms have a special value, for they
> explicitly safeguard crucial positive truths. . . . Infallible signi-
> fies the quality of neither misleading nor being misled and so
> safeguards in categorical terms the truth that Holy Scripture is a
> sure, safe, and reliable rule and guide in all matters. . . . Similarly,
> inerrant signifies the quality of being free from all falsehood or
> mistake and so safeguards the truth that Holy Scripture is en-
> tirely true and trustworthy in all its assertions.[5]

The concepts of infallibility and inerrancy are modern words that arose under duress. The Roman Catholic Church adopted the doctrine of papal *ex cathedra* infallibility as it was losing its papal states in the late 1800s. American fundamentalism adopted the doctrine of biblical infallibility as its traditional beliefs were being challenged by the rise in historical and scientific knowledge in the early 1900s. Without irony, they ascribed tremendous authority to traditional authorities that were losing author-ity, in different times and different places for different reasons.

Regarding scriptural interpretation, while no one in first-century Judaea would have used such terminology, analogous options for inter-preting the Hebrew Bible did exist. As we shall see, Jesus did not adopt them, preferring more wide-ranging interpretative strategies. In this chapter we will analyze how Jesus of Nazareth interpreted his own Scrip-tures. This investigation proceeds on the premise that *Christ's method of interpretation is appropriate for Christians*. If Christians want to know how to interpret and enact Scripture, then we should study how Christ interpreted and enacted Scripture.

Jesus Was a Rabbi Who Practiced Midrash

Jesus was considered a rabbi (Mark 14:45; Matt 26:25; John 3:2; etc.). The Newer Testament frequently depicts Jesus debating with Pharisees, a re-ligious and social group within Second Temple Judaism known for their emphasis on the observance of Torah. In the Gospel accounts, Jesus and

---

5. "Chicago Statement," "Infallibility, Inerrancy, Interpretation," §C.

the Pharisees disagree about how to interpret and apply religious law.[6] Many passages unfairly depict all Pharisees as strict *legalists*, those who rigorously obey and enforce the law in all circumstances without regard to outcome. In truth, the Pharisees practiced a range of interpretative strategies, and Jesus overlapped with them in many ways.[7]

Jesus's interpretation of his own Scripture is best understood as *midrash*. Jesus's Jewish tradition denied to Scripture a fixed meaning that could be determined. Instead, Jews ascribed (and ascribe) to Scripture an inexhaustible meaning that invites perpetual investigation, allows perpetual discovery, and demands perpetual debate. Hence, the point of exegesis is not so much to *get it right* as to *never stop*.[8] Along the way, only openness and respect will reveal the hidden meanings that are unavailable to any isolated human mind.

The term *midrash* is based on the Hebrew root *d-r-sh*, "to investigate." It is an expansive form of biblical interpretation that attempts to discover the latent meanings within Scripture. To do so, midrash can take many different forms: expanding on briefly mentioned events, providing character backstories, applying general laws to specific cases, interpreting historic events allegorically as timeless morality tales, etc. The practice of midrash began during the Second Temple period, roughly 516 BCE to 70 CE, but became a pervasive practice within rabbinic Judaism, beginning after the destruction of the Second Temple in 70 CE.[9]

How are the teachings of Jesus similar to the Jewish practice of midrash? One midrashic practice is the juxtaposition of discrete passages, stringing together the "pearls" of the Torah in new ways that reveal new meanings, thereby fostering scriptural discovery through scriptural play. Originally, in their order of appearance in the Torah, these pearls are placed in a particular order on a particular string. However, for purposes of exposition, that order can be rearranged. Jewish expositors take pearls from different places on the string, which were previously isolated from one another, and place them into relation, fostering new discoveries of meaning. Jewish tradition encourages this novel juxtaposition of separated pearls. At its most successful, such comparison reveals their primordial unity, "recovering the originary moment of Revelation itself."[10]

6. Mansoor, "Pharisees," 16:30–31.

7. Falk, *Jesus the Pharisee*, 54, 149.

8. Stern, "Midrash and Parables," 707.

9. Herr, "Midrash," 14:182.

10. Boyarin, "Allegory and Midrash," 114–15.

Jesus employs this strategy. When a contemporary asks Jesus to name the greatest commandment, Jesus instead names two—the commandment to love God (Deut 6:5) and neighbor (Lev 19:18). These he declares to be similar but not identical (Matt 22:34–40). In so doing, he integrates two commandments that can, in certain situations, conflict. Is it more important to rest on the Sabbath or practice compassion on the Sabbath? Is it more important to maintain ritual purity or help a bloodied assault victim? Jesus sides with his contemporaries, such as the Jewish sage Hillel, who advocate observance of the law *alongside* compassionate pragmatism.[11] Jesus's integration of two commandments that conflict in certain situations generates an open interpretation that resists algorithmic applications and predetermined outcomes. Jesus proclaims both theism *and* humanism, placing them into an unresolved relationship that demands discernment.

Like the midrashic expositors, Jesus communicates wisdom through stories.[12] For example, after Jesus associates love of God with love of neighbor, a listener presses him: "But who is my neighbor?" Rather than providing an authoritative definition of "neighbor," Jesus tells the story of the good Samaritan. This brief story provides a certain insight into the term *neighbor*, revealing a universalist ethic in which *one chooses to become a neighbor to everyone*. It rejects restrictive geographic or ethnic definitions of "neighbor," offering instead a sweeping moral one. The audience is invited to apply this ethical and experiential possibility in their own lives, which are their own stories. In this way, Jesus transforms our life together by infusing it with universalist hope, while always leaving it open to new meanings, through the elasticity of narrative.

Midrashic stories provide concrete illustrations of general principles.[13] For example, the Scriptures had long referred to God as father, the "redeemer of old" (Isa 63:16). But this metaphor requires explication. Some earthly fathers are wrathful, some forgiving; some negligent, others engaged. What is YHWH like? Jesus responds that YHWH is Abba, our affectionate father, and tells the story of the prodigal son (Luke 15:11–32), in which a negligent and disrespectful son is welcomed home by a merciful and forgiving father. This story adds a new layer of significance to the inherited biblical testimony and presents new opportunities for understanding God.

11. Bowker, *Jesus and the Pharisees*, 34–37.

12. Neusner, *Midrash*, 174–76.

13. Neusner, *Midrash*, 122–23.

The quest to understand the Torah was also (and remains today) a quest to join human minds to the mind of God: to reason as God reasons, with Scripture providing the divine substance for our human reasoning. For the midrashists, this reasoning resulted sometimes in the *amplification* of certain injunctions, rather than their mere acceptance and observation.[14] Jesus also practices such amplification. For example, Exod 20:13 forbids murder, but Matt 5:22 forbids both murder and the anger that might lead to it. Exodus 20:14 proscribes adultery, but Matt 5:27–30 proscribes adultery and the lust that might lead to it. And Lev 24:17–20 prescribes proportionate retribution (an eye for an eye, in a noble attempt to protect society from disproportionate retribution), but Matt 5:38–42 prescribes unlimited mercy (turn the other cheek).

Such amplification accords with the midrashists' emphasis on the *ethical* implications of Torah, which was scrutinized to determine which human behaviors best fulfilled the will of God.[15] Jesus joins in this ethical emphasis by citing the Golden Rule as a summary of Torah itself: "In everything do to others as you would have them do to you, for this is the Law and the Prophets" (Matt 7:12). There is no record of any interaction between Jesus and his elder contemporary, the sage Hillel. Still, Jesus echoes and adapts Hillel's summary of Torah: "That which is hateful to you, do not do to others, the rest is commentary; go now and study."[16]

Finally, midrashists engaged contradictory and difficult passages, attempting to resolve them so that the Jewish mind might be drawn into the consistency of the divine mind.[17] Jesus also engaged in this effort, aiming to harmonize the *seemingly* conflicting aspects of Scripture. For example, Jesus prioritized certain principles over others: although he observes the Sabbath, he prefers Hosea's call to mercy (Hos 6:6) over any rigorous observance of Sabbath law (Matt 12:1–8). Even though the Hebrew Scriptures prescribe sacrifice through the priesthood (Lev 1:1–5) *and* honor of father and mother (Exod 20:12; Deut 5:16), Jesus prioritizes honor of father and mother over sacrifice through the priesthood by insisting that financial care of parents take precedence over temple support (Matt 15:1–9).

---

14. Neusner, *Midrash*, 105–6.

15. Fonrobert, "Ethical Theories," 57.

16. Bokser and Bokser, *Talmud*, Shabbat 31a, 87.

17. Neusner, *Midrash*, 216–18.

Jesus's Practice of Midrash Disavows
Contemporary Inerrantism

Jesus's midrashic interpretation of Scripture is different from the interpretative strategy propounded by the Chicago Statement on the inerrancy of Scripture. If we accept the Chicago Statement as a thorough
declaration of biblical inerrancy, and if we apply it retroactively to Jesus's
own interpretation of his Hebrew Scriptures, we find that Jesus is not an
inerrantist.

Jesus himself explicitly rejects any global inerrantism when he declares, commenting on the Jewish laws for divorce, "It was only because
you were so hard-hearted that Moses allowed you to divorce your wives"
(Matt 19:8a). This passage suggests that *the Scriptures aren't revealed perfection but contain concessions to human brokenness, concessions that may
need later revision.*

Inerrantist Christians may simply respond that the "New" Testament is superior to the "Old" Testament, and if there is a conflict between
the two, then the "New" Testament is infallible. But even Paul, who made
the first contributions to the Christian Scriptures, sometimes denies that
his words are from Jesus or directly inspired: "To the rest I say—*I and not
the Lord*, that . . ." (1 Cor 7:12a [emphasis added]). Later in the letter, he
again writes as a human advisor, not an instrument of revelation: "I have
no command of the Lord, but I give my opinion as one who by the Lord's
mercy is trustworthy" (1 Cor 7:25).

Based on this analysis, we can make several observations about Jesus's interpretative strategy. As we have seen above, Jesus does not submit
to Scripture in its entirety, nor does he declare it thoroughly absolute
in truth value, nor does he construct theological arguments through the
accumulation of relevant biblical texts. Jesus does not "proof text" by offering isolated scriptural verses as evidence in support of his preaching.
He illustrates abstract principles with concrete stories, spiritualizes ethical commands, prioritizes some passages over others, and amplifies other
teachings. These are not the practices of contemporary infallibilists, who
vaunt the entire Bible as the infallible word of God, equal in truth value
and without error. Jesus's approach to Scripture is also not compatible
with the fundamentalist doctrine of *sola scriptura*, or "Scripture alone,"
which resists the expansion of scriptural meaning that midrash facili-
tates. As followers of Jesus choose their own method for interpreting the

Bible, we conclude that *since Christ is not an infallibilist, Christians should not be either.*

Christ Interprets the Bible Agapically, so Christians Should Interpret the Bible Agapically

Jesus focuses on agape within his Bible. Where the biblical emphasis on agape conflicts with any other biblical command, Jesus prioritizes agape over the command. He does not reject the law, but he subordinates all law to the law of love. He sees the love of Abba for all creation and shares that love with those around him. If necessary, Christ *transgresses* Scripture to reveal agape. If necessary, Christians should transgress Scripture to reveal agape.

Today, Sophia is leading Christians into an ever more agapic world. Jesus himself says so: "I still have many things to say to you, but you cannot bear them now. When the Spirit of truth comes, [she] will guide you into all truth" (John 16:12–13a [feminized]). Sophia, the Spirit of love, is speaking to us, revealing those ways through which we can become more loving. She is making us aware of those we have harmed, that we might help them. She is reminding us of those we have pushed aside, so that we might invite them in. Since Pentecost she has never been silent, and she never will be silent. Our duty is to listen: "Let anyone who has an ear listen to what the Spirit is saying to the churches" (John 2:7a).

Given the truth of ongoing revelation by Sophia, and the priority of agape in the life and teaching of Jesus, we can develop a standard for faithful assessment of particular Bible passages: *Any passage that coheres with the revelation of God as agapic love advocating peace and justice is true. Any passage that does not cohere with the revelation of God as agapic love advocating peace and justice is not true.*

Throughout this book, in the practice of this standard, I have interpreted the Bible as agapically as possible. To do so, I have highlighted egalitarian passages, extolled universalist passages, rejected oppressive passages, ignored misogynistic passages, abbreviated passages to fit my argument, searched for translations to fit my argument, downplayed violent language, and explicitly feminized or gender neutralized masculine language. I have done so shamelessly: literally, without shame or embarrassment, but with a profound sense of duty to interpret in the service of God, who declares, "I have loved you with an everlasting love" (Jer 31:3).

The divine love is *for all*; therefore, our interpretation of the Bible should be *for all*. Others will disagree and interpret the Bible in a violent, classist, racist, sexist, xenophobic, homophobic, or transphobic manner. Their arguments are *biblical*, even *rigorous*, but they are not *agapic*. Therefore, they are wrong.

Agape Must Win the Clash of Interpretations

The tension between agape and rigorism creates a clash of interpretations. The clearest historical example of this clash of interpretations is the issue of slavery. The Bible was written during a time when slavery was morally acceptable. There are biblical regulations for slavery, but no condemnations of slavery. One thousand eight hundred years after the Newer Testament was written, American enslavers quoted this passage from the Bible, from Peter's First Letter, to justify their enslavement and mistreatment of Africans:

> Slaves, be subject to your masters with all fear, not only those who are good and gentle but also those who are dishonest. For it is a commendable thing if, being aware of God, a person endures pain while suffering unjustly. If you endure when you are beaten for doing wrong, what credit is that? But if you endure when you do good and suffer for it, this is a commendable thing before God. For to this you have been called, because Christ also suffered for you, leaving you an example, so that you should follow in his steps. (1 Pet 2:18–21)

That is horrible advice. What happens when enslaved persons are abused by their enslavers? Does such abuse fulfill their God-given self or demonically distort it?

Frederick Douglass tells us how slavery changes a person, distorting them into that which God never intended. His enslaver, Mr. Thomas Auld, sent the spirited Douglass to a brutal slave breaker, Mr. Covey, who was known for dispiriting his charges. Douglass writes:

> I was somewhat unmanageable when I first went there, but a few months of this discipline tamed me. Mr. Covey succeeded in breaking me. I was broken in body, soul, and spirit. My natural elasticity was crushed, my intellect languished, the disposition to read departed, the cheerful spark that lingered about my eye

died; the dark night of slavery closed in upon me; and behold a man transformed into a brute![18]

According to 1 Peter, Douglass's suffering during this time was commendable. As unearned, unwarranted, and useless, it made him Christlike. Indeed, if Douglass had continued to allow his enslavers to afflict him, then he would have earned more merit in the eyes of God.

But Douglass didn't. When Covey tried to subdue Douglass for a beating, Douglass fought back. Confused and angered, Covey got another enslaved person, Hughes, to help subdue Douglass, who fought them both off. Covey then asked a second enslaved person, Bill, to help, but Bill refused despite Covey's threats. Finally, Covey and Douglass fought alone for two hours, and Douglass bested Covey. Afterward, Covey never admitted defeat or spoke of the fight, for fear of his reputation.[19]

Peter may *not* have been pleased by Douglass's spirit, but Jesus—who sought to elicit the image of God in everyone—would have been. Jesus's consciousness was structured by the exodus narrative, God's rescue of the Israelites from Egypt, through which God expresses their preference for captive over captor: "Then the Lord said, 'I have observed the misery of my people who are in Egypt; I have heard their cry on account of their taskmasters. Indeed, I know their sufferings, and I have come down to deliver them from the Egyptians and to bring them up out of that land to a good and spacious land, to a land flowing with milk and honey'" (Exod 3:7–8a).

The enslavers turned to 1 Peter to justify their brutality. The enslaved turned to Exodus to resist their captors. The enslavers' use of the Bible was wrong because it was cruel. The enslaved persons' use of the Bible was correct because it was liberating. In other words, arguments *for* slavery are biblical; arguments *against* slavery are biblical; but only the arguments against slavery are *agapic*. The Bible is not the standard of truth. Agape is the standard of truth.

We may consider the issue of slavery to be settled, but biblical infallibilism produces zombie moralities. We are surprised to encounter these long dead ethics staggering across our intellectual landscape in a resolute quest for certainty they will never find. A prominent infallibilist website, GotQuestions.org, defends the Bible's allowance of slavery. They do not excuse the Bible because it was written in a different time and place

---

18. Douglass, *Autobiographies*, 58.

19. Douglass, *Autobiographies*, 63–64.

when slavery was taken for granted. Instead, they insist that the Bible is by nature transcendent of time and place. Therefore, its authority cannot be challenged: slavery was a divinely sanctioned practice then, and may even be permissible now.[20]

Slavery has been wrong ever since the first tribe abducted a child from their neighbors, then exploited that child for the rest of their life. This action offended God, who came to us in Jesus to clarify God's will. Somewhere, along the way, Jesus's message was lost. Physical abuse is wrong and should be stopped, always, even if the Bible condones it. Biblical infallibilism does not produce the most agapic interpretation of the Bible, nor does it express deeper faith, nor does it promote moral acuity. Biblical infallibilism just leads us astray. Fortunately, biblical *agapism* holds great promise.

Agapic Interpretation of the Bible Promotes Flourishing

Above, we noted that the Jewish tradition deems Scripture to be of inexhaustible meaning, and this inexhaustible meaning invites perpetual discovery. The *surface* meaning exists only to be surpassed. Likewise, we will deem Christian Scripture to be of inexhaustible meaning—*and that inexhaustible meaning is agapic.* In the Spirit of Christ, we will plumb the Bible for its agapic implications. Interpretatively, we will practice *agapism*.

Agapism conflicts with infallibilism. The clearest *contemporary* example of this clash of interpretations is the issue of LGBTQ+ rights, in particular the issue of same-sex marriage. Christian opponents of same-sex marriage cite about seven passages in the Bible, which they interpret as forbidding it. They also declare that the purpose of sexuality is reproduction, and same-sex couples can't reproduce, so same-sex marriage is unnatural.

Neither argument stands up to scrutiny. The passages that ostensibly forbid same-sex relations were written thousands of years ago in cultures very different from our own. They require historical knowledge of those cultures for interpretation, since they are deeply tied to practices unfamiliar to us like temple prostitution in fertility rites designed to produce good harvests, pederasty (the taking of a young male lover by older males, in a process of sexual initiation), and the humiliation of defeated

20. Got Questions Ministries, "Why Does Bible Allow."

enemies in wartime. They do not address same-sex emotional intimacy, or the sexual expression of that emotional intimacy, since these concepts were unfamiliar to the biblical authors.

Familiar to the biblical authors were concepts of sexuality and marriage that we would consider abhorrent today. A bride who could not prove her virginity could be stoned to death (Deut 22:20–21). Virgins who were raped had to marry their rapist (Deut 22:28–29). Polygamy was practiced; in Genesis, for example, Lamech, Abraham, Esau, and Jacob had two or more wives. Some of these "wives" were concubines, secondary wives whose children had less hereditary status; King Solomon had three hundred concubines (1 Kgs 11:3). On the command of Moses, the Israelites slew the Midianite men, women, and boys, leaving alive only the unmarried girls to take as wives (Num 31:1–18).

So, the concept of "biblical marriage" is complicated, but so is animal sexual behavior. Increasing knowledge of zoology has disproved the claim that same-sex relations are "unnatural." In fact, nature is rife with same-sex relations, which have now been observed in hundreds of species. They seem to serve a variety of purposes, such as male bonding and female bonding for intensified social support, reconciliation after conflict, experimentation with social organization, or the simple pursuit of pleasure in a painful world. Such exchanges frequently occur within a bisexual framework, although in some species a percentage of members will never seek out heterosexual copulation. Heterosexual members of these species seem unbothered by same-sex behavior. So, if we survey nature with open eyes, then we will see that same-sex attraction is natural and part of God's plan, while opposition to same-sex attraction is unnatural and not part of God's plan.[21]

Even if same-sex relations were unbiblical or unnatural, which they are not, progressive Christians would still support same-sex marriage for theological reasons: God the Trinity is love, and humans are made in the image of God the Trinity, for love. Romantic relationships characterized by emotional intimacy fulfill the image of God within us. According to the self-report of gay men and lesbians, *which is to be trusted*, they can achieve such intimacy only within same-sex relations. To *condemn* these relations denies the image of God within them; to *celebrate* these relations fulfills the image of God within them. Therefore, we should approve of same-sex intimacy and celebrate it within the institution of marriage.

---

21. Poiani, *Animal Homosexuality*, 178–80.

This issue is of great importance, as young people are currently flee-ing a religion they see as oppressive of LGBTQ+ persons. So adamant is fundamentalist objection to same-sex marriage that most young people consider Christianity to be *inherently* anti-LGBTQ+, rather than *acciden-tally* anti-LGBTQ+. Christ never mentioned same-sex marriage, so it's unclear why some Christians are so vigorously opposed to it, while being quite tolerant of conspicuous consumption, rapacious greed, and social injustice, all of which Jesus explicitly and repeatedly condemned.[22]

Scripture Functions Best When It Stays in Its Lane

The authors of the Newer Testament were writing the *gospel.* The gospel is "good news" for all, not bad news for some. Hence, the Bible should be interpreted as good news for all, not as a science or history textbook for infallibilists. At the beginning of this chapter, I wrote of my student who had been told that any apparent conflict between science and the Bible should be resolved in favor of the Bible. This teaching created for her a false opposition between science and religion. Alas, this is not the first time in history that religion has not stayed in its lane or that the Bible has been misapplied to scientific questions.

For those who assert that science and religion conflict by nature, the most frequently cited proof of such conflict is the Galileo affair. In the popular interpretation of that unfortunate event, the famous physicist, inventor, and astronomer Galileo Galilei (1564–1642) was sentenced to lifelong house arrest by the Catholic Church for asserting that the Earth orbited the Sun. The ecclesiastical authorities also forced him to recant his heliocentric (Sun-centered) theory and promise not to advance it any longer.

For those who believe that science and religion are incompatible, this event provides one powerful example of the darkness of religion relative to the brilliance of science. The only solution, they propose, is to reject all religious belief and usher in a new age of unshackled reason, scientific investigation, and technological advance. These advocates of scientism are poor historians, simplifying a complex historical event to suit their arguments . . . a practice which is, ironically, not very scientific.

In truth, the church's response to Galileo's heliocentric theory of the solar system was not monolithic. He had admirers and detractors, and

22. Kinnaman with Hawkins, *You Lost Me,* 163–64.

his trial became a proxy battle for these rival factions. Among those who most deeply opposed his views were biblical *literalists*. Biblical literalists interpret Scripture according to the plain, simple meaning of the text. For literalists, the Bible is true to fact and to be interpreted as the word-for-word word of God. According to them, to interpret the Bible as poetry or metaphor dilutes meaning and prioritizes human imagination over divine revelation.

Biblical literalism is most strongly associated with twentieth-century American Protestant fundamentalism, and it has been generally rejected by the Roman Catholic Church. Nevertheless, in the Galileo affair, certain opponents of Galileo's theories utilized a literal interpretation of the Bible to argue against heliocentrism. For example, literalist interpretations of several biblical texts suggested that the Earth must be stationary and the Sun in orbit around it. Psalm 93:1 states: "God has made the world firm, not to be moved" (see Ps 96:10 and 1 Chr 16:30 as well). Psalm 104:5 states: "The Lord set the earth on its foundations; it can never be moved," and Eccl 1:5 declares: "The sun rises and sets and returns to its place" (see also Ps 18:4–6). If these passages are regarded as science rather than poetry, then the Earth cannot orbit the Sun; the Sun must orbit the Earth.[23]

As a man of sincere faith, Galileo had taken considerable time to argue that his heliocentric theory was compatible with the Bible, arguing that the Bible teaches us about salvation, not the nature of the cosmos. Galileo quoted a contemporary, Cardinal Cesare Baronius, who supported astronomical investigations by arguing, "The Bible tells us how to go to heaven, not how the heavens go." Galileo also maintained that Scripture is not about "science" but about faith. Science and faith have different modes of discourse and different methods of argument. He referred to Augustine's *accommodationism*—the belief that God reveals to humans only what they can handle at that time in history; God *accommodates* revelation to our level of preparation.[24] Augustine himself was developing Paul's own accommodationism, which he explicitly admitted to the Corinthians: "I fed you with milk, not solid food, for you were not ready for solid food" (1 Cor 3:2).

Tragically, the misapplication of Scripture to science drives thinking persons out of faith. Science helps us to understand the material universe;

23. Langford, *Galileo, Science, and Church*, 52–53.
24. Langford, *Galileo, Science, and Church*, 65–66.

Scripture helps us to understand the spiritual universe. If we can know something by means of science, then we need not address Scripture on that question. And if Scripture declares that fire is cold or ice is hot, then we should ignore it.[25]

Scripture should also stay in its lane with regard to history. Historical study is a modern practice characterized by original research, broad perspective, rigorous reasoning, and cautious conclusions. A modern historian of the biblical period will consider data from a variety of disciplines—archeology, geology, paleoanthropology (the study of human remains from that period), linguistics, genetics, and ancient writings from all intertwined cultures.

The Bible was not written in this way. It provides data about what people thought had happened, usually very much from their own perspective. Their primary source was stories passed down from generation to generation, such as the story of Balaam and the ass. In that story, God prevents the pagan prophet Balaam from cursing Israel by placing an armed angel on his path. Balaam is riding his donkey toward Israel and approaches the angel, but the donkey can see the angel and Balaam can't. When the donkey refuses to proceed, Balaam beats it mercilessly, at which point the donkey begins to argue its case with him in an explicit, verbal exchange. On hearing the donkey's argument, Balaam's eyes are opened and he sees the angel, at which point he very prudently decides to retreat (Num 22).

GotQuestions.org insists that the story of Balaam and his donkey actually happened and should be seriously probed for moral and theological lessons.[26] Yet stories such as this were meant to entertain and instruct, not to be taken as historical events. We should imagine this story being told around a campfire, with the listeners laughing at the hapless Balaam and his protesting donkey, in gleeful community. Over the course of many such evenings and thousands of such stories, the Israelites learned the beliefs and values that knit them together as a nation, all while having a good time. This story was *not* meant to be heard with life-denying solemnity.

25. Rambachan, "What Is Advaita," 16.

26. Got Questions Ministries, "Did Balaam's Donkey."

Scripture Offers a "Surplus of Meaning" That Overflows Any One Interpretation and Provides Different Guidance in Different Situations[27]

Agapic love assumes different forms in different situations, sometimes expressing itself as comfort, sometimes as challenge, sometimes as joy, sometimes as lament. Likewise, the meaning of Scripture arises only within a situation. Abstraction renders Scripture insignificant because Scripture was not created for abstract persons in abstract situations. Felt human realities, and their capacity for enrichment, offer Scripture its reason for existence, so it must be related to these realities to gain meaning. There, in dynamic relationship to dynamic contexts producing dynamic interpretations, Scripture gains its dynamic significance. Only the particular is universal.

As Jesus moves from particular situation to particular situation, he illustrates unifying love while always leaving play in his interpretation of Scripture. Unchained from rigorism, he preserves the freedom to spontaneously express agape in his next encounter. Each interpretation is provisional, specific to that situation, and no interpretation is normative, to be applied blindly to another situation. Aristotle argues that plot twists should be surprising but, after the fact, seem obvious. Similarly, Jesus's interpretations of the Hebrew Scriptures are always surprising but, after the fact, seem self-authenticating. This authentication is the work of the Holy Spirit: Spirit ratifies Christ, Wisdom ratifies Truth, Sophia ratifies Jesus.

Given Jesus's genius, his disciples could never know exactly how he would express the divine love within Scripture next. They knew only that it would be expressed again, freely and variably, as elicited by the particular situation.[28] For example, Jesus does not shun lepers; in an expression of loving relationality, Jesus dines with Simon the leper to express God's universalism and the kingdom's inclusion of the excluded. He teaches women and prioritizes their religious education over their traditional duties (Luke 10:38–42). He heals on the Sabbath. Again and again, Jesus's interpretative strategy is humanistic, intended to increase human well-being in every situation, including the well-being of those whom Jesus condemns for greed, elitism, and hard-heartedness.

---

27. Ricoeur, *Interpretation Theory*, 45.
28. Fletcher, *Situation Ethics*, 75–77.

Biblical Interpretation Is Never Closed

Because the infinite God offers continuing revelation to our finite minds, our understanding of God must always be open. Jesus preserves this openness by telling many different stories, all of which leave us open to new stories. While philosophical and theological claims exclude one another and compete for space, stories accommodate one another and welcome newcomers.

The human quest for comprehensive systems seeks climax in totality, stability, and order. We seek to *understand* totally that we might *control* totally. However, such totality limits potential, conforming the future to an unchanging norm inherited from the past. In contrast, the Bible points us toward the kingdom of God, an unfolding future that replaces our despondency with anticipation. The bitter past cannot determine this wondrous future, nor can a totalizing interpretative strategy constrain it.

Openness to the kingdom of God prohibits any strategy of control that claims mastery of the Bible. For that reason, we must distrust understandings of the Bible that are too tidy and determinate. As Witold Gombrowicz argues, "Serious literature does not exist to make life easy but to complicate it."[29] Complications challenge the pat answers that limit us; they ask us new questions that reveal greater potential. Complications are a source of increase.

Therefore, with regard to interpretations of the Bible that claim authority for themselves, we must be suspicious. And our suspicion must be directly proportionate to the certainty of the claims we confront; the more authority claimed, the more scrutiny needed. Because the Bible is often used to claim power *over*, we must ask of any interpretation, "Who benefits?" The Bible itself, through the revelation of the prophets, forbids utilization of the text to preserve one's own advantageous position in a stratified society.

The Bible also forbids manipulation of the text to deify one's own preexisting opinions. That is, sometimes people have a deeply felt conviction that they then ratify by scouring the Bible for affirmation: "I feel strongly about this, so God must agree with me." Agreeable passages are exalted, disagreeable passages ignored, and meanings massaged in a highly selective manufacture of certainty. These interpreters then propound their preexisting opinion, now sprinkled with proof texts, as the revealed will of God. Rarely are these biblically affirmed prejudices

29. Gombrowicz, *Diary*, 291.

imitative of Christ in their generosity or inclusiveness. More often, they attempt to preserve society as the interpreter knows it rather than create society as God imagines it.

Given my extensive reference to Scripture throughout this book, always in support of my own argument, I could be accused of proof texting. However, I have no intention of "proving" my arguments by citing biblical "facts," as American fundamentalists began to do in the early twentieth century, in imitation of the scientific method. Instead, this book is playful, creative, and exploratory, more like a Jewish midrash. I'm not trying to "get it right." Instead, *my intention is to create a collage of scriptural passages, illustrative anecdotes, and reasoned arguments within which Christians and their communities can flourish.* I hope that the cumulative effect of these efforts will be life giving, helping readers to find more joy, and possibly even more challenge, while trusting that the emergent meaning and purpose will themselves make sense of life. This trust is what the Christian tradition calls faith.

Strict Literalism Is a Modern Innovation

If someone invites you to a white elephant party, you shouldn't bring a white elephant. Strict literalism can be quite embarrassing, as Augustine pointed out in the fourth century:

> It not infrequently happens that something about the earth, about the sky, about other elements of this world, about the motion and rotation or even the magnitude and distances of the stars, about definite eclipses of the sun and moon, about the passage of years and seasons, about the nature of animals, of fruits, of stones, and of other such things, may be known with the greatest certainty by reasoning or by experience, even by one who is not a Christian. It is too disgraceful and ruinous, though, and greatly to be avoided, that he [the non-Christian] should hear a Christian speaking so idiotically on these matters, and as if in accord with Christian writings, that he might say that he could scarcely keep from laughing when he saw how totally in error they are.[30]

In the end, the intellectual gymnastics necessary to hold a view of biblical infallibility—to reject evolution for creationism, for example—is more

---

30. Augustine, "Literal Interpretation of Genesis," 82.

anxiety-producing than reassuring. Literal interpretation cannot make any sense of passages such as 1 Sam 2:8: "For the pillars of the earth are the Lord's, and on them he has set the world." Such passages beg allegorical interpretation: Abba creates and sustains the universe. Jesus himself endorses allegory through his allegorical preaching, and he gets frustrated with the disciples when they can't understand his allegorical meaning (Mark 8:14–21). Later, Paul himself argues for and provides an allegorical interpretation of Genesis (Gal 4:21–31).

Augustine further develops these interpretative strategies by developing the four senses of Scripture, an approach intended to plumb the various meanings of a text, and the depth of those meanings, while also leaving room for further development in understanding. The first sense is the *literal* sense, the plain meaning of the text, which provides the bedrock upon which the next three senses rest. The second sense is the *allegorical* or *symbolic* meaning of the text. For instance, in the story of the good Samaritan, Augustine identifies the beaten man with humanity, the robbers with the devil, and the good Samaritan with Christ. The *moral* sense extracts practical ethics from the text as guidelines for life; the story of the good Samaritan teaches us to extend kindness to everyone we meet, in the imitation of Christ. And the *anagogical* sense relates to our final spiritual destiny; the inn represents the church, which brings the beaten man to wholeness, i.e., salvation.[31]

The Bible Should Be Interpreted as Spiritually as Possible

Given the richness of Augustine's approach, we can see how a strictly literal interpretation of the Bible evaporates meaning. Literalism impoverishes the text, but it also bespeaks an inner disquiet, a thirst for certainty that God has intentionally denied us. Unchanging, static meaning arrests our development, but God always invites us *forward* into new meanings that ever approach the divine, agapic mind. On this journey, *we are invited to place our faith in God, not the Bible.*

We began this chapter by reflecting on the needless conflict between science and religion created by literal interpretation of Genesis, and how that conflict is driving many young people out of faith. As a corrective to this needless conflict, we can counter-assert that *the Bible should be*

---

31. Clark, "Reversing the Ethical Perspective," 308–9.

interpreted as spiritually as possible, emphasizing the existential implications of any passage, unbothered by concerns about historical or scientific accuracy.

The best category through which to interpret the Bible spiritually is that of *myth.* The word *myth* is highly problematic in English, as it holds two contradictory meanings: a myth is an untrue story, an "old wives' tale," something that people believe to be true but isn't. But a myth can also be an ancient tale, passed down for millennia, that has shaped culture by shaping the minds that constitute it.

We will prefer the second meaning of myth. In our definition, a myth is a story with sufficient existential power to transform consciousness. A myth, thus defined, alters our interpretation of reality. Without changing the facts, it changes how we *feel* about those facts; it changes *us.* It may not be historically or scientifically accurate, but it is experienced as *true* because it helps us to negotiate our emotional and spiritual lives. A myth opens us up to energies within reality that we would have otherwise overlooked. It reveals *the more,* both within the universe and within us. In the words of Joseph Campbell, "I think of mythology as the homeland of the muses, the inspirers of art, the inspirers of poetry. To see life as a poem and yourself participating in the poem is what the myth does for you."[32]

Myth helps to integrate our interpretation of life, granting us wholeness. It appeals to our intuition and creative imagination, which do not *contradict* law and logic, but lie *beyond* law and logic. In this way, myth attempts to make us spontaneously wiser. As a story, myth resists fixed signification—a single, exhaustive interpretation—which would only sterilize it. It seeks to produce skillful, intuitive action within the infinite situational plenum, the overflowing abundance that defies the blind application of unbending rules.

How can human beings integrate their experience of reality into a harmonious unity? Consider the myth of the exodus, the Israelite flight from captivity in Egypt, through the wilderness, into the promised land, led by Moses, Aaron, and Miriam (Mic 6:4). This journey, from a bad situation through a worse situation to a better situation, is a universal human experience. Often, we become so accustomed to the bad situation, or we so fear the worse situation, that we refuse to undertake the journey. The exodus story then speaks, empowering us to overcome our fears and

---

32. J. Campbell with Moyers, *Power of Myth,* 65.

promising us companionship along the way, the accompaniment of all those who have persevered through hardship, in hope.

The exodus story applies to any human situation that moves *from despair through trial to deliverance*. During the period of American slavery, it emboldened enslaved persons to flee from captivity through danger to freedom. Decades later, it inspired suffragettes to leave their homes and fight for the right to vote. Today, it inspires closeted LGBTQ+ persons to come out to their family and friends. Survivors of childhood abuse refer to the story as they move from repression through psychotherapy to mental health, survivors of domestic abuse refer to the story as they move from physical danger through divorce to safety, people with substance abuse disorders rely on it as they move from addiction through rehabilitation to sobriety, and patients draw strength from it as they move from cancer through chemotherapy to health. The exodus myth is inexhaustibly relevant, *more so as a transformative story than historical event.*

Biblical Agapists Are No Less Faithful Than Biblical Infallibilists

To interpret the Bible so selectively and spiritually may seem less faithful than the biblical infallibilists' blanket endorsement of Scripture. After all, we are proposing a canon within the canon—a selection of passages within the Bible that we prioritize over or even against other passages. The standard by which we select these passages is the agapic love of Abba for the world, as revealed by Jesus and continually endorsed by Sophia.

Infallibilists may say that subjecting divine Scripture to human reason is arrogant, but they too have a canon within the canon—though unacknowledged. I was once in a very wealthy and fundamentalist church that placed a banner behind the pulpit reading, "No one comes to the Father except through the Son," a paraphrase of John 14:6b and a favorite of exclusivists, those who believe that only Christians can be saved. I wondered what would have happened if I had replaced the banner with one that read, "Cursed are you who are rich, for you have received your consolation" (Luke 6:24). I doubt it would have stayed up long, infallibilism aside.

In practice, infallibilist interpretation of the Bible is wildly inconsistent as they focus on texts that reinforce their worldview and ignore texts that challenge their worldview. For example, the Ethics and Religious

Liberty Commission of the Southern Baptist Convention opposes trans-sexual surgery that aligns a person's genital identity with their neurological identity.[33] In so doing, they cite Deut 23:1: "No one whose testicles are crushed or whose penis is cut off shall come into the assembly of the Lord" (although here, we may prefer the KJV: "He that is wounded in the stones, or hath his privy member cut off, shall not enter into the congregation of the Lord"). This text is considered authoritative, but texts that forbid eating shellfish (Lev 11:11) are overridden by the new covenant in Christ (Mark 7:18–19).

Likewise, Lev 11:7–8 forbids eating or even touching pig flesh, yet fundamentalists still eat pork and toss the football around, which for many years was made of pigskin (admittedly, these days most are synthetic leather). People get Lev 18:22 tattoos to express their opposition to same-sex marriage, apparently unaware that Lev 19:28 forbids tattoos. Many fundamentalists support the separation of undocumented immigrant families at the border, in tragic disobedience of Lev 19:33–34, which states: "When an alien resides with you in your land, you shall not oppress the alien. The alien who resides with you shall be to you as the native-born among you; you shall love the alien as yourself, for you were aliens in the land of Egypt: I am the Lord your God."

While infallibilists quote the Bible in opposition to LGBTQ+ rights, many passages regarding family, gender, and sexuality are problematic for them. Generally, Protestant infallibilists promote large, traditional families in which the husband works and the wife cares for the "quiverful" of children. Their arguments are biblically based and generally pro-sex, within the confines of marriage. But there are some passages that they don't quote very often, such as Luke 20:34–35: "Jesus said to them, 'Those who belong to this age marry and are given in marriage, but those who are considered worthy of a place in that age and in the resurrection from the dead neither marry nor are given in marriage.'" Jesus also suggests that his followers become eunuchs for the kingdom of heaven (Matt 19:11–12). John the Revelator explicitly links *male* virginity to salvation: "Then I looked, and there was the Lamb, standing on Mount Zion! And with him were one hundred forty-four thousand who had his name and his Father's name written on their foreheads. . . . It is these who have not defiled themselves with women, for they are virgins" (Rev 14:1–4).

33. Schrock, "Transgendered Persons."

Virgins, male or female, generally don't produce families, but if they did, Jesus would be somewhat disruptive: "Whoever comes to me and does not hate father and mother, wife and children, brothers and sisters, yes, and even life itself, cannot be my disciple" (Luke 14:26). Fundamentalist Christians frequently cite the Bible in support of traditional gender roles within the family, while ignoring passages that challenge traditional gender roles. The most ardent male fundamentalists ignore Paul's repeated instruction to "greet one another with a holy kiss" (Rom 16:16; 1 Cor 16:20; 2 Cor 13:12; 1 Thess 5:26), and they always will. The Southern Baptist Convention is infallibilist, but they use grape juice instead of wine for communion, even though Jesus used wine. And good for them—using grape juice allows people with alcohol abuse disorders to participate in communion without fear of relapse. Jesus would approve of this pastoral move in defiance of biblical rigorism.

Omega Texts Render the Bible Perpetually Transformative

If our reading of the Bible is so selective, if there are many texts that we reject as antiquated, then why refer to the Bible at all? Why should progressives refer to a text so rooted in the past? We continually refer to the Bible *because the Bible offers a plentitude of passages that link us to the past, comfort us in the present, and lure us into a better future.* These are the omega texts of the Bible, those that are forever relevant to human well-being, upon which we can build community, through which we are less lonely, and with which we can repair the world.

Humanity will never outgrow these omega texts. In a thousand years, if humans are still around, they will still refer to them and benefit from them. In some ways, this book is already a compendium of omega texts. Space does not allow me to list every such text, but consider what a world informed by such wisdom, and truly structured by its truth, would be like: What if the world truly realized that God is love (1 John 4:8b)? What would society look like if its members truly trusted God and enacted the divine love? Certainly, it would be universalist: Paul's observation that in Christ there is no longer Jew nor Greek, slave nor free, male nor female would be extended to all divided groups, not to create a colorless homogeneity, but to promote a flourishing diversity.

For this to happen we would need to love God *more*, to actually love God with all our heart, as Jesus commanded (Mark 12:30). Such love would necessarily produce a deepened love of neighbor, thereby fulfilling Jesus's second commandment (Mark 12:31). It would also produce a more peaceful world in which Isaiah's dream is fulfilled and resources for armaments are directed toward human well-being (Isa 2:4). But this dream doesn't just require love of neighbor; it will ultimately require love of enemies (Matt 5:44a), a solidarity as surprising as that of the wolf and the lamb or the leopard and the goat (Isa 11:6). For this peace to arrive, we must forego our thirst for justice, *when that thirst is only masked revenge.* Collectively, if we prioritize our children's future over our ancestors' vengeance, then we will have to turn the other cheek (Matt 5:39).

As we build that world, we will continue to need the support of community and the comfort of faith. Those who trust in God can grieve confidently, knowing that nothing can separate us from the love of God (Rom 8:39), who will one day wipe the tears from our eyes (Isa 25:8) in a better life to come (1 Cor 15:54–57).

On this journey we are supported by a cloud of witnesses (Heb 12:1), our ancestors who have gone before us in faith. Life is difficult, and trusting God is difficult, but we are reassured that we are not alone: Jacob wrestled with God, through which he became Israel (Gen 32:22–32), as have billions since then, as will billions more. Doubt is a correlate of faith, and the greater the faith, the greater the doubt. We are all like the father of that sick child, who cries out with tears, "I believe; help my unbelief!" (Mark 9:24b). The psalms record every sacred emotion that human beings have ever had. We find ourselves in their world and discover that we are not alone. In every situation, we are joined by the psalmist and every reader who has drawn sustenance from the beauty of the psalms, which assure us that we are not isolated; we belong.

Scripture Is Intended to Heal, Not Harm

Those are a few of the omega texts that will draw us into God's imagination and guide us in our co-creation of the kingdom. The Bible can produce well-being for all if we interpret it by its own standard: "Love does no wrong to a neighbor; therefore, love is the fulfilling of the law" (Rom 13:10).

Our understanding of God's love unfolds through time. For Scripture to be life-giving it cannot become a Procrustean bed into which our preconceptions and prejudices are jammed. Instead, it must be capacious, as capacious as the kingdom it commends. Alas, algorithmic, controlling interpretations of the Bible such as infallibilism and rigorism curve in on themselves. They enervate a book that was meant to give life. No algorithm can cage Jesus's Bible, just as no tomb could hold Jesus's body.

Jesus's scriptural interpretation is pastoral. It helps the person in their situation—it heals, it forgives, it includes. Christians' scriptural interpretation should do the same—heal not hurt, love not fear, include not exclude. To the extent that we interpret Scripture in these ways, to that extent we are interpreting Scripture as Jesus did.

10

Now Is the Beginning

Eternity isn't some later time. Eternity isn't a long time. Eternity has nothing to do with time. Eternity is that dimension of here and now which thinking and time cuts out. This is it. And if you don't get it here, you won't get it anywhere. And the experience of eternity right here and now is the function of life. There's a wonderful formula that the Buddhists have for the Bodhisattva, the one whose being (sattva) is illumination (bodhi), who realizes his identity with eternity and at the same time his participation in time. And the attitude is not to withdraw from the world when you realize how horrible it is, but to realize that this horror is simply the foreground of a wonder and to come back and participate in it.

—JOSEPH CAMPBELL[1]

Apparently, I Am Going to Hell

I ATTENDED A CHURCH meeting in northern Mexico many years ago, while I was interim codirector of Programa Nogalhillos, a Presbyterian Border ministry site. At the beginning of the meeting, we sat in a circle

1. J. Campbell with Moyers, *Power of Myth*, 81.

and everyone recounted how they had become a Christian. Most of the ministers gathered at this meeting came from hard backgrounds and had converted to Christianity in a sudden flash of revelation, usually during a particularly traumatic time in their life. Each of them could provide a precise date and location that marked their entry into faith. Their stories were emotional and compelling. For them, their conversion to Christianity marked a change in their life from lost to found, from sin to salvation, from death to life. None of their stories were boring.

Then the conversation came to me. I talked about how I had grown up in the church, and how my dad was a minister, but that I had struggled with some aspects of faith, like the relationship between science and religion, or whether the stories in the Bible were literally true or not. So, I had kind of wandered from the faith for a few years, and considered some other ways of understanding life, but eventually worked out most of the kinks in my theology, and now considered myself a Christian and was even going to seminary next fall.

There were so many eyes looking at me with so much pity. I knew that I had said something wrong, but I wasn't sure what. Certainly, these men (and they were all men) had more interesting stories than my own, but I didn't realize that the stories were required, and that I hadn't met the requirement. A bit unsettled, I defaulted to my proud lineage: "Like I said, my father's a minister, and my parents are coming to visit in a few weeks, and some of you might meet them!" The man sitting next to me smiled gently and said, "I'm glad your father's a minister. But you have to remember: God has children, but no grandchildren." This was a polite reminder that to become a child of God, I needed to have my own conversion experience, not my dad's (who, incidentally, never had one—he was just a Christian all his life). I had to get myself saved. I had to be born again. If not, I was going to hell.

These warnings, and others I've received throughout my life, have never triggered me. Since I wasn't raised in a church that taught hellfire and damnation, I have no childhood trauma regarding my eternal destiny. We didn't talk about the afterlife much, except when loss in this life made those conversations necessary. When that happened, we learned to trust in the goodness of God.

Others, raised in more threatening churches, perpetually fret over their salvation. Their religion gives them anxiety about the future instead of trust in the present. In this chapter, we will discuss the relationship between God, time, and destiny, both individual and social. We will do so in the conviction that faith should be life giving, not anxiety-producing. *Anxiety-producing religion needs reform.* We will point out the reforms that can make faith itself an exercise in trust rather than fear.

As we discuss the purpose and future of time, we can divide our discussion into three subtopics: the physical destiny of the universe, the moral purpose of time, and the question of life after death. The physical destiny of the universe will not be our concern here; that is a matter for astrophysicists and cosmologists. Our concerns are religious.

Religious truths reveal new ways of being, but to be discovered they must first be *asked.* Asking implies an unknown, a more that awaits discovery. In discussing the relationship between God, life, and time, we are joining a long tradition of asking, "What is possible?" This question is among the most powerful because it implies that what we know, what we are familiar with and used to, does not exhaust possibility. There is always unrealized potential.

Creative Destruction Characterizes Time

Hindu worshipers of Shiva have a remarkably honest understanding of the relationship between God and time because they understand Shiva to be both Creator *and* Destroyer. This combination of functions is inevitable if we accept that God sustains time, a ceaseless process of creation and destruction, appearance and disappearance, birth and death. By divine decree, the future is forever dying to become the past, thereby rendering the present everlastingly new. Throughout this process, every newly appearing "thing" eventually becomes old, then disappears. God, *who loves us*, has placed us within continuous gain and unremitting loss so that we might revel in ceaseless novelty.

Analysis reveals that we are not *in* time so much as we *are* time.[2] Reality is not a collection of permanent objects; it is a flow of ever-changing experiences, like waves that arise from and disappear back into the sea. Because some things last tremendously longer than we do, we mistake them for permanent. And because we think that other things will make us permanently happy, we ascribe permanence to them. All the time, this craving for permanence amid impermanence causes us to suffer.

Wisdom recognizes that everything vanishes as soon as it appears, like dewdrops at sunrise. We may cling to them, but we cannot possess

2. Stambaugh, "Existential Time," 53.

them, any more than we can possess the circle formed by a whirling firebrand.[3] Reality consists of transitory events, not permanent things. We are one of those transitory events, as are each and every one of our experiences:

> All flesh is grass,
>   and all its beauty is like the flower of the field.
> The grass withers, the flower fades,
>   when the breath of the Lord blows upon it;
>   surely the people are grass.
> The grass withers, the flower fades,
>   but the Word of our God shall stand forever. (Isa 40:6–8)

We may crave a steady-state universe that is stable and predictable and abiding, but God has placed us within a dynamic universe, full of suspense and surprise and challenge. Reality, as an expression of God's own being, is more verb than noun. We are not an object among objects within an object; we are a process among processes within a process. If we try to construct unchanging substance out of ever-changing process, then we will misinterpret life, and to interpret clumsily is to live clumsily.

Existence through Time Produces Bereavement

Because time consists of positive and negative aspects, we are free to focus on the negative aspects. Everything we have we will lose, including the affection of a toddler, our physical vitality, and those rare moments in life when all the stars align and we feel ourselves to be on the way up. Our mistakes are sealed in the past and continue to echo through our own and others' lives. We cannot relive the good or undo the bad.

Perhaps most painfully, time presses us toward our inevitable demise: "What is your life? For you are a mist that appears for a little while and then vanishes" (Jas 4:14a). Time is cruel in its relentlessness. Given these painful aspects of time, we can develop, to a greater or lesser degree, *chronophobia*—fear of time, extreme lamentation over the passage of time, or obsessive anxiety about our ever-approaching mortality.

Blessed with a situation that grants us unceasing novelty and meaningful adventure, we too easily condemn ourselves to fear of the future. This self-condemnation renders time disjointed, jarring, and graceless. The Greeks had a word for ordinary time that produces anxiety: *chronos*,

---

3. Gethin, *Foundations of Buddhism*, 190.

from which we get our words *chronometer*, *chronological*, and *chronopho-bia*. In Greek myth, the god of time, Chronos, is allegorically associated with the chief Titan, Cronus. Cronus was the father of the Olympians who, fearing their ascendancy, devoured his own children. Just as the past devours the future, just as time gives life and takes it away, so Chronos/Cronus became the source of both being and nonbeing, birth and death.[4] The myth of Chronos scorns any naive sentimentality about time.

End-Time Fantasies Produce Maladjustment

There are multiple ways to avoid full acceptance of our being through time. Our awareness of aging and mortality can drive us to fantasize about eternity, *defined as timelessness*. The eternalist tradition defines the soul as our true, eternal self, and the body as our false, temporal self. Salvation then becomes release of the soul from the body.

More prosaically, we can anesthetize ourselves to the reality of death with the intoxicant of busyness, preventing any thought of death from leaking through the gaps in our daily schedule.

One of the unhealthiest reactions to our existential situation is to thirst for the end of time as we know it, to fantasize about a supernatural disruption of time so profound that the future becomes unrecognizable. In religion, this belief is called *millennialism*. In American Christianity, millennialism takes the form of *dispensationalism*. Dispensationalists believe that we are in the final stages of the sixth dispensation, the dispensation of grace, which will soon be replaced by the rapture of the church prior to an era of tribulation under Satanic forces. The tribulation will be followed by the one-thousand-year reign of Christ and conclude with the final judgment of God on all persons. Everyday parlance refers to these various events as the rapture, second coming, end-time, judgment day, doomsday, apocalypse, Armageddon, etc.

Dispensationalists utilize a peculiarly apocalyptic interpretation of the Bible that prioritizes passages regarding the end of time. The system was generated by John Nelson Darby in the 1850s and popularized by C. I. Scofield in the early twentieth century through his reference Bible.[5] Despite continually predicting the impending judgment day, and

4. Sallustius, "On the Gods," 343–44.
5. Stancil, "Dispensational Theology," 4:776.

that judgment day never arriving, dispensationalism still garners millions of adherents.

Biblically, dispensationalism attempts to reconcile a variety of apocalyptic passages into one coherent prediction of the future. One of the most important comes from Matthew, who places these words in the mouth of Jesus:

> You will hear of wars and rumors of wars, but see to it that you are not alarmed. Such things must happen, but the end is still to come. Nation will rise against nation, and kingdom against kingdom. There will be famines and earthquakes in various places. All these are the beginning of birth pains. . . . Then you will be handed over to be persecuted and put to death, and you will be hated by all nations because of me. At that time many will turn away from the faith and will betray and hate each other, and many false prophets will appear and deceive many people. Because of the increase of wickedness, the love of most will grow cold, but the one who stands firm to the end will be saved. (Matt 24:6–13)

American dispensationalists combine this passage with others in which Christians "will be caught up together in the clouds to meet the Lord in the air" (1 Thess 4:17), such that "there will be two men in the field; one will be taken and one will be left" (Matt 24:40). More disturbingly, there will be a beast who "causes all, both small and great, both rich and poor, both free and slave, to be given a brand on the right hand or the forehead, so that no one can buy or sell who does not have the brand, that is, the name of the beast or the number for its name" (Rev 13:16–17). The dispensationalist map of end-time verses creates a vivid story with compelling imagery and high drama. It has profoundly influenced both American church life and the entertainment industry.

Dispensationalism Harms Its Captives

Dispensationalism is the scourge of American Christianity. It promotes the fear of God over the love of God, turns Christians away from proper care for this world, and grants preachers hypnotic power over their congregations. Although Jesus declared "Blessed are the peacemakers," many dispensationalists hallow conflict since "wars and rumors of wars" are signs of the end-time. (But when, in human history, have there not been wars and rumors of wars?) Likewise, many dispensationalists hallow earthquakes and famines as signs of the end-time.

Why this thirst for apocalypse? Why do so many Christians want time as we know it to end? Perhaps because, to put it most simply, life is difficult. To the best of our current knowledge, we are the only animal that can consider life and doubt its worth. As conscious beings, we can evaluate ourselves, compare that evaluation with an imagined ideal, and loathe our imperfection. In the arena of activity, we must decide and act in an infinitely complex world that offers no guaranteed outcome to our most consequential endeavors. We are always selves in community, striving to balance our self-interest with the community's interests, especially those of our closest relations. We are plagued with regrets about a past we cannot change. Persian poet Omar Khayyám reminds us: "The Moving Finger writes; and, having writ / Moves on: nor all thy Piety nor Wit / Shall lure it back to cancel half a Line / Nor all thy Tears wash out a Word of it."[6]

For struggling persons (and we are all struggling persons), when time ends our suffering will end. Instead of integrating the negative, we can fantasize about its defeat in a final battle. Rather than guide history toward peace, we can hope to become subject to a victorious God of war (Rev 19:17–21). Rather than decide to act, we can wait to obey. Rather than confront death, we can hope to be raptured out of its grasp, like Elisha (2 Kgs 2:11).

All these stratagems avoid the work. They deny the freedom that Abba grants us, reject the counsel that Sophia offers us, and delay the healing that Jesus extends to us. In God's plan, we are participants not spectators. God never intended to resolve all our problems in one fell swoop. Such overwhelming intervention would not be a fitting climax to a story that we have always cowritten with God.

The film *1917* graphically depicts what it means to do the work.[7] Unique among movies, the climax of the film is not a battle, but *the avoidance of a battle.* Two British corporals race against time to deliver a message to the front lines calling off a futile attack that will result in nothing but slaughter. One of the corporals is killed, but the other successfully reaches the frontline, saving the lives of thousands, including his own brother. In the final scene of the movie, the surviving corporal opens a

6. Khayyám, *Rubáiyát*, 194.

7. Mendes, *1917*.

letter from home that includes a photo of his wife and children, and her handwritten message on the back of the picture, "Come back to us."

What if the purpose of time is not to end, but to go on indefinitely? Jesus calls for peaceful continuance, not martial climax. We fantasize about death for the enemy, while he dreams of life for all. Jesus talks about the kingdom of God *as if* it is coming tomorrow because he knows that, if we live as if the kingdom of God is coming tomorrow, then it will come today. His eschatological (end-time) preaching communicates the importance of *decisive action for God now*, not passively waiting for God *then*. In the Gospel of Thomas, when the disciples ask Jesus when the kingdom will come, he replies, "It is not by being waited for that it is going to come."[8]

Martin Luther King faced repeated calls to wait, be patient, and trust that race relations would improve on their own. In response, he translated Jesus's prophecy of the kingdom of God into a nonviolent call for civil rights in America, not at some point in the future, but *now*. Speaking to a quarter of a million people gathered on the National Mall in 1963, King declared: "Tomorrow is today. We are confronted with the fierce urgency of now. In this unfolding conundrum of life and history, there is such a thing as being too late. Procrastination is still the thief of time."[9]

Millennialism fantasizes about a war to end all wars, that perennial human fantasy which always produces the next war. It encourages existential and political procrastination, delaying pressing concerns into an indefinite future. More dangerously, it sears souls with religious trauma. For power-hungry leaders, Jesus's message of love, healing, and peace offers little leverage over their flock. They need a different message, one that offers more power *over* and control *of*, so they create a perverse message of judgment, damnation, and warfare. Hell is kept at the forefront of parishioners' minds, keeping them afraid, which is to keep them docile.

Children's young minds are scarred with imagery from the hell industry, be it the *Left Behind* series of books and movies, or threats of damnation from the pulpit, or parents who use hell language to frighten their kids into obedience, or "hell houses," fundamentalist "haunted houses" that vividly depict the consequences of disbelief. Caregivers tell their children that, if they are not raptured, they will be left behind to suffer through the seven-year tribulation, divinely condemned to an

---

8. "Gospel of Thomas," §113, in Layton, *Gnostic Scriptures*, 588.
9. M. L. King, *Testament of Hope*, 243.

anarchic world of looting, rape, and murder, defenseless and alone, while
the rest of their family reposes in heaven with Christ. Eventually, according to dispensationalist theology, a leader will arise to impose order, but
he will force Christians to receive the mark of the beast; any who refuse
will be killed. Those who give in and receive the mark will be safe during
the reign of terror but will then suffer everlasting torture in hell for their
apostasy.[10]

What does this toxic theology, so graphically depicted in countless
movies, TV shows, and novels, do to the young minds that absorb it?
It constantly warns them that their safety and security are fragile and
can be replaced at any moment with unspeakable horror. Youth raised
in this toxic theology fear the world, which (so say their mentors) is replete with ascendant evil. They fret over the future and its unstoppable
approach. They place everyone they know into the binary of saved and
unsaved, then worry that all their friends who are unsaved—whom they
have failed to save—will burn for eternity. They are taught to doubt their
salvation, then they are assured of their salvation, if only they will obey.
Josiah Hesse, who grew up immersed in apocalypticism, writes, "I still
dream of demons, hell, the Mark of the Beast and the Lake of Fire a few
times a week, sometimes sleepwalking—or sleep running—out the front
door, convinced the Antichrist is coming to tattoo 666 on my forehead,
followed by an eternity of torture in hell."[11]

The End-Times Love Money

Inculcating this guilt and its resultant religious terror is an immensely
profitable industry. Hal Lindsey's *The Late Great Planet Earth*, published
in 1970, argued that the reestablishment of the state of Israel, as well as
the rise of communism and an increase in wars and famines, heralded
the impending apocalypse. When the end-times failed to appear in the
70s, he published a sequel entitled *The 1980s: Countdown to Armageddon*,
which spent twenty weeks on the *New York Times* bestseller list. In 1991,
he published *Israel and the Last Days*. In 1999, he published *Planet Earth:
The Final Chapter*. In 2017, he graciously provided a foreword to Thomas
J. Hughes's book *America's Coming Judgment: Where Is Our Hope?*

10. Sweetman, "Defining Dispensationalism," 207–11.
11. Hesse, "I Grew Up Evangelical," para. 23.

Jesus states that the exact timing of his second coming is unknowable (Matt 24:36), and Hal Lindsey was prudent enough to never give a time window for Armageddon, after which his prophecies (and book sales) would expire. Other Christian prophets have not been so wise, beginning with Paul, who writes, "We who are alive, who are left, will be caught up in the clouds together with them [the deceased raised to life] to meet the Lord in the air, and so we will be with the Lord forever" (1 Thess 4:16–17). In the early Christian church, the Montanists predicted that the new Jerusalem would descend in the late second century. Hippolytus, an early Christian theologian, calculated that the second coming would occur six thousand years after the creation of the world, or around the late third century. In the twelfth century, Joachim de Fiore gathered a utopian community in anticipation of Armageddon, which he predicted would begin by 1260. In the early fifteenth century, the militant Taborites (followers of the reformer Jan Huss) arose to cleanse the world of sin in preparation for the second coming. In the 1530s, Anabaptists took over the German city of Münster, declared it the new Jerusalem, invited in anyone who wanted to escape judgment day, and expelled everyone who wouldn't get rebaptized. In the 1800s, William Miller used biblical numerology to predict Christ's return on October 22, 1844, leading to "the Great Disappointment."[12]

Regarding end-times prediction, according to its practitioners, past performance is no guarantee of future results. It doesn't matter if they've been wrong every time—they might be right next time, and that's *scary*. Picking up the baton after Hal Lindsey, the apocalyptic *Left Behind* novels, first appearing in 1995, have sold tens of millions of copies in numerous languages, spawned multiple movie adaptations, and can be played as a video game. The original novels were so successful that the authors created children's versions called *Left Behind: The Kids*, which are kind of like *Home Alone* except the parents have been raptured instead of gone on vacation, and the adversary is Satan instead of two incompetent thieves.

Given the short-term framework of the dispensationalists, we would expect them to give most of their money away and live in material simplicity, secure in the knowledge that the second coming, not this-worldly wealth, would deliver their crown. (Indeed, I do know of some middle-class millennialists who never saved for retirement, so sure were they of the impending judgment day. Alas, they had to move in

---

12. Weber, "Millennialism," 371–76.

with their daughter in their old age.) Oddly, those who profit from the ever-approaching, never-arriving millennium tend to plan financially for the long term, taking mortgages, hiring estate lawyers, and setting up trust funds. In 1977, *Publishers Weekly* noted that Hal Lindsey sported a Porsche racing jacket, tooled around Los Angeles in a Mercedes 450 SI, and maintained a suite of offices for the personal management firm that invested his royalties.[13] When a reporter asked Tim LaHaye, coauthor of the *Left Behind* series, if he intended to sell all he had and give it to the poor, per the instruction of Christ, he responded, "You know how much I pay in taxes?"[14]

Dispensationalism is a money-making racket with a captive audience who need to escape. To be spiritually healthy, we must accept responsibility for our emotional well-being and personal destiny. Dispensationalism denies us responsibility for either. It disempowers people, encouraging the repression of personal problems based on the fantasy that Jesus will return to do all the work for us. It devalues this world, painting it as demonically treacherous and politically irredeemable. Within its escapist framework, neglect of this life for the next is the only religious option. Its leaders instill in their followers a deep suspicion of outsiders, thereby ensuring information control, groupthink, rejection of dissent—and the leaders' hold on power.

What if, instead of thirsting for the end of time, we said *yes* to its continual unfolding? What if, instead of craving resolution, we honored the freshness of life to be found in every new moment? Any peace to be had in life will not arise from wishing it otherwise. We cannot achieve a timeless eternity, and Jesus is not coming back to solve all our problems. Our peace will arise only from openness to reality as it is, and reality is *temporal.* The temporal, time-full nature of reality is good, because permanence cannot change. Only impermanence grows, thrives, and pulses with potential.

Time Is the Medium of Loving Relationship

The Trinity heals us through story. Creation, incarnation, crucifixion, and resurrection all take place within time. The divine preference for story is to be expected: If God is internally related, and the creation bears

13. E. A. Smith, "*Late Great Planet Earth* Made the Apocalypse a Popular Concern."
14. Gates, "Religion," para. 15.

the impress of God, then the universe will be suffused with being-toward, being-with, and being-for. The universe will be suffused with relationality, and relationality manifests only through time.

This insight calls for a celebration of life *as it is*. So much philosophy has preferred the abstract to the concrete, the universal to the particular, and the absolute to the relative. But our situation is concrete, particular, and relative. To celebrate our situation *and its limitations* is to trust God. By divine design, our specific characteristics make us specifically ourselves, granting us a specific contribution to make, thereby granting us a specific value. No one else is who we are, so no one can offer precisely what we offer. If we were unlimited, then none of us would have such specific value. We would subsist within a universal omnicompetence, needless of one another, needless of community, and needless of love.

For this reason, the infinitely particular exceeds the Infinite Absolute. Love demands the limitedness that allows us to participate in productive relationships. Through these relationships, the self overflows itself. The boon of limitedness allows us to exceed our limitations, thereby transcending all absolutes. The network exceeds its field, the community exceeds its members, and the concrete exceeds the abstract.

This Moment Pulses with the Entire Purpose of Time

In chapter 3, we discussed continuous creation, the belief that Abba is sustaining the universe at every moment of its existence: "Thou, even thou, art Lord alone; thou hast made heaven, the heaven of heavens, with all their host, the earth, and all things that are therein, the seas, and all that is therein, and thou preservest them all" (Neh 9:6a KJV). Abba didn't create the universe, place it on a shelf, and walk away. Abba is sustaining it now. Hence, Abba is both Creator and Sustainer, fully present everywhere and everywhen, for without God there is nowhere and nowhen. If Abba hides their face, all vanish (Ps 104:29).

Christian millennialists have long awaited the perfection of history in the end-time, but the doctrine of continuous creation shifts the perfection of time from the future into the present. In other words, a continuous creation is a continuous eschaton. *Eschaton* is a Greek word that refers to the final destiny of the universe in time. This destiny need not lie in the future. Instead, the purpose of time lies in this very moment. To quote Jesus again: "Once [Jesus] was asked by the Pharisees when the

kingdom of God was coming, and he answered, 'The kingdom of God is not coming with things that can be observed; nor will they say, 'Look, here it is!' or 'There it is!' For, in fact, the kingdom of God is among you" (Luke 17:20–21 NRSV).

Thought about the end-time (Greek: *eschaton*) is called *eschatology*. Jesus suggests that the purpose of time is here, now. Traditionally, embedding the goal of time in the present moment, declaring the fullness of time to be immediately available, has been called *realized eschatology*.[15] In the 1800s, British theologian C. H. Dodd found himself surrounded by *premillennialists*, apocalyptic preachers who prophesied that, because the millennium had not yet appeared, the end-time was approaching. Dodd considered these prophets to be charlatans and argued for *postmillennialism*: that the hinge of time (the millennium) had already occurred in Christ, who had fulfilled the spiritual potential of the universe and offers us the very same fulfillment today. No greater climax to time could occur because no greater climax was possible. Time would stretch indefinitely into the future, perpetually offering Christians the religious realization that Jesus had exemplified and offered in first-century Judaea.[16]

As noted above, Dodd's postmillennialism was called realized eschatology, but the past participle "realized" has never served Dodd's doctrine well. If the potential for *kairos* (time as blessed, time as eternity) pulses in each and every moment, then his concept of time is better served by the continuous participle "realizing." To be "realized" places the event in the past. To be "realizing" places the event in the present, and every present that will ever come. Therefore, Dodd's doctrine of time is better described as a *realizing eschatology*, an actualization of spiritual potential ceaselessly available to everyone, everywhere, all the time.[17] For this reason Martha confesses to Jesus, "I have come to believe that you are the Messiah, God's Only Begotten, the One who *is coming* into the world" (John 11:27 [emphasis added]). The English present progressive "is coming" translates the Greek present participle *erchomenos*, implying a continuous process that is always available yet never finished.

This realizing eschatology demands a rejection of any controlling divine providence. In the words of Thomas Jay Oord, God's love is *uncontrolling*. If we co-create with God, then the next moment is as blank

---

15. Barbour, *Religion and Science*, 216–18.

16. Ladd, *Theology of New Testament*, 56.

17. Jeremias, *Parables of Jesus*, 21, 230. Jeremias uses the expression *sich realisierende Eschatologie*, as noted in Ladd, *Theology of New Testament*, 56–57.

as the artist's canvas. Divine love limits divine power over, just as human love limits human power over. Hence, time and its inhabitants are not coercively controlled by God. Instead, time is the means by which God bestows freedom. Time keeps our future open, so that when we close ourselves off from one another and God, redemption still awaits us.[18]

Faith believes in transformation, an unlimited experiential potential embedded within reality, which is symbolized linguistically by the word *salvation*. Compared to realizing eschatology, millennialism and dispensationalism are reprehensible since they delay transformation indefinitely into the future. Realizing eschatology, on the other hand, does not delay healing, reconciliation, or joy; it asserts the urgency of the now and accepts the divine invitation to live out this very moment in the fullness that is available to us.

The concept of realizing eschatology offers another advantage. Even if the divine plentitude is available now, observation suggests that we have not achieved it in either our individual or social lives. There is a *not yet* embedded in time, a perennial opportunity to be realized. This *not yet* can be approached but not possessed, thereby bestowing both direction, purpose, and eros to time's progression. We have not *realized* the kingdom, but we can always *be realizing* the kingdom.

In the process of realizing the kingdom, we reject *declinism*. Declinism believes that everything is getting worse, yearns for an idealized past, and interprets all change as deterioration. Declinism begins its reminiscences with "in the good old days" and ends every lament with "these days." Since the past shines, the present seethes, and the future threatens, for the declinist the only rational course of action is to *go back*. If regression can't be achieved, then the declinist will at least resist all change since stasis will at least slow our descent.

Thorough knowledge of history disallows declinism. Things were not simpler back then; they were just as complicated, perhaps even more so. Maybe people think that the world was a better place when they were children because they were children then and didn't read the newspaper. Some people are so nostalgic for their childhood innocence that they seek to extend it into adulthood, granting their allegiance to institutions and leaders who make decisions for them. The leaders present their decisions as clear and certain, never sharing the reasoning process that went into them, never imposing the ambiguity of decision making on the led.

18. Oord, *Uncontrolling Love of God*, 94.

Opaque institutions may grant their members an agreeable innocence, but opacity is just a cover for corruption. *Institutions are as corrupt as they are opaque, and they are as honest as they are transparent.*
Ignorance about what takes place behind closed doors may preserve
our innocence, but always at the cost of bad things happening. Be they
the closed doors of church, government, industry, or home, secrets hide
shame. Still, some people would rather remain ignorant of suffering than
reduce suffering. Instead of building the kingdom, they sigh for Eden.
Instead of working *with* the advance of time, they try to turn it around,
demanding that the river run uphill.

This Moment Is the Beginning

To confront and reduce suffering is difficult. Exhausted by the effort, we
may yearn for the end of time, but *God moves from beginning to beginning*.
There is no finish line and, as experiencing beings, this endlessness is a
blessing: "It is the dimension of time wherein [we] meet God, wherein
[we] become aware that every instant is an act of creation, a Beginning,
opening up new roads for ultimate realizations. Time is the presence of
God in the world of space, and it is within time that we are able to sense
the unity of all beings," writes Abraham Joshua Heschel.[19]

Reality is unfinished. God does not seek the closure of time; God
seeks its consummation, *through us*. We tend to declare the beginning of
the universe to be the Big Bang scientifically or Genesis spiritually, but a
realizing eschatology declares that the beginning is *now*. Time is eternal
birth: every instant is an act of creation, the Giver is ever present in the
given, and the experience of living is never complete. God is declaring, at
this very moment, "I am about to do a new thing; now it springs forth; do
you not perceive it?" (Isa 43:19).

Trust in God produces a love for tomorrow, and tomorrow prefers
the possible over the received. For Christians, the great possibility is the
kingdom of God, which is the reign of love. By working toward this vision, *faith reverses causality*. Rather than being caused by the darkness
of the human past, faithful work is caused by the brilliance of the divine
future. Origin is no longer essence. Thus, God is hope for the future, not
nostalgia for the past: "Do not say, 'Why were the former days better than
these?' For it is not from wisdom that you ask this" (Eccl 7:10).

19. Heschel, *Sabbath*, 92 (gender neutralized).

Hope for the new thing demands our renunciation of the old order. What we are *used to* is not normative. Only what *should be* is normative. We may be used to injustice, but we should work for justice. We may be used to war, but we should work for peace. Such change is terrifying, as it calls for the end of safety, the loss of identity, and the breakup of the world as we have always known it.[20] But Sophia, in all her wisdom, counsels us to *let go.*

In this vision, God saturates time. While God's activity in the past inspires awe, and God's activity in the present inspires gratitude, God's futurity *invites.* This invitation to accomplish the divine imagination grants direction to time and purpose to human activity. Each moment offers the beginning of a pilgrimage toward more God—more justice, more hope, more peace, and more love. Now, time allows us to yearn, to receive, to develop—to rise, and thus to experience ourselves as having risen: "The way is the goal."

Every symphony has a key signature, every painting has a tone, and every life has a mood. For Christians, the underlying mood of life is *hope.* Hope is what love looks like in time, and hope trusts that God "is able to accomplish abundantly far more than all we can ask or imagine" (Eph 3:20). Cynics may dismiss such hope as mere dreaming. Certainly, realism recognizes that humankind is not perfectible. But anything within time can be changed, and anything that can be changed can be *improved.* We are free, and because we are free, we can shepherd the world into the reign of love. Indeed, that struggle is our mission. Our participation in this mission must be thoroughgoing and enthusiastic, for only here will we find the compassion, joy, and peace that God desires for us, until the kingdoms of this world serve the reign of love (Rev 11:15).

The purpose of life-in-time is to enjoy God-in-time and enact their will on earth. This purpose is difficult, as life inevitably presents tragedy, be it physical, emotional, or spiritual. For some, tragedy suggests the impossibility of any loving God. But for others, God is the support who sustains us through tragedy, especially tragic loss.

We All Walk in the Valley of the Shadow of Death

My wife, Abby, performed her first funeral only one month into her first pastorate. She wasn't even ordained yet. The deceased was Wesley Ward,

---

20. Baldwin, *Nobody Knows My Name,* 117.

a twenty-four-year-old man, a recent college graduate, on a weekend road trip to see a professional football game. On the way home there was a car accident. No one was drunk, no one was irresponsible, no one broke the law. But they were young and didn't have enough money for a hotel, so they decided to return home that night, even though it was late. Another young man, the driver, fell asleep at the wheel. The car drifted to the left, into oncoming traffic, with Wesley in the passenger seat sleeping. He took the brunt of the impact from the car that hit them, and he did not survive.

Children are supposed to bury their parents; parents aren't supposed to bury their children. The death of a parent in their old age is sad. The death of a child in their youth is tragic. Throughout this book, I have attempted to hallow this-worldly life as much as possible, without romanticism or denial. But realism demands that we acknowledge the horrific tragedy that can occur due to accidents, natural events, and worst of all, human evil. In a dangerous world, how can we risk the terrifying tenderness of love?

The afterlife is a subject that prudent theologians don't discuss often. In this respect it is much like theodicy, the attempt to explain why bad things happen to good people in a universe created and sustained by a loving God. Some questions are over our heads and their answers beyond our imaginations. Discussion of the afterlife also risks egoism. If the afterlife becomes a reward we seek or a punishment we avoid, then our conduct cannot escape the prison of selfishness.

Nevertheless, like my wife Abby, pastors must care for those who have experienced tragedy, and theology must guide them in comforting the bereaved. To do so, we must address that which we don't understand, and quite possibly can't understand: here, death and afterlife. Regarding these topics we will have no clear answers, only enigmatic assurances. Sometimes Sophia's counsel comes as intimation, and that in the softest of whispers, but faith deems her quiet truth sufficient.

Everything that I'm about to write could be wrong, either because it's flat out wrong or because it is simply inadequate to God's plans for us. If, for example, we tried to communicate to an unborn child what life would be like—what colors are, how a mango tastes, the subtle harmonies of a symphony, the complexity of human emotional life—we would fail because the unborn child would have no referents by which to understand our descriptions. The effort would be futile. Quite possibly, considerations of the afterlife confront the same difficulty, and we can no more imagine ultimate healing than we can imagine a fifth dimension. Thus, caught in the vise of pastoral necessity and theological impossibility, we proceed.

Death Serves Life

Struck by personal loss and guaranteed our own personal demise, our natural tendency is to interpret death as a curse. Closer examination suggests benefits to death that we might overlook in our state of existential terror. Simply from the perspective of biology, death and its natural correlate, aging, have important functions. If, for example, most complex organisms did not age unto death, if they died due only to trauma or illness, then reproductive rates (set as replacement rates) would be lower and evolutionary adaptation would take place more slowly. Given the deep time necessary for evolution to produce significant change, without aging and death humankind would probably not exist.

Moreover, if complex organisms died only from trauma and illness, and not aging, then there would be less need for reproduction, and less need for its correlate, sexual intercourse, which would be disappointing.

Moreover, if reproductive rates were much lower, then life would recover more slowly from mass extinction events. But since extinction events happen to a biosphere constantly churning with death and reproduction, life recovers from them relatively quickly, often with profound adaptations that produce entirely new species. In this way, both the constancy of death and the disruption of the extinction event combine to produce new forms of life, a combination that eventually produced us.[21]

Humans also benefit from death *culturally*. Because our social mores are plastic, not fixed, they can evolve over time, but this evolution relies on the constant replacement of older generations by younger generations. On average, older generations want to preserve society *as it is*, while younger generations want to mold society *as it should be*. These emerging adults thus tend to be more open to new ways of structuring society, thereby producing cultural evolution.[22]

Our recent rate of cultural evolution is startling. We can deem the human species to have fully evolved one hundred thousand years ago, which is a conservative estimate. Let us take, for example, a White,

21. Sterelny and Griffiths, *Sex and Death*, 302–4.
22. Sterelny and Griffiths, *Sex and Death*, 331–33.

cisgender, heterosexual, American male from two hundred years ago, 0.2 percent of our species' history, and propel him forward into today's world. What would he be shocked by? Slavery has been abolished. Interracial marriage is legal and largely accepted. America has had a Black president. Women go to college, not finishing school, and can become doctors, lawyers, business leaders, etc.; they serve in Congress and on the Supreme Court. Husbands can go to jail if they hit their wives. Parents can go to jail if they beat their children. Men can marry men, women can marry women, and once we explained to our disoriented man from the past about nonbinary and transgender people, we would have to explain that they too can marry each other. America has a very large population of Jews, Muslims, Buddhists, Hindus, nonreligious, and atheists, and everything is all right, unless you're disturbed by these facts *in themselves*, which our beleaguered time traveler probably would be. He may even try to explain to us everything that's wrong and why we should go back, but we won't go back.

From a religious perspective, perhaps the greatest benefits of death are *spiritual*: "What is good, if kept short, is twice as good," observes Baltasar Gracián.[23] The awareness that life is transitory encourages us to take it seriously and resist triviality. My wife and I had a parishioner who was estranged from her sister through no fault of her own. A very dutiful person, every year she invited her sister to Thanksgiving dinner and every year her sister declined. After many years of this perseverance, our parishioner was diagnosed with terminal cancer. She wouldn't make it to the next Thanksgiving. On being told of the diagnosis, and realizing that time was short, the sister reconciled and took good care of our parishioner until her death—cooking, cleaning, talking, managing medicines, etc.

Now, if you had asked the estranged sister, at any point prior to the diagnosis, if our parishioner would die one day, she would have said, "Yes, of course. We all die." But only the *reality* of death, enforced through a diagnosis of terminal illness, awakened her to the urgency of the now. Only undeniable, impending separation could evoke her authenticity.

Awareness of death fosters our attentiveness to every moment, helping us to cherish what we should cherish and overlook what we should overlook. Fighting on the Eastern Front of World War Two, Soviet Army surgeon Olga Nikitichna Zabelina reminisced:

---

23. Gracián y Morales, *Art of Worldly Wisdom*, 60.

> Sometimes I hear music . . . a woman's voice . . . or a song. And
> there I find what I felt then. Something similar . . . But I watch
> films about the war—not right. I read a book—not right. No,
> not it. It doesn't come off. I start talking, myself—that's also not
> it. Not as frightening and not as beautiful. Do you know how
> beautiful a morning at war can be? Before combat . . . You look
> and you know: this may be your last. The earth is so beautiful . . .
> And the air . . . And the dear sun . . .[24]

Acknowledgment of death quickens us, even amidst the horror of war.
The denial of death, on the other hand, diminishes us. Mortality and
vitality are inseparable. Today will never come again; *this* moment is
precious; it is the key moment in which we can realize life and answer
the call to a higher possibility. For this reason, those who seek the full
intensity of life are grateful to be reminded that we are dust, and to dust
we shall return (Gen 3:19).

Finally, from an interpersonal perspective, death is our gift to future
generations. It is how we make room for them, after a life well lived, so
that they might share in the gladness. Previous generations died to give
us our days in the sun, and we will die to give future generations their
days in the sun. Certainly, this gift is enforced; we have no choice but to
die for others. But if we recognize the necessity of death, including our
own, then we can accept it with peace. We need not die under compulsion; we can embrace death as an act of generosity toward others, those
whom we love, whom we have not yet met: "No one has greater love than
this, laying down one's life for one's friends" (John 15:13).[25]

Awareness of death has the potential to be vitalizing, while the denial of death will always produce pathology. The Christian tradition resists
the denial of death by confessing Christ crucified. This event was a tragic
death caused by extreme trauma, of a rabbi who would have preferred to
grow old and die in peace, but whose passion for humanity made him the
object of empire's hatred. By declaring the suffering of Christ to be the
suffering of God, we acknowledge the presence of God within our worst
suffering, such as that of combatants in war, parents mourning a child, siblings suffering estrangement, or adolescents scorned for their difference.

Having communicated the divine solidarity with our human predicament, having revealed the universal, unconditional love of God for
all, and on the verge of subjecting God in Christ to the darkness of the

24. Alexievich, *Unwomanly Face of War*, 208 (ellipses original).
25. Zizioulas, *Being as Communion*, 112.

tomb, Jesus declares the completion of his work: "It is finished" (John 19:30). Now, God is fully united with humankind, life is fully united with death, and love infuses every aspect of reality. Through this transformation, the emergent reality of faith takes root, and new being can move forward in hope.

The Next Life Is for This Life

God the Trinity was not finished. Through the story of Christ, God communicates the love that grants us freedom and God's own vulnerability to trauma. But God also desires to heal our woundedness, a desire that God communicates through the resurrection, in which God repudiates moral evil and reveals the overwhelming power of divine love. So powerful is the promise of an afterlife that, for many, it takes priority over this life, reducing our earthly existence to a holding cell. Neither the Bible nor experience offer any evidence that God meant for this life to be so downgraded. God declares it "very good," to be enjoyed, not devalued. Striving to turn her contemporaries' attention to this world, the Islamic mystic Rabia Basri walked the streets of Basra, Iraq, with a bucket of water in one hand and torch in the other. When people asked her why, she replied, "I want to pour water into hell and cast fire into paradise, that these two veils disappear, so it becomes clear who worships God purely out of love."[26]

Those who, contra Rabia, focus on entrance to heaven and avoidance of hell will insist that this life, though transitory, is highly consequential because it determines our eternal destiny. Unfortunately, such obsession with "salvation" places us in a self-imposed spiritual bind. God is love, of both self and others, and we are made in the image of God, to love self and others. Thus, active love concerns itself with universal solidarity, not individual destiny; a selfish thirst for private salvation hobbles the spirit. From this perspective, the actions of a virtuous atheist are preferable to those of a heaven-obsessed Christian since they arise from a pure heart.

The height of faith is a willingness to be damned for the glory of God.[27] In literature, Huckleberry Finn was willing to be so damned. He had been floating down the Mississippi river with his trusted friend, the runaway slave Jim. Immersed in a culture that sacralized slavery,

26. M. Smith, *Rabi'a the Mystic*, xxvii.
27. Hartshorne, *Omnipotence*, 122.

concerned about his own wayward life, and determined to go straight, Huck decided to turn Jim in to his "owner," the widow Miss Watson. Every cultural cue that Huck had ever received told him that protecting Jim from capture was a sin, so Huck wrote a letter telling Miss Watson where Jim was and how to get him back. Huck immediately felt his conscience clear, knowing that he was going to turn Jim in, until he thought about the days he had spent with Jim, the situations they had wriggled out of, and the courage and honesty of his friend. Finally, more concerned about Jim's freedom than his own soul, Huck rips up the letter, declaring, "All right, then—I'll *go* to hell!"[28]

Elder-Son Theology Is Resentful

Undoubtedly, most Whites in Huck's world would have condemned his decision. They cherished the established order, which gave them power and prestige even as it ate away at their souls. To them, any challenge to the received social structures, no matter how kind, constituted a threat. People should behave as expected, and God would punish those who didn't.

This worldview is that of the elder son, who receives second billing to the prodigal son in Jesus's parable (no doubt, this secondary status bothers him). The elder son is dutiful, staying home to run the farm while his brother goes off and blows his inheritance in the city. The elder son is responsible and works hard, tending what the prodigal neglects. When the prodigal (wasteful) son returns, so destitute that he seeks only to work as a laborer, his father *runs* to him, and the prodigal falls into the arms of forgiveness. Overjoyed, the father orders a celebration for all (Luke 15:11–32).

The elder son is dismayed, and not without reason: "Listen! All these years I've been working like a slave for you, and I have never disobeyed your command, yet you've never even given me a young goat so that I could celebrate with my friends. But when this 'son' of yours comes back, who has wasted your money on prostitutes, you kill the fatted calf for him!" (Luke 15:11–22).

Why was his father more overjoyed by the prodigal's returning than the elder's staying? Jesus reveals a truth about God unpalatable to the rigidly righteous: God inclines to grace, not condemnation; mercy, not judgment. We are supposed to empathize with the prodigal and thank

28. Twain, *Huckleberry Finn*, 499–500.

God for clemency. Unfortunately, for those of us who have lived life with steady discipline and constant care, divine clemency can seem mere leniency, and this leniency creates resentment.

Resentment Demands Exclusion

Jesus taught, "Judge not, that you be not judged"(Matt 7:1 NKJV). Nevertheless, we can see elder son theology—a preference for punishment over forgiveness—throughout Christian history. At its worst, elder son theology manifests itself as *eschatological exclusivism*: the belief that we (the good) will go to heaven and they (the evil) will go to hell. God's judgment *includes* some and *excludes* others, usually those we consider undeserving. For many, this exclusion can rise to the level of nightmarish fantasy.

Throughout this book we have noted the mutually amplifying contrasts that constitute and intensify reality, giving it a topography of meaning and consequence. These contrasts are *nondual*—interdependent, complementary, and co-arising (productive of one another). In making this argument, we are not trying to fetishize nondualism, *which is itself nondual*. If nondualism is absolutized, then it ceases to be nondual. Put simply, nondualism can be taken so far that it ceases to be agapic.

Thomas Aquinas makes this mistake when he describes the blessedness of the saints in heaven, a blessedness that relies on the cursedness of souls in hell:

> Nothing should be denied the blessed that belongs to the perfection of their beatitude. Now everything is known the more for being compared with its contrary, because when contraries are placed beside one another they become more conspicuous. Wherefore in order that the happiness of the saints may be more delightful to them and that they may render more copious thanks to God for it, they are allowed to see perfectly the sufferings of the damned.[29]

Aquinas goes on to explain that the saved are not rejoicing in the sufferings of the damned so much as they are rejoicing in the justice of God and their own salvation through it. Seeing hell produces gratitude, not pity, because pity is associated with unhappiness, and the redeemed can be only happy. Nevertheless, the redeemed perceive the suffering of others and experience no compassion.

29. Aquinas, *Summa Theologica*, 2960, §94.1 Suppl.

Unfortunately, Aquinas expresses a common theme in Christian theology. The early-American Calvinist Jonathan Edwards agrees: "The misery of the damned in hell is one of those great things that the saints in their blessed and joyful state in heaven shall behold and take notice of."[30] And in the early 1800s, Scottish Presbyterian Robert Murray M'Cheyne described a judgment day that foreshadows Stalin's purges:

> There can be no doubt but that ministers and people will stand together, and be witnesses to one another's acquittal or condemnation—that parents shall stand and be witnesses to the acquittal or condemnation of their children—that children shall stand and be witnesses to the acquittal or condemnation of their parents—that husbands shall stand and be witnesses to the acquittal or condemnation of their wives, and that wives shall stand and be witnesses to the acquittal or condemnation of their husbands. Then, dear brethren, it follows immediately from this, that it will be no grief to the righteous to see the wicked condemned. Their tears will be over, their sorrows will be past, and yet they will see them condemned, they will hear their agonizing cry—they will see their sad countenances, and yet they will not shed a tear.[31]

In the Christian tradition, God is Trinity—three distinct persons perfectly united through love into one God. Each person within this interdependent God is perfectly compassionate and perfectly open. As the children of God, our purpose in life is *theosis*: growth in God, toward God, for God. To grow in God is to grow in love, not for some, but for all, because God loves all into being. Hence, *Trinitarian theology demands universal affection.* This affection expresses itself in our valuation of persons, our treatment of persons, and our hope for the destiny of persons. Exclusivism misses the mark because it denies that our destinies are entwined.

In November of 2022, the United States men's national soccer team defeated the Iranian team 1–0 in World Cup qualifiers, eliminating Iran from the international competition. At the final whistle, the US teammates embraced one another in celebration, jubilant over their narrow victory. Then, they noticed the disappointment of the Iranian team, particularly that of Saeid Ezatolahi, who had collapsed onto the field

30. Jonathan Edwards, "Sermon on Isaiah 66:23," preached June 1742; quoted in Gerstner, *Jonathan Edwards,* 34.

31. M'Cheyne, *Basket of Fragments,* 27.

weeping. While the Iranians' disappointment could have intensified the Americans' joy, the US team chose a different path, that of compassion.

Attacker Josh Sargent kneeled next to Ezatolahi, hugged him, and offered words of consolation, soon to be joined by Brenden Aaronson and DeAndre Yedlin. Defender Tim Weah walked over, and as he approached, Weah's face changed from one of "beaming delight" to sympathy. "As Ezatolahi tried to collect himself, Weah took him by the hands and pulled him to his feet, before hugging him and whispering in his ear."[32] Their countries were sworn enemies, but these players weren't having it. Fellowship could be achieved on the pitch, if not in international relations.

When asked about his conduct later, Weah stated, "I think the United States and Iran have had so many issues politically and I just wanted to show that we are all human beings and we all love each other.[33] . . . He is still my family, he is still my brother and I love him the same way as the guys I grew up with."[34] Brenden Aaronson added, "I could feel the emotion from him on the ground. . . . It's hard to see that from a player. All you want to do is go and console them and tell them that everything is going to be OK. It's just a human thing."[35]

Any theology in which the redeemed show less compassion than international soccer players needs reform. Thankfully, we can base this reform on the tradition itself. The early church theologian Origen argued for the salvation of all, including even Satan in the final redemption. In the early 1800s, German theologian Friedrich Schleiermacher argued that salvation had to be universal, because no one could enjoy heaven if they knew there were souls in hell, a point emphasized by his Greek Orthodox contemporary, Silouan the Athonite:

> A certain hermit declared [to Silouan] with evident satisfaction: "God will punish all atheists. They will burn in everlasting fire." Obviously upset, [Silouan] said: "Tell me, supposing you went to paradise and there looked down and saw somebody burning in hellfire—would you feel happy?" "It can't be helped. It would be their own fault," said the hermit. The Staretz answered him with a sorrowful countenance, "Love could not bear that. We must pray for all."[36]

32. M. Rogers, "Team USA Players," para. 5.

33. M. Rogers, "Team USA Players," para. 6.

34. M. Rogers, "Team USA Players," para. 7.

35. M. Rogers, "Team USA Players," para. 10.

36. Louth, "Eastern Orthodox Eschatology," 246.

God is love, and love demands that time consummate itself in reunion. Nightmarish fantasies about a final, eternal separation arise from human fear and insecurity, not agape.

A God of Love Could not Create or Sustain a Hell of Everlasting Punishment

Why is exclusion so attractive to us? Consider how often the word *exclusive* occurs in advertising: we are intrigued to receive an exclusive offer, we are excited about an invitation to an exclusive club, we like to be seen in exclusive restaurants. If someone is being *ex*cluded, but we are being *in*cluded, then we are *in*—with all the privileges that being an insider entails. The higher we climb insider mountain, and the more people we leave behind, the more benefits we accrue. This ascent is so dizzying that all too frequently those who are excluded seek to be included, not so that they can include, but so that they too can exclude.

The binary of heaven and hell is a spiritualization of our desire to exclude, at the expense of our neighbors whom we are called to love. The binary itself never dovetailed with the vision of Christ, who expressed instead a universal, unconditional, inclusive love of *all*. Such agapic universalism cannot culminate in everlasting exclusion. Agapic universalism can culminate only in universal salvation.

Moreover, the absolute either/or binary of heaven and hell never made judicial sense. We can imagine a heaven for the perfectly good and a hell for the abjectly evil, but most of us—all of us, really—are somewhere in between. If we shift the determining factor from ethical conduct to faith in God, which is the orthodox Christian approach, most of us are somewhere on the spectrum of faith and doubt, not perched securely at either end. In either case, where would God draw the line of judgment, lifting those on one side to heaven while casting those on the other side to hell?

The application of black-and-white binaries to a shades-of-gray world produces confused thought, clumsy action, and coarse feeling. Noting this truth, Jesus declares, "You judge by human standards; I judge no one" (John 8:15). Yet the thought of a spiritual universe without everlasting torment threatens many spiritual leaders. When my wife was being considered for ordination, a member of her ordination committee, an ordained minister himself, asked her about heaven and hell. Abby said that she rejected the concept of hell and believed in universal salvation. Dumbfounded and flabbergasted, the committee member exclaimed, "Then what are we doing as ministers?!?"

The Christian tradition has been so addicted to false binaries for so long that some Christians can't imagine faith without them. Their worldview is entirely based on the dualisms of heaven and hell, God and Satan, angel and demon, saints and sinners, saved and condemned. Without these dualisms there's no categorical grid by which to organize reality and no mission for the church. For these Christians, who seek to save non-Christians from hell by converting them to Christianity, universalism denies the church any mission.

But in the context of Trinitarianism—of interpersonal relationship perfectly united through divine love—*resistance to dualism is the mission of the church*. Since all persons are children of God and inseparable from one another, ethics becomes universalist—all are treated equally (Matt 5:43–48). Since God is the divine mother who births all creation (Job 38:29; Isa 66:7; etc.), and no mother rejects her sinful child, salvation is universal (1 Tim 2:3–4). *Universalism challenges the church to replace every dualism with nondualism, thereby healing division through reconciliation.* God creates connection, God preserves connection, and God *restores* connection. Hell has no rehabilitative function. Of what use is hell to a God of restorative love?

Sophia invites us to trust in God, not believe in hell. To place wrath in the heart of God places wrath at the heart of being and robs the universe of its beauty. To posit a demon for every angel and Satan as the enemy of God places creation, which God has declared very good, on a teeter-totter that can tip either way. True faith in God induces love instead of obsessing over evil. Faith declares, with Rabia, "My love for God leaves no room for hating Satan."[37]

The Bible Provides the Basis for Christian Universalism

Exclusivists argue for final *exclusion* based on the Bible. Universalists argue for final *inclusion* based on the Bible. The exclusivist arguments are coherent, but the universalist arguments are agapic. The universalist arguments are also spiritually useful because they resist our temptation

37. M. Smith, *Rabi'a the Mystic*, 99.

to self-promoting exclusivism, which never cohered with divine agape. God is God of the cosmos, not of the tribe, and God will bring the whole cosmos to fruition, not just a tribe within it. Abba creates and sustains all; we are "fearfully and wonderfully made" (Ps 139:14) in the image of God, who is "good to all, whose tender mercies extend over all creation" (Ps 145:9). This extravagant promise pervades the Bible. At the risk of repetitiveness, let us consider a few of those passages.

The universalist story begins, of course, with the story of Adam and Eve, which implicitly argues that we are one human family. This theme runs throughout the Hebrew Scriptures and receives especially powerful expression in the prophet Isaiah, who prophesies: "The glory of YHWH shall be revealed, and *all* flesh shall see it together, for the mouth of YHWH has spoken (Isa 40:3–5 [emphasis added]). In case this passage might be applied only to the Jews, Isaiah elsewhere clarifies:

> On this mountain the Lord of hosts will make for *all* peoples
>   a feast of rich food, a feast of well-aged wines,
>   of rich food filled with marrow, of well-aged wines strained clear.
> And he will destroy on this mountain
>   the shroud that is cast over *all* peoples,
>   the covering that is spread over *all* nations;
>   he will swallow up death forever.
> Then the Lord God will wipe away the tears from *all* faces.
>   (Isa 25:6–8a NRSV [emphasis added])

And, in case anyone doubts the power of God to achieve the reign of love, Isaiah insists, writing in the voice of God, "My purpose shall stand, and I will fulfill my intention" (Isa 46:10).

The church interprets Jesus as the fulfillment of Isaiah's prediction. Indeed, when John the Baptist prophesies about the coming of Christ, he quotes Isaiah explicitly: "*All* flesh shall see the salvation of God" (Luke 3:4–6 [emphasis added]). Jesus then picks up the thread by insisting, "I do not judge anyone who hears my words and does not keep them, for I came not to judge the world but to save the world" (John 12:47), because "it is the will of your Father in heaven that *not one* of these little ones should be lost" (Matt 18:13 [emphasis added]). Then, explicitly advocating universalism, he prophesies, "And I, when I am lifted up from the earth, will draw *all* people to myself" (John 12:32 [emphasis added]).

The early church writers continued to insist that Abba is the Parent "from whom every family in heaven and on earth takes its name" (Eph 3:14–15). Naturally, the Parent of all "desires *everyone* to be saved and to come to the knowledge of the truth" (1 Tim 2:3 [emphasis added]). To achieve this goal, Abba will "bring all things—in heaven and on earth—together in Christ" (Eph 1:10 [emphasis added]). And, for those of us who do not want a soul excluded from heaven, we have the assurance that Abba "accomplishes all things" (Eph 1:11).[38]

Universal Salvation Demands Radical Transformation

Universalism is frequently criticized, not without reason, as neglectful of God's justice. Where is justice if both oppressor and oppressed, both the cruel and the merciful gain equal entrance into the vision of God? If salvation is universal, then why not conduct ourselves selfishly, since even our most despicable acts will be wiped clean?

But the function of universalism is not to produce nihilism; it is to produce universalism. That is, a universalist worldview values all equally, treats all equally, and hopes for all equally. Such comprehensive universalism transforms individuals and societies, prodding them to mutual regard, thereby rendering them more just. In other words, *comprehensive universalism is the passkey to social justice.*

Nevertheless, any doctrine of universal salvation must acknowledge the reality of abject evil. Rulers gladly kill children to increase their power. Sadists torture people to death, film the event, then watch it later for pleasure. Generals take pregnant women as prisoners, wait for them to give birth, then kill them and raise the children as their own. These are all concrete, historical events. The list could go on forever.

Such evil could not withstand the full presence of God. Eventually, God will free us from all that separates us from God. Thus, we can infer that *universalism entails annihilationism*, the divine overcoming of all fear, hatred, and anger. Evil should anticipate its own defeat: "But who can endure the coming day? Who can stand firm when the One appears? That day will be like a smelter's fire or a launderer's soap, when the One will preside as refiner and purifier" (Mal 3:2). God promises to be a swift witness "against those who cheat the hired laborers of their wages, and oppress the widow and the orphan, who rob foreigners of their rights and have no respect for me" (Mal 3:5b).

---

38. Macdonald, *Evangelical Universalist*, 81–83.

To faith, hope, and love, the full presence of God is like water to the desert, a refreshing rain that brings new life. But to fear, anger, and hatred, the full presence of God is agony. The godless are not *deprived* of the love of God; they are *antagonistic* to it.[39] They cling to their enmity like a battlefield corpse clings to its sword.

Those who have deformed the image of God within them must, by God's own mercy, be made aware of that deformation. They must realize that they have denied their own soul, which is to deny themselves. When they look within, they will find that the moral beauty that should be present, and could be present, is absent, by their own choice, and they will experience horror. To hatred, love is a scourge.[40]

Ultimately, the patience of God overwhelms the stubbornness of evil, as water wears down the rock. Resistance to our deepest desire eventually exhausts itself. *The elimination of evil is an act of restoration, not retribution, and it is temporary, not eternal.* Through this cleansing, we will finally choose to become who we are, in an act of divinely graced self-creation.[41]

Love Conquers Death through Resurrection

"The essential nature of death is relationlessness," claims Eberhard Jüngel.[42] God as Trinity abhors relationlessness. God has chosen to be loving relationship, and God has summoned the universe out of nothingness to participate in God's very own dynamism. Death is the disappearance of relationship into the nothingness of relationlessness. This disappearance offends God as much as our nonbeing did prior to creation. In response, just as God summons us out of nonbeing into being, so God summons us out of death into life.

In the Christian tradition, Jesus's resurrection reveals that death is a broken power. It does not have the last word; instead, we will rise, transformed and yet the same, into a world of glad surprise. Resurrection consecrates the body as the means of our relationship with one another and the cosmos. Through the body, we are freed from our isolation in the self. The body is how the soul gives and receives love. It is the soul as

39. Bulgakov, *Bride of the Lamb*, 492.
40. Bulgakov, *Bride of the Lamb*, 474–75.
41. Bulgakov, *Bride of the Lamb*, 499.
42. Jüngel, *Death*, 135.

communion, the soul as movement, the soul as lover, the soul as dance. Without the body, the soul would lose life.[43]

Resurrection affirms the unity of soul and body, recognizing that a person is not just the combination of the two; a person is their emergent co-creation. Hence, the soul cannot be separated from the body because such separation would deny our personhood; you cannot separate one from the other and still have a person any more than you can separate hydrogen from oxygen and still have water. Likewise, we cannot say "a person is most truly spirit" or "a person is most truly body" any more than we can say "water is most truly hydrogen" or "water is most truly oxygen."

Recognizing this fundamental inseparability, the Bible's affirmation of resurrection as embodiment is absolute. When the risen Jesus appears to the disciples, who are somewhat flabbergasted at his reappearance, he simply responds, "'Have you anything here to eat?' So, they gave him a piece of broiled fish and he ate it" (Luke 24:41).

Unfortunately, as Christianity grew in the Roman Empire, it adopted the sky god imagery of the Roman pantheon. In so doing, it abandoned the garden god imagery it had inherited from Judaism, which resolutely valued embodiment, and replaced it with imagery more suited to a purely spiritual existence. Because it adopted Greco-Roman religious imagery, Christian art tends to depict God, angels, and redeemed souls in the clouds, with nowhere to go and nothing to do, unless they happen to be playing a lute. Garden imagery, on the other hand, provides resurrected persons with pleasure and purpose in a material paradise. For this reason, garden imagery would better dovetail with Christian views of the resurrection.

Resurrection Is an Act of Perfect Healing

Now, we will consider some of the basic qualities of resurrected life. Speculation about the exact nature of the afterlife inevitably leads into conundrums and contradictions that shred the coherence of any theology. Smart theologians avoid it, but bereaved parishioners need it, so pastoral theology demands it.

We are fully healed at the resurrection, both physically and spiritually. Our bodies and souls will be perfect. We trust this assertion due to the appearance of Jesus to his disciples, *wounds healed*. His scars declare

43. Schmemann, *O Death*, 42.

that the pain of the passion was real, and his death on the cross was real, but both were overcome by the restorative power of God the Trinity. We may anticipate the same: "I am going to bring [them] recovery and healing; I will heal them and reveal to them an abundance of well-being and security" (Jer 33:6).

Divine Dance
(sculpture by Scotty Utz, photograph by Daniel Weatherby)
The sculptor writes, "Relationship and community are the central
themes of this cross. . . . The three crosses can only be seen when you
look through the steel structures, into the negative space, and recognize
their relationship to each other from different places on the field."

Healing is a subjective word that begs definition. For example, certain Christian groups insist that gender fluidity, transgender identity, and same-sex attraction are unnatural, contrary to the plan of God, and result from psychological harm in childhood. For this reason, according to these groups, the LGBTQ+ community needs "reparative therapy" (also known as conversion therapy or sexual orientation change efforts) to heal those wounds. This "repair" will make them gender conforming and heterosexual. "Reparative therapy" has been condemned as inherently harmful by the American Psychological Association, American Psychiatric Association, National Association of Social Workers, American Counseling Association, American Medical Association, American Academy of Pediatrics, and World Health Organization. Nevertheless, its proponents persist in propagating injury.

Whereas God created us to become who we are, the advocates of reparative therapy demand that LGBTQ+ persons become who they are not. Whereas Jesus restored people to visibility, the advocates of reparative therapy demand LGBTQ+ persons hide. Reparative therapy seeks return to an old world in which sexual and gender minorities were closeted. We are arguing, on the contrary, that diversity is God's plan. God didn't just make a tree; God made over sixty thousand different species of trees. God didn't just make a butterfly; God made over twenty thousand different species of butterflies. Diversity being divinely planned, we may anticipate that *diversity will not be eradicated at the beginning; diversity will be consummated.* In the fullness of God, in the *kairos*, in the commonwealth where eternity infuses all time, personal fulfillment arises alongside universal fulfillment:[44] *LGBTQ+ persons will remain LGBTQ+.* Healing will come to those cisgender, heterosexual persons who are uncomfortable with sexual and gender diversity, and they will thank God for that healing.[45]

Healing will come to all. Those who were depressed, and whose depression tainted every moment of joy in their lives, will experience pure joy for the first time. Psyches scarred by childhood trauma will be restored to wholeness. People suffering from substance abuse disorders will be freed. Lonely people will find accompaniment. Those weighed down by hatred will forgive, and those weighed down by guilt will be forgiven. Healing will come to wounds we didn't know we had.

44. Tillich, *Love, Power, and Justice,* 65.

45. MacDougall, "Bodily Communions," 182–83.

Through Resurrection,
We Will Be Reunited with Loved Ones

My friend was working in a hospital as a chaplain intern when he was confronted with an extremely difficult situation. On his rounds, a six-month-old baby was actively dying of cancer. Twice, the baby went into cardiac arrest, at which point the mother and aunts would start crying, begging the baby to come back to them. Twice, without medical intervention, the baby revived. My friend knew that this cycle couldn't continue, so he gathered the family together, spoke with them about the diagnosis, reminded them of God's care, and prayed with them for the strength to let their child go. The family recognized that begging their terminally ill child not to die wasn't helping, and they resolved to assist in a peaceful transition. The next time the baby went into cardiac arrest, they spoke soothingly, telling her to go toward the light and reassuring her that loved ones on the other side were there waiting. Surrounded by calm prayer and gentle weeping, the baby passed over.

"Blessed are those who are mourning, for they will be consoled," promises Jesus (Matt 5:4). This promise implies that, in the words of Mark Heim, "Eternal life, salvation, will have an interpersonal character."[46] The comfort of a parent who has lost a child is reunion with that child. God cannot abide the severing of love by death, so God responds with reunion. The promise of reunion does not remove pain but transfigures it, granting us the hope that God will redeem our present suffering through future healing—physical, emotional, and spiritual. This great hope secures all lesser hopes. As Paul writes, "Hope does not disappoint, for the love of God has been poured into our hearts through the Holy Spirit" (Rom 5:5).

We Cannot Reunite without Reconciling

Just as God brings persons back into physical relation, so God will bring persons back into spiritual relation. The restoration of spiritual relation depends on reconciliation. Abba as love sustains the universe, rendering love the moving power of life. This love drives everything that is toward everything else that is. Thus, our experience of love is an experience of the most basic nature of the universe, which loves unity and abhors separation. All that is estranged strives for reunion, sensing that self-fulfillment

46. Heim, *Depth of the Riches*, 57.

lies in the other, just as other-fulfillment lies in the self: "Love manifests its greatest power where it overcomes the greatest separation."[47]

Faith strives to restore the primordial unity, energized by the appeal of unsurpassable love. We feel the divine beauty and cannot help but respond accordingly.[48] The great act that allows reconciliation, and the great experience for which we all are destined, is forgiveness. From a this-worldly perspective, forgiveness denies the past lordship over the future. As a symbol, forgiveness does not just point to the coming harmony; it mediates that harmony. It is a foretaste of universal accord, an appearance of God's future in our present.[49]

At the resurrection, the forgiveness of God will free us from our loathing, both of self and others, in an act of immediate and absolute healing. Every wrong will be wiped clean, every scar will be healed, and every regret will vanish into a sea of mercy. At that point, we may barely recognize ourselves.

We fling words at God like children throw rocks at the sun. Our discussion of the afterlife has been just as futile. Words fail us; we rely on metaphor and simile, until metaphor and simile themselves become useless. God's glorious intention for us lies beyond the reach of language. Dante struggled with this limitation as he concluded the *Divine Comedy*. His poetic genius served him well as he described the inferno and purgatory, but all language evaporated before the beauty of God. Pausing before the highest celestial sphere, he hears a sound he had never heard before, which he can describe only as "the laughter of the universe," the joy of a cosmos healed, the final reunion of all that had been separated, the defeat of hatred by love. Perhaps this vision is too much to hope for, but why would we hope for anything less?[50]

Faith Embraces Paradox

I have dug myself a bit of a hole here. I have accepted death as a correlate to life, yet most concepts of the afterlife are deathless. Have I accidentally committed myself to reincarnation? That would solve some of the conundrums created as I have attempted to celebrate earthly existence without self-deception. But in most denominations of Buddhism and Hinduism,

47. Tillich, *Love, Power, and Justice*, 25.
48. Hartshorne, *Omnipotence*, 14.
49. Moltmann, *Trinity and the Kingdom*, 116–18.
50. Cox, *When Jesus Came*, 294.

the goal of religious practice is not to be reincarnated; it is to achieve release (moksha) from reincarnation because life is difficult. Release, too, is a deathless state.

The Buddha, wise man that he was, explicitly refused to describe nirvana, and not without reason. What is there to do in a deathless afterlife? The American theologian Charles Hartshorne refused to believe in an afterlife because he thought it would be boring.[51] I think that God, being the creative type, could probably solve that problem and give us meaningful work and perpetual growth in a world less cruel than this one, but I'm not smart enough to speculate how. Faith doesn't *know*; faith *trusts*.

Earlier, we discussed the tragic death of Wesley Ward, the twenty-four-year-old man who died in a car accident. When they went through his belongings, they found in his wallet a hand-written card with Wesley's favorite Bible verse on it: "Be strong and of good courage; be not frightened, neither be dismayed; for the Lord your God is with you wherever you go" (Josh 1:9). His parents printed copies of this card and handed them out at his funeral, with a description on the back: "Wesley M. Ward / December 2, 1977–December 9, 2001 / Hand written bible verse, Joshua 1:9 / Found in Wesley's wallet."

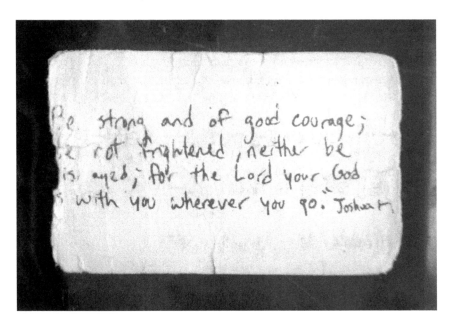

---

51. Hartshorne, *Omnipotence*, 35.

Wesley M. Ward
Dec.2, 1977-Dec.9, 2001
Hand written bible verse, Joshua 1.9
Found in Wesley's wallet

I have carried that card in my own wallet for the past twenty-two years. It brings me comfort. I don't expect life to be easy, and no life is immune from suffering. Wesley reminds me that I can trust God, even through tragedy. Nowhere does God promise a life without trial, but everywhere God promises to accompany us through both the agony and the ecstasy, not at a distance, but nearer to us than we are to ourselves.

Through trust of God we can sing, even in the darkness. We can laugh in anticipation of weeping and weep in anticipation of laughter, always sheltered in faith. Along the way, as we are parted from one another, we can remember Jesus's parting words to his disciples, "Yes, you are grieving now; but I will see you again and then you'll rejoice, and no one will take your joy from you" (John 16:22).

Afterword

Do you already know that your existence—who and how you are—is in and of itself a contribution to the people and place around you? Not after or because you do some particular thing, but simply the miracle of your life? And that the people around you, and the places, have contributions as well? Do you understand that your quality of life and your survival are tied to how authentic and generous the connections are between you and the people and places you live with and in?

—ADRIENNE MAREE BROWN[1]

THIS BOOK IS INCOMPLETE. Desiring to produce a thorough interpretation of agapic nondualism, I had originally planned to include chapters on Trinitarian ethics (what conduct the Trinity commends), Trinitarian epistemology (how we come to knowledge in a Trinitarian framework), and Trinitarian theology of religions (how a Trinitarian Christian interprets the fact of religious pluralism). I then intended to conclude the book with a reflection on theological method (the sources of theological thinking and the criteria by which theological thinking is evaluated). Alas, including those chapters in this book would have severely taxed me, my publisher, and you (I fear). They will have to be a separate effort, which is tentatively entitled *God Is Love: Love Is Something You Do.*

The foregoing book addresses the deeply ambiguous question: How should we live? For Socrates, this vital question is the beginning of all

---

1. brown, *Emergent Strategy*, 90.

philosophy. Every human being, even the most unreflective, must answer the question through the living of their lives. We can give an unexamined answer by living a trivial life, or we can give a profound answer by living life well. Socrates forcefully advocates the latter. So does Jesus, who passionately taught his disciples to live *engodded* (vital, vibrant, vigorous) lives. Engodded life is the opposite of ineffectual life. It is spiritually alive, not spiritually dead; bright eyed, not hollow eyed.

For Jesus, living truth boils down to love of God, self, neighbor, and world. Together, these four loves produce a comprehensive love of life. Love is the way, the halakah, the path through life that leads to fulfillment. A life lived *lovingly* best expresses this truth, more so than any combination of words. We tend to think of God as a noun, but this grammar limits the limitless God, who always overflows our theological concepts. God is love, and language best expresses the immanence of God when God permeates all language: God is love (noun), God is the pure act of loving (verb), God is persons who are loving (adjective), God is activity performed lovingly (adverb). These grammatical terms symbolize the divine saturation of the universe: God is everything, everywhere, *in every way*, always within, and always beyond.

To act Godfully is to act lovingly, and to live Godfully is to live lovingly. To associate any inert substance with God is wrong; God is empty of substance and empty of inertia. God is becoming, and becoming in a certain direction—towards love, through love, for love. Our greatest honor is that we are invited to *become with* God, to co-create love. This co-creating is our highest vocation, and in it we will find our deepest gratification.[2]

I have argued that, for Christians, fully Trinitarian thought accompanied by fully Trinitarian language best expresses the sacred potential within life. This change will come as a shock to many, who might accuse Trinitarians of *tritheism*. Tritheism is belief in three gods, making it a form of polytheism. The early disciples of Jesus were *monotheistic* Jews in a *polytheistic* Greco-Roman context, worshippers of the one God who treasured their monotheism. But, as the developing Christian tradition struggled to understand exactly who Jesus Christ and the Holy Spirit are, and what they are doing, it developed *Trinitarian* thought that asserted the co-eternity, co-divinity, and co-equality of all three persons. In response to divine self-revelation, the church developed the concept of the Trinity.

2. Cobb and Griffin, *Process Theology*, 28.

The Great Open Dance
(side view; sculpture by Scotty Utz, photograph by Katherine Brooks)

Declaring that God is both three and one would, we would expect, produce a conviction that God is neither monotheistic nor tritheistic but Trinitarian. Or, embracing paradox, it might produce a concept of God as monotheistic, tritheistic, *and* Trinitarian. Instead, the declaration that God is both three and one produced a forceful assertion that God is *triune* and monotheistic, but most definitely *not* tritheistic. God is one and three, but more one than three. Oddly, in a Trinitarian context, monotheism became orthodox, and tritheism heretical.

This imbalance produced some confusion: the church rejected *subordinationism*, the belief that the Son or Holy Spirit is subordinate to the Father. Yet the Nicene Creed, the most universally accepted creed in the Christian tradition, asserts that both the Son and Holy Spirit *depend* ontologically on the Father, the Son being *begotten* (not created) by the Father and the Spirit *proceeding* from the Father. We can infer that the Father in no way *depends* on the Son or Spirit. This move was intended to ensure one, single source of divinity and preserve Christianity's monotheistic bona fides.

Simultaneously, the Nicene Creed asserts the shared divine *substance* of the Father, Son, and Holy Spirit, yet states, "I believe in one God, the Father, Almighty." The creed does not refer to the Son as God or the Spirit as God. But if the Son and Spirit share in the divine substance, then what happened to their divinity?

According to tradition, the Son and Spirit cannot be mere *modes* of the Father, because the church also rejected *modalism*, the belief that God just appears to be three persons but is really one person in three different guises. Nevertheless, fear of tritheism pushes many theologians into a modalistic interpretation of the Trinity. In the twentieth century, Karl Barth writes: "The meaning of the doctrine [of the Trinity] is not, then, that there are three personalities in God. This would be the most extreme expression of tritheism, against which we must be on our guard. . . . But in it we are speaking not of three divine 'I's,' but thrice of the one divine I."[3]

How does one divine "I" produce three distinct manifestations without falling into modalism? Following the Barthian critique is Stephen Holmes, who argues that the emphasis of the Jewish Bible is on monotheistic resistance to polytheistic impulses. According to Holmes, since the church chose to preserve the "Old Testament" as the Scripture to which Jesus extensively referred, we should preserve the integrity of its primary emphasis and treat the triune "New Testament" as "a brief coda or appendix" to an essentially monotheistic Scripture.

But Holmes's demotion of the Newer Testament's incipient Trinitarian language denies the authenticity of the disciples' experience of Christ and the Holy Spirit, both of which transcended their experience of *created* reality, both of which seemed *divine*. In response to its tripersonal soteriology (doctrine of salvation), the church developed a tripersonal theology, the Trinity. Anything less would have reduced Jesus to a prophet and the Spirit to a feeling.

The assertion that three persons cannot unite perfectly to become one God denies numerous analogies in the physical and experiential world. By way of extension, these critics of tripersonal Trinitarianism

---

3. Barth, *Doctrine of Word*, 410–11.

would have to declare that three tones cannot unite to form one chord, and that three sides cannot unite to form one triangle, and that three colors cannot unite to form one flag, and that three atoms cannot unite to form one molecule, and that three particles cannot unite to form one atom. None of these declarations holds true, nor does the declaration that three persons cannot unite to form one God.

Taking a different tack, Karen Kilby argues that robust Trinitarianism is a mere act of projection—a reading of liberal politics into the heart of God, a covert deification of progressive ideology.[4] As such, it rejects traditional theology and the biblical witness to declare the Trinitarian theologian's ethics to be God's ethics. Then, having projected their ethics *onto* God, Trinitarian theologians argue that their ethics are *from* God, divinely justified, to be universally instituted.

Certainly, Trinitarian ethics dovetails with Trinitarian theology. But this coherence need not suggest hypocritical bombast. Instead, the consistency of Trinitarian ethics with Trinitarian theology could be just that: *consistency*, a trait generally praised in theological circles. Fundamentalist theology is consistent with fundamentalist ethics. I disagree with both, not because they are inconsistent, but because I think they obstruct the abundance of life that God intends. Fundamentalists can accuse me of projecting, and I can accuse them of projecting, but any clarification of our positions will be achieved only by respectful, rational argumentation, not mutual dismissal for our shared consistency.

Opponents of robust Trinitarianism also note that, if the Trinity serves as a source for Christian ethics, then it should produce *similar* Christian ethics, which it doesn't. Different Trinitarian theologians offer different doctrines of the church, which often cohere with their denominational affiliation: Moltmann, a Protestant, proposes democratic governance; Zizioulas, an Orthodox, believes the bishop to be essential; Boff's focus is socioeconomic; LaCugna's is interpersonal; Volf's is ecclesiastical. Of what value is Trinitarian theology if it cannot produce a consistent Trinitarian ethic?[5]

This critique would be fair if it were applied consistently across all Christian theologies and their resultant Christian ethics, but it isn't. The Roman Catholic tradition produces a variety of ethical systems; Protestant biblical fundamentalists produce a variety of ethical systems; Presbyterian denominations that share the Westminster Confession produce

4. Kilby, "Perichoresis and Projection," 439.
5. S. Holmes, "Three versus One," 82.

a variety of ethical systems. The variety of ethics produced by any one category of theology does not imply the bankruptcy of that category; it reveals the freedom of human thought even when limited in its sources. Trinitarian ethics vary because Trinitarian theologians write from a wide variety of life experiences, church teachings, and biblical emphases; Trinitarians need not be embarrassed by these riches.[6]

Karen Kilby also argues that the Trinity in itself is not a *subject* of Christian reflection, but instead provides a *grammar* for reflection on the activity of the Father, Son, and Holy Spirit. According to Kilby, the doctrine of the Trinity informs us how we should practice *first*-order theology, our doctrines of God, Christ, and Spirit, but the Trinity itself is a *second*-order doctrine, informative to the primary doctrines, but not itself one of them. We can speculate about it, but that speculation is not essential to Christian theology or church practice.[7]

This solution is puzzling. A monotheistic Trinitarian will produce a very different Christology (doctrine of Christ) from a tripersonal Trinitarian. If the Trinity is the controlling grammar of Christian theology, influencing every aspect thereof, then we should pay extremely close attention to it. Kilby's own argument, intended to decenter the Trinity in Christian theology, instead renders it the *foundation* of Christian theology, implicitly insisting that we make that foundation sure.

In interreligious dialogue, when a practitioner of another religion respectfully asks us how God can be both three and one, the response "That is just our grammar for God" will produce only a puzzled look that implicitly requests clarification. The more descriptive response "The Trinity is three persons perfectly united through love into one God" may produce some consternation, especially on the part of our monotheistic neighbors, but also a more fruitful conversation.

Nor is declaring the Trinity an impenetrable mystery legitimate. Certainly, our understanding of God is severely limited, and the Trinity is a subject of revelation, not reason. But if Christianity declares that God is one and three, then refuses to address *how* they are one and three, we are inviting an immediate dismissal of our most foundational assertion. Avoidance never helps the avoider.

Finally, if our strictly monotheistic conversation partner asks if we are tritheists, then we can reply that our Trinitarian theology avoids both modalism (I'm sorry, we're not pure monotheists) and tritheism (really,

6. Van den Brink, "Social Trinitarianism," 338.

7. Kilby, "Perichoresis and Projection," 443.

we're not polytheists) by positing the three persons as interdependent, co-creating, and mutually open to one another. Thankfully, their perfect unity does not depend on any underlying similarity; they incorporate diversity into divinity, celebrating difference itself as holy, *as should we*. Abba, the Architect of the universe, provides the physical laws that weave the cosmos into one beautiful fabric and the moral laws that weave humankind into one loving family. Jesus, the Empath of the universe, ratifies Abba's artwork and communicates the divine truth through his celebration of embodied life. Sophia, the Perfector of human experience, continually inspires us toward the practice of wisdom and heights of spirit. Their specific roles are unique but complementary, granting them different emphases, activities, and memories, all of which harmonize within the perfect community that is God. Salvation, therefore, is communion in difference.[8]

The above may sound disorienting to those who are familiar with the Christian tradition, but the familiar never exhausts the possible. *Our vocation is to actualize the imagination of God.* Sometimes, disruption is beneficial. As the archbishop of Canterbury Rowan Williams reminds us, "If you genuinely desire union with the unspeakable love of God, then you must be prepared to have your 'religious' world shattered."[9]

If God is unifying love, then religion that divides is irreligious. Faith demands that we think in a way that integrates, not separates. Traditionally, Christian theology has relied on four different sources: the Bible, tradition, reason, and experience. Different denominations emphasize different sources over others. Some will ask: Is it biblical? Others will ask: Is it traditional? And so on. Problematically, none of these four sources provides a reliable criterion for evaluating the faithfulness of any particular theology. In addition to beautiful passages that extol peace, justice, and love, the Bible contains violent, misogynistic, and violently misogynistic passages. The Christian tradition has nurtured souls and healed bodies, but at times harmed both. Reason provides guardrails that, if used skillfully, protect against tribal insanity, but reason is hollow in itself: egoists can rationalize their egoism as easily as altruists can rationalize their altruism. Human experience inevitably informs how we interpret the Bible, how we interpret tradition, and how we reason,

8. Heim, *Depth of the Riches*, 62.
9. R. Williams, *Being Disciples*, 50.

but bad experience—racist culture, militaristic values, sexist upbring-ing—can produce bad theology. So, by what criterion should we evaluate Christian theology?

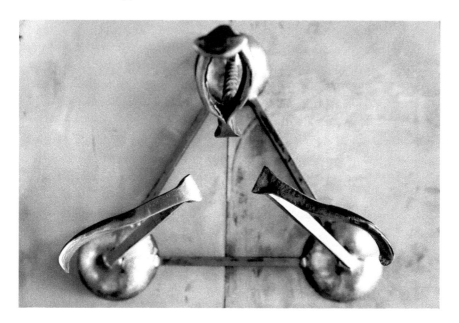

The Great Open Dance
(top view; sculpture by Scotty Utz, photograph by Katherine Brooks)

As you consider the ideas presented in this book, I hope that you will evaluate them by the standard of agape. *Agape is the measure of all things.* Jesus reveals this truth, and Paul restates it in one of the most beautiful passages ever written, 1 Cor 13:1–13. We may be dulled to the radicality of these words due to their overuse at weddings, but Paul wasn't writing just about marital love. He was writing about love as the abiding ground of human flourishing. For Paul, love is the source of our being, the goal of our becoming, and our sustenance along the journey:

> If I speak in the tongues of humans and of angels but do not have love, I am a noisy gong or a clanging cymbal. And if I have prophetic powers and understand all mysteries and all knowl-edge and if I have all faith so as to remove mountains but do not have love, I am nothing. If I give away all my possessions and if I hand over my body so that I may boast but do not have love, I gain nothing. Love is patient; love is kind; love is not envious or boastful or arrogant or rude. It does not insist on its own way; it

is not irritable; it keeps no record of wrongs; it does not rejoice in wrongdoing but rejoices in the truth. It bears all things, believes all things, hopes all things, endures all things. Love never ends. But as for prophecies, they will come to an end; as for tongues, they will cease; as for knowledge, it will come to an end. For we know only in part, and we prophesy only in part, but when the complete comes, the partial will come to an end. When I was a child, I spoke like a child, I thought like a child, I reasoned like a child. When I became an adult, I put an end to childish ways. For now we see only a reflection, as in a mirror, but then we will see face to face. Now I know only in part; then I will know fully, even as I have been fully known. And now faith, hope, and love remain, these three, and the greatest of these is love.

In many ways, this book is an exposition of this passage by Paul. In the conviction that faithfulness to God entails faithfulness to love, I have tried to write a Christian theology saturated in love. As a word, *love* runs the risk of exhaustion and enfeeblement, but its truth is transformative. *Love changes everything, all the time.* To the extent that we understand love and are open to it, to precisely that extent will we be transfigured, both individually and collectively.

I request that you judge this work by the criterion of love, the only legitimate criterion in the Christian tradition. As an exposition of agape, this book should help individuals to feel more at home in the universe, more confident in life, less afraid of death, more peaceful within struggle, and more hopeful, even while acknowledging the darkness. For communities, I pray that this book would grant them more unity, purpose, and patience with one another, an opportunity ever presented by our imperfections.

I hope that the church will eventually progress beyond this book as the church becomes ever more agapic, which is to become ever more inclusive, universalist, and egalitarian. When this book is forgotten, which it will be, I pray that it will be forgotten because it has been replaced by more loving theologies that are more faithful to our loving God. These theologies will correct every accidental offense I have committed due to my own immersion in a specific place at a specific time with a specific set of blinders. For those theologies, and for their eventual appearance, I thank God, who is forever leading us into the reign of love.

About the Artist

SCOTTY UTZ IS A blacksmith who works in the mountains of North Carolina. Raised by the artist Thornton Utz, and having earned a master of divinity degree from Princeton Theological Seminary, through his work Scotty explores the intersections between theology and craftsmanship, contemplating ideas about God through metal. He creates objects and spaces that mingle spirit and matter—sometimes the sculpture is the focal point in a gathering place, sometimes it is a spiritual exploration, and sometimes it is a whimsical, functional item. Regarding the works that appear in this book, Scotty writes, "Wrestling with concepts of the Trinity since adolescence has left me with a kind of limp that keeps showing up in my work. But sometimes a limp is a sign of blessing" (Gen 32:22–32). Pictures of Scotty's art appear courtesy of Katherine Brooks Photography.

Bibliography

Alexievich, Svetlana. *The Unwomanly Face of War: An Oral History of Women in World War II*. New York: Random House, 2018.

Ali, Mukhtar. "Islam and the Unity of Being." In *Nondualism: An Interreligious Exploration*, edited by Jon Paul Sydnor and Anthony J. Watson, 109–26. Studies in Comparative Philosophy and Religion. New York: Lexington, 2023.

Almalech, Mony. "Cultural Unit Red in the Old Testament." *Language and Semiotic Studies* 9 (2023) 104–42. DOI: 10.1515/lass-2022–2010.

American Psychiatric Association. *Diagnostic and Statistical Manual of Mental Disorders [DSM-5]*. Washington, DC: APA, 2013.

Annan, Kent. *After Shock: Searching for Honest Faith When Your World Is Shaken*. Downers Grove, IL: InterVarsity Press, 2011.

Anselm. *Basic Writings*. Edited and translated by Thomas Williams. Cambridge, MA: Hackett, 2007.

Aquinas, Thomas. *Summa Theologica*. Translated by Fathers of the English Dominican Province. Vol. 5. London: Burns, Oates & Washbourne, 1912. https://www.documentacatholicaomnia.eu/03d/1225-1274,_Thomas_Aquinas,_Summa_Theologiae_%5B1%5D,_EN.pdf.

Artemi, Eirini. "The Term *Perichoresis* from the Cappodocian Fathers to Maximus Confessor." *International Journal of European Studies* 1 (2017) 21–29. DOI: 10.11648/j.ijes.20170101.14/.

Athanasius. "Life of St. Anthony." Translated by H. Ellershaw. From *Nicene and Post-Nicene Fathers*, edited by Philip Schaff and Henry Wace, 2nd ser., 4. Buffalo, NY: Christian Literature, 1892. Revised and edited for New Advent by Kevin Knight. https://www.newadvent.org/fathers/2811.htm.

Augustine. *Confessions*. Translated by Henry Chadwick. Oxford: Oxford World Classics, 1991.

———. "Homily 7 on the First Epistle of John (1 John 4:4–12)." Translated by H. Browne. From *Nicene and Post-Nicene Fathers*, edited by Philip Schaff, 1st ser., 7. Buffalo, NY: Christian Literature, 1888. Revised and edited for New Advent by Kevin Knight. https://www.newadvent.org/fathers/170207.htm.

———. "On the Literal Interpretation of Genesis." In *The Faith of the Early Fathers*, edited by William Jurgens, translated by John Hammond Taylor, 3:82–87. Collegeville, MN: Liturgical, 1970.

————. *On the Trinity*. Edited by Gareth B. Matthews. Translated by Stephen McKenna. Cambridge: Cambridge University Press, 2002.

Avery-Peck, Alan, and Jacob Neusner, editors. *The Routledge Dictionary of Judaism*. New York: Taylor & Francis, 2004.

Bacon, Hannah. "'Thinking' the Trinity as Resource for Feminist Theology Today?" *CrossCurrents* 62 (2012) 442–64. http://www.jstor.org/stable/24462298.

Bahm, Archie J. "Polarity: A Descriptive Hypothesis." *Philosophy and Phenomenological Research* 21 (1961) 347–60. DOI: 10.2307/2105151/.

Baldwin, James. *The Fire Next Time*. New York: Modern Library, 2021.

————. *Nobody Knows My Name: More Notes of a Native Son*. New York: Knopf Doubleday, 1992.

Baloyi, Elijah. "A Re-Reading of John 8:1–11 from a Pastoral Liberative Perspective on South African Women." *HvTSt* 66 (2010) 1–7. DOI: 10.4102/hts.v66i2.838/.

Baravalle, Hermann von. "Conic Sections in Relation to Physics and Astronomy." *Mathematics Teacher* 63 (1970) 101–9. DOI: 10.5951/MT.63.2.0101.

Barbour, Ian G. *Religion and Science: Historical and Contemporary Issues*. San Francisco: HarperSanFrancisco, 2013.

Barna Group. "Six Reasons Young Christians Leave Church." Barna, Sept. 27, 2011. https://www.barna.com/research/six-reasons-young-christians-leave-church/.

————. "What Americans Think about Women in Power." Barna, Mar. 8, 2017. https://www.barna.com/research/americans-think-women-power/.

Barnard, Ian. "Toward a Postmodern Understanding of Separatism." *Women's Studies* 27 (1998) 613–39. DOI: 10.1080/00497878.1998.9979235.

Barnstone, Willis, and Marvin W. Meyer, eds. *The Gnostic Bible*. Boston: Shambhala, 2006.

Barr, James. "Interpretation, History of." In *Oxford Companion to the Bible*, edited by Bruce M. Metzger and Michael D. Coogan, 305–24. Oxford Companions. New York: Oxford University Press, 1993.

Barth, Karl. *The Doctrine of the Word of God*. Vol. 1, pt. 1 of *Church Dogmatics*. London: T. & T. Clark International, 2004.

Bauckham, Richard. "Jürgen Moltmann and the Question of Pluralism." In *The Trinity in a Pluralistic Age: Theological Essays on Culture and Religion*, edited by Kevin J. Vanhoozer, 155–64. Grand Rapids: Eerdmans, 1997.

Baylis, C. A. "The Philosophic Functions of Emergence." *Philosophical Review* 38 (1929) 372–84.

Bazzano, Manu. "Deathlife, lifedeath." *Person-Centered & Experiential Psychotherapies* 15 (2016) 256–62. DOI: 10.1080/14779757.2016.1204348.

Bermejo, A. M. "Circumincession." In *New Catholic Encyclopedia*, edited by Berard L. Marthaler, 1:741–42. 2nd ed. New York: Gale, 2002.

Biale, David. "The God with Breasts: El Shaddai in the Bible." *History of Religions* 21 (1982) 240–56. DOI: 10.1086/462899/.

Blowers, Paul M. "Maximus the Confessor, Gregory of Nyssa, and the Concept of 'Perpetual Progress.'" *VC* 46 (1992) 151–71. DOI: 10.2307/1583788.

Boff, Leonardo. *Trinity and Society*. Translated by Paul Burns. 1988. Reprint, Eugene, OR: Wipf & Stock, 2005.

Bokser, Ben Zion, and Baruch M. Bokser, eds. *The Talmud: Selected Writings*. Classics of Western Spirituality. Mahwah, NJ: Paulist, 1989.

Bourgeault, Cynthia. *The Wisdom Jesus: Transforming Heart and Mind—A New Perspective on Christ and His Message*. Boston: Shambhala, 2008.

Bowker, John. *Jesus and the Pharisees*. Cambridge: Cambridge University Press, 1973.

Bowman, Donna. "God for Us: A Process View of the Divine-Human Relationship." In *Handbook of Process Theology*, edited by Donna Bowman and Jay McDaniel, 11–24. St. Louis: Chalice, 2006.

Boyarin, Daniel. "Allegory and Midrash in Origen." In *The Oxford Handbook of Origen*, edited by Ronald E. Heine and Karen Jo Torjesen, 100–117. Oxford Handbooks. Oxford: Oxford University Press, 2022.

———. "John's Prologue as Midrash." In *The Jewish Annotated New Testament*, edited by Amy-Jill Levine and Marc Zvi Brettler, 688–91. 2nd ed. Oxford: Oxford University Press, 2017.

Boyd, Gregory. "The Self-Sufficient Sociality of God: A Trinitarian Revision of Hartshorne's Metaphysics." In *Trinity and Process: A Relational Theology of God*, edited by Joseph A. Bracken, SJ, and Marjorie Hewitt Suchocki, 73–94. New York: Continuum, 1997.

brown, adrienne maree. *Emergent Strategy: Shaping Change, Changing Worlds*. Emergent Strategy. Chico, CA: AK, 2017.

Brunner, Emil. *The Christian Doctrine of God*. Translated by Olive Wyon. Vol. 1 of *Dogmatics*. Philadelphia: Westminster, 1950.

Buber, Martin. *I and Thou*. Translated by Walter Kaufmann. New York: Simon & Schuster, 1970.

Buechner, Frederick. *The Magnificent Defeat*. San Francisco: HarperCollins, 1985.

Bulgakov, Sergeï Nikolaevich. *Bride of the Lamb*. Translated by Boris Jakim. New York: Bloomsbury Academic, 2002.

———. *Churchly Joy: Orthodox Devotions for the Church Year*. Translated by Boris Jakim. Grand Rapids: Eerdmans, 2008.

Burke, Kenneth. *The Philosophy of Literary Form*. Berkeley: University of California Press, 1974.

Burton, David. "Is Madhyamaka Buddhism Really the Middle Way? Emptiness and the Problem of Nihilism." *Contemporary Buddhism* 2 (2001) 177–90. DOI: 10.1080/14639940108573749.

Butler, Judith. *Frames of War: When Is Life Grievable?* New York: Verso, 2016.

———. *Gender Trouble: Feminism and the Subversion of Identity*. New York: Taylor & Francis, 2011.

———. *Undoing Gender*. London: Routledge, 2004.

Butler, Octavia E. *Parable of the Sower*. New York: Seven Stories, 2017.

Byrom, Thomas. *The Heart of Awareness: A Translation of the Ashtavakra Gita*. Boston: Shambhala, 1990.

Calvin, John. *Institutes of the Christian Religion*. Edited by John T. McNeill. Translated by Ford Lewis Battles. Philadelphia: Westminster, 1960.

Campbell, Joseph, with Bill Moyers. *The Power of Myth*. New York: Knopf, 2011.

Campbell, W. Keith, and Joshua Miller. "Narcissism." In *International Encyclopedia of the Social Sciences*, edited by William A. Darity Jr., 5:369–70. 2nd ed. Detroit: Macmillan Reference USA, 2008. Gale eBook.

Cattoi, Thomas. "Response to 'Buddhist Musings on Nondualism.'" In *Nondualism: An Interreligious Exploration*, edited by Jon Paul Sydnor and Anthony Watson, 83–84. Studies in Comparative Philosophy and Religion. New York: Lexington, 2023.

Center for Action and Contemplation. "Distilled Wisdom." Center for Action and Contemplation, Aug. 14, 2019. https://cac.org/daily-meditations/distilled-wisdom-2019-08-14/.

"Chicago Statement on Biblical Inerrancy." Evangelical Theological Society, 1978. https://www.etsjets.org/files/documents/Chicago_Statement.pdf.

Clark, Patrick M. "Reversing the Ethical Perspective: What the Allegorical Interpretation of the Good Samaritan Parable Can Still Teach Us." *Theology Today* 71 (2014) 300–309. DOI: 10.1177/0040573614542308.

Clooney, Francis X., SJ. *Comparative Theology: Deep Learning across Religious Borders.* New York: Wiley-Blackwell, 2010.

———. *Seeing through Texts: Doing Theology among the Śrīvaiṣṇavas of South India.* Toward a Comparative Philosophy of Religions. New York: State University of New York Press, 1996.

———. *Theology after Vedanta: An Experiment in Comparative Theology.* Toward a Comparative Philosophy of Religions. New York: State University of New York Press, 1993.

Coakley, Sarah. *God, Sexuality, and the Self: An Essay "On the Trinity."* Cambridge: Cambridge University Press, 2013.

———. "'Persons' in the 'Social' Doctrine of the Trinity: A Critique of Current Analytic Discussion." In *The Trinity: An Interdisciplinary Symposium on the Trinity*, edited by Stephen T. Davis et al., 123–44. Oxford: Oxford University Press, 1999.

Cobb, John B., Jr., and David Ray Griffin. *Process Theology: An Introductory Exposition.* Philadelphia: Westminster, 1976.

Cohen, Leonard. "Anthem." Track 5 on Cohen, *The Future.* Recorded Jan.–June 1992. Columbia 472498-2, 1992, compact disc.

Coleman, Monica A. *Not Alone: Reflections on Faith and Depression.* New York: Inner Prizes Incorporated, 2012.

Commission on Worship of The Lutheran Church—Missouri Synod. *Lutheran Service Book.* St. Louis: Concordia, 2006.

Cone, James H. *The Cross and the Lynching Tree.* Maryknoll, NY: Orbis, 2011.

Congregazione per la Dottrina della Fede, La. "'Responsum' della Congregazione per la Dottrina della Fede ad un dubbio sulla validità del Battesimo conferito con la formula 'Noi ti battezziamo nel nome del Padre e del Figlio e dello Spirito Santo,' 06.08.2020." Vatican, June 8, 2020. https://press.vatican.va/content/salastampa/it/bollettino/pubblico/2020/08/06/0406/00923.html#rispostein.

Cook, Francis H. *Hua-Yen Buddhism: The Jewel Net of Indra.* University Park: Pennsylvania State University Press, 1977.

Copenhaver, Brian T., ed. *The Greek "Corpus Hermeticum" and the Latin "Asclepius" in a New English Translation.* Attributed to Hermes Trismegistus. Reprint, Cambridge: Cambridge University Press, 1995.

Cottrell-Boyce, Aidan. "Soteriological Uncertainty and the Development of Religious Resistance Identities." *Review of Faith & International Affairs* 15 (2017) 10–23. DOI: 10.1080/15570274.2017.1329387.

Coughenour, Courtney, et al. "Estimated Car Cost as a Predictor of Driver Yielding Behaviors for Pedestrians." *Journal of Transport & Health* 16 (2020) 100831. DOI: 10.1016/j.jth.2020.100831.

Council Fathers. *Decrees of the First Vatican Council.* Papal Encyclicals Online, 1868. https://www.papalencyclicals.net/councils/ecum20.htm.

Cox, Harvey. *When Jesus Came to Harvard: Making Moral Choices Today.* New York: Houghton Mifflin, 2006.

Crossan, John Dominic. *Jesus: A Revolutionary Biography.* San Francisco: HarperCollins, 1994.

Cullerne, John. *The Penguin Dictionary of Physics.* 4th ed. Penguin Reference Library. New York: Penguin, 2009.

Danby, Herbert, ed. and trans. *The Mishnah: Translated from the Hebrew with Introduction and Brief Explanatory Notes.* Oxford: Oxford University Press, 1933.

David, Ariel. "Byzantine Basilica with Graves of Female Ministers and Baffling Mass Burials Found in Israel." *Haaretz,* Nov. 15, 2021. https://www.haaretz.com/archaeology.

Delio, Ilio, OSF. *A Hunger for Wholeness: Soul, Space, and Transcendence.* Mahwah, NJ: Paulist, 2018.

De Mille, Agnes. *Martha: The Life and Work of Martha Graham.* New York: Vintage, 1992.

Dennett, Daniel C. *Darwin's Dangerous Idea: Evolution and the Meaning of Life.* New York: Simon & Schuster, 2014.

Descartes, René. *Descartes: Selected Philosophical Writings.* Translated by John Cottingham et al. Cambridge: Cambridge University Press, 1988.

———. *Meditations on First Philosophy.* Translated by Michael Moriarty. Oxford World's Classics. New York: Oxford University Press, 2008.

Douglass, Frederick. *Autobiographies.* Edited by Henry Louis Gates Jr. New York: Library of America, 1994.

Drake, Harold A. "Monotheism and Violence." *Journal of Late Antiquity* 6 (2013) 251–63. DOI: 10.2373/journal/837.78/.

Driver, Tom F. "Transformation: The Magic of Ritual." In *Readings in Ritual Studies,* edited by Ronald L. Grimes, 170–87. Englewood Cliffs, NJ: Prentice Hall, 1996.

Dunne, Frank, and Arthur Segal. *A Spiritual and Ethical Compendium to the Torah and Talmud.* Charleston, SC: BookSurge, 2009.

Duns Scotus, John. *Four Questions on Mary.* Translated by Allan B. Wolter. New York: Franciscan Institute, 2000.

Dupuis, Jacques, SJ. *Toward a Christian Theology of Religious Pluralism.* Maryknoll, NY: Orbis, 1997.

Dyson, Freeman. *Infinite in All Directions.* London: Penguin, 1989.

Edmondson, Stephen. "Opening the Table: The Body of Christ and God's Prodigal Grace." *AThR* 91 (2009) 224–37.

Edwards, Rem B. "Axiological Reflections on Infinite Human and Divine Worth." *Journal of Formal Axiology* 11 (2019) 11–38.

El Saadawi, Nawal. *Memoirs from the Women's Prison.* Translated by Marilyn Booth. Literature of the Middle East. Berkeley: University of California Press, 1994.

Ephrem the Syrian. *Ephrem the Syrian: Hymns.* Translated by Kathleen E. McVey. Classics of Western Spirituality. Mahwah, NJ: Paulist, 1989.

Episcopal Church, The. *The Book of Common Prayer and Administration of the Sacraments and Other Rites and Ceremonies of the Church, Together with The Psalter or Psalms of David; According to the use of The Episcopal Church.* New York: Church, 2006.

Fackenheim, Emil L. *The Religious Dimension in Hegel's Thought.* Bloomington: Indiana University Press, 1971.

Falk, Harvey. *Jesus the Pharisee: A New Look at the Jewishness of Jesus.* 1985. Reprint, Eugene, OR: Wipf & Stock, 2003.

Farley, Wendy. *Eros for the Other: Retaining Truth in a Pluralistic World.* University Park: Pennsylvania State University Press, 2010.

Farrugia, E. "The Iconic Character of Christian Language: Logos and Icon." *MelT* 45 (1994) 1–17. https://www.um.edu.mt/library/oar/handle/123456789/37182.

Feynman, Richard P. *The Pleasure of Finding Things Out: The Best Short Works of Richard P. Feynman.* Edited by Jeffrey Robbins. New York: Basic, 2005.

Fiddes, Paul S. "Suffering in Theology and Modern European Thought." In *The Oxford Handbook of Theology and Modern European Thought*, edited by Nicholas Adams et al., 169–91. Oxford Handbooks. Oxford: Oxford University Press, 2013.

Fisher, George P. *An Unpublished Essay of Edwards on the Trinity: With Remarks on Edwards and His Theology.* New York: Scribner's Sons, 1903.

Fletcher, Joseph. *Situation Ethics: The New Morality.* Louisville: Westminster, 1966.

Fonrobert, Charlotte Elisheva. "Ethical Theories in Rabbinic Literature." In The *Oxford Handbook of Jewish Ethics and Morality*, edited by Elliot N. Dorff and Jonathan K. Crane, 51–70. Oxford Handbooks. Oxford: Oxford University Press, 2016.

Frank, Priscilla. "30 Years Later, a Sculpture of Jesus as a Nude Woman Finally Gets Its Due." *Huffington Post*, Oct. 6, 2016. https://www.huffpost.com/entry/christa-edwina-sandys-art_n_57f55296e4b0b7aafe0b8999.

Freeman, R. David. "Woman, a Power Equal to Man: Translation of Woman as a 'Fit Helpmate' for Man Is Questioned." *BAR* 9 (1983) 18–32.

Freud, Sigmund. *The Future of an Illusion.* Translated by Peter Gay. New York: Norton, 1989.

———. *Totem and Taboo: Some Points of Agreement between the Mental Lives of Savages and Neurotics.* Translated by Peter Gay. New York: Norton, 1989.

Gadamer, Hans-Georg. *Truth and Method.* 2nd ed. Translated by Joel Weinsheimer and Donald G. Marshall. New York: Continuum, 2000.

Gamow, George. *One, Two, Three—Infinity: Facts and Speculations of Science.* London: Dover, 1988.

Gates, David. "Religion: The Pop Prophets." *Newsweek*, May 23, 2004. https://www.newsweek.com/religion-pop-prophets-127971.

Geary, James. *I Is an Other: The Secret Life of Metaphor and How It Shapes The Way We See the World.* New York: Harper Perennial, 2012.

Gerstner, John H. *Jonathan Edwards on Heaven and Hell.* Grand Rapids: Baker, 1980.

Gethin, Rupert. *The Foundations of Buddhism.* Oxford: Oxford University Press, 1998.

Gilmer, John. "Joy in the End." Sermon given at International Christian Fellowship Church, Nairobi, Mar. 29, 2015.

Girard, René. *Evolution and Conversion: Dialogues on the Origins of Culture.* London: Bloomsbury, 2017.

Gleick, James. *Genius: The Life and Science of Richard Feynman.* New York: Vintage, 1993.

Gombrowicz, Witold. *Diary.* Translated by Lillian Vallee. Margellos World Republic of Letters. New Haven: Yale University Press, 2012.

Gordon, Ernest. *To End All Wars: A True Story about the Will to Survive and the Courage to Forgive.* Grand Rapids: Zondervan, 2013.

Gordon, Peter. "Numerical Cognition without Words: Evidence from Amazonia." *Science* 306 (2004) 496–99. DOI: 10.1126/science.

Got Questions Ministries. "Did Balaam's Donkey Really Talk to Him?" Got Questions, n.d. https://www.gotquestions.org/Balaam-donkey.html.

———. "Why Does the Bible Allow Slave Owners to Beat Their Slaves?" Got Questions, n.d. https://www.gotquestions.org/beating-slaves.html.

Gracián y Morales, Baltasar. *The Art of Worldly Wisdom*. New York: Macmillan, 1892.

Gray, James M. "The Inspiration of the Bible—Definition, Extent and Proof." From *The Fundamentals: A Testimony to the Truth*, edited by R. A. Torrey. Chicago: Testimony, 1910. https://www.godrules.net/library/torrey/NEWtorrey_b2.htm.

Greene-McCreight, Kathryn. *Feminist Reconstructions of Christian Doctrine: Narrative Analysis and Appraisal*. New York: Oxford University Press, 2000.

Gregory of Nazianzus. "To Cledonius the Priest against Apollinarius. (Ep. CI.)." Translated by Charles Gordon Browne and James Edward Swallow. From *Nicene and Post-Nicene Fathers*, edited by Philip Schaff and Henry Wace, 2nd ser., 7. Buffalo: Christian Literature, 1893. Revised and edited for New Advent by Kevin Knight. https://www.newadvent.org/fathers/3103a.htm.

———. "Fifth Theological Oration (Oration 31)." Translated by Charles Gordon Browne and James Edward Swallow. From *Nicene and Post-Nicene Fathers*, edited by Philip Schaff and Henry Wace, 2nd ser., 7. Buffalo: Christian Literature, 1894. Revised and edited for New Advent by Kevin Knight. http://www.newadvent.org/fathers/310231.htm.

Gregory of Nyssa. "Against Eunomius." Translated by W. Moore et al. From *Nicene and Post-Nicene Fathers*, edited by Philip Schaff, 2nd ser., 5. Buffalo: Christian Literature, 1893. Revised and edited for New Advent by Kevin Knight. https://www.newadvent.org/fathers/2901.htm.

———. "On 'Not Three Gods.'" Translated by H. A. Wilson. From *Nicene and Post-Nicene Fathers*, edited by Philip Schaff, 2nd ser., 5. Buffalo: Christian Literature, 1893. Revised and edited for New Advent by Kevin Knight. https://www.newadvent.org/fathers/2905.htm.

Gunton, Colin E. *The One, the Three and the Many: God, Creation and the Culture of Modernity; The 1992 Bampton Lectures*. Cambridge: Cambridge University Press, 1993.

Guthrie, W. K. C. "Pythagoras and Pythagoreanism." In *Encyclopedia of Philosophy*, edited by Donald M. Borchert, 8:181–84. 2nd ed. Detroit: Macmillan Reference USA, 2006. Gale eBook.

Habito, Ruben L. F. *Living Zen, Loving God*. Boston: Wisdom, 1995.

Haines, Valerie A. "From Organicist to Relational Human Ecology." *Sociological Theory* 3 (1985) 65–74. https://www.jstor.org/stable/i210390/.

Hampson, Daphne. "The Theological Implications of a Feminist Ethic." *Modern Churchman* 31 (1989) 36–39. DOI: 10.3828/MC.31.1.36.

Hall, Douglas John. *God and Human Suffering: An Exercise in the Theology of the Cross*. Minneapolis: Fortress, 1987.

Hart, David Bentley. *The Beauty of the Infinite: The Aesthetics of Christian Truth*. Grand Rapids: Eerdmans, 2004.

Hartshorne, Charles. *Creative Synthesis and Philosophic Method*. Chicago: Open Court, 1970.

———. "The Dipolar Conception of Deity." *Review of Metaphysics* 21 (1967) 273–89. http://www.jstor.org/stable/20124563.

———. *The Divine Relativity: A Social Conception of God*. New Haven: Yale University Press, 1948.

———. *Omnipotence and Other Theological Mistakes*. New York: State University of New York, 1984.

Hartshorne, Charles, and William L. Reese, eds. *Philosophers Speak of God*. Chicago: University of Chicago Press, 1953.

Hedges, Paul. "The Old and New Comparative Theologies: Discourses on Religion, the Theology of Religions, Orientalism and the Boundaries of Traditions." *Religions* 3 (2012) 1120–37. DOI: 10.3390/rel3041120.

Heim, S. Mark. *The Depth of the Riches: A Trinitarian Theology of Religious Ends.* Sacra Doctrina: Christian Theology for a Postmodern Age. Grand Rapids: Eerdmans, 2001.

Heraclitus. *Fragments: A Text and Translation with a Commentary.* Translated by T. M. Robinson. Phoenix Presocractic Series. Toronto: University of Toronto Press, 1991.

Herr, Moshe David. "Midrash." In *Encyclopaedia Judaica,* edited by Michael Berenbaum and Fred Skolnik, 14:182–85. 2nd ed. Detroit: Macmillan Reference USA, 2007. Gale eBook.

Heschel, Abraham Joshua. *Man's Quest for God: Studies in Prayer and Symbolism.* New York: Crossroad, 1982.

———. *Moral Grandeur and Spiritual Audacity: Essays.* New York: Farrar, Straus and Giroux, 1997.

———. *The Prophets.* New York: Harper & Row, 1962.

———. *The Sabbath: Its Meaning for Modern Man.* Boston: Shambhala, 2003.

Hesiod. "Hymn 2." In *The Homeric Hymns and Homerica,* translated by Hugh G. Evelyn-White, 288–323. LCL 496. Cambridge, MA: Harvard University Press, 1914.

———. *Theogony. Works and Days. Testimonia.* Edited and translated by Glenn W. Most. LCL 57. Cambridge: Harvard University Press, 2006.

Hesse, Josiah. "I Grew Up Evangelical. Terrifying Rapture Films Scarred Me Forever." *Guardian,* Feb. 1, 2023. https://www.theguardian.com/world/2023/jan/31/rapture-films-left-behind-evangelical.

Hikota, Riyako Cecilia. "The Christological *Perichōrēsis* and Dance." *Open Theology* 8 (2022) 191–204. DOI: 10.1515/opth-2022-0202/.

Holmes, Barbara. *Joy Unspeakable: Contemplative Practices of the Black Church.* Minneapolis: Fortress, 2004.

Holmes, Stephen R. "Three versus One? Some Problems of Social Trinitarianism." *Journal of Reformed Theology* 3 (2009) 77–89. DOI: 0.1163/156973109X403732.

Homer. *The Iliad of Homer.* Translated by Richmond Lattimore. Ancient Studies. Chicago: University of Chicago Press, 2011.

Hua, Hsüan. *The Śūraṅgama Sūtra: A New Translation.* San Francisco: Buddhist Text Translation Society, 2009.

Hughes, Langston. *Gospel Plays, Operas, and Later Dramatic Works.* Edited by Dolan Hubbard. Vol. 6 of *The Collected Works of Langston Hughes.* Columbia: University of Missouri Press, 2001.

Huxley, Aldous. *The Perennial Philosophy.* New York: Harper and Row, 1944.

Irenaeus of Lyons. "Against Heresies (Book IV, Chapter 20)." Translated by Alexander Roberts and William Rambaut. From *Ante-Nicene Fathers,* edited by Alexander Roberts et al., vol. 1. Buffalo, NY: Christian Literature, 1885. Revised and edited for New Advent by Kevin Knight. www.newadvent.org/fathers/0103420.htm.

Isenberg, Wesley W., trans. "Gospel of Philip." In *The Nag Hammadi Library in English,* edited by James M. Robinson, 131–51. New York, Harper & Row, 1977.

James, M. R., trans. "Acts of John." In *The Apocryphal New Testament,* edited by J. K. Elliott, 228–69. Oxford: Oxford University Press, 2005.

Jennings, Theodore W. "On Ritual Knowledge." In *Readings in Ritual Studies,* edited by Ronald L. Grimes, 324–34. Englewood Cliffs, NJ: Prentice Hall, 1996.

Jeremias, Joachim. *The Parables of Jesus*. 3rd ed. Hoboken, NJ: Pearson, 1972.

John of Damascus. "An Exposition of the Orthodox Faith." Translated by E. W. Watson and L. Pullan. From *Nicene and Post-Nicene Fathers*, edited by Philip Schaff and Henry Wace, 2nd ser., 9. Buffalo, NY: Christian Literature, 1899. Revised and edited for New Advent by Kevin Knight. https://www.newadvent.org/fathers/3304.htm.

Johnson, Elizabeth A. *Creation and the Cross: The Mercy of God for a Planet in Peril*. Maryknoll, NY: Orbis, 2018.

————. "Redeeming the Name of Christ." In *Freeing Theology: The Essentials of Theology in Feminist Perspective*, edited by Catherine Mowry LaCugna, 115–38. San Francisco: HarperCollins, 1993.

————. *She Who Is: The Mystery of God in Feminist Theological Discourse*. New York: Herder and Herder, 2017.

————. *Women, Earth, and Creator Spirit*. Madeleva Lecture in Spirituality. Mahwah, NJ: Paulist, 1993.

Johnston, Robert K. *Evangelicals at an Impasse: Biblical Authority in Practice*. Atlanta: John Knox, 1979.

Juel, Donald. "The Trinity and the New Testament." *ThTo* 54 (1997) 314–24. DOI: 10.1177/004057369705400303.

Julian of Norwich. *In Love Enclosed: More Daily Readings with Julian of Norwich*. Edited by Robert Llewelyn. Translated by Sheila Upjohn. 3rd ed. London: Darton, Longman and Todd, 2004.

Jüngel, Eberhard. *Death, the Riddle and the Mystery*. Translated by Iain and Ute Nicol. Louisville: Westminster, 1975.

Kang, D. C. "Why Was There No Religious War in Premodern East Asia?" *European Journal of International Relations* 20 (2014) 965–86. DOI: 10.1177/1354066113506948.

Katagiri, Dainin. *Each Moment Is the Universe: Zen and the Way of Being Time*. Boston: Shambhala, 2008.

Katz, Mordechai. *The Babylonian Exile to the Era of the Chassidim and Misnagdim*. Vol. 2 of *Yesterday, Today, and Forever*. New York: Feldheim, 1997.

Keating, Daniel A. "Trinity and Salvation: Christian Life as an Existence in the Trinity." In *The Oxford Handbook of the Trinity*, edited by Gilles Emery and Matthew Levering, 442–53. Oxford Handbooks. Oxford: Oxford University Press, 2012.

Keller, Catherine. *On the Mystery: Discerning Divinity in Process*. Minneapolis: Fortress, 2008.

Kepler, Johannes. *The Harmony of the World*. Translated by E. J. Aiton et al. Memoirs 209. New York: American Philosophical Society, 1997.

Khayyám, Omar. *The Rubáiyát of Omar Khayyám*. Translated by Edward Fitzgerald. London: Quaritch, 1859.

Kilby, Karen. "Perichoresis and Projection: Problems with Social Doctrines of the Trinity." *NBf* 81 (2000) 432–45. https://www.jstor.org/stable/43250486

King, Larry, interviewer. "Karla Faye Tucker: Born Again on Death Row." *CNN*, Mar. 26, 2007. cnn.com/2007/US/03/21/larry.king.tucker/.

King, Martin Luther, Jr. *A Call to Conscience: The Landmark Speeches of Dr. Martin Luther King, Jr.* Edited by Clayborne Carson and Kris Shepard. New York: Grand Central, 2002.

————. *A Testament of Hope: The Essential Writings and Speeches of Martin Luther King, Jr.* Edited by James Washington. New York: HarperCollins, 1986.

King, Richard. "Early Yogācāra and Its Relationship with the Madhyamaka School." *Philosophy East and West* 44 (1994) 659–83. DOI: 10.2307/1399757.

King, Ursula. *Women and Spirituality: Voices of Protest and Promise*. New York: Macmillan, 1993.

Kinnaman, David, with Aly Hawkins. *You Lost Me: Why Young Christians Are Leaving Church . . . and Rethinking Faith*. Grand Rapids: Baker, 2011.

Kitarô, Nishida. *Last Writings: Nothingness and the Religious Worldview*. Translated by David A. Dilworth. Honolulu: University of Hawai'i Press, 1993.

Klyve, Dominic. "Darwin, Malthus, Süssmilch, and Euler: The Ultimate Origin of the Motivation for the Theory of Natural Selection." *Journal of the History of Biology* 47 (2014) 189–212. http://www.jstor.org/stable/43863375.

Kohl, Christian Thomas. "Buddhism and Quantum Physics: A Strange Parallelism of Two Concepts of Reality." *Contemporary Buddhism* 8 (2007) 69–82. DOI: 10.1080/14639940701295328.

Kragh, Helge. "An Anthropic Myth: Fred Hoyle's Carbon-12 Resonance Level." *Archive for History of Exact Sciences* 64 (2010) 721–51. https://www.jstor.org/stable/41134335.

Kreitzer, Larry. "Apotheosis of the Roman Emperor." *BA* 53 (1990) 210–17. DOI: 10.2307/3210166.

LaCugna, Catherine Mowry. *God for Us: The Trinity and Christian Life*. San Francisco: HarperCollins, 1993.

Ladd, George Eldon. *A Theology of the New Testament*. Rev. ed. Grand Rapids: Eerdmans, 1993.

Lamott, Anne. *Bird by Bird: Some Instructions on Writing and Life*. New York: Knopf Doubleday, 2007.

Langford, Jerome J. *Galileo, Science, and the Church*. 3rd ed. Ann Arbor Paperbacks. Ann Arbor: University of Michigan Press, 1992.

Lao Tzu. *Tao Te Ching*. Translated by D. C. Lau. Penguin Classics. New York: Penguin, 1963.

Lapidge, Michael. "Stoic Cosmology." In *The Stoics*, edited by John M. Rist, 161–85. Berkeley: University of California Press, 1978.

Lawlor, F. X., et al. "Infallibility." In *New Catholic Encyclopedia*, edited by Berard L. Marthaler, 7:448–53. 2nd ed. Detroit: Gale eBooks, 2003.

Layton, Bentley. *The Gnostic Scriptures: A New Translation with Annotations and Introductions*. AYBRL. New Haven: Yale University Press, 1995.

Levine, Amy-Jill. *Light of the World: A Beginner's Guide to Advent*. Nashville: Abingdon, 2019.

Lewis, C. S. *The Four Loves*. Reprint, New York: Harcourt Brace Jovanovich, 1991.

Longenecker, Richard N. *Biblical Exegesis in the Apostolic Period*. 2nd ed. Grand Rapids: Eerdmans, 1999.

Lott, Bernice. "Cognitive and Behavioral Distancing from the Poor." *American Psychologist* 57 (2002) 100–110. DOI: 10.1037/0003-66X.57.2.100.

Loughlin, Gerard. "What Is Queer? Theology after Identity." *Theology & Sexuality* 14 (2008) 143–52. DOI: 10.1177/1355835807087376.

Louis, Jacobs, and Benjamin De Vries. "Halakhah." In *Encyclopedia Judaica*, edited by Fred Skolnik, 8:251–58. Detroit: Macmillan Reference USA, 2007. Gale eBook.

Louth, Andrew. "Eastern Orthodox Eschatology." In *The Oxford Handbook of Eschatology*, edited by Jerry L. Walls, 233–47. Oxford Handbooks. Oxford: Oxford University Press, 2007.

Loy, David. "The Nonduality of Life and Death: A Buddhist View of Repression." *Philosophy East and West* 40 (1990) 151–74. https://www.jstor.org/stable/i260893.

Luti, Mary. "Divinized." United Church of Christ, Dec. 3, 2021. ucc.org/daily-devotional/divinized.

MacDonald, Gregory. *The Evangelical Universalist: The Biblical Hope That God's Love Will Save Us All.* London: SPCK, 2012.

MacDougall, Scott. "Bodily Communions: An Eschatological Proposal for Addressing the Christian Body Problem." *Di* 57 (2018) 178–85. DOI: 10.1111/dial.12415.

Maclean, Norman. *"A River Runs through It" and Other Stories.* 25th anniv. ed. Chicago: University of Chicago Press, 2001.

Madigan, Kevin J., and Jon D. Levenson. *Resurrection: The Power of God for Christians and Jews.* New Haven: Yale University Press, 2009.

Makransky, John. *Awakening through Love: Unveiling Your Deepest Goodness.* Somerville, MA: Wisdom, 2007.

Mallek, Raanan. "Historical Developments of the Term Ger Toshav and the Halakhic Implications Therein for Relating to Non-Jews." In *Jews in Dialogue: Jewish Responses to the Challenges of Multicultural Contemporaneity,* edited by Magdalena Dziaczkowska and Adele Valeria Messina, 15–52. Studies in Jewish History and Culture 61; Free Ebrei 2. Leiden, Neth.: Brill, 2020. DOI: 10.1163/9789004425958_003.

Mansoor, Menahem. "Pharisees." In *Encyclopaedia Judaica,* edited by Michael Berenbaum and Fred Skolnik, 16:30–32. 2nd ed. Detroit: Macmillan Reference USA, 2007. Gale eBook.

Marenbon, John. *The Philosophy of Peter Abelard.* Cambridge: Cambridge University Press, 1999.

Margalit, Natan. *The Pearl and the Flame: A Journey into Jewish Wisdom and Ecological Thinking.* Boulder, CO: Albion Andalus, 2022.

Mascaro, Juan. *The Upanishads.* Penguin Classics. New York: Penguin, 1965.

Matarazzo, James M., Jr. *The Judgment of Love: An Investigation of Salvific Judgment in Christian Eschatology.* Distinguished Dissertations in Christian Theology. Eugene, OR: Pickwick, 2018.

Mbiti, John S. *African Religions & Philosophy.* 2nd rev. and enlarged ed. New York: Pearson Education, 1990.

McCabe, Herbert. *God, Christ, and Us.* New York: Continuum, 2003.

McCagney, Nancy. *Nāgārjuna and the Philosophy of Openness.* Lanham, MD: Rowman & Littlefield, 1997.

M'Cheyne, Robert Murray. *A Basket of Fragments: Being the Substance of Sermons.* London: Murray, 1848.

McCoy, Terrence. "What Happened When This Feisty Woman Got Fined $2,000 for Feeding the Homeless." *Washington Post,* Apr. 20, 2015. https://www.washingtonpost.com/news/acts-of-faith/wp/2015/04/20/what-happened-when-this-feisty-woman-got-fined-2000-for-feeding-the-homeless/.

McDougall, Joy Ann. *Pilgrimage of Love: Moltmann on the Trinity and Christian Life.* AAR Reflection and Theory in the Study of Religion. New York: Oxford University Press, 2005.

McFague, Sallie. *Models of God: Theology for an Ecological, Nuclear Age.* Minneapolis: Fortress, 1987.

McInroy, Mark J. "How Deification Became Eastern: German Idealism, Liberal Protestantism, and the Modern Misconstruction of the Doctrine." *Modern Theology* 37 (2021) 934–58. DOI: 10.1111/moth.12700.

Mendes, Sam, dir. *1917.* Universal City, CA: Universal, 2019.

Merton, Thomas. *New Seeds of Contemplation*. Boston: Shambhala, 2003.

———. *Raids on the Unspeakable*. London: New Directions, 1966.

———. *Thomas Merton: Spiritual Master; The Essential Writings*. Edited by Lawrence Cunningham. Mahwah, NJ: Paulist, 1992.

Meyer, Marvin. *The Gospel of Thomas: The Hidden Sayings of Jesus*. San Francisco: HarperCollins, 1992.

Michaels, Axel, and William S. Sax. "Performance." In *The Oxford Handbook of the Study of Religion*, edited by Michael Stausberg and Steven Engler, 304–15. Oxford Handbooks. New York: Oxford University Press, 2016. DOI: 10.1093/oxfordhb/9780198729570.001.0001.

Miralles, Antonio. "A New *Response* of the Congregation for the Doctrine of the Faith on the Validity of Baptism." Vatican, Feb. 1, 2008. https://www.vatican.va/roman_curia/congregations/cfaith/documents/rc_con_cfaith_doc_20080201_validity-baptism-miralles_en.html.

Moltmann, Jürgen. *Creating a Just Future: The Politics of Peace and the Ethics of Creation in a Threatened World*. Translated by John Bowden. Philadelphia: Trinity International, 1989.

———. *The Crucified God: The Cross of Christ as the Foundation and Criticism of Christian Theology*. Minneapolis: Fortress, 1993.

———. "God Is Unselfish Love." In *The Emptying God: A Buddhist-Jewish-Christian Conversation*, edited by John B. Cobb, Jr., and Christopher Ives, 116–24. Maryknoll, NY: Orbis, 1994.

———. *The Trinity and the Kingdom: The Doctrine of God*. San Francisco: Harper and Row, 1981.

Moody, Anne. *Coming of Age in Mississippi: The Classic Autobiography of Growing Up Poor and Black in the Rural South*. New York: Random House, 2011.

Morrison, Toni. *Beloved*. New York: Penguin, 1998.

Muir, John. *My First Summer in the Sierra*. San Francisco: HMH, 1998.

———. *The Wild Muir: Twenty-Two of John Muir's Greatest Adventures*. Edited by Lee Stetson. San Francisco: Yosemite Conservancy, 2013.

Murdoch, Iris. *A Fairly Honourable Defeat*. Penguin Twentieth-Century Classics. New York: Penguin, 2001.

———. *The Sovereignty of Good*. Routledge Great Minds. New York: Taylor & Francis, 2013.

Nash, Bruce, creator. *Modern Marvels*. Season 13, episode 9, "Barbarian Battle Tech." Aired Mar. 4, 2007, on the History Channel.

Neusner, Jacob. *The Midrash: An Introduction*. Lanham, MD: Aronson, 1994.

New York Times. "Bishop Attacks Display of Female Christ Figure." *New York Times*, Apr. 25, 1984. https://www.nytimes.com/1984/04/25/nyregion/bishop-attacks-display-of-female-christ-figure.html.

Nietzsche, Friedrich. *Ecce Homo*. Translated by Walter Kaufmann. New York: Vintage, 1989.

Nikodimos of the Holy Mountain, St., and St. Markarios of Corinth, compilers. *The Philokalia: The Complete Text*. Edited and translated by G. E. H. Palmer et al. 5 vols. New York: Faber and Faber, 1979–2023.

Nouwen, Henri J. M. *Henri Nouwen: Writings Selected*. Edited by Robert A. Jonas. Modern Spiritual Masters. Maryknoll, NY: Orbis, 1998.

———. *The Wounded Healer: Ministry in Contemporary Society*. New York: Crown, 2013.

Obama, Barack. "Remarks by President Obama at Memorial Service for Former South African President Nelson Mandela." Obama White House, Dec. 10, 2013. https://obamawhitehouse.archives.gov/the-press-office/2013/12/10/remarks-president-obama-memorial-service-former-south-african-president-.

Olivelle, Patrick, trans. *Upaniṣads*. Oxford World's Classics. Oxford: Oxford University Press, 1998.

Oliver, Mary. *Evidence: Poems*. Boston: Beacon, 2009.

Olson, Roger E., and Christopher Hall. *The Trinity*. Guides to Theology. Grand Rapids: Eerdmans, 2002.

O'Neill, Mary. "The Mystery of Being Human Together." In *Freeing Theology: The Essentials of Theology in Feminist Perspective*, edited by Catherine Mowry LaCugna, 139–60. San Francisco: Harper San Francisco, 1993.

Oord, Thomas Jay. *Pluriform Love: An Open and Relational Theology of Well-Being*. Grasmere, ID: SacraSage, 2022.

———. *The Uncontrolling Love of God: An Open and Relational Account of Providence*. Downers Grove, IL: IVP Academic, 2015.

Ouspensky, Leonid. *Theology of the Icon*. 2 vols. Yonkers, NY: St. Vladimir's Seminary Press, 1992.

Pagels, Elaine. *The Gnostic Gospels*. 1979. Reprint, New York: Random House, 2004.

———. "What Became of God the Mother? Conflicting Images of God in Early Christianity." *Signs: Journal of Women in Culture and Society* 2 (1976) 293–303.

Paine, Thomas. *Collected Writings*. Edited by Eric Foner. Library of America 76. New York: Library of America, 1995.

Phan, Peter C. "Relations, Trinitarian." In *New Catholic Encyclopedia*, edited by Berard L. Marthaler, 12:45–46. 2nd ed. Detroit: Gale eBooks, 2003.

Philo. "Who Is the Heir of Divine Things?" In *The Works of Philo*, translated by C. D. Yonge. LCL 261. Peabody, MA: Hendrickson, 1993. DOI: 10.4159/DLCL.philo_judaeus-who_heir_divine_things.1932.

Pinnock, Clark. "Systematic Theology." In *The Openness of God: A Biblical Challenge to the Traditional Understanding of God*, by Clark Pinnock et al., 101–25. Downers Grove, IL: IVP Academic, 1994.

Plato. *The Republic*. Edited by G. R. F. Ferrari. Translated by Tom Griffith. Cambridge Texts in the History of Political Thought. Cambridge: Cambridge University Press, 2000.

Poiani, Aldo. *Animal Homosexuality: A Biosocial Perspective*. Cambridge: Cambridge University Press, 2010.

Presbyterian Church (U.S.A.). *Book of Confessions*. Rev. study ed. Louisville: Presbyterian, 2017.

Priests for Equality, trans. *The Inclusive Bible: The First Egalitarian Translation*. Lanham, MD: Rowman and Littlefield, 2007.

Primavesi, Anne. *Gaia and Climate Change: A Theology of Gift Events*. London: Taylor & Francis, 2008.

Pritscher, Conrad P. *Re-Opening Einstein's Thought: About What Can't Be Learned from Textbooks*. Bold Visions in Educational Research 24. Leiden, Neth.: Brill, 2008.

PRRI Staff. "Religion and Congregations in a Time of Social and Political Upheaval." PRRI, May 16, 2023. https://www.prri.org/research/religion-and-congregations-in-a-time-of-social-and-political-upheaval/.

Pseudo-Macarius. *Fifty Spiritual Homilies and the "Great Letter."* Translated by George A. Maloney, SJ. Classics of Western Spirituality. Mahwah, NJ: Paulist, 1992.

Rabinowitz, Louis Isaac, and Warren Harvey. "Torah." In *Encyclopedia Judaica*, edited by Michael Berenbaum and Fred Skolnik, 20:39–46. Detroit: Macmillan Reference USA, 2007. Gale eBook.

Ramanuja. *Vedartha Sangraha of Sri Ramanujacharya*. Translated by S. S. Raghavachar. Mysore: Sri Ramakrishna Ashrama, 1978.

Rambachan, Anantanand. *A Hindu Theology of Liberation: Not-Two Is Not One*. SUNY Series in Religious Studies. New York: State University of New York Press, 2015.

———. "What Is Advaita (Not-Two)?" In *Nondualism: An Interreligious Exploration*, edited by Jon Paul Sydnor and Anthony J. Watson, 13–30. Studies in Comparative Philosophy and Religion. Lanham, MD: Lexington, 2023.

Ratcliffe, Susan, ed. *Oxford Treasury of Sayings and Quotations*. 4th ed. Oxford: Oxford University Press, 2011.

Rea, Michael. "Gender as a Divine Attribute." *RelS* 52 (2016) 97–115. DOI: 10.1017/S0034412514000614.

Rice, Richard. "Trinity, Temporality, and Open Theism." *Philosophia* 35 (2007) 321–28.

Ricoeur, Paul. *Interpretation Theory: Discourse and the Surplus of Meaning*. Abilene: Texas Christian University Press, 1976.

Rico-Uribe, Laura Alejandra, et al. "Association of Loneliness with All-Cause Mortality: A Meta-Analysis." *PLoS ONE* 13 (2018) e0190033. DOI: 10.1371/journal.pone.0190033/.

Rogers, Carl. *On Becoming a Person: A Therapist's View of Psychotherapy*. New York: Houghton Mifflin, 1995.

Rogers, Martin. "Team USA Players Share Emotional Embrace with Iran's Saeid Ezatolahi." *Fox Sports*, last updated Nov. 30, 2022. https://www.foxsports.com/stories/soccer/team-usa-players-share-emotional-embrace-with-irans-saeid-ezatolahi.

Rohr, Richard. *Adam's Return: The Five Promises of Male Initiation*. New York: Crossroad, 2004.

———. *Everything Belongs: The Gift of Contemplative Prayer*. Rev. and updated ed. New York: Crossroad, 2003.

———. "Leaving the Garden." July 31, 2022. https://cac.org/daily-meditations/leaving-the-garden-2022-07-31/.

———. *Wondrous Encounters: Scripture for Lent*. Cincinnati: St. Anthony Messenger, 2011.

Ross, Susan A. "God's Embodiment and Women." In *Freeing Theology: The Essentials of Theology in Feminist Perspective*, edited by Catherine Mowry LaCugna, 185–209. San Francisco: HarperSanFrancisco, 1993.

Rounds, David, and Ronald B. Epstein, trans. *The Śūraṅgama Sūtra: A New Translation with Excerpts from the Commentary by the Venerable Master Hsuan Hua*. Ukiah, CA: Buddhist Text Translation Society, 2012.

Sahinidou, Ioanna. "Christological Perichoresis." *Open Journal of Philosophy* 4 (2014) 552–59. DOI: 10.4236/ojpp.2014.44057.

Salazar, Maritza R., et al. "Diversity and Team Creativity: Exploring Underlying Mechanisms." *Group Dynamics* 21 (2017) 187–206. DOI: 10.1037/gdn0000073.

Sallustius. "On the Gods and the Cosmos." In *Anthology of Classical Myth: Primary Sources in Translation*, edited and translated by Stephen M. Trzaskoma et al., 342–44. Boston: Hackett, 2004.

Sampsell-Willmann, Kate. *Lewis Hine as Social Critic*. Oxford: University Press of Mississippi, 2009.

Sanders, John. "Historical Considerations." In *The Openness of God: A Biblical Challenge to the Traditional Understanding of God*, by Clark Pinnock et al., 59–100. Downers Grove, IL: IVP Academic, 1994.

Sayers, Dorothy L. *Christian Letters to a Post-Christian World: A Selection of Essays*. Grand Rapids: Eerdmans, 1969.

Schiffman, Lawrence H. "Sadducees." In *Encyclopedia of Religion*, edited by Lindsay Jones, 12:654–55. 2nd ed. Detroit: Macmillan Reference USA, 2005. Gale eBook.

Schleiermacher, Friedrich. *Christian Faith: A New Translation and Critical Edition*. Edited by Terrence N. Tice and Catherine L. Kelsey. Translated by Terrence N. Tice et al. 2 vols. Louisville: Westminster John Knox, 2016.

Schmemann, Alexander. *O Death, Where Is Thy Sting?* Yonkers, NY: St. Vladimir's Seminary Press, 2003.

Schrock, David. "What the Gospel Has to Say to Transgendered Persons." Ethics & Religious Liberty Commission, July 20, 2015. erlc.com/resource-library/articles/what-the-gospel-has-to-say-to-transgendered-persons/.

Schüssler Fiorenza, Elisabeth. *Jesus: Miriam's Child, Sophia's Prophet: Critical Issues in Feminist Christology*. T&T Clark Cornerstones. New York: Bloomsbury, 2015.

Schwartz, Hans. *Christology*. Grand Rapids: Eerdmans, 1998.

Schweig, Graham M. *Dance of Divine Love: India's Classic Sacred Love Story; The Rasa Lila of Krishna*. Princeton, NJ: Princeton University Press, 2018.

Shoemaker, Sydney. *Identity, Cause, and Mind: Philosophical Essays*. Expanded ed. Oxford: Oxford University Press, 2003.

Siderits, Mark. "On the Soteriological Significance of Emptiness." *Contemporary Buddhism* 4 (2003) 9–23. DOI: 10.1080/1463994032000140158.

Siderits, Mark, and Shoryu Katsura. *Nagarjuna's Middle Way: Mulamadhyamakakarika*. Classics of Indian Buddhism. San Francisco: Wisdom, 2013.

Simpson, Albert B. *Days of Heaven upon Earth*. New York: Christian Alliance, 1897.

Smith, Betty. *A Tree Grows in Brooklyn*. San Francisco: HarperCollins, 2001.

Smith, Erin A. "*The Late Great Planet Earth* Made the Apocalypse a Popular Concern." *Humanities* 38 (2017). https://www.neh.gov/humanities/2017/winter/feature/the-late-great-planet-earth-made-the-apocalypse-popular-concern.

Smith, Margaret. *Rabi'a the Mystic and Her Fellow-Saints in Islam: Being the Life and Teachings of Rabi'a al-Adawiyya Al-Qaysiyya of Basra Together with Some Account of the Place of the Women Saints in Islam*. Cambridge: Cambridge University Press, 1984.

Sobrino, Jon. *Jesus the Liberator: A Historical-Theological Reading of Jesus of Nazareth*. Maryknoll, NY: Orbis, 1993.

Soelle, Dorothee. *The Inward Road and the Way Back*. Translated by David L. Scheidt. 1979. Reprint, Eugene, OR: Wipf & Stock, 2003.

———. *The Silent Cry: Mysticism and Resistance*. Translated by Barbara and Martin Rumscheidt. Minneapolis: Fortress, 2001.

———. *Suffering*. Translated by Everett R. Kalin. Minneapolis: Fortress, 1989.

———. *Thinking about God: An Introduction to Theology*. Translated by John Bowden. 1990. Reprint, Eugene, OR: Wipf & Stock, 2016.

Song, Bin. "A Ru Theology of Nondualism." In *Nondualism: An Interreligious Exploration*, edited by Jon Paul Sydnor and Anthony J. Watson, 243–60. Lanham, MD: Lexington, 2023.

Stambaugh, Joan. "Existential Time in Kierkegaard and Heidegger." In *Religion and Time*, edited by Anindita Niyogi Balslev and Jitendra Nath Mohanty, 46–60. Numen Book Series 54. Leiden, Neth.: Brill, 1993.

Stancil, W. T. "Dispensational Theology." In *New Catholic Encyclopedia*, edited by Berard L. Marthaler, 4:775–76. 2nd ed. Detroit: Thomson/Gale, 2010. Gale eBook.

Stark, Rodney. "Secularization, R.I.P." *Sociology of Religion* 60 (1999) 249–73. DOI: 10.2307/3711936.

Steindl-Rast, David. *Deeper Than Words: Living the Apostles' Creed*. New York: Crown, 2010.

Stephenson, A. A. "Marcion." In *New Catholic Encyclopedia*, edited by Berard L. Marthaler, 9:142–43. 2nd ed. Detroit: Thomson/Gale, 2010. Gale eBook.

Sterelny, Kim, and Paul E. Griffiths. *Sex and Death: An Introduction to Philosophy of Biology*. Science and Its Conceptual Foundations. Chicago: University of Chicago Press, 2012.

Sterk, Andrea, and John Wayland Coakley, eds. *Earliest Christianity to 1453*. Vol. 1 of *Readings in World Christian History*. Maryknoll, NY: Orbis, 2004.

Stern, David. "Midrash and Parables." In *The Jewish Annotated New Testament*, edited by Amy-Jill Levine and Marc Zvi Brettler, 707–10. 2nd ed. Oxford: Oxford University Press, 2017.

Strathern, Alan. "Religion and War: A Synthesis." *History and Anthropology* 34 (2023) 145–74. DOI: 10.1080/02757206.2022.2060212

Streng, Frederick J. *Emptiness: A Study in Religious Meaning*. Nashville: Abingdon, 1967.

Sweetman, Mark S. "Defining Dispensationalism: A Cultural Studies Perspective." *JRH* 34 (2010) 191–212. DOI: 10.1111/j.1467-9809.2010.00862.

Sydnor, Clement A. III. "Letter." To Dr. Benjamin L. Rose of Union Theological Seminary, Virginia, Mar. 24, 1965. In the author's possession.

————. "Trust and Tragedy." Unpublished sermon, Bow Creek Presbyterian Church, Virginia Beach, VA, Apr. 12, 1991. In the author's possession.

Sydnor, Jon Paul. "Blessed Transgression: On Serving Communion to Jews." *Journal of Interreligious Studies* 22 (2018) 64–87.

————. "The Dance of Emptiness: A Constructive Comparative Theology of the Social Trinity." In *Comparing Faithfully: Insights for Systematic Theological Reflection*, edited by Michelle Voss Roberts, 23–45. Comparative Theology: Thinking across Traditions 1. New York: Fordham University Press, 2016.

————. "God in All Things: Ramanuja's Divine Ontology for Christian Panentheism." *Interreligious Studies and Intercultural Theology* 6 (2023) 153–71. DOI: 10.1558/isit.19095.

————. "Interformation: The Ethics of Interreligious Ritual Participation." *Interreligious Studies and Intercultural Theology* 1 (2017) 187–205. DOI: 10.1558/isit.33604.

————. *Rāmānuja and Schleiermacher: Toward a Constructive Comparative Theology*. Princeton Theological Monograph. Eugene, OR: Pickwick, 2011.

Tagore, Rabindranath. *Stray Birds*. New York: Cosimo Classics, 2004.

Tallchief, Maria, with Rosemary Wells. *Tallchief: America's Prima Ballerina*. Ashland, OH: Baker & Taylor, 2009.

Tanner, Norman P., ed. "Fourth Lateran Council: 1215." Documenta Catholica Omnia, [1990]. From *Decrees of the Ecumenical Councils* (Washington, DC: Georgetown University Press, 1990), 2 vols. http://www.documentacatholicaomnia.eu/o3d/1215-1215,_Concilium_Lateranum_IIII,_Documenta_Omnia,_EN.pdf.

Teilhard de Chardin, Pierre. *The Making of a Mind: Letters from a Soldier-Priest, 1914–1919.* Translated by René Hague. New York: Harper & Row, 1965.

Tertullian. "Against Praxeas." Translated by Peter Holmes. From *Ante-Nicene Fathers*, edited by Alexander Roberts et al., vol. 3. Buffalo, NY: Christian Literature, 1885. Revised and edited for New Advent by Kevin Knight. http://www.newadvent.org/fathers/0317.htm.

Tetlow, Joseph A. *Considering Jesus: The Human Experience of the Redeemer.* Chicago: Loyola, 2022.

Thatamanil, John. *The Immanent Divine: God, Creation, and the Human Predicament; An East-West Conversation.* Minneapolis: Fortress, 2006.

Thatcher, Margaret. "Interview for *Woman's Own* ('No Such Thing [*as Society*]')." Margaret Thatcher Foundation, Sept. 23, 1987. www.margaretthatcher.org/document/106689.

Theophilus. "Apology to Autolycus." Translated by Marcus Dods. In *Ante-Nicene Fathers*, edited by Alexander Roberts et al., vol. 2. Buffalo, NY: Christian Literature, 1885. Revised and edited for New Advent by Kevin Knight. https://www.newadvent.org/fathers/0204.htm.

Thibodeau, Paul H., and Lera Boroditsky. "Natural Language Metaphors Covertly Influence Reasoning." *PLoS ONE* 8 (2013) 1–7. DOI: 10.1371/journal.pone.0052961.

Tillich, Paul. *Dynamics of Faith.* New York: Harper Colophon, 1957.

———. *Love, Power, and Justice: Ontological Analyses and Ethical Applications.* Oxford: Oxford University Press, 1954.

Tracy, David. *Plurality and Ambiguity: Hermeneutics, Religion, Hope.* Chicago: University of Chicago Press, 1994.

Tuggy, Dale. "Metaphysics and Logic of the Trinity." Oxford Academic, Dec. 5, 2016. From *The Oxford Handbook of Topics in Philosophy.* Oxford Handbooks. https://doi.org/10.1093/oxfordhb/9780199935314.013.27.

Twain, Mark. *Mark Twain's "Tom Sawyer" and "Huckleberry Finn."* Modern Library Giant 49. New York: Modern Library, 1998.

United States Catholic Conference. *Catechism of the Catholic Church.* Merrimack, NH: Thomas More College Press, 1994.

Van den Brink, Gijsbert. "Social Trinitarianism: A Discussion of Some Recent Theological Criticisms." *International Journal of Systematic Theology* 16 (2014) 331–50. DOI: 10.1111/ijst.12053.

Van Oort, Johannes. "The Holy Spirit as Feminine: Early Christian Testimonies and Their Interpretation." *HvTSt* 72 (2016) 22–45. DOI: 10.4102/hts.v72i1.3225.

Vasko, Elisabeth. "Redeeming Beauty? Christa and the Displacement of Women's Bodies in Theological Aesthetic Discourses." *Feminist Theology* 21 (2013) 195–208. DOI: 10.1177/0966735012464151.

Volf, Miroslav. *After Our Likeness: The Church as the Image of the Trinity.* Sacra Doctrina: Christian Theology for a Postmodern Age (SACRA). Grand Rapids: Eerdmans, 1998.

Voss Roberts, Michelle. *Body Parts: A Theological Anthropology.* Minneapolis: Fortress, 2017.

———. *Dualities: A Theology of Difference.* Louisville: Westminster John Knox, 2010.

Walker, Alice. *The Color Purple.* Penguin Classics. New York: Penguin, 2019.

———. *The World Has Changed: Conversations with Alice Walker.* New York: New Press, 2010.

Washington Post Staff. "Nov. 10–Dec. 1, 2022, Washington Post-KFF Trans in America Survey." *Washington Post,* Mar. 22, 2023. https://www.washingtonpost.com/tablet/2023/03/23/nov-10-dec-1-2022-washington-post-kff-trans-survey/.

Watson, Alan. *The State, Law, and Religion: Pagan Rome.* Athens: University of Georgia Press, 1992.

Weber, Timothy P. "Millennialism." In *The Oxford Handbook of Eschatology,* edited by Jerry L. Walls, 365–83. Oxford Handbooks. Oxford: Oxford University Press, 2007. DOI: 10.1093/oxfordhb/9780195170498.003.21.

Weil, Simone. *Letter to a Priest.* Routledge Great Minds. New York: Routledge, 2014.

———. *Selected Writings.* Edited by Eric O. Springsted. Modern Spiritual Masters. Maryknoll, NY: Orbis, 1998.

Wells, H. G. *The Outline of History: Being a Plain History of Life and Mankind.* Garden City, NY: Doubleday, 1971.

Westerhoff, Jan. *Nāgārjuna's Madhyamaka: A Philosophical Introduction.* New York: Oxford University Press, 2009.

Whitehead, Alfred North. *Religion in the Making: Lowell Lectures, 1926.* New York: Macmillan, 1926.

Williams, Arthur H. "The Trinity and Time." *SJT* 39 (1986) 65–81. DOI: 10.1017/S0036930600044665.

Williams, Rowan. *Being Disciples: Essentials of the Christian Life.* London: SPCK, 2016.

Winell, Marlene. "Understanding Religious Trauma Syndrome: Trauma from Religion." *CBT Today* 39 (2011) 23–25. DOI: 10.1083/cbt/73829.32.

Wisse, Frederick, trans. *Apocryphon of John.* Edited by James M. Robinson and Richard Smith. Nag Hammadi Library in English. Leiden: Brill, 1988.

Wolterstorff, Nicholas. *Lament for a Son.* Grand Rapids: Eerdmans, 1987.

Wright, N. T. *Surprised by Hope: Rethinking Heaven, the Resurrection, and the Mission of the Church.* San Francisco: HarperCollins, 2008.

Zhai, Yujia (Sam). "Nondualism and Christian-Jewish Relations: Toward a Nondualist Covenantal Theology." In *Nondualism: An Interreligious Exploration,* edited by Jon Paul Sydnor and Anthony J. Watson, 185–204. Studies in Comparative Philosophy and Religion. Lanham, MD: Lexington, 2023.

Zheng, Liling, et al. "Color Adaptation Induced from Linguistic Description of Color." *PLoS ONE* 12 (2017) 1–17. DOI: 10.1371/journal.pone.0173755/.

Zizioulas, John. *Being as Communion: Studies in Personhood and the Church.* Contemporary Greek Theologians 4. Crestwood, NY: St. Vladimir's Seminary Press, 1985.

Index

Printed in the USA
CPSIA information can be obtained
at www.ICGtesting.com
LVHW021729140824
788087LV00009B/86